Venetian vernacular
architecture

Venetian vernacular architecture

Traditional housing in the
Venetian lagoon

Richard J. Goy

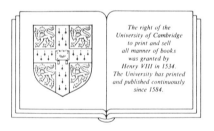

The right of the
University of Cambridge
to print and sell
all manner of books
was granted by
Henry VIII in 1534.
The University has printed
and published continuously
since 1584.

Cambridge University Press

Cambridge
New York   New Rochelle
Melbourne   Sydney

Published by the Press Syndicate of the University of Cambridge
The Pitt Building, Trumpington Street, Cambridge CB2 1RP
32 East 57th Street, New York, NY 10022, USA
10 Stamford Road, Oakleigh, Melbourne 3166, Australia

First published 1989

Printed in Great Britain at
Redwood Burn Limited, Trowbridge, Wiltshire

British Library cataloguing in publication data

Goy, Richard J. (Richard John), *1947–*
Venetian vernacular architecture:
traditional housing in the Venetian lagoon.
1. Italy. Venice. Vernacular houses.
Architectural features
I. Title
728.3′0944′31

Library of Congress cataloguing in publication data

Goy, Richard J. (Richard John), *1947–*
Venetian vernacular architecture.

Bibliography: p.
Includes index.
1. Architecture, Domestic – Italy – Venice.
2. Vernacular architecture – Italy – Venice.   3. Venice
(Italy) – Buildings, structures, etc.   I. Title.
NA7594.G6 1988   728′.0945′31   88–18155

ISBN 0 521 34581 2

RB

To Barbara and to Catherine

Contents

Illustrations

List of illustrations

Preface

This book is an attempt to provide an introduction to the vernacular architecture of the Venetian lagoon. It is intended to form a companion and complementary volume to my earlier work, *Chioggia and the Villages of the Venetian Lagoon*, which surveyed the origins and development of these communities as a whole, and which placed considerable emphasis on their social and economic history as well as analysing their characteristic urban structure. This first book thus provided a framework – social, demographic, economic – in which the present work may be set. Nevertheless, I hope that it will be used in its own right as a survey of the architecture of these modest but very rewarding settlements, which for so many centuries have lain under the political (and architectural) shadow of the *Dominante* itself.

Our awareness of the richness, variety and importance of vernacular styles of architecture has increased enormously in the last two or three decades. Similarly, few architects or historians are still unaware of the need to preserve the totality of historic urban environments rather than simply concentrate their attentions (and funds) on the more outstanding individual buildings. It thus appears timely that a general survey of these villages should be published in order to reinforce the awareness of those concerned as to their condition, and to learn about the homes of these more modest Venetians who lived beyond the world-famous *centro storico* of the sea-city.

It is also gratifying to record that the physical condition of these historic communities is now a matter of considerable concern to the various authorities responsible for their preservation and restoration. Whilst the difficulties remain formidable, it should be noted that all of these villages have the status of conservation areas and that much progress has been made in restoration work since the disastrous floods of 1966 finally provided an impetus for a series of long overdue measures to be begun. As the survey in Part III shows, a considerable number of the more noteworthy individual houses have been recently restored or are undergoing restoration at present (1987). It is to be hoped that these efforts will be expanded to include the many more lesser houses and cottages which provide the essential fabric that knits these communities together.

The present work is thus aimed principally at the architectural historian and to some extent at the well-informed layman. As will be seen, there are a number of more specialised fields that are discussed only in the most general terms insofar as they affect the development of the lagunar vernacular style. Many of my conclusions as to the socio-economic structure of the villages and also their demographic patterns are based on earlier research for *Chioggia and the Villages of the Venetian Lagoon*, and I do not claim to present further academic conclusions of consequence in this present work. However, general surveys, too, have their place, and I hope that this one will be found to serve a purpose with some degree of success.

Acknowledgements

Among the various official bodies in Venice, I must offer thanks to Dottoressa Tiepolo and the staff of the Archivio di Stato; to the staff of the Biblioteca Nazionale Marciana; to those of the Biblioteca Querini-Stampalia and the Biblioteca Civica Correr. Special thanks are due to Arch. Claudio Barbini and his colleagues at the Ufficio di Urbanistica of the Comune di Venezia for their invaluable survey plans of the lagoon villages, and particularly of Burano.

In London, thanks are due to the staff of the Department of Prints and Drawings of the Victoria and Albert Museum, and to those of the Drawings Collection of the British Architectural Library at Portman Square.

On a more personal level, I must thank a number of professional friends and colleagues for their advice and assistance, and particularly Sir John Hale, Professor of Italian History at University College London; Brian Pullan, Professor of Modern History at Manchester University; Dr Deborah Howard, Lecturer in Architectural History at the University of Edinburgh, who made many helpful suggestions while the book was in draft; and to Dr Richard Mackenney, Lecturer in History also at the University of Edinburgh, for specific advice on the trade guilds and for his enthusiastic encouragement.

Thanks for their support are also due to several close friends in Venice, especially Giovanni and Maria Borella, Primo Zambon and Giulio Vianello, and to Jane Jones in London.

Finally, and certainly most importantly, thanks to Barbara, who became my wife while this book was being written and without whom it would probably have never been completed.

All of the illustrations are by the author, with the exception of the following:
    Figs. 4 and 8: Archivio di Stato di Venezia
    Figs. 20 and 66: Victoria and Albert Museum, London
    Figs. 90, 147, 150, 151, 152, 154: Drawings Collection, British Architectural Library
    Figs. 114 and 120: Museo Civico Correr, Venice

Thanks are due to all of the above bodies for permission to reproduce these illustrations.

Glossary of architectural and other terms

abbaino	skylight, dormer window or garret in roof
affresco	fresco, painting onto wet plaster
altana	roof terrace, almost always of timber
androne	the ground-floor central hall of a Venetian *palazzo*
architrave	lintel to a door or window
Arsenale	the state-run shipyards in Castello, eastern Venice
arte	a trade or craft guild
banda	parapet
barbacane	a jetty or cantilevered upper storey; beams that support such a storey – see text
barchessa	an outbuilding, often arcaded, attached to a villa, usually for storing farm equipment or as stables
bordonal	architrave
bottega	a retail shop, but also a workshop for any craft or trade
cà	common Venetian abbreviation for *casa*, house; often somewhat perversely applied to the largest *palazzi*
calle	a narrow Venetian street or alley (dim. *calletta, callesella*)
camino	chimney
campo	in Venice, a square; derived from the fact that the *campi* were originally grassed (It. *campo* – field) (dim. *campiello*)
càneva	as *cantina*, a wine store or warehouse
capitello	capital of a column
casa colonica, *casa padronale,* *villa, casìno*	these four terms have similar but not identical meanings, and can be broadly defined thus: a villa is the country house of a patrician, usually with fairly substantial lands attached, and at least with a garden or orchard. The villas of Murano and the Giudecca were suburban rather than rural, but generally conform to the type, as being places of resort and/or working farms. The term *casa colonica* is usually applied to the nobles' houses on the further islands of the lagoon, hence the adjective *colonica*; they were often used as hunting and fishing bases. The term *casa padronale* is usually used solely to describe the farmhouse-villas of Pellestrina, where the *padroni* were not noble, but merely successful local farmers. *Casìno* is a term

often applied to a more urban form of construction, and is defined by Boerio as a building for entertainment and conversation, rather like a *ridotto*. A *casìno di campagna* is thus a small country house for the *villeggiatura*, but probably not a 'serious' farmhouse. There is naturally a good deal of overlapping between these terms.

cason (e)	a building primarily built as a hunting-lodge; sometimes a substantial permanent structure, sometimes only a temporary shelter
cavanna	a boat shed or a roofed dock for storing small boats
centinate	the centring of an arch
chiave di volta	keystone
cortile	courtyard
cotto, in	constructed of brickwork
davanzale	window sill
extrados	upper or outer curve of an arch
fabbro	a smith
finestra	window
fòndaco, fòntego	warehouse for storage of goods; often applied to the ground floor of a Venetian *palazzo*, which was used for this purpose; also to the depositories of foreign trading communities in the city
fondamenta	quay or waterfront
fondamento	foundation of a building
frontone	gable
garzon (e)	apprentice in a trade
intrados	the inner curve of an arch
lido	capital of a column
loggia	a covered arcade
manoalo	a labourer, unskilled worker
marangono	a carpenter (Italian: *falegname*)
mariegole	the Statutes of a trade guild or *arte*
mensola	a corbel
merlatura	battlements or crenellation
modioni	modillions, or projecting corbels, usually carrying a cornice
montante	a mullion
muratore	a bricklayer; also a general builder – see text
napa	chimney-pot
palazzo	generally any large or monumental building, but here refers to the large city houses of the Venetian nobility (dim. *palazzetto*)
palo	a timber stake or pile; *palafitta*: an assembly of piles to form the foundation of a building
pergolo	balcony

piano	floor or storey of a building (*pianterreno*: ground floor)
piano nobile	the principal storey of a house of substance; almost always the first floor, but occasionally the second
piastrella	floor tile
pietra, pietra viva	natural stone
pietra cotta	brickwork or brick (literally 'cooked stone')
ponte	bridge
pontile	jetty or landing-stage
pòrtego	the great hall of a Venetian palace, nearly always forming the central axis on the first floor, with ancillary rooms on either side
pozzo	a well; *vera da pozzo*: a well-head
proto	the architect or chief surveyor of a major building or other project – see text
quattrocento	the fifteenth century
rio	a minor canal; *rio terrà*: a reclaimed canal
riva	quay or waterfront
ruga	an important street or *calle*
sacca	a bay or enclosed basin of water
sagoma	profile, especially of stone-carving
salizzada	a paved street, an important thoroughfare
scala	staircase
scuola	in Venice either a religious confraternity or a trade guild
seicento	the seventeenth century
Serliana	a type of window said to have originated with Serlio, consisting of a three-light opening, the central light of which is larger and has a semi-circular head; the outer lights have square heads, sometimes with smaller square openings above them
sestiere	one of the six administrative districts into which Venice is divided: S. Marco, Castello, S. Polo, Dorsoduro, Cannaregio, S. Croce
settecento	the eighteenth century
soler, solaio	floor or pavement
sottopòrtego	an arcade, supported on columns, with accommodation above
squero	yard for the construction and repair of small boats
tagliapietra, taiapiera	a stonemason
tavola, tola	a table; in building often means a slab of stone or marble or a large flat plank of timber
tegola, tegolina	a roof tile
terrazzo	floor finish consisting of small pieces of crushed stone, marble etc., in a lime mortar, sometimes coloured with brick dust – see text
teza, tettoia	a shed or outbuilding

traliccio	a roof truss
trave	a beam
vetrero, veriero, vetraio	a glassworker, maker of glass objects
villeggiatura	a sojourn at a country villa by the nobility, usually in summer

Part I

Building in the Venetian lagoon

1

General introduction

This book is divided into three parts; when I began to write the first drafts, my intention was simply to compile a fairly straightforward but comprehensive survey of the historic buildings that survive today in the lagoon villages surrounding Venice. Such a survey would be useful since none had yet been published in English and most of the guides to Venice (even the indispensable Lorenzetti) dwell only briefly on these lesser islands. The survey thus formed the original *raison d'être* for the present work. However, as I began to compile it certain questions came to mind constantly, and I was sure that the same questions would arise in the reader's mind when confronted with such a catalogue of vernacular buildings. And so the book developed into three parts, the intention of the first two being to answer many questions about the general development of vernacular architecture in the lagoon.

Part I deals with the fundamental difficulties of building in the Venetian environment and the matters discussed are all applicable to Venice itself as well as to its satellite villages. In this section I examine the physical context of the lagoon, its subsoil and topography; outline the available sources of building materials and their means of transport to the lagoon; analyse the methods of construction that were developed here in response to this unique and difficult environment; I also make some observations on the development of the building trades and guilds and on the rôle of the architect; and finally summarise the economic constraints that determined the types of houses that were built. It is naturally necessary to refer constantly to building in Venice, the lagunar capital and metropolis of the region, the political and cultural centre from which all power devolved.

In Part II I enter the city itself and outline the development of that most seminal and influential of all house types in the region, the city *palazzo-fòntego* of the merchant aristocrats who formed the body of the Venetian state. I summarise its form and function and then see how this extraordinarily influential house type was adopted and then adapted by the lesser social classes to produce a wide range of house forms, from the suburban villas of Murano and the Giudecca to the *case padronali* of Pellestrina's farmers and the modest *borghese* houses of Burano.

Finally, in the third part of the book I survey the lagoon villages and describe and illustrate all of the important individual historic houses as well as typical examples of the lesser house types to provide a comprehensive picture of this vernacular style of architecture.

In compiling this book, and in particular the survey, certain decisions had to be made at an early stage to define its scope and limitations. As can be inferred from the above, I have concentrated solely on domestic architecture, together with the very small (though important) group of public buildings that survive in these communities today. Ecclesiastical architecture is not discussed, since here – as elsewhere – it is so completely different from the domestic vernacular and represents the imposition of a building typology from above, from a powerful, complex and essentially 'foreign' organisation, the Church.

A more difficult limitation to impose on such a work is its geographical scope. My earlier book dealt with the whole of the ancient *Dogado*, the Adriatic littoral almost as far as Trieste, in its attempt to define the extent of traditional lagunar urban forms. In the present book, however, I have restricted the scope to the Venetian lagoon proper, chiefly for topographical convenience, but also because the outer limits of the spread of vernacular architecture are very difficult to define with precision and an attempt to do so would have resulted in far too bulky and diffuse a work.

In Part III, therefore, I have covered all of the lagunar satellites with the rather reluctant omission of Chioggia. This reluctance is chiefly because Chioggia is quintessentially a lagunar settlement, and its history formed a key part of my earlier study. However, Chioggia is not a village but an important town, with a rich variety of monumental buildings and a very high density of development that makes it much more akin to central Venice than to any of the lesser villages; the town thus really deserves a separate study of its own to do full justice to this density and variety.

The settlements examined in Part III thus include three sizeable villages (Murano, Burano, Pellestrina) together with three lesser settlements (Torcello, Mazzorbo, Malamocco) all within the Venetian lagoon and all closely related in their vernacular style to the middle rank and lesser houses of the capital. Their housing has considerable richness and variety despite the modest size of many of the houses.

In drawing the attention of the reader to these villages I would hope that they will achieve something of the recognition first given to the lesser domestic architecture of Venice when Egle Trincanato published her seminal *Venezia Minore* over thirty years ago. I am greatly indebted to that work in this present study, as I am also to the analyses of Maretto and Muratori; unfortunately Paolo Maretto's magnificent *La Casa Veneziana* was published too late for me to consult when researching for the present book, although it seems destined to become the definitive work on the housing of the city centre.

2

The lagunar environment

The Venetian lagoon is a large but shallow body of water lying between the Italian mainland and the northern end of the Adriatic Sea, the Gulf of Venice. The lagoon measures some eight to ten kilometres in width by about fifty in length; it is separated from the sea by a chain of long, narrow islands, known in dialect as *lidi*; between these *lidi* are gaps known as *porti*, through which the tides and all shipping enter and leave the lagoon. The total area of the lagoon covers some 55,000 hectares, although this area is divided into various zones. Firstly there is the deepest part of the lagoon, consisting chiefly of salt water brought in by the tides, and generally known as the *laguna viva*. Further towards the mainland shore is the part of the lagoon consisting predominantly of fresh water, and subject to comparatively little tidal movement; this is the *laguna morta*. Finally there is the broad fringe of marshes and swamps around the landward edge of the lagoon which are virtually unaffected by tides, and many of which now consist of *valli* or enclosed basins of water for the cultivation of fish.

The *laguna viva* is divided into three major basins corresponding to the three chief *porti* into the Adriatic, the *Bacino di Chioggia*, *Bacino di Malamocco* and *Bacino di Lido*. The main navigable channels are fairly narrow but often quite deep, and a few are able to take very large shipping indeed; most of the rest of the lagoon is shallow, however, with an average depth of barely a metre. The levels of land around its perimeter and on the islands within it are also very low, and virtually all of this land is less than two metres above median tide level. The tidal range here is the largest of the whole Adriatic shoreline; at periods of new and full moons there are two high and low tides every 24 hours, and then the tidal range is greatest. At the first and last lunar quarters there is only one tide every 24 hours and the range is at its minimum. The highest tide recorded to date was the infamous inundation of November 1966, when a level of 1.94 metres above median water level was recorded; the lowest was in February 1934, at 1.21 metres below median level.

The Venetian lagoon was originally formed by a complex interaction between geological forces on land and the action of the sea. The series of important rivers that rises in the eastern Alps and the Dolomites flows south and east across the great plain of the Veneto towards the upper Adriatic, bringing with it large quantities of silt. The rivers are at their most active, and destructive, in spring, when they are in flood not only with heavy rain but with vast quantities of melted snow from the mountains. The chief of these rivers are the Brenta, Sile and Piave, although there are others further east that flow from the Dolomites towards the lagoons of Caorle, Marano and Grado – the chief of these are the Livenza and Tagliamento.

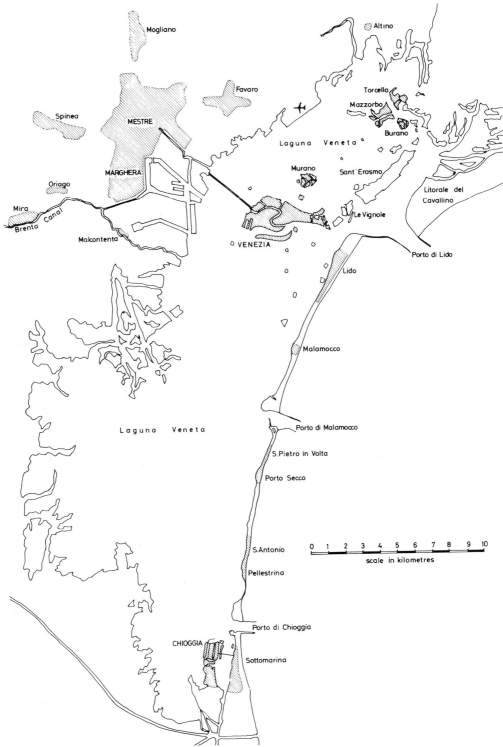

1 Sketch map of the Venetian lagoon indicating the location of the settlements discussed in the text.

The other natural force that formed the lagoon was the sea, together with the winds that act with it; the currents of the upper Adriatic move in an anticlockwise direction around the Gulf of Venice and these currents and tides deposit sand along the littoral. The lagoon of Venice (and the others along this coast) was thus formed by the meeting of these two forces, the mainland rivers laden with silt and the Adriatic currents laden with sand.

A further factor in this process is the wind, and two winds in particular: firstly there is the Scirocco which has its origins in the deserts of North Africa and blows northwards straight up the Adriatic. The Scirocco is notable for its effect on the tides and when a strong Scirocco coincides with a particularly high tide, it pushes the waters of the Adriatic (which is basically a huge cul-de-sac) high above their normal levels, consequently causing widespread flooding and damage. The second wind is the Bora, the cold northerly wind that blows southwards from the Dolomites and the mountains of northern Yugoslavia. The Bora has a less dramatic effect on the tides, but is often very strong, and has a considerable effect in 'sculpting' the dunes and low-lying soils along the gulf shoreline. Together with the anticlockwise currents of the sea, it has produced notable changes in the shoreline even in quite recent times. The littoral of Cavallino, for example, is today about five kilometres longer than it was in the sixteenth century, and this extension is entirely the result of the natural accumulation of dunes brought around the coast by the sea and the wind.

The formation of the Venetian lagoon was thus originally the result of these interactions but in geological terms it has never been a stable environment. There is a third factor to consider in its development over the centuries and that is the slow, natural lowering of land levels over the whole of this part of north-eastern Italy. This process has been continuing for many centuries, but has accelerated in recent decades because of disturbances to the substrata by the activities of man. It is possible that before the major alterations to the geography of the region by man the lagoon was indeed kept approximately in a state of equilibrium, with silt deposits brought down by the rivers (which would have rendered the lagoon shallower and eventually silted it completely) at least partly offset by the general lowering of land levels throughout the region.

Such a thesis can never be proved, however, as the Venetian government many centuries ago realised the potential danger of silting of the lagoon by the Brenta, Sile and Piave, and devised enormously complex hydraulic projects to divert these rivers so that they discharged directly into the sea.

An account of all of these works of diversion and canalisation is far too complex to detail here, but in principle they consisted of the diversion of the Brenta, the southernmost of the three, so that it circumvented the lagoon just south of Chioggia and discharged into the sea at Brondolo. The lower course of the Sile was similarly diverted around the northern end of the lagoon where it joined the lower Piave and reached the sea at Iesolo. Finally the Piave itself was also diverted and its lowest section canalised immediately below San Donà, so that it now enters the sea at Cortellazo, just below Eraclea. The only remaining streams whose courses now naturally discharged into the Venetian lagoon

2 and 3   The lagunar environment. 2: The lagoon near Torcello, a mixture of shallows, low-lying *barene* and firmer islets on which settlements can be built. 3: The lagoon off the lee shore near Pellestrina. With the exception of the deeper channels, much of the lagoon's surface is very shallow, and is staked for the cultivation of shellfish. The shed supported on timber piles forms a base for the villagers of Pellestrina to 'farm' the lagoon.

were the very modest Dese (and its tributary, the Zero) and the old Brenta Canal, neither of which posed a significant threat of silting.[1]

There were many other aspects of the lagoon's condition that required monitoring and maintenance; the Venetian Republic had an entire ministry or agency, the *Magistrato alle Acque*, whose sole purpose was to regularly survey the lagoon and its associated *lidi*, rivers, *porti* and canals, and to organise all works of repair and maintenance whenever necessary. One of their most important fields of activity was the maintenance of the sea defences along the outer shores of the *lidi*, those narrow, precarious strips of land that protected the lagoon from storm and flood. Until the middle of the eighteenth century the sea defences consisted chiefly of a large number of stone breakwaters projecting into the sea, together with embankments and palisades of timber – long rows of large stakes, with the spaces between the rows filled with stones, rocks or sand.[2]

These palisades required frequent repair, and regularly cost enormous sums of money; the timbers sometimes had to be brought down to the lagoon from the forests of Cadore, 100 km. away, and they were often floated down the Piave in great rafts, in the same way that the piles for the foundations of the city's buildings were transported.

Such palisades, together with such additional measures as the planting of tamarisks to stabilise the sandy soil, were the only sea defences for centuries until the great stone *Murazzi* were finally completed in the eighteenth century. The stone sea walls were later extended so that by the early years of the nineteenth century almost the whole length of the *lidi* from S. Nicolò down to Chioggia was protected by this great barrier of Istrian stone. For centuries until their completion, however, these *lidi* were subject to frequent storms and inundations, and on a number of occasions the sea broke right across them to flood unhindered into the lagoon. The land levels of all of these *lidi* remain extremely low even today, and most of the littoral of Pellestrina is less than 1.2 metres above median tide level.

The other aspects of the seaward shore of the lagoon that were of vital concern to the Republic were the *porti* between the lagoon and the sea. Today there are only three *porti*, all of them fairly wide and deep, although the Porto di Lido is by far the most important since it gives direct access to Venice itself. The Porto di Chioggia similarly provides the Adriatic's chief fishing port with direct access to the sea, while the third *porto*, that of Malamocco, historically the least important, has today been dredged to provide a deep water channel for oil tankers to dock directly at Marghera.

In earlier centuries there were more *porti* than the present three, and in Roman times there may have been as many as six or seven. The gate at Treporti was formerly a true *porto*, a rôle that it has lost in the last three centuries with the natural elongation of the Cavallino peninsula. Until the early fifteenth century, too, the littoral of Pellestrina

[1] See various references in R. J. Goy, *Chioggia and the Villages of the Venetian Lagoon* (Cambridge 1985). On the topography of the lagoon generally, the primary sources are the magnificent maps and plans in Archivio di Stato di Venezia (A.S.V.), particularly those of Sabbadino. Among secondary sources there are: R. Albertini, *I Porti Minori del Litorale Veneto* (Naples 1957); A. Averone, *Sull'Antica Idrografia Veneta* (Mantua 1911); R. Cessi, ed., *Antichi Scrittori d'Idraulica Veneta*, 2 vols. (Venice 1930); G. A. Zanon, *Sulla Formazione dei Cordoni Litorali*, etc. (Venice 1892); B. Zendrini, *Memorie Storiche dello Stato Antico e Moderno della Laguna di Venezia* (Padua 1811). See also bibliography to the present work.
[2] See Goy, *Chioggia*, esp. Part II. See also L. Lanfranchi *et al.*, *Mostra Storica della Laguna Veneta* (Venice 1970).

4 Map of the central part of the Venetian lagoon, drawn in the sixteenth century, possibly under *proto* Cristoforo Sabbadino. It covers the city of Venice, Murano, the Lido and the mainland

shoreline around Fusina and Marghera. The navigable channels are all carefully delineated and named (A.S.V. Savi ed Esecutori alle Acque; Laguna Series, No. 36).

consisted of two separate islands with a fairly narrow *porto* between them; this was filled in soon after the War of Chioggia but it gave its name to the present village of Porto Secco and its former site can still be traced today. It is possible that the littoral of Venice Lido also once consisted of two smaller *lidi*, and a number of sixteenth-century surveys indicate a very vulnerable section of shoreline, possibly another lost *porto*. The Republic had to ensure that the chief *porti*, those of Venice and Chioggia, were kept free of silting which might impede navigation and reduce the efficiency of the tides that regularly scoured the main channels and took all the city's effluent safely out to sea. From time to time attempts were made to reduce or fill in the lesser *porti*, with the intention of concentrating the force of the tides through the chief ones and thus ensuring that they did not silt up. Porto Secco was filled in partly for military reasons but also no doubt with this principle in mind; a little later, attempts were also made (unsuccessfully) to fill in the *porto* of Malamocco.

The two chief problems in maintaining the stability of the lagunar environment, therefore, were the reduction of silting and the maintenance of the sea-defences. In all other respects, the Republic, via the *Magistrato alle Acque*, pursued a consistent policy of non-intervention in the natural balance of the lagunar ecology. It was forbidden to private individuals to make any alteration whatsoever to the lagoon, the *palude* (marshes), the channels and watercourses, the shoreline and the sea-defences. Heavy fines were imposed, for example, on anyone who took sand from the foreshore for building purposes, or who cut down the trees that bound the soil together along the littoral. On the landward shore of the lagoon, there was a large area of marshes and *valli*, but even here no interference with the natural environment was tolerated, and the *Magistrato alle Acque* carefully recorded the landward limits of the lagoon with a series of stone markers or *cippi*, which were placed at intervals around the entire perimeter, from Treporti, via Iesolo, Altino, Marghera, the Brenta Canal, and thence to Chioggia, a distance of about 100 km. It was forbidden to anyone with lands on the landward side of this boundary to encroach on the lagoon in any way.

The lagoon itself was well surveyed and charted from an early date; in particular, the sixteenth century was a very active era for the surveyors of the *Savii ed Esecutori alle Acque*, as they were then known. Many hydraulic works were undertaken to reduce problems of silting, and a series of magnificent maps was produced, many under Cristoforo Sabbadino, who was *proto* or Chief Surveyor of the agency in the middle of the sixteenth century.

With the exception of the great hydraulic works to divert the silt-bearing rivers, and of purely natural phenomena (such as the elongation of the Cavallino peninsula), one of the most striking aspects of the sixteenth-century lagoon is that it so closely resembles its present topography, chiefly as a direct result of this consistently highly conservationist policy of the Republic. Examining Sabbadino's great survey of 1556, for example, there are only a few localised zones where any significant topographical differences may be identified.[3] The width of most of the *lidi* has increased in the last four centuries, partly because of a residual slow accumulation of silt, and partly because of local reclamation, chiefly undertaken because their extreme narrowness made them so vulnerable to flood. We may

---

[3] See Goy, *Chioggia*, fig.1. The map itself is in A.S.V. *Savii ed. Esecutori alle Acque Laguna* series no. 13.

also note one or two areas where the slow lowering of land levels has led to the loss of a number of islands and their transformation into *barene*.[4]

A particularly notable zone lies immediately north of Torcello where, in the medieval period, a number of significant communities stood. They declined for several reasons, partly because of silting, but also because of the natural lowering of land levels; several sixteenth-century surveys indicate the vestiges of this cluster of lost villages, as they slowly became more and more uninhabitable and were eventually abandoned to their fate.

It is not appropriate here to discuss in detail the complex geological processes that led to the formation of the various substrata beneath the lagoon, although a summary description of these strata will provide an appreciation of the technical difficulties involved in building not only in the *centro storico* of Venice itself but in all of the lagunar settlements.[5]

The bed of the lagoon is generally covered with a layer of silty deposits, much of which have accumulated as a result of human activity. These deposits may be broadly described as sedimentary or alluvial and have the appearance of fine silty mud; this contains a considerable amount of decayed vegetable matter as well as waste and rubbish from all the human settlements in the lagoon area. It is this superficial layer that requires quite frequent dredging and removal, particularly in the narrow, shallow *rii* of the city centre and the major villages. This alluvial layer varies in depth from less than a metre up to several metres and is naturally not capable of carrying very high loads.

Zuccolo has described the typical subsoil structure that lies below this layer thus:

> Below these superficial deposits of fairly recent origin there are strata of clayey mud or of very soft clay of organic origin. In general, below this there follows a stratum of clay of medium consistency, which usually in turn rests on a stratum of dense sand; sometimes, however, it bears upon bands of very densely compacted clay (*caranto*), but of quite limited thickness. At a greater depth, there are successive layers of clay of low and medium density, and of strata of sand with a very fine grain. Usually, therefore, the mechanical characteristics of these clays and clayey muds are very poor, mixed as they often are with organic material, and which comprise the superficial strata down to a depth of 5 or 6 metres, but which in areas of recent reclamation reach a thickness of about 8 to 10 metres.[6]

As we will see, the buildings of the city and its surrounding villages are all founded either on these more superficial layers of sand or sandy clay, or on the layer of *caranto*, the level of the surface of which, however, is sometimes too deep; in such cases the loads are carried on it indirectly via the less dense layers of clay above it.

[4] *Barene* are low banks in the lagoon visible at low tides but normally covered with water at high tides.
[5] See note 1 above. See also A. Giordani-Soika, *Ricerche sull'Ecologia e sul Popolamento delle Dune del Litorale di Venezia* (Venice 1959).
[6] G. Zuccolo, *Il Restauro Statico nell'Architettura di Venezia* (Venice 1975), p. 67.

3

An historical introduction

In the eighth and ninth centuries, the period of the emergent Venetian Republic, Venice itself was only one of a series of settlements in the lagoons that stretch around the crescent of the Adriatic gulf from the Po delta almost as far as modern Trieste. The earliest Republic was a confederation of twelve of these settlements, and its first headquarters was not at Venice but at Eraclea, several miles north-east of the Venetian lagoon.

All of the twelve were lagoon towns, built either on low islands within the lagoons themselves or else on the *lidi* that protected these lagoons from the sea. The southernmost town of the twelve was Chioggia, and the easternmost was Grado, built on a *lido* site directly opposite the remains of the great Roman city of Aquileia. Among the other settlements, four directly concern us here – Torcello, Murano, Malamocco and Rivo Alto. Torcello became a major ecclesiastical centre and an important port and trading base. Murano (Morianus) also became a significant town, while Malamocco for a few decades was the headquarters of the lagunar confederation, after its transferral from Eraclea. Old Malamocco eventually disappeared under the sea and the later medieval settlement was never more than a compact little village; but the fourth of these towns, Rivo Alto, was to have a far greater future than all of the others. The capital of the confederation was transferred once again from Malamocco in AD 810 and this time the move was to be longer-lasting. It lasted for almost ten centuries, in fact, and Rivo Alto slowly grew to become Rialto and then took the name of Venezia, capital of the Veneti.[1]

The site of Rivo Alto was almost ideal for the purposes of defence from mainland aggression although extremely difficult for the establishment of a major city. It lies precisely in the centre of the Venetian lagoon, on a group of low but firm islets; the mainland shore lies two miles away to the west while the open sea is barely a mile to the east. This natural 'moat' provided a degree of security from aggression that was quite unparalleled in any other large city in the Italian peninsula. Throughout the medieval period, while Florence, Rome and Milan were confined behind massive defensive walls, and while the palaces of their great families remained private fortresses, the Venetian patricians were building their own city palaces directly out of the water, with rows of delicate stone-traceried windows, with balconies and terraces, and with their private barges moored directly outside. This extraordinary security that the lagoon provided had such a profound effect on the medieval architecture of the city and its satellites that its importance can hardly be over-emphasised.

---

[1] For a small selection of standard histories, see general bibliography to the present volume.

It may be simply illustrated, however, by referring to two roughly contemporary buildings, the Palazzo della Signoria in Florence, completed in about 1315, and the south wing of Venice's Palazzo Ducale, begun just after the former was built, and constructed for a very similar purpose. The Palazzo della Signoria is still basically a castle, albeit a very imposing and luxuriously appointed one; the Palazzo Ducale is by no stretch of the imagination a castle, and there is no element of defence in any aspect of its design. Even its crenellations are an elaborate, refined decoration, with no military purpose whatsoever. This is an important theme in this survey: the architecture of the Venetian lagoons in all periods is based on function, practicality and on beauty, but never on considerations of security.[2]

Rialto slowly consolidated its position as the capital of the lagunar confederation and, despite many vicissitudes, it grew and prospered. The further lagunar settlements, such as Caorle and Grado, remained within the Dogado, the strip of territory along the edge of the Gulf that formed the core of the Venetian state, and they were sufficiently far from Venice to remain important towns in their own right.

The settlements closer to Venice slowly became satellites of the capital as it grew in power and influence. Several of them became, and remained, important towns, major sub-centres for trade and commerce. They also developed some degree of specialisation; Chioggia, for example, was pre-eminent firstly in the production of salt and, later, as that industry slowly declined, it grew to become the largest fishing port in the Adriatic, a rôle that it continues to hold today, some 1200 years after the foundation of the Republic.[3] Murano, the closest of these other towns to the capital, naturally had the closest social and economic ties, but after 1292 it became the centre for glass production, again a rôle that it has retained to our own day. Torcello, too, from its earliest days an important religious centre, also grew to become a major focus of monastic life and culture, and at its medieval peak contained several famous and extremely wealthy monasteries.

Although there are certain factors in common in the history of these lagunar settlements, therefore, we cannot easily generalise about their socio-economic development, and when we later consider the villages individually, we will see a number of key differences in these fields that are closely reflected in the architecture that survives today.

The pattern of development within the lagoon as a whole was initially quite random, in that the natural topography lent itself to colonisation only in certain places. Rialto was built on a cluster of over a hundred small islets divided by narrow canals, and with one broader channel, the later Grand Canal, dividing the group roughly in half.[4] Chioggia, too, was built on a compact group of islets, roughly rectangular in overall form, just inside the lagoon in its southern corner.[5] However, there were no other groups of islets in the lagoon south of Venice that were suitable for colonisation, and so Chioggia was, and

[2] For a useful general urban history of Florence, see G. Fanelli, *Firenze* (Rome 1980) in the excellent series Le Città nella Storia d'Italia. For the Palazzo Ducale of Venice see: G. Mariacher, *Il Palazzo Ducale di Venezia* (Florence 1950); E. Arslan, *Venezia Gotica* (Milan 1970); E. R. Trincanato 'Il Palazzo Ducale' in *Piazza S. Marco* (various authors; Venice 1970), with very useful drawings.

[3] See Goy, *Chioggia*.

[4] Essential as an attempt at analysing the early urbanisation of the Realtine group is S. Muratori, *Studi per una Operante Storia Urbana di Venezia* (Rome 1959).

[5] See Goy, *Chioggia*. Also E. Concina *Chioggia: Saggio di Storia Urbanistica* (Treviso 1978); more general is D. Razza, *Storia Popolare di Chioggia* (Chioggia 1898).

remains, the only major town here; its site was so restricted, however, that as it grew and prospered in the twelfth and thirteenth centuries, it spread onto the adjacent *lido*, where a suburb community, Clugia Parva or Lesser Chioggia, grew up and where Sottomarina presently stands.

The whole of the southern lagoon is thus devoid of any other settlements apart from those on the *lidi*. These narrow strips of land were always very precarious places to settle, though, and none of the *lido* settlements ever grew to prosperity as did the intra-lagunar settlements of Venice, Chioggia, Murano and Torcello.

In the northern lagoon, the topography was rather different, and north of Venice a number of important communities arose. Firstly there was Murano, also built on a cluster of small islets and, like Venice, divided into two parts by a broader channel.[6] Further north again was an extensive zone of islands and channels, where in the early and high middle ages a large cluster of settlements grew – Torcello, Mazzorbo, Burano, Costanziaca, Ammiana, S. Cristina. Some were so close together as to be virtually contiguous, and Mazzorbo and Burano today are still linked by a footbridge. Some of them had communities largely based on the considerable number of religious houses, whereas others, notably Burano, were more simple fishing communities. Most of them reached a peak of importance in the early medieval period, after which there began a long, slow period of decline; this was due in part to Venice's pre-eminence as the capital of what was now a great trading empire and a sophisticated international culture. Torcello, Mazzorbo and the rest simply could not compete with Venice any longer on economic terms, although some of these islands remained important centres of religion and culture long after their economic importance had gone.

The chief reason for their decline, however, was silting in the lagoon, and the difficulty of communications; in addition, the lowering of land levels, particularly acute at Ammiana, Costanziaca and S. Cristina, led to ever more frequent flooding.[7] The large quantities of silt brought into the lagoon by the Sile (before its later diversion) made navigation more and more difficult, particularly to Torcello, and so slowly these islands declined and their sea-borne trade was diverted to Venice. As silt reduced the navigability of the lagoon channels, the waters became more stagnant and malaria became widespread. Eventually, some islands were completely abandoned, while others, such as Torcello, survived only as the relics of once-rich and flourishing communities. Ammiana and Costanziaca have now long since disappeared below the waters of the lagoon, and even the original sites of some of these earlier settlements are now difficult to locate with precision. Of all of them, only Burano remains a living and substantial community today.

As the Venetian Republic evolved, a complex system of government developed, with numerous specialised committees and ministries. Although the Republic had a very extensive trading empire, with communities and agencies all over the Middle East as far as the Black Sea, and in northern Europe in Flanders, Paris and London, its territorial empire

---

[6] There is no comprehensive and satisfactory history of Murano; the most useful work is V. Zanetti, *Guida di Murano* (Venice 1866; new facsimile edn Venice 1984).

[7] See note 1 to chapter 2 above. See also bibliog. in Goy, *Chioggia*.

was very small.[8] The basic core of the state consisted simply of the coastal strip, the Dogado, which extended from just south of Chioggia (with boundary forts at Loreo and Cavarzere) north-east to Grado, a distance of about 130 km.

However, this coastal strip was extremely narrow, and its confines on the landward side roughly coincided with the line of the old Roman trunk roads, the Via Annia and Via Popilia, which skirted the edges of the lagoons along this coastline. This was the heartland of the Venetian state, and for a very long time, until the great era of Terraferma expansion in the fifteenth century, this was indeed the modest extent of the *Serenissima* in Italy; a state in which much of the territory was lagoon or marsh, and in which almost all communications had to be effected by boat.

The further towns of the Dogado – Caorle, Grado – were governed by officials (quasi-military governors) directly appointed by the *Signoria*, the ruling body of the state. Within the Venetian lagoon itself there were four governors, known as *podestà*, and based at Chioggia, Murano, Malamocco and Torcello. The *podestà* were always patricians, again appointed by the *Signoria*, and with a term of office usually of sixteen months. They presided over the administration of the towns or villages under their jurisdiction and may best be described as civil governors. The communities under their governorship had their own councils, consisting of locally elected citizens or villagers. In the smaller villages there was a single all-purpose council, but in a larger town such as Chioggia, there was a more complex administration based on that of central government. Here there were two councils, a *Maggior Consiglio* or Great Council, consisting of every eligible male citizen, and a smaller executive committee or *Minor Consiglio* consisting of either six or twelve men.[9] Chioggia's *Maggior Consiglio* was large, comprising on occasion more than 200 men, and was the chief debating chamber for all major local issues – the election of officials, expenditure of funds on public works, the airing of grievances – a very wide range of matters indeed.

Like almost all aspects of the Venetian system of government, the administration of the lagoon, once established, was a very stable institution for an extremely long period of time. The *podestà* were originally appointed towards the end of the thirteenth century, and the locally elected councils were almost certainly virtually contemporaneous with them; this form of administration survived with only minor variations until the fall of the Republic over 500 years later. The four *podestà* of the lagoon required living accommodation in these villages, of course, and the village councils required halls in which to meet, and the buildings constructed for these two purposes in the medieval period provide us today with a small but valuable group of gothic structures. The most important civic building in the lagoon outside Venice was the *Palazzo Comunale* at Chioggia, which is unfortunately lost to us, as it was replaced by the present town hall in the middle of the last century; the *Palazzo* of Murano is also gone. However, we still have two of the original

[8] See the general histories cited, in bibliog. to the present book. For the trading empire, see esp. F. Lane, *Venice: a Maritime Republic* (Baltimore 1973).
[9] For the structure of central government, see the general histories; also G. Maranini, *La Costituzione di Venezia*; 2 vols. (Florence 1974); for a contemporary description of the government in *c.* 1500 see M. Sanudo, *La Città di Venetia*, A. C. Arico ed. (Milan 1980). For a later contemporary description see F. Sansovino, *Venetia Città Nobilissima*; new facsimile edition, based on the third edition, which incorporated the additions of G: Martinioni in 1663 (Venice 1968).

three public buildings at Torcello, two at Burano and two at Malamocco to provide us with at least a partial picture of the physical context in which these medieval communities were administered. The *Palazzo* of Chioggia, as we might imagine, was a more imposing structure than any of these survivors, as befits the second city of the lagoon, and we have several illustrations of it in the town archive.

The relationship between the lagoon islands and the capital was a slightly paradoxical one. On one hand, they were the closest of all of the Venetian 'colonies', literally in the *Serenissima*'s own aquatic backyard, and thus very closely tied to the city in political, economic and social terms. The produce of the islands and of the villagers' fishing boats all went to Rialto to be sold; many Venetian patricians had houses, estates or other interests in the lagoons. The churches and monasteries also had close links in both directions – churches in the city owned land in the lagoons, and monasteries in the lagoons owned property in the capital. Communications, too, could sometimes be very rapid if the necessity arose. On the other hand, the *podestà* system gave the communities a high degree of autonomy in dealing with their own local affairs, even though the law of the state was always paramount. And the fact that the villages were all built on self-contained islands also gave them a higher degree of day to day autonomy, even of isolation, that would not have been so pronounced if the communities had been the same distance apart on the Terraferma. The lagoon exaggerates distances: even from Burano the towers and spires of Venice can be clearly seen, but they appear to be far more than five miles away, and in this historical context, those five miles of water gave rise to a completely different form of community, a series of such communities, in fact, joined together by the navigable channels but at the same time divided by the open expanses of the lagoon.

Despite this autonomy, Venetian government in general was highly centralised, although power was never concentrated in individuals. All decisions of government policy were made at S. Marco, and all business was conducted at Rialto. The latter was literally the meeting point of all communications within the lagoon; here all of the complex network of canals came together, and here were the markets – the fish market, the fruit and vegetable market, the market for spices and precious stones, for gold and silver, the market for international banking. The fishermen of the lagoons and the market-gardeners were obliged by law to sell their produce here, and so it was to Rialto that they looked for their livelihoods, just as they looked to S. Marco for their laws and their governors.

The importance of the waterway network cannot be over-stressed. The Venetian lagoon was, and to a large extent still is, a different world from the 'normal' world of the Terraferma, just a couple of miles away. Boats were the only means of communication for everyone, from the doge to the humblest fisherman; all goods, for whatever purpose, had to be transported by water, and often trans-shipped onto barges from the more conventional carts of the mainland. Timber for building construction, for piles, for shipbuilding, had to be floated down the rivers and across the lagoon in great rafts to the Arsenal, or towed down the Grand Canal to the building site. Barges full of sand, bricks and lime carried the other basic building materials. In times of drought, even water had to be transported by boat from the mainland. Barges full of grain came along the inland waterway network from the flatlands beyond the Po delta to watermills on the Àdige and Brenta; ships similarly laden brought grain from further south, from the Abruzzi and

5 The lagoon and the city: the view of the northern shoreline of Venice seen from Burano, divided by the waters but joined by the navigable channels which are today all marked with timber *bricole* as seen on the right.

Puglia. Venice was linked to most of the other major cities of the great Po plain by river and canal, and similarly linked to the other towns of the Dogado; it was possible to reach Grado in one direction, and Mantua, Ferrara and even Milan in the other, by an extensive system of rivers, canalised rivers and artificial channels.

Within the lagoon itself, the smaller communities varied considerably, not only in their social and economic structure, but also in their size and in their overall pattern of development. Apart from the slow changes wrought by the lowering of land levels and silting, the villages were naturally not static in their size or in population. Venice itself was one of the largest cities in Europe by the middle decades of the fourteenth century, but in the spring of 1348 the plague, the 'Black Death', arrived in the city and brought to an abrupt end a long period of urban growth and prosperity in the city and its satellites, indeed throughout northern Italy and much of western Europe. Recovery was slow, and this first devastating plague was followed at varying intervals over the next three centuries by many other outbreaks, several of which (notably those of 1575 and 1630) were particularly severe in the lagoon. The plague was more responsible than any other single factor for the patterns of growth and decline within the lagoon communities; as we will see later, the longer periods of freedom from the disease are also marked by numerical expansion and building activity in both the lagunar capital and its surrounding satellite villages. For this reason much of the architecture that survives in the lagoon today dates from the first decades of the seventeenth century and from the first half of the eighteenth, both periods of rapidly expanding population, and at least to some extent of increased prosperity as well.

The Venetian lagoon was a special environment, and the architecture that evolved there had a number of notable features which, when seen together, make Venetian vernacular architecture quite distinct from that of even its close neighbours on the Terraferma, of Padua, Vicenza or Verona. We have mentioned the very high degree of security that the lagoon itself offered, and the consequent lack of any defensive element in the local vernacular style. Perhaps the two other most important purely practical aspects of Venetian architecture are firstly the extraordinary physical difficulties of building in such an environment, and secondly the fact that there were so few naturally available building materials in the vicinity with which to construct a great city and its satellite settlements. These difficulties, and the ways in which they were overcome, will be examined in the next two chapters.

4

Building materials and their sources

The range of building materials traditionally used in Venetian architecture is quite small. This may appear surprising when we examine the extraordinary richness and variety of the built fabric of the city and its satellites. However, a large part of that variety derives from stylistic variations which cover a very long span of time, from the later Veneto-Byzantine style to the baroque and beyond, to the neo-classicism of the first part of the nineteenth century. And it is also based in large part on countless 'variations on a theme', of different rhythms of fenestration, of proportion, of decoration, rather than on a wide range of basic materials. For example, there is only one type of stone that is used in a significant quantity, and that is white Istrian 'marble' and there are only very small quantities of other, true marbles as detailed decoration. Most Venetian buildings are of brick, although this is very often finished either with a veneer of stone, or rendered or stuccoed and it is often this veneer (in some cases originally painted or frescoed) that provides the colour and variety of the buildings' surfaces.

The very earliest structures in the lagoon were simple huts or sheds of timber, with roofs thatched with osiers, and this most basic form of construction can still be seen today in a few isolated *valli*, where *casoni* have been built for use as hunting or fishing bases. The number of these surviving *casoni* has diminished rapidly in recent years, but while a few remain they are valuable reminders of the simplest of all lagunar building forms, a square or rectangular one-roomed hut with a pitched, thatched roof.

However, other than its original littoral pinewoods and the osiers of the lagunar margins, the lagoon itself offered no other natural building materials, and even brick, the most basic, essential material, had to be brought from the mainland. In this chapter, and that which follows, we will briefly discuss these materials and the ways in which they were assembled to form the archetypal lagunar vernacular style. The quotations that I have inserted at various places in these two chapters are short excerpts from Francesco Sansovino's *Venetia Città Nobilissima*,[1] in which he summarises, usually with great clarity, the major features of the domestic architecture of the city and its villages; written in 1580, it is still useful today.

---

[1] F. Sansovino, *Venetia Città Nobilissima*, book IX, p. 382. This and all the other excerpts are from the facsimile edition, published Venice 1968. This facsimile is of the 1663 original edition, and thus includes the additions of Stringa and Martinioni.

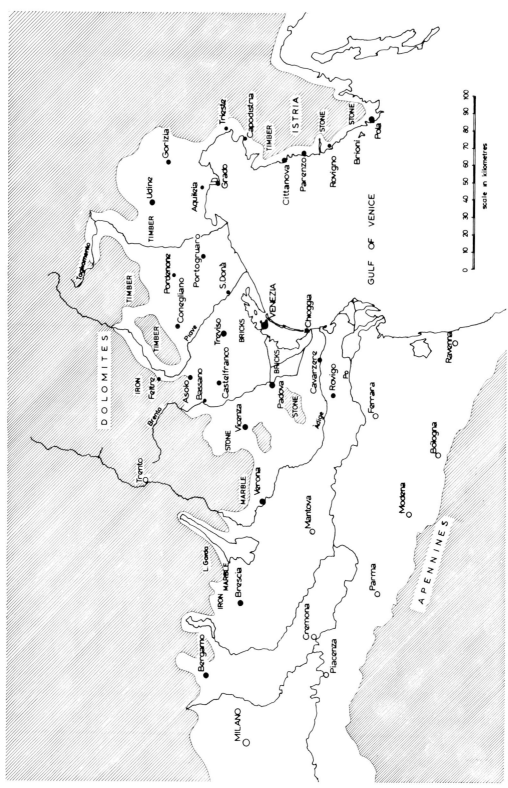

6 Sketch map of north-eastern Italy indicating the major towns and cities and the principal sources of building materials for Venice and its satellites. Towns indicated with a solid black circle were within Venice's Terraferma empire for all or most of the period from about 1400 to the end of the sixteenth century, and in most cases remained so until the fall of the Republic in 1797.

Bricks and tiles

Bricks or burned stones and lime are obtained from the lands of Padua, Treviso and Ferrara, but the most highly esteemed are those of Padua; this is not only because the clay is better but also because the bricks are better seasoned, and are well burnt, and in addition because the moulds for the tiles, bricks and hollow tiles[2] are of greater size than the others, and a boat manned generally by not more than two persons may transport on most occasions all of the materials necessary to build each large new building.

Palladio, in the *Quattro Libri*, also briefly summarises the manner in which bricks should be made:

> The stones which are made by the hand of man are commonly known as *quadrelli* because of their form; these have to be made from clay soil, which is . . . easily workable; gravelly or sandy soil should be left where it is found. The clay should be extracted in the Autumn, and worked in the winter, and thus the bricks may be well formed in the following Spring.
>
> But if it becomes necessary to make them in Winter or Summer, in Winter they are to be covered with dry sand and in the Summer with straw. To form them [well] it is necessary to allow [the clay] to dry for a considerable time, and it is best to dry it in the shade, so that not only the surface dries thoroughly, but also the inner parts as well, so that all is equally dry; this cannot be done in less than two years.[3]

Clay for brickmaking was available in large quantities virtually all over the flat fertile plains of the Venetian Terraferma. As we saw, the original Dogado included only a narrow mainland strip along the edge of the lagoons, but even here in the vicinity of Mestre suitable clay could be found, and Mestre remained a useful centre for brickmaking because of its convenience for a very long time.[4] Later, in 1405, Padua became a permanent part of the Terraferma Empire and thus the fine clay to which Sansovino refers also became a part of the patrimony of raw materials for the Venetian state. A little later again, the Empire had expanded to embrace a large part of the entire great plain of northern Italy, so that supplies were now secure over a very wide area. In practice, however, the bulk and weight of bricks, and hence the cost of transport, meant that most supplies for the lagoon were drawn from a comparatively small area, and a line drawn from Cavarzere, through Padua, Treviso and S. Donà, was probably the usual limit for regular bulk deliveries to the capital and its satellites.

Brickworks were usually small and scattered, many being run almost literally as 'cottage industries', family enterprises with a kiln and drying shed attached to the house. Little detailed research has yet been undertaken on this fundamental aspect of Venetian building, although the principles of traditional brickmaking by hand have not changed in a significant way from Palladio's day to our own. However, the supply of large quantities of bricks was often irregular and there were undoubtedly shortages from time to time as the result of wars, or other natural disasters such as famines or plagues. In particular, supplies prior to the beginning of the fifteenth century were not always readily available

---

[2] '& si perché il morello del tegolo, del mattone, & della tavella e di maggior misura de gli altri' (ibid.).

[3] A. Palladio, *I Quattro Libri dell'Architettura*, book I, p. 8. This and all the other excerpts are from the facsimile edition, published Milan 1969.

[4] In fact, there were brickworks right on the banks of the Canale Salso, which joins Mestre to the lagoon, via the fort of Marghera. The canal was excavated in 1361 and formed a useful part of the Terraferma waterway network. Some of the works survived at least until the early eighteenth century, and may be seen on a survey of 1721 in A.S.V. S.E.A. Diversi no. 61 (reproduced in *Altobello* [Comune di Venezia, 1985]).

7 Bricks: the apse of S. Donato at Murano represents a *tour de force* of the skills of the Venetian bricklayers; it was completed in about 1140.

for the reason noted above; government decrees as early as the 1320s legalised their production only at certain times of the year, in accordance with Palladio's observations on good practice, a restriction that must on occasion have exacerbated shortages.[5]

Timber

> Timber is brought in great quantities down the rivers in the form of rafts, from the mountains of Cadore, from the Friuli, and from the [Marca] Trevisana . . .[6]

Timber was the next essential building material, and was required in very large quantities not only for the upper floors of buildings and for joinery. Millions of timber piles were required for foundations, and there was a further enormous demand for the *palificate* (palisades) for the sea defences, as well as the requirements of the great ship-building industry of the Arsenal. Palladio, as a true follower of Vitruvius, also diligently follows the Roman's recommendations for the felling and seasoning of timber:

> Timber should be cut in the Autumn, and throughout the Winter . . . It should be cut only halfway through to the heartwood and thus left to drain out . . . in this way the bad [substances] will drain away . . . Once cut, it must be left in a place where it is not affected by hot sun, nor by impetuous winds, nor by rain; [after seasoning] . . . not before three years should it be used for flooring, for doors or windows. . . .[7]

Originally much of the coastal strip was covered with pine forests and a number of fragments of these formerly extensive forests remain today. Pines flourished on the light, sandy soil of the littoral and even in Roman times the special qualities of certain of these species were well known. Vitruvius described the excellent qualities of alder (always found along the banks of rivers) that made it particularly useful for foundations:

> Hence, in swampy places, alder piles driven close together beneath the foundations of buildings take in the water that their own consistency lacks, and remain imperishable forever, supporting structures of enormous weight and keeping them from decay . . . One can see this at its best in Ravenna; for there all the buildings, both public and private, have piles of this sort beneath their foundations.[8]

Vitruvius was also well aware of the special qualities of larch for building construction:

> The larch, known only to the peoples of the towns on the banks of the river Po and the shores of the Adriatic, is not only preserved from decay and the worm by the great bitterness of the sap, but also it cannot be kindled with fire nor ignite of itself.[9]

The larch (which according to Vitruvius was named after the town of Larignum where it was identified) was 'transported by way of the Po to Ravenna, and is to be had in Fano, Pesaro, Ancona and the other towns in that neighbourhood'. One of the difficulties in transporting larch (to Rome, for example) was that it is so dense that it does not float, and

[5] Zuccolo, *Il Restauro*, pp. 50–1 and notes 83 *et seq*. See also A. Sagredo, *Sulle Consorterie delle Arti Edificative in Venezia* (Venice 1856); he notes specific decrees passed by the government in respect of the seasons permitted for taking clay for brickmaking, on 20 January 1326, 17 March 1327 and 12 March 1331.
[6] Sansovino, *Venetia Città Nobilissima*, book IX, p. 383.
[7] Palladio, *I Quattro Libri*, book I, p. 7. As he concedes, his recommendations are based on chapter 9 of the second book of Vitruvius's *Ten Books on Architecture*. The latter's own advice is in fact far more detailed.
[8] Vitruvius, *Ten Books*, book II, chapter 9, para. 10.
[9] *Ibid.* para 14.

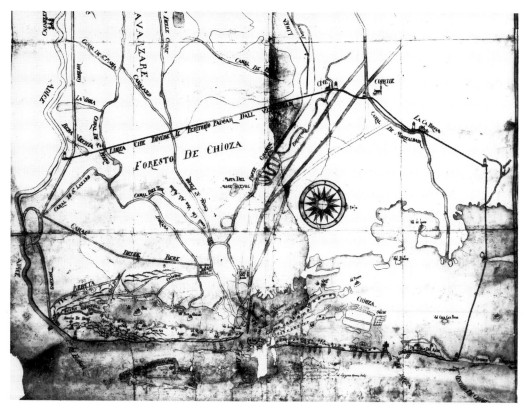

8 Timber supplies: a seventeenth century map of the environs of Chioggia, indicating the borders of the Dogado and the complex network of canals and diverted rivers. Much of this zone was now a carefully conserved forest (A.S.V. Misc. Mappe no. 823).

hence had to be carried by ship rather than simply floated to its destination in the form of a raft, as other timbers were, both by the Romans and later by the Venetians.

All of Vitruvius's observations were relevant to the Venetians' own situation, of course. Regarding the medieval forests of the Venetian hinterland, several documents from the thirteenth century confirm that in that period these forests still remained extensive, and a number of local place names still evoke the formerly sylvan nature of the nearby Terraferma.[10] Some of these forests were cleared as demand rose in Venice, and slowly it became necessary to search further and further afield for certain types of timber. By the later sixteenth century (as Sansovino notes) it was often necessary to obtain timber for repairs to the sea-defences and for general construction work from as far as Pordenone and Belluno, some of the closest extensive upland forests that remained. (The Euganean Hills near Padua were another, more convenient, source, but they were not extensive, and demand in Padua itself was significant.) Indeed, apart from the complex political considerations, one of the major economic reasons for the great Terraferma expansion of the Republic in the fifteenth century was an attempt to guarantee state control over a far

[10] E. Concina, *Chioggia: Saggio di Storia Urbanistica* (Treviso 1978) p. 4 and footnotes.

greater area to ensure regular supplies of basic foodstuffs and commodities to the capital; among these were grain, vegetables and wine, but there is no doubt either that control over the vast mountainous forests of the Bellunese and much of the Friuli was another key consideration.

Timber was also essential to build and repair the merchant shipping fleets on which the Republic's economic survival still to a large extent depended, while its security similarly depended on equally imposing fleets of war galleys. It is difficult to document with precision the slow process of the destruction of much of the coastal pine forest and the progressive exploitation of forests further afield. Lane has suggested that significant deforestation of the woods closest to the lagoon began as early as the tenth or eleventh centuries.[11] Apart from the narrow band of coastal pinewoods, the adjacent Terraferma plain contained a mixture of hardwoods, among them oak, ash and beech. We may conclude that convenient supplies of oak, for example, would have been depleted quite rapidly, as it is a timber with so many uses.

We may attempt to cast a little light on the deforestation process by examining a handful of documents in the Chioggia archive: Chioggia's hinterland was extensively forested, and there are a number of twelfth-century references to the woods of this zone, particularly around the villages of Conché, Codevigo, Rosara, Corte and Boion, the last two situated near the western shore of the lagoon, opposite Padua.[12] Undoubtedly some of these woodlands were lost in this period as both Chioggia and Venice expanded significantly.

By the latter part of the fourteenth century there was a large warehouse at Chioggia specifically for storing timber, chiefly for work to embankments, mooring posts and for urgent repairs to the sea defences.[13] In 1397 a resolution was passed in the Town Council prohibiting the further deforestation of the immediate hinterland of the town, a prohibition that extended to the then limits of the Dogado, the 'first mouth of the Brenta' and the border with the lands of Padua.[14]

Despite considerable pressures on these remaining local forests, therefore, the government and its agencies attempted to resist their complete removal, and a number survived in the environs of Chioggia well into the sixteenth century. There were woods at Fogolana (near Conché) in 1468,[15] while a ducal decree a few years later , in 1486, made further restrictions on cutting timber.[16] By now much of the timber for building construction and shipbuilding came from considerable distances from the lagoon, and this fact is verified by several ducal decrees which specify where timber for repairs to the sea-defences was to be obtained. One such decree, in 1556, ordered that 2,000 stakes of oak were to be obtained,

[11] F. Lane, *Venice: A Maritime Republic* (Baltimore 1973) p. 8.

[12] See note 9 above.

[13] Archivio Comunale di Chioggia (A.C.) 26 c.34t.

[14] Ibid. c. 97t. The decree in effect put a moratorium on the signing of any new leases or tenancy agreements 'pro conservatione vinum comunis et omni allio bono respectu'.

[15] A.C. 12 (Ducal Letters) c.34.

[16] Ibid. c.86. A decree of the Council of Ten dated 28 November 1601 is revealing of the government's attitude towards timber supplies; it reads in part: 'intendendosi ogni giorno gli continui e grandissimi danni . . . ordina di coniare un nuovo bollo per i roveri che interessano l'Arsenale che non debbono essere tagliati in alcun modo ne con licentia, ne senza licentia ma restino riservati per il bisogno di essa casa [i.e. the Arsenal]'.

some procured locally from Pragin near Padua and from Teolo in the Euganean Hills; the rest, however, was to be taken from Camisano near Vicenza and from as far as Pordenone in the Friuli.[17]

By the mid-sixteenth century the remaining zones of woodland in the vicinity of the lagoon were carefully demarcated and preserved. The Sabbadino-Minorelli map,[18] drawn in 1556 and transcribed a century later, still shows considerable surviving woods, most of them around the southern end of the lagoon, although there were also a number of smaller patches of forest at Marghera, Altino and Tessera and fragments of these have survived today.

Stone

But a beautiful and marvellous thing is the stone which is brought from Rovigno and Brioni, a fortress on the coast of Dalmatia; it is white in colour and resembles marble; but it is solid and strong such that it will last for an extremely long time against both the ice of winter and the rays of the sun; from it are made statues, which are polished with felt as one would polish marble, so that when polished they indeed have the appearance of marble. And with this material the entire façades of Palaces and Churches are decorated, with columns that can be made in a single piece, as tall, as broad and as long [*sic*] as one would desire;[19] because the quarries of Rovigno have a great abundance of this type of stone, known as Istrian, or Liburnica by the ancient writers . . .

There are also façades covered with fine marble, but from Greece, transported from the islands of the Archipelago [i.e., the Cyclades], and especially from Paros, but it is not as white as our own [Istrian], and quite different from the marble of Carrara in Tuscany. The stone of Verona is also of high renown because it is red; since it has various figurings on it, the stone gives great beauty to buildings; and from this stone are built the pavements of Churches and Palaces, in a chessboard pattern [with Istrian stone], and it can also be worked further to produce sinks,[20] fireplaces, cornices and other similar things. Nevertheless, the red stone of Cattaro[21] is the most beautiful and the most durable for pavements.[22]

Of stone, there are two varieties, that which is provided by nature, and the other made by the industry of man; the natural is taken from quarries and is used either for lime or for building walls . . . Those stones which are used in building walls are either of marble and hard stones, which are called *pietre vive*, or are of soft stone . . . The marbles and *pietre vive* may be worked as soon as they have been quarried . . . and may immediately be placed in the work. But the soft stone . . . must be quarried in the Summer, and kept in the open and should not be put into the work for two years; it is quarried in the Summer so that, since it is not accustomed to the effects of wind, rain and ice, it may little by little become more and more durable, and thus become more used to resisting the similar injuries inflicted on it by the passage of time . . .[23]

As may be inferred from Sansovino and Palladio, there is no stone or marble available in

[17] A.C. 14 (Ducal Letters) c. 44.
[18] A.S.V. Map Archive S.E.A. Laguna Series no. 13.
[19] 'con colonne alte, grosse & lunghe di un pezzo quanto si vuole'; Sansovino, *Venetia Città Nobilissima*, book IX, p. 383.
[20] *Acquari* are perhaps sinks or cisterns, tanks or decorative troughs.
[21] Cattaro (modern Kotor) lies on the Dalmatian coast south of Dubrovnik. It was a long-established Venetian foothold in Dalmatia although the hinterland was controlled by local clans with which the Serenissima waged a long, intermittent war.
[22] All of the above from Sansovino, *Venetia Città Nobilissima*, book IX, p. 383.
[23] Palladio, *I Quattro Libri*, book I, chapter 3, pp. 7–8. The stones made by the industry of man, bricks, were usually called *pietre cotte*, literally 'cooked stones'. This passage is loosely based on Vitruvius (*Ten Books*, book II, chapter 7).

the immediate vicinity of the lagoon; the closest places from which stone may be obtained are the Euganean Hills, south-west of Padua. This stone is a volcanic trachite, usually grey or dark grey (sometimes almost black) in colour and with a distinctive texture. While very durable, its sombre appearance does not lend itself to decorative sculptural work and indeed it does not seem to have been used in the lagoons much before the eighteenth century, when it became very popular for general paving purposes.[24] Piazza S. Marco was repaved with trachite (and a pattern of white Istrian stone) in the eighteenth century, and it is today universally used to pave the *calli* and *campi* throughout the city and its satellite villages.

Further afield, however, both further west into the Veneto and north-east to the Friuli, there was a wide variety of building stones available, with many different colours and textures. Some are highly decorative, and although much prized both today and in the past, their texture and grain makes most of them unsuitable as general building stones.

Verona and Vicenza are both surrounded by quarries producing valuable stones and marbles. There is a white stone from Vicenza, S. Gottardo, suitable for general building purposes, although it is fairly light and rather porous. It is thus fairly easy to work, but is not suitable for conditions of high exposure or for fine carving. However, its accessibility and workability mean that it has been widely used on the Terraferma.

Verona has always been an important centre for decorative marbles; the best known is 'Rosso di Verona', which can be seen in all parts of the Veneto and in the lagoons. It was often used for paving, as Sansovino notes, frequently in a pattern with a stone of contrasting colour. It was also used in the form of decorative paterae or inlays on façades and sometimes for individual pieces of sculpture; an example of the latter is the monumental fireplace designed by Vittoria for Palazzo Trevisan at Murano. 'Rosso di Verona' is very hard, but also has a pronounced grain, which makes it difficult to work; in conditions of high exposure, too, it tends to eventually deteriorate along this grain, producing a pocked, uneven surface. However, its warm rich colour has always made it highly prized as a polished sculptural stone and, like that of Istria, it has a variety of shades depending on the finish given to it. With a high polish it is deep crimson, while on prolonged exposure to the elements it 'bleaches' to a paler, pinkish colour.

We may summarise here the other decorative stones and marbles available in the Venetian hinterland, chiefly from the environs of Vicenza and Verona. From the former city, in addition to S. Gottardo, there is a group of stones known as Chiampo, from the village of that name, a few miles north-west of Vicenza. They are mostly fairly fine-grained marbles, usually yellowish-buff in colour, although pink and stronger yellows are also found; some varieties have pronounced veining, while others are even-grained with no figuring.

From the Veronese there was available a range of very beautiful, strongly figured and coloured marbles, of which Rosso di Verona is simply the best known among many. None were suitable for general building purposes, and all have similar qualities to Rosso in their structure and workability. They were thus used for specialised sculpture, for inlays, paterae and similar work, but not for more humdrum purposes. In colour these marbles range from the golden yellow of Gialetto through the deep pinkish-gold of Giallo Reale, to

---

[24] Euganean trachite is not specifically mentioned by Vitruvius, Palladio or Sansovino, although the Roman does refer to the 'white tufa from Venetia' which I cannot identify with certainty.

9 Stonework: detail of the Porta della Carta, the principal formal entrance to the Palazzo Ducale, the work of the Bon family, and executed in *c.* 1440–5. (The figure of doge Foscari and the winged lion are nineteenth century copies.)

the pale pink of Pietra Persichina, the strongly-figured rose pink of Breccia Pernice and the deep, strong figuring of Rosso di Verona itself.[25]

Further west again, another important producer of fine marbles was the city of Brescia, whence came the famous Breccia (Brescia) Aurora and the internationally known Botticino. This last has an extremely fine, even grain and was particularly highly regarded for the finest works of sculpture; in colour it is usually very pale cream or buff.

It is clear therefore that there were many fine decorative stones available within about 100 km. of Venice, but very few were suitable for general building purposes, for the day-to-day requirements of masons for such work as door and window surrounds, steps, arches and thresholds.

The one stone that proved ideal for all these and many other purposes in Venice and throughout the lagoon came from Istria, the peninsula across the Venetian Gulf. Istria was one of the first and longest-lasting of all the *Serenissima*'s overseas possessions; since the tenth century the doge had had, among other sonorous titles, that of *Dux Totus Istriae*, a title often challenged but never permanently overturned. From the twelfth century the Republic had its chief fortress at Capodistria (modern Koper), and the peninsula was to prove an invaluable part of the maritime empire. Istria is very close to the capital, only 100 km. directly across the gulf, and ships could easily sail across in a day and a night; the colony was to be not only an indispensable source of building stone, but also a major supplier of timber, charcoal and fish, as well as manpower for the Venetian navy.

[25] Many of these and other rare stones only came into widespread use with the Renaissance, for the decoration of façades. They were used particularly extensively on the buildings of the 'Lombard' Renaissance such as Palazzo Dario, S. Maria dei Miracoli and the Scuola Grande di S. Marco.

10 Brick and stone: the combination of these two key materials is seen at its simplest in work such as this – detail of the Ponte del Diavolo at Torcello, the characteristic bridge built with no parapets and with inclined steps to permit the crossing of horses.

Istrian stone is often referred to as marble, although it is not a true marble; it has several properties that make it suitable for almost all forms of building work. It has a fine, even grain, and so it is suitable for detailed sculpting, and it is comparatively easy to work. It absorbs little water, so it is invaluable in foundations and any other element that is in contact with water – steps, quays, thresholds. It is strong and can support high loads, certainly very much higher than are possible using the local 'stock' bricks. Istrian stone can also be highly polished if such a finish is required or it can be given a coarser finish for more general building uses. It is fairly resistant to the atmosphere and the effects of air-borne pollution, although the increase of certain acidic and industrial pollutants in the last few decades has inflicted considerable damage on many of the stone sculptures of the city.

In all, Istrian stone was an almost ideal material with which to embellish the buildings of Venice and its satellites, and it was indeed used extensively. Apart from the ubiquitous red brick (the colour of which it admirably complements), Istrian stone is the material which more than any other gives the city's architecture its characteristic brilliance. In colour it is usually said to be white, although in fact there are a number of shades, some of which incline towards cream, while others have a very pale pink cast. The masons and architects of the lagunar capital exploited this gleaming colour to the full over the centuries, and together with the contrasting colour and texture of the brickwork, this stone and the strong sunlight upon it are key elements in the development of the sculptural, three-dimensional qualities of Venetian façades.

Istrian stone was quarried in several places in the peninsula, although much of it originated at Rovigno (Rovinj) and the small town of Orsera (Vrsar) a few miles north up the coast; other supplies came from the offshore islet of Brioni (Brijuni), which lies just north-west of Pola, and these supplies were shipped to Venice from the latter port. In the city and its lagoon it was used quite literally everywhere. Even the most humble cottages sometimes had window lintels and sills of Istrian stone; in larger houses it was used for framing every type of external opening, for doors, gates, windows; for the foundations that supported the principal walls of the great *palazzi*; for columns and window tracery; for coats of arms and other embellishments; for keystones and rustications; for rainwater gutters and well-heads. It was used for some of the finest sculpture in the city and it was used for the gulleys in the *campi* where the rainwater was collected. It was used for countless heraldic imperial Venetian lions – from the Arsenal to Corfù – on castles, forts and palaces in many parts of the Empire; it was also used to build the quays from which the mercantile greatness of that Empire derived. In short, it became the stone of Venice.

The lesser building materials: sand, metals and lime

Sand

Sand, or rather *arena* of three different types can be obtained, that is, from sand pits, from rivers and from the sea [shore]. That from sand pits is always the best, and it is black or white or red, or *carboncino*, which . . . is found in Tuscany. In the territory . . . of Baia and Cuma there is found a powder called by Vitruvius *Pozzolana*, which sets very quickly with water and renders buildings extremely strong . . . By long experience it can be seen that, among the sand from pits, the white is the worst, and among those obtained from rivers the best is that from torrents, which can be found below cliffs (or rapids) where the water rushes down, because it is the best cleaned. Sand from the sea is the worst of all types . . . it must be cleaned so that it is like clear glass; but the best is that which is found nearest to the shore and is the largest [grained].[26]

Palladio's description, like his other recommendations, is taken almost *verbatim* from Vitruvius. His mentor then continues thus:

[sand from the sea] has these defects when used in masonry: it dries slowly; the wall cannot be built up without interruption, so from time to time there must be pauses in the work; and such a wall cannot carry vaults. Furthermore, when sea sand is used in walls and these are coated with stucco, a salty efflorescence is given out which spoils the surface.

. . . But pit sand used in masonry dries quickly, the stucco coating is permanent, and the walls can support vaultings . . . Fresh pit sand however, in spite of all its excellence in concrete structures, is not equally useful in stucco, the richness of which, when the lime and

---

[26] Palladio, *I Quattro Libri*, book I, chapter 4, p. 8.

straw are mixed with such sand, will cause it to crack as it dries on account of the great strength of the mixture . . .[27]

Of Palladio's three types of sand, the Venetians had plenty of sea and river sand, but no pits in the immediate vicinity. Sea sand required very careful washing to remove the salts, (often apparently unsuccessfully) and the salinity of the Adriatic here is particularly high. In fact, the Republic forbade the taking of sand from the littoral for building purposes for fear that its removal would weaken the sea-defences, and there were only a couple of places, specifically described, where sea sand could be taken; these were zones where a large mass of dunes had accumulated and there was thus no immediate danger of breaching the dykes.[28] Most sand was obtained from the beds of the major rivers of the Venetian Terraferma, the Piave, Sile, Àdige and Po; it was dredged from the river bed and brought to the city in barges. This process had the sometimes useful side effect of deepening channels for navigation at the same time.

Lime

The stone for making lime is either excavated from the mountains or else it is taken from the rivers. All stone from the mountains is good if it is dry, well cleansed, and free from any other materials . . . There are also certain sorts of spongy stones, the lime of which is extremely good for rendering walls. In the hills of Padua (Euganean Hills) are also excavated certain schist rocks, the lime of which is excellent for works that are to remain in the open or in water, because it cures quickly and lasts for a very long time . . . All types of stone, whether from the mountains or rivers . . . should be well burned for sixty hours. When 'cooked' (the stone) should be bathed in water, not soaked immediately, but rather wetted continuously so that it is not burned, until it is well tempered. Then it should be put into a humid place in the shade [until required for use] . . . To make mortar, it must then be mixed with sand, which is taken from a sand pit; three parts of sand should be mixed with one of lime; if the sand is from the river or the beach, then there should be two parts of sand to one of lime.[29]

Once again, Palladio's description closely follows that of Vitruvius, although interestingly he omits the latter's suggestion that when using river or sea sand a third part of burned brick, pounded up and sifted, may be added to the mixture 'to make your mortar of a better composition to use.'[30] The omission is a little surprising since this form of mixture was common in Venice and the Terraferma particularly for the external rendering of house walls.

Lime was generally brought to the city, therefore, from the Euganean Hills, from the upper courses of some of the major mainland rivers and also sometimes from the hills of Carnia.

Metals

Metals used in building construction consisted chiefly of nails, hinges and brackets and, in more *signorile* work, wrought iron for gates, grilles and so on. The only significant metals were iron and lead; the use of copper was extremely limited because

[27] Vitruvius, *Ten Books*, book II, chapter 4.
[28] One such place was Cà Roman at the southern tip of the littoral of Pellestrina.
[29] Palladio, *I Quattro Libri*, book I, chapter 5, pp. 8–9.
[30] Vitruvius, *Ten Books*, book II, chapter 5.

of its cost, and only a very few buildings in the city centre have copper roofs.

Iron

Iron is used for making nails, for hinges, for bolts, with which the doors are secured, for making the said doors, for shutters and similar works.[31]

The main centre of domestic ironwork was the town of Feltre in the Dolomites, where there were local supplies of ore; a lesser centre, a little further north, was Agordo in the Valle Cordevole. The requirements of the building industry for iron were not extensive, however, and the ironworks were far more widely concerned with other sectors of industry such as shipbuilding and the manufacture of arms.

Pre-eminent in iron and steel production in northern Italy was the city of Brescia in Lombardy, which was a member of the Lombard League until 1426, when it became part of the Venetian Terraferma Empire; it remained under the flag of S. Marco until the fall of the Republic in 1797, and the city, together with the nearby Val Trompia, supplied much of the *Serenissima*'s specialised iron and steelwork, particularly armaments – swords, armour, guns and so on.

Lead

Once again the use of lead in building construction was usually confined to fairly small fixtures and accessories; again, as Palladio noted, it was used for such purposes as securing the glazing in windows, for water pipes, and other more minor metalwork. Fixings for stone – ties and cramps – were usually of iron but they were located in pockets that were then run with molten lead in order to secure them. The major use of lead was for roofing, but it was very expensive in such quantities, and was usually only used for major public buildings or churches and roof shapes that could not be finished easily with tiles. The domes of S. Marco and the Salute, for example, and of many lesser churches, are finished with lead, and it was also sometimes used at a fairly shallow pitch on public buildings such as the Ducal Palace, the Mint, and Biblioteca Marciana, on the Rialto Bridge and the adjacent Palazzo dei Camerlenghi.

However, it is no coincidence that this short list includes the most important and prestigious buildings in the city; the very large majority of buildings of all types in the city and all its satellites are roofed with clay tiles.[32]

---

[31] Palladio, *I Quattro Libri*, book I, chapter 6.
[32] Palladio distinguishes between three types of lead, white, black and grey, of which the white was considered the best.

5

Methods of construction and vernacular details

Introduction

Almost all elements of traditional Venetian building construction allowed for structural movement and settlement, and for the resolution of stresses by means of joints with a degree of elasticity. This principle was essential given the topographical context in which the buildings were constructed – any structural system based on rigid joints would inevitably have led to widespread cracking and failure. Certain forms of construction were difficult in this context, and two that always posed specific problems were very high point loads or concentrated loads, and also vaulted systems which imposed not only high point loads at the springing of arches but also often imposed lateral thrusts as well. Perhaps the most obvious field in which heavy concentrated loads could not be avoided was in the case of church *campanili*, and many of them collapsed over the centuries, or had to be taken down and rebuilt. The surviving *campanile* at Burano is a well-known example of the problem, with its considerable inclination which has theoretically rendered it liable to collapse at any time. In other forms of building it was essential that high point loads were avoided or dispersed, usually by means of large beams or strip foundations bearing on rows of timber piles.

The elasticity inherent in all key elements of construction can be seen in the fact that mortar always had a heavy lime content, that the bricks of which most buildings were built were very soft, and that all upper floors and roofs were of timber. Principal floor beams were set close together to carry a load as evenly as possible onto the wall, and the same principle was followed with roof trusses. High point loads, if unavoidable, were usually carried on columns of Istrian stone, or occasionally on columns of timber.

Once again I have illustrated this chapter with excerpts from Francesco Sansovino's *Venetia Città Nobilissima*, where appropriate.

The elements of building

Foundations

Now, the foundations of all of the buildings are built of extremely strong piles of oak [*quercia o rovere*] which will last eternally if it is kept below water . . . These piles are driven into the ground and then held with large [cross-] beams and the spaces between one pile and another are filled with broken stones and cement in order to consolidate and render the foundations stable and firm, such that they may sustain the weight of any great wall, however thick or tall, without moving so much as a hair's breadth . . .[1]

[1] Sansovino, *Venetia Città Nobilissima*, book IX, p. 382.

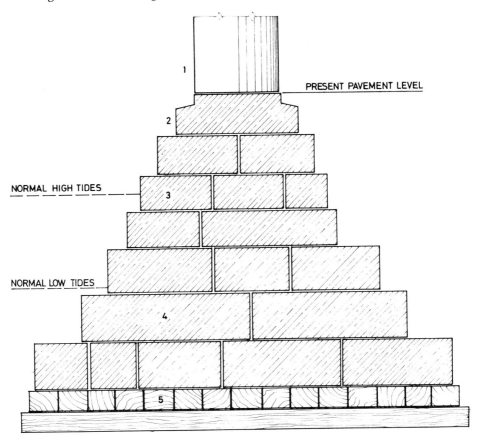

PRESENT PAVEMENT LEVEL

NORMAL HIGH TIDES

NORMAL LOW TIDES

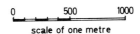

scale of one metre

11 A simple direct foundation, although one of considerable size – this is a section through the foundation to the colonnade of the Doges' Palace, on the side facing the Piazzetta (that to the Molo is only slightly different). The drawing is diagrammatic in that the main blocks of stone are not ashlar and there are many small gaps filled with rubble.

1 Columns of Istrian stone forming the colonnade.
2 Bases to the columns, approx. 400 mm. deep, but all now below present pavement level.
3 Three narrower courses of Istrian stone, each course about 300 mm. deep.
4 Three larger courses of stone, each approx. 400 mm. deep.
5 *Zattaron*, consisting of two layers of beams of red larch, with an overall depth of 380 mm. Each individual beam is approx. 190 mm. deep by 250 mm. wide and 4 metres long, this being the width of the footing at its base. Although laid down over 500 years ago, the *zattaron* remains in excellent condition today.

But if the ground is found to be soft and settles considerably, as is found in marshy places, then it is necessary to construct piles, the stakes of which are to have a length equal to the eighth part of the wall [to be carried] and are to have a thickness equal to one twelfth of their length. It is necessary to position the piles such that there is no space to insert any additional piles between them; and they must be driven in with blows sufficiently heavy so as to consolidate and strengthen the ground. These piles are to be driven not only beneath the

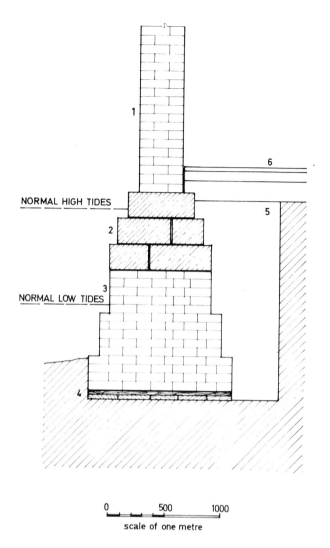

NORMAL HIGH TIDES

NORMAL LOW TIDES

0   500   1000

scale of one metre

12 A direct foundation of the simplest kind, and the type that was in widespread use for most buildings up to the fifteenth century, and continued to be the most common type for minor buildings thereafter. The *zattaron* is composed of three, or sometimes only two layers of timber planking. The brick perimeter wall of the house might be either two or only one and a half bricks in thickness.

> perimeter walls which stand on the canal front but also to carry the landward walls and those that divide the buildings [internally]. Because if the foundations to the intermediate walls are of a different type to those of the perimeter walls, when the beams are placed so that one end is supported on one wall and the other on another (with different footings) often the intermediate walls will settle while those at the perimeter, supported on piles, will not do so; and the walls will open up, thus destroying the structure and disfiguring its appearance . . .[2]

[2] Palladio, *I Quattro Libri*, book I, chapter 7, pp. 10–11. If we apply his rules for pile sizes to Palazzo Trevisan at Murano (see chapter 11) the piles supporting the main walls should have been about 1.7 m. long and 150 mm. in diameter; these dimensions are rather small for a house of this size.

Many major buildings in the city and lagoons are indeed supported on timber piles driven into the clay. In a few rare places it was possible to build directly off the firm stratum of clay, the *caranto*, but it is generally too deep for walls to bear on directly, and in these cases it was necessary to first consolidate the entire area of the building before construction began. This was undertaken by building a bulkhead or *tura*, consisting of a temporary walling of timber, forming a coffer dam around the perimeter. This dam was then sealed with clay and the water removed from the interior. The area was then consolidated using rough piles of oak or larch, the dimensions of which were usually in the order of 200 × 200 mm. or 200 × 250 mm. and approximately three or four metres in length. The piles were driven into the clay in a spiral manner, beginning at the perimeter and working in towards the centre, with an average of nine piles to each square metre of floor area. Pile-driving was traditionally undertaken by hand, with two men standing on a timber platform and using a heavy drop-hammer or *mazzuolo*; the method was in occasional use until quite recent times. The timbers normally used, oak and larch, are extremely durable, although long, careful seasoning was necessary before use, and it was essential that after seasoning in salt water for many months, the piles were always kept below the low-water line so that they were never exposed to the air.

For the strip foundations to the major structural walls of a large house, the piles were driven so close together as to form a virtually continuous wall, usually four or five rows deep. Once they had been levelled, a thick decking of timber planks was laid on top to form the first part of the footing itself. This deck was known as the *zattaron* (from *zattere* – raft), and consisted of two, or sometimes three layers of thick larch planking, each layer at right angles to the one below. The planks were usually about 250 to 300 mm. wide and from 25 to 50 mm. in thickness; walnut or mahogany was also occasionally used. Non-structural walls were often built directly off this decking, although for main structural walls several courses of squared Istrian stone, or a mixture of brick faced with stone, were used to bring the wall up to a level significantly higher than that of normal high tides. Foundations for the lesser houses of the city and the villages naturally had far less load to carry and were thus simpler; in such cases, the builder of the house had far more limited resources to spend on such unseen works as foundations. Here timber piling was rarely adopted, and a simple base or *zattaron* was laid, onto which the strip foundation was directly built.

The chief disadvantage in building directly off the *zattaron* with brick is that the local brick clay is fairly soft and porous and absorbs a significant amount of water. This is less critical at the lower levels where the brick is permanently submerged, but far more so at higher levels, where it is subject to frequent cycles of wetting and drying by the tides and also to far greater extremes of temperature. It was therefore the practice in the very largest houses to build all foundations below water level in large blocks of Istrian stone, which is not only far more durable (and expensive) than brick, but also acts as a horizontal damp-course to prevent water rising up the wall by capillary action. One of the chief difficulties in restoring houses in the city and the lagoon today is the greatly increased frequency of *acque alte*, exceptionally high tides that rise above the level of the top of the stone and saturate the bricks above, degrading them and damaging surface decorations.

In most cases, whether footings are of brick or stone, they are stepped so that the top course has the same thickness as the wall built onto it. Footings of stone had an additional advantage over those of brick: because the stones were so much larger than the bricks above them, they not only ensured the even distribution of loads onto the footings but also helped to tie the entire structure together, particularly at the external corners.

From information recently published by Zuccolo[3] we may conclude that piled foundations were comparatively rare until about the fifteenth century, when they began to be used more and more frequently, although still only for the larger palaces of the city, and partly as a direct result of the need to build higher and greatly increase loads on the footings. Before this period, foundations were generally of the direct type, as can be found even in such large, monumental buildings as the Ducal Palace.

By the time of the Renaissance, piled footings were in general use in the city, but still probably fairly rare outside it, chiefly because loads remained very much lower, and there were still very few buildings in the lagoons with more than two storeys. In the city itself, the elaboration of the main façades of palaces and the extensive use of decorative stone again contributed to the increase in dead loads, rendering piling essential in many cases. By the later sixteenth century, it was almost universal; the later editions of Sansovino by Stringa and Martinioni record the famous examples of the new Rialto Bridge, completed in 1591 and supported on 12,000 piles of elm, each three metres long, and the church of the Salute, reputedly supported by 1,156,657 piles of oak, larch and other species.[4]

Beyond the magnificent reaches of the Grand Canal, and out in the lagoons, foundations remained much simpler. In most cases a *zattaron* of timber was built, on which a stepped footing of brick rose to ground-floor level. Such a form of construction was quite adequate for the modest loads that most walls were required to carry, and it is probably only at Murano that some of the larger Renaissance villas required piled footings.

---

[3] G. Zuccolo, *Il Restauro*. We may note here that pile-driving in Venice seems to have always been executed by hand, although counter-balanced machines were used elsewhere. Vasari mentions (in his *Lives*) that Sansovino renewed the piles to the Tiepolo family house at the Misericordia while the family remained in occupation.

[4] Sansovino, *Venetia Città Nobilissima*, book VIII, p. 365 (Rialto Bridge) and book VI, p. 278 (S. Maria della Salute). Zuccolo has published considerable detail of traditional foundation types; we may summarise his notes on the original footings for two of the most notable buildings in Venice, the Palazzo Ducale and the *campanile* of S. Marco. The foundations to the colonnade of the former consist solely of a *zattaron* positioned 3 m. below modern pavement level, or 2 m. below mean high tide level. This *zattaron* consists of two courses of planks of red larch, one orthogonal to the other, with an overall thickness of 38 cm., and a width of 4 m. There are no piles at all. When recently inspected the *zattaron* was in excellent condition after 450 years (the Piazzetta wing was begun in 1424). Diminishing courses of stone are built onto the *zattaron*, each course 40 cm. deep. There are three such courses on the Molo façade and two to that on the Piazzetta. At a level of 40 cm. below present pavement level a single large padstone forms the base for the columns to the arcade; this stone is 1.39 m. square and 40 cm. deep. The original pavement level was thus at the base of this padstone. The dead load on each padstone has been calculated at 224 tonnes, or 1.60 kg. per sq. cm. The present *campanile* of S. Marco is the modern reconstruction of 1903 but is a copy of the original tower. This original *campanile* had a total dead weight of 14,400 tonnes, supported on an area of 222 sq. m. It was also built on a square *zattaron* but in this case below the *zattaron* was a *palificata* of timber piles, which were only 1.5 m. long but which covered the whole area of the footing. The piles bore directly onto the stratum of *caranto* which at this point is quite close to the surface, at about 6 m. below present pavement level. The piles were of poplar, 26 cm. in diameter, and on top of them the *zattaron* was 12 cm. thick. There was evidence of considerable differential settlement when the foundations were examined in 1902, with an inclination towards the north-east. Taking into account the large wind loads on the structure, Zuccolo states that the net load onto the foundations was from 4.16 to 8.64 kg. per sq. cm., or up to five times the load on the colonnade of the Ducal Palace (Zuccolo, *Il Restauro*, pp. 59–62).

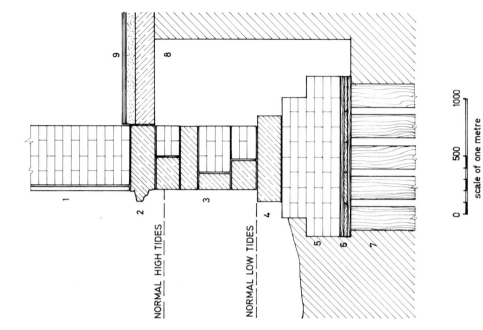

Fig. 14

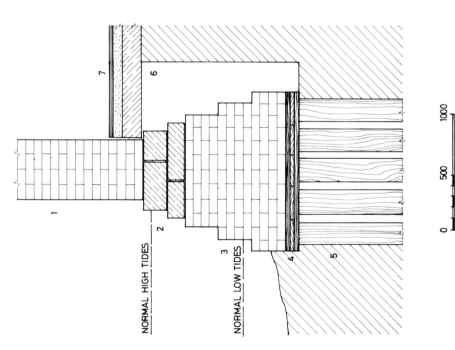

Fig. 13

Walls

The universal walling material was brick, the soft, orange-red 'stock' brick of the Venetian hinterland. Main structural walls were usually between 400 and 500 mm. thick, although occasionally less on upper floors. Trincanato[5] has identified three common brick sizes; the older hand-made bricks usually had dimensions of $400 \times 300 \times 60$ mm., while some of the other earliest buildings were constructed using *altinelle*, very small bricks of only $200 \times 100 \times 50$ mm. They are called *altinelle* because they are said to have come from the Roman city of Altino, on the edge of the lagoon near Torcello, and there is no doubt that at least some of these smallest bricks are indeed re-used Roman bricks. After about the fourteenth century, a universal brick size of $260 \times 130 \times 65$ mm. was established and almost all of the buildings in the latter part of this study are built of these bricks. Many façades, particularly in the thirteenth and fourteenth centuries, were intended to be fair-faced, but later it became more and more common to finish the wall with a coating of mortar or render. There were two chief reasons for this: firstly, it helped to protect the soft brickwork from the ravages of the weather, and secondly it provided a plain surface which could then be decorated, and sometimes frescoed.

The bricks were always bedded in lime mortar, which had sufficient elasticity to allow for differential settlement, and a similar mixture was used on the façades. Often a light grey finish was obtained, known as *rovigno* (from the town in Istria), by mixing pulverised Istrian stone into the mortar, and this light grey was particularly suitable as a backing for frescoes.

Another technique involved mixing into the mortar a quantity of terracotta powder together with a little sand, producing a reddish colour known as *pastellone*. Other shades could be obtained by the addition of different natural pigments. In later periods, instead of traditional rendering a more complex finish, *marmorino*, was occasionally adopted; this was a form of imitation marble, of slaked lime applied to a base coat of stucco or render.

[5] E. R. Trincanato, *Venezia Minore* (Milan 1948) p. 94.

13 and 14   Two forms of indirect foundation. The second is more elaborate, and is of the type that may be found supporting a large city palace.
Key to 13
1 Brick perimeter wall of the building, two bricks, or approx. 520 mm. thick.
2 Spreading courses of Istrian stone.
3 Brick foundations stepped out to approx. 1.5 metres thick at the base.
4 *Zattaron* of three layers of thick planking on which the foundation is raised.
5 Timber piles.
6 Clay lining to the inner face of the footings.
7 Ground floor consisting of bricks or clay tiles on a thick bed of mortar on well-consolidated clay or earth.
Key to 14
1 Brick perimeter wall of house, faced with thin slabs of stone.
2 Stone string course with moulded profile.
3 Lower courses of wall faced with stone but with brick backing.
4 Foundation course of Istrian stone.
5 Lowest courses of the foundation of brick, stepped out to the width of the *zattaron*.
6 *Zattaron* as described on Fig. 13.
7 Timber piles.
8 Clay lining to inner face of footings.
9 Floor finish as that on Fig. 13.

15 Venetian brickwork: detail of a house on Campo S. Agnese, showing degradation of the soft bricks by frequent *acque alte*. The characteristic relieving arch above the openings may also be noted as well as the unusually robust frames of Istrian stone.

Later still a more modern form of sand and cement render came to be used, although a significant proportion of lime was still necessary to retain flexibility, and the sand was often a simple replacement for powdered marble. In some buildings, as we will see below, the entire façade was decorated with stone or marble, but this was naturally a very expensive finish, and most such façades conceal a brick structure.

As we will see in chapter 8, the plans of most city palaces and of many lesser buildings are regular and symmetrical, and the pattern of structural walls is simple to establish. The almost universal pattern of construction in these cases consists of four parallel structural walls, two of which formed the outer, flank walls of the house, while the inner pair divided the central hall or *pòrtego* from the secondary rooms on either side of it. These four walls all carried roughly similar loads: the two outer ones carried part of the upper floors and a major part of the roof. In fact, if the roof had the usual four-way pitch, one quarter of its load was carried by each of the four outer walls. The two inner walls only rarely carried a part of the roof (if it was a false truss: see below), but a larger proportion of the upper floors. The four major parallel structural walls are usually thus all of the same thickness, a dimension corresponding to either one and a half or two bricks in thickness, that is, approximately 400 mm. or 520 mm. respectively.[6]

The front façade was also fairly substantial, not because it carried considerable loads, since generally it did not, but because it was the principal elevation, and was often adorned with cornices, balconies and other features; in addition, the central section, which lit the *pòrtego*, often consisted of a large multi-light window, so that to some extent this façade was a framed construction rather than a simple loadbearing wall.[7] In many cases, the bond between this front façade and the two flank walls was unsatisfactory, and another of the difficulties of restoration today is that of significant differential settlement

[6] For comprehensive structural analyses of many *palazzi* and their load patterns see Zuccolo, *Il Restauro*.
[7] See below pp. 44–5.

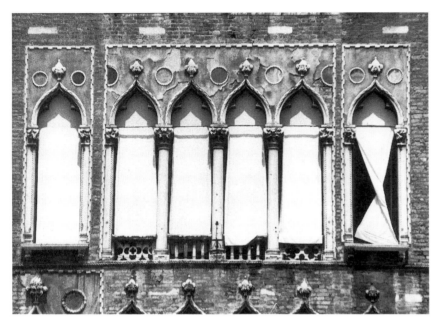

16 Brickwork and stonework: detail of the façade of Palazzo Gritti in Campo S. Angelo. The brickwork is generally fair-faced but is rendered in the window panels which are framed by the typical medieval narrow band of stone.

between the two elements, partly as a result of their different static load patterns, and partly because of inadequate tying at the external corners. Many of the larger medieval houses have 'stitching courses' of large blocks of Istrian stone at the corners for precisely this purpose; in addition to their decorative value they strengthen these vulnerable corners of the structure.

Internal walls, other than the two spine walls, were generally of light construction, except those that framed a stairwell. None of the lateral walls between rooms carried any load other than its own weight, and so, if they were of brick, they were generally only 260 mm., or one brick, in thickness. In many cases these and other non-structural partitions were of timber studwork, roughly squared posts and struts, usually about 100×100 mm. in size, which were then finished with plaster, either on timber laths or on a lath of dried reeds.

Floors

Ground floors in the most humble houses consisted simply of beaten earth. In larger houses, the flooring would consist of brick, or perhaps *terrazzo* (see below) or, in the most imposing houses, of stone. Usually this was Istrian, but it was often alternated with black trachite or other marble of a contrasting colour to form geometrical patterns.

> The beams, because of the thickness of the timber, are spaced so that the gaps between them are equal to their width, rendering great delight to the eye, while also providing strength, so that they may sustain any great load; and there is no vibration when walking on these floors.[8]

[8] Sansovino, *Venetia Città Nobilissima*, book IX, p. 383.

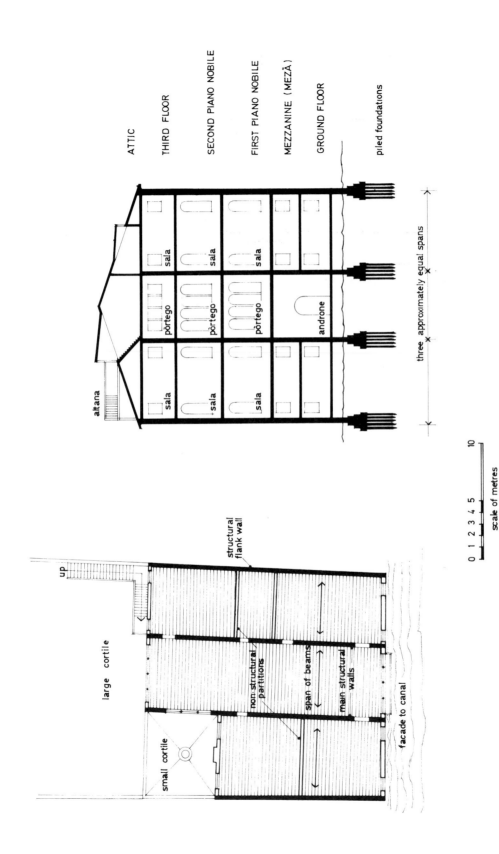

ATTIC

THIRD FLOOR

SECOND PIANO NOBILE

FIRST PIANO NOBILE

MEZZANINE (MEZÀ)

GROUND FLOOR

piled foundations

altana

sala | pòrtego | sala

sala | pòrtego | sala

sala | pòrtego | sala

| | | androne |

three approximately equal spans

0 1 2 3 4 5   10

scale of metres

large cortile

up

small cortile

structural flank wall

non-structural partitions

span of beams

main structural walls

facade to canal

17 Plan (at first-floor level) and cross-section of a typical city *palazzo*. The structural principles are applicable to nearly all of the smaller *palazzetti* and the villas of Murano and the Giudecca, as well as many more modest houses. The primary features are the four parallel loadbearing walls (shown solid black) and the floor beams all spanning onto them; this arrangement applies to all floor levels. The section is typical of the larger city palaces but again its principles apply to many smaller houses.

18 Elevation of Palazzo Gritti to Campo S. Angelo. Apart from the unusual off-centre portal, the façade conforms precisely to the classic tripartite arrangement shown in Fig. 17.

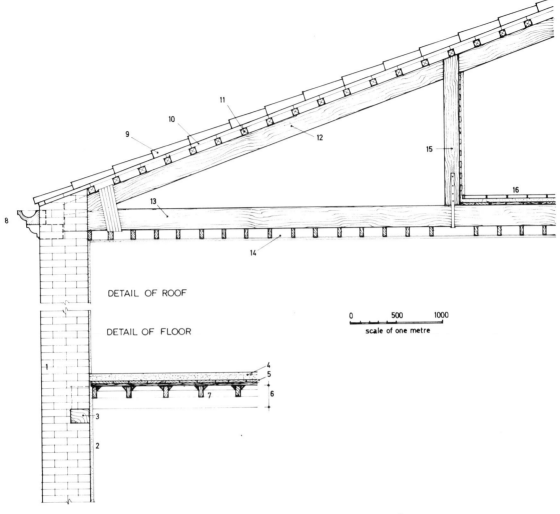

DETAIL OF ROOF

DETAIL OF FLOOR

scale of one metre

19 Details of typical floor and roof construction in the larger Venetian houses.

Floor detail
1 Perimeter wall of brick, two bricks in thickness.
2 Plaster wall finish.
3 Wall-plate of timber, to which the main beams are spiked.
4 Floor finish of terrazzo.
5 Floor boarding of one or sometimes two layers, closely fitted and nailed to main joists.
6 Main floor joists or beams, usually from about 150 mm. × 180 mm. to 250 mm. × 200 mm. in size and from 250 mm. to 500 mm. apart.
7 Smaller transverse joists with decorative fillets forming one of several types of coffered or Sansovino ceiling.

Roof detail
8 Stone gutter supported on corbels built into the wall.
9 Half-round clay roof tiles.
10 Flat bricks or clay tiles forming the roof lining.
11 Purlins usually about 70 mm. square and at about 250 mm. centres.
12 Main rafters, commonly placed at about 700 mm. to 900 mm. centres, and usually about 200 mm. × 100 mm. in section.
13 Roof tie-beam, bearing on perimeter wall, and connected to the rafters by straps of iron; the size of the tie-beam is usually about 200 mm. × 250 mm.
14 Ceiling of plaster on a lath of reeds, which are fixed to small ceiling joists about 50 mm. × 75 mm. in size and at around 250 mm. centres.
15 Truss post strapped to lower tie-beam and usually 150 mm. × 150 mm. in section. In this example, there is an attic room on the right of the post, with walls lined with plaster on laths fixed to the posts.
16 Attic floor of flat clay bricks or tiles bedded in mortar, on a layer of timber boarding. Attics often contained kitchens, and hence the non-combustible floor finish.

Upper floors were of timber. Vaulting is extremely rare for the reasons mentioned earlier; it was also a good deal more difficult to build than a simple beam floor. Upper floors were thus almost always built of beams of oak (sometimes larch or fir) the typical dimensions of which were 200 × 200, 200 × 150 or 180 × 150 mm. The maximum section of timber usually available was in the order of 300 × 200 mm. The spans between the main structural walls were naturally also limited by the maximum lengths of such beams available, but they usually fell within the range of 4.5 metres up to about 7 metres. The most common spans in the medium-sized and larger houses were in the narrower range of from 5 to about 6.5 metres; spans longer than about 7 metres are rare, not simply because of the difficulty of obtaining timber but, equally importantly, because of the need to minimise deflection at mid-span, especially under the load of a *terrazzo* floor finish. Longer spans thus required the use of *barbacani* (see below), which in turn meant more large sections of expensive timber.

As Sansovino states, the beams were placed at close centres, the gaps between them being one or one and a half times the width of the beam, an arrangement that gave the most evenly distributed load onto the wall. This load was often (but not always) taken by a large timber wall-plate, built into the brickwork, the floor beams being spiked to it. This wall-plate was of considerable size (200 × 150 mm. being a typical section) and ensured the full distribution of the load onto the whole length of the wall. With time, some of these wall-plates have deteriorated, and given rise to local settlement, and the consequent development of concentrations of load that the original design was intended to prevent.

The close spacing of the floor beams gave rise to the Sansovino or coffered ceiling popularised by Francesco's father Jacopo. This was a ceiling in which the main beams were all left exposed but highly decorated and painted; the ceiling was further elaborated by the insertion of smaller transverse timbers between the main beams to create a coffered soffit, which was often further elaborately gilded and decorated.

On top of the floor beams were usually laid two layers of timber boarding, one at right angles to the other, and closely nailed down to produce a monolithic structure. In the more *signorile* houses a further finish was laid onto this boarding.

Floor finishes

Venetian *terrazzo* is one of the most justly renowned features of lagunar vernacular architecture. The earliest form of *terrazzo* consisted of a layer of *paston*, a mixture of crushed bricks or clay roof tiles, together with lime and crushed Istrian stone, which made a pavement elastic enough to accommodate structural settlement without cracking. The later, universally known, *terrazzo* is essentially a modification of this finish; once again, Sansovino's description is clear and succinct:

> For the upper rooms and for the Hall [i.e. the *pòrtego*] the floors or pavements are built not of brick but of . . . *terrazzo*; the which material lasts for a very long time, is attractive to the eye and easy to clean. It is made with lime and with bricks or tiles that are well crushed and mixed all together. Then there is added one part of small flakes of Istrian stone, well pulverised, and this mixture, fully compacted, is spread over the floor deck of timber planks, which are closely fitted together and nailed down, so that they cannot distort and can support the weight. And

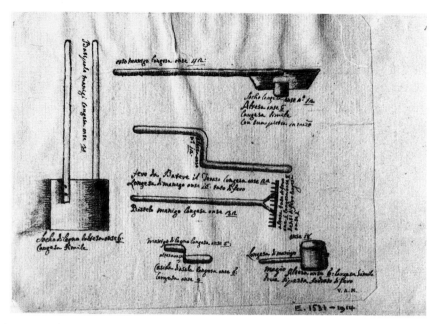

20 The tools of the trade: a drawing of the implements used in the specialised craft of terrazzo-laying, from a collection of sketches by Richard Norris in 1769 (V. & A. Mus., London; ref. 95.A.17). Among them can be identified a heavy drop-mallet for pounding the stone or brick; a smaller mallet; a rake for spreading the mixture on the floor; and a heavy cranked iron bar for beating the terrazzo down to form a compact layer.

then, with bars of iron, the mixture is beaten and pressed down over a period of several days. And when it has been completely levelled and hardened, another layer of the same material is laid on top, into which has been incorporated cinnabar or [other] red colouring. And then, after it has been left to set for several days, it is coated with linseed oil, with which the *terrazzo* achieves such a lustrous finish that a man may see himself reflected in it, as in a mirror. And although this mixture may have a reputation for being unwholesome because of its coldness, however there is no finer material for pavements, none more beautiful or gracious or more durable than this; it is maintained by scrubbing with either a cloth or sponge, and for those who wish to retain its lustrous appearance, it can be covered with rugs or carpets [*tele*] so that it is not damaged by shoes, and in this way when one enters a room thus appointed, one would think that one was entering a fine and beautifully clean Church kept by nuns. And if on occasion it breaks up, either because of excessive cold or any other reason, it can easily be made good by putting another layer on top, but thinner than the first, although of the same composition. And the specialists and masters of this particular craft are usually the Friulani.[9]

The *terrazzo* floor finish is characteristically Venetian, its advantages being its elasticity and the possibility of a wide variety of colours and tones by means of selection of the aggregates of which it is composed. The only disadvantage is its weight, and although the very large floor beams used were more than capable of carrying such loads, they often distorted considerably with time (especially if a second layer was added) although they usually retain their structural integrity. The use of *barbacani* on longer spans again helped to reduce this deflection.

[9] Ibid.

Another type of flooring occasionally used in certain specific areas was the *steler*, which consisted simply of large slabs of red Verona marble, laid directly onto the floor beams; these slabs were up to about 1.8 × 1.0 metres in size and 70 mm. in thickness. According to Trincanato[10] such floors were often used up to the fifteenth century, particularly on terraces, balconies or for a *liagò* (see p. 56), but were rare after that date, probably because of the expense in selecting slabs of sufficient size and free from defects.

Ceilings

The exposed structure or Sansovino ceiling was very common, and may be found in houses of all types and classes. In the humblest houses, there was no decoration to this structural soffit at all. However, in slightly larger houses a traditional ceiling of plaster on a lath of timber or of reeds was almost universal. In the *palazzi* such a ceiling was often very elaborate, with carved and gilt timber, with oil paintings on canvas within complex frames, and with very luxurious decoration. The variety of ceiling finishes is thus considerable and closely echoes the general status of the house in which it is found. In the medium-sized and smaller houses with which Part III of this book is concerned, the large majority of ceilings are either of a fairly simple Sansovino type or else they have a straightforward plaster finish.[11]

Staircases

Staircases exhibit a considerable variety in their form in Venetian vernacular architecture, although a clear pattern of evolution can be discerned in their location and in their design. In the earliest medieval houses, stairs were often external; although many of the oldest examples have been lost, a number of fine examples of external stairs survive in the great gothic *palazzi* as well as a group of lesser houses, including the two open stairs to the *Palazzi Comunali* at Torcello. In the larger gothic houses, they were usually in two flights, and served the first *piano nobile* directly from the private courtyard at the rear of the house. They thus gave direct access to the main floor of private accommodation without the necessity of passing through the ground floor, which was given over to trade and commerce; they also saved space within the house itself. Such stairs are usually built on a series of brick arches with stone treads and balustrades.[12]

Later, they fell from favour and the Renaissance, particularly in the sixteenth century, gave rise to the development of the grand internal stair. This development can be seen partly as a reflection of the reduced importance of the ground-floor *androne* or Hall as a place for directly conducting business, but also partly in the desire for increased comfort,

---

[10] Trincanato, *Venezia Minore*, p. 110. She cites as examples Palazzo Vallaresso (Albergo Monaco) and Palazzo degli Avogadori.

[11] For illustrations of a number of highly decorated ceilings in houses not accessible to the public, see E. Bassi, *Palazzi di Venezia* (Venice 1976); for example, Palazzo Grimani at S. Maria Formosa (p. 232) and Palazzo Zenobio ai Carmini (p. 350).

[12] There are far too many of this type to enumerate; for illustrations of examples see E. Arslan, *Venezia Gotica* (Milan 1970) figs. 143–5; see also P. Maretto, *L'Edilizia Gotica Veneziana* (2nd edn Venice 1978) pp. 67, 81, 86, 96, 99, 103.

21 Ceilings: one of the most ornate forms consists of elaborate *trompe l'œil* work in fresco, such as this baroque example in the main hall at Palazzo Giustinian, Murano.

and the obviation of the necessity to climb up a very long flight of external stairs, in the open air and often in the rain.

The internal stair was generally built on one side of the *androne*, usually about halfway down its length, with two flights at right angles to the axis of the Hall, and with the half-landing thus on the flank wall. Such an arrangement appears to have originated in Venice with Codussi at the Corner-Spinelli and Vendramin-Calergi palaces (at the end of the fifteenth and first years of the sixteenth centuries), although the feature was adopted generally by Sansovino, Sanmicheli and others soon afterwards. Once established, it became almost universal in all of the larger and medium-sized houses throughout the lagoon communities. It was an efficient arrangement and one that could be easily accommodated within the traditional overall form of the Venetian house.

Such stairs, however, did occupy a significant amount of space, an element always at a premium in the lagoon islands. Two other forms of stair were developed with this fact in mind: the spiral stair and the interlocking or Leonardo stair. The former was not widely used, although a number of interesting examples survive, and it undoubtedly had sculptural possibilities as well as saving space. We may mention here not only the famous *scala del bovolo* in Palazzo Contarini at S. Luca but also that in Palazzo Bernardo at S. Polo.

Interlocking stairs became more widespread, particularly in the houses of the middle and lower classes. In such less imposing buildings (with lower storey heights) it was possible to build a stair from one floor to another in a single straight flight, with the additional aesthetic advantage of regular patterns of fenestration, as well as saving considerable space. The Leonardo stair thus consisted of two quite separate, interlocking staircases, with a wall down the centre between them, giving access to two separate apartments on different floors. It also gave each stair a separate entrance from the street, a much appreciated feature in the crowded city centre.[13] This stair was particularly popular in the seventeenth century, when there was acute pressure on land for redevelopment,

---

[13] For examples of interlocking stairs see G. Gianighian and P. Pavanini, *Dietro i Palazzi* (Venice 1984); also Palladio, *I Quattro Libri*, book I, chapter 28, pp. 60–6.

22 Staircases: the best-known external stair in Venice is the helical *scala del bovolo* in Palazzo Contarini at S. Luca. Spiral stairs were rarely as elaborate as this but were very economical of space.

and when owners were anxious to maximise the return on their developments. In this period many blocks of apartments were built in the city centre; they varied widely in size, some being quite spacious and *signorile*, and occupied by quite wealthy *borghesi*, while others were much more modest and intended for artisans. In such blocks plans were often very complex and ingenious, and interlocking stairs were widespread.

Most internal stairs in the houses of the middle and lower classes were of timber, although in the *palazzi* they were nearly always of structural stone. Their detailing is generally fairly simple, with the exception of the balustrading, which was of stone in the great *palazzi*, of timber or sometimes of iron in the middle rank houses, and always of timber in the lesser houses.

Roof construction

Roofs to private houses were always pitched, apart from the small areas often occupied by terraces or *altane*, although even here, the *altana* was usually built above a pitched, tiled roof. The construction was always of timber, usually larch or pine. As we will see in more detail later, most of the plans of medium-sized and larger houses were regular and symmetrical, apart from a small gap formed by a light well or *cortile*. However, the main body of the house had a plan that was often close to a square and a four-way pitch was the most common form of roof – hence Sansovino's phrase 'I colmi delle fabriche sono per lo più in quattro acque', that is, the roof falls in all four directions to a perimeter gutter.

The design of the roof truss was such that in some cases it was a true truss, spanning

23 Roofs: view from the top of the Torre dell'Orologio in Piazza S. Marco over the roofs of the Merceria – a typically crowded collection of terraces, *altane* and chimneys. The half-round clay tile is the universal roof finish.

right across between perimeter walls, and in other cases was a false truss, with part of the load of the roof taken by the two internal spine walls, on either side of the *pòrtego*. In either case, however, the chief rafters were usually placed at 700 to 900 mm. centres and were about 200 × 100 mm. in size; the diagonal rafters at the corners were of similar size, and sometimes rather larger. The principal tie-beam that formed the bottom chord of the truss (whether true or false) was of timber about 200 × 250 mm. in section, and where this met the principal rafters at the eaves, the two timbers were bound together with straps of iron. Quite often the truss was developed to form a queen-post roof, with truss-posts on either side of the ridge, and with a counter-tie at high level to prevent spreading. Such a roof had the great advantage that it could all be built of timbers none of which was more than about 5 metres long, although scarf-joints were necessary if the lower tie-beam was to have a clear span (see Fig. 19).

Above the principal rafters, purlins were fixed at about 250 to 300 mm. centres, and in section they were usually about 70 × 70 mm.; this large size was chiefly necessary because of the considerable weight of the roof finish, which consisted firstly of a complete layer of sheathing of thin, flat tiles or bricks onto which the roof tiles were laid. These were the typical half-round clay tiles that are still used in all parts of the lagoon today. They were originally made of much the same clay as the bricks for the walls, but today they are often pressed or extruded to form a denser, more long-lasting finish.

Rainwater was collected by means of a gutter of semi-circular cross-section, all of Istrian stone, and supported on a row of stone corbels. Istrian stone was ideal as it was very durable and almost impervious, but such an apparently expensive detail (often seen on quite humble houses) was necessary because of the perennial problems of water supply and the need to conserve rainwater for re-use (see below). In most larger houses, the water was taken to the ground in vertical downpipes, often semicircular in section, and built into the fabric of the external wall. In the small cottages, the rainwater often discharged directly into the *campo* or *cortile* where, however, it would still percolate down into the communal well-sump. It was thus not lost, but still re-cycled for later use. Smaller houses had roofs simpler in design than the four-way pitch and the Palladian or queen-post truss; very often they were roofed with a simple double pitch, with the ridge parallel with the longer axis of the building, to reduce the lengths of timber required. In many freestanding houses this long axis was parallel with the quay or *fondamenta* as we see in many houses at Murano and Pellestrina. Later, narrower cottages, built on more restricted sites, had a deep plan and hence there is either a triangular gable on the façade and a double-pitched roof behind it or a simple monopitch is used. This is a very common type among the smaller, narrower cottages of Pellestrina and Burano, where many houses are only one room (or four or five metres) wide and could thus be roofed with a monopitch using quite small timber sizes.

The altana

The *altana* is a characteristic feature of Venetian vernacular architecture, most commonly found in the central zones of the city, although a number may also be seen at Chioggia, Murano and Pellestrina. The *altana* is a roof terrace, constructed all of timber, and approached by a flight of steps and a hole or dormer in the roof. The terrace is supported on a number of short brick piers which are built off the tops of the structural walls of the house. The terrace itself is framed in timber, with a floor of open wooden boards to facilitate drainage, and a surrounding balustrade also of timber, chiefly to minimise the overall weight of the structure.

The chief practical function of the *altana* was for drying washing; in practice, and in particular on the houses of the nobility, it became a sun-terrace, and was used in much the same way as these terraces are today: for taking the air on summer evenings, for bleaching one's hair (once a very fashionable pastime), or for simply sitting outside and conversing. Many houses and apartments in the city and its larger satellites had no gardens or even courtyards, and so the only possible place in which one could breathe fresh air in privacy (and dry the washing) was here on the roof among the chimneys.[14]

---

[14] The paintings of Bellini and Carpaccio show that *altane* already existed in the city in large numbers by the later fifteenth century; they must have required regular replacement as they were so vulnerable to atmospheric degradation, although their design has hardly changed at all in 500 years.

24 The *altana*: acute shortages of space led to the spread of roof terraces throughout the city and its major satellites – an *altana* and a more conventional roof terrace on Casa Gatti on the Grand Canal at S. Marcuola.

The abbaino

The *abbaino* is a form of dormer in the roof, and in dialect is known as a *baroal*. The simplest and the most common form of *abbaino* is merely a raised section of roof, with a small rectangular window or windows in the front face. In this form it is found in almost every type and size of house, lighting garrets and other storage facilities in the roof space. Larger *abbaini* are developed to become true dormers or gables (*frontoni*) with a small double-pitched roof, and a façade that is often pedimented. In the seventeenth and eighteenth centuries these gables were sometimes quite elaborately decorated, and became aedicules, with elaborate tympani, volutes and scrolls on either side and heavy classical cornices, as we will see in later chapters. They are particularly widespread in the middle-rank houses of the *seicento* and *settecento*, such as the *case padronali* of Pellestrina, and a number of houses at Murano as well as examples throughout the capital. In these more substantial houses the gable is in the centre of the façade, directly above the *pòrtego*, and usually lights one or two good-sized rooms in the roof.

25 to 27 Roof gables: these take a wide variety of forms, as these three examples show, although the aedicule with a triangular pediment is the most widespread. Fig. 25 is a baroque example from a house on Rio dei Vetrai at Murano; Fig. 26 is a detail of the central bay of the Michiel-Deste villa at Burano, more restrained in its detailing; Fig. 27 is from a cottage at Burano, where the enthusiasm of the builder exceeded his skill in execution.

The *liagò*

This is a very rare feature of which only a few examples exist in the city centre, and probably none outside it. The *liagò* is a form of covered *loggia*, usually in the top storey of a house, with the roof above it supported on a row of timber or stone columns. It may have originated with the continuous colonnades of the early Veneto-Byzantine palaces, such as Cà Loredan and the Fondaco dei Turchi, and its practical function seems to have been akin to that of the *altana*. Unfortunately there remain so few examples today (if indeed any at all are original) that their origin and detailed evolution must remain uncertain.[15]

Fireplaces, chimneys and chimneypots

> All of the rooms [of the houses] have chimneys, but the Hall (*pòrtego*) does not. And this is certainly with reason, so that, when one rises from bed, there is a fire nearby, which not only drives away excessive humidity which would otherwise affect one at night when asleep, but also warms the room, and purges it of unpleasant vapours that may be borne in on the air, or by other means.[16]

Chimneys and chimney-pots are a notable and characteristic aspect of Venetian architecture at all levels, from the great *palazzi* to the smallest cottages. In the *palazzi*, as Sansovino states, the fireplaces (and hence chimneys) were almost always located down the two flank walls of the house and served the smaller 'habitable' rooms that gave off from both sides of the *pòrtego*. Virtually every room had an open fireplace and the hearth itself was formed in the almost universal manner, with the timber floor beams trimmed around the hearth, which was usually supported on a low vault of brickwork. The chimney usually projected beyond the outer face of the wall, and is thus expressed externally by its widening out behind the fireplace in a pyramidal shape tapering upwards to the stack itself. The hearth is usually about 1.5 metres wide overall. In bedrooms and living rooms the fire served the functions described by Sansovino, but a very similar arrangement in the kitchen would provide space for a range with spits and other culinary accessories.

Externally, if it is on an upper floor, the fireplace is often supported on low arches formed in brick, and these arches in turn are supported by large stone corbels. Such features are found in all parts of the city and its satellites and in all classes of house. The *pòrtego* very rarely had any form of heating at all, relying for some nominal background heat on that supplied by the rooms on either side. The great hall was only used to the full for a large party or celebration on fairly rare occasions, and then, we may assume, mostly in summer. When not in use for such 'public' events it merely served as a very spacious access corridor.

In the lesser houses and cottages, the fire or range formed the focal point for the entire household. In such houses very often the kitchen-living room was the only room that had a fireplace, and the range thus combined the functions of heating the main room of the

---

[15] Trincanato (*Venezia Minore*, p. 100) shows a sketch of a *liagò* by Jacopo Bellini, in the form of a covered balcony projecting from a façade and supported on timber brackets. The Albergo del Salvadego in Bocca di Piazza has a top-floor *liagò*, probably a reconstruction, but it does not project beyond the face of the building.

[16] Sansovino, *Venetia Città Nobilissima*, book IX, p. 383.

cottage and as the means of heating water and cooking. In a few of the more isolated *casoni* we may still see the very large range recessed into an inglenook, where it may also incorporate an oven for baking bread. A good example of such a range may be seen in a farmhouse at Torcello, on the central canal. We may discuss the more particular arrangements that pertained in the various types of lagoon houses later, but a note on chimney-pots is also appropriate here.

The traditional Venetian chimneypot is unique to the city and its lagoon. The *fumaiolo* (or *comignolo*) evolved specifically to reduce the danger of the spread of fire from flying cinders; the risk of fire was considerable in the extremely congested city centre, as it was to a slightly lesser extent at Chioggia and Murano. The *fumaiolo* has a variety of sometimes quite complex shapes; the most characteristic is an inverted truncated cone, on top of a cylindrical stack. It is also found with a square plan, and hence has the form of an inverted truncated pyramid on top of a square stack. In either form it is sometimes found grouped in pairs, threes or even fours, thus producing very complex shapes. The conical form was originally the most common, although many examples have been lost over the centuries and replaced with less imaginative shapes. The *fumaiolo* is built of brick, and rendered; its form is a cinder-trap and the smoke usually escapes from small vents around the corbelled-out base of the pot.

The pot itself is capped with a small two-way pitched roof of tiles. The surface of the pot was often decorated, and it is clear that in certain periods (particularly the time of Carpaccio and Bellini) this decoration had become a status symbol and was often rich and elaborate. Many chimneys today are capped with a more simple, square *fumaiolo*, although a significant number of the older, cone-shaped pots still survive.[17]

The introduction of stone façades

If we now briefly consider the principal façade of the Venetian house as a whole (before summarising its chief component parts), one of the major transformations in its appearance was the introduction of stone as an 'all over' cladding material. It had been used for a long time up to the fifteenth century for detailing specific items and features; the great gothic *palazzi* had all their doors, windows, string courses, cornices and quoins picked out in finely carved stone, but the general wall surface remained either fair-faced brickwork or stucco. The overall use of stone on façades dates only from the latter part of the fifteenth century, and in particular from the period after about 1480.

The Cà d'Oro is a unique example of a 'high' gothic private house which is faced entirely with fine stone, much of which was originally painted. But it was only under the direct influence of the Lombard masters, particularly Pietro Lombardo, and then Codussi, that the concept of the façade as a veneer of marble and precious stone became widely accepted. The earliest such works were probably Palazzo Dario, S. Maria dei Miracoli and the Scuola Grande di S. Marco, all of the period *c.*1482–95; in all three cases not only is

---

[17] The famous Venetian chimneypots are first shown in the cycle paintings of Carpaccio and Bellini; see esp. Carpaccio's Miracle of the Cross (Venice, Accademia) and also Mansueti's True Cross at S. Lio (ibid.). Palazzo Dario, contemporary with these pictures, has a fine collection today, although mostly restored or rebuilt.

28

29

30

28 to 30 Chimneys: the fireplace within the house is expressed clearly on the wall surface outside, as these three examples show. Fig. 28 is a tiny cottage at Burano, where the chimney is the dominant feature of the exterior; Fig. 29 is a recently modernised house at Malamocco, with one ground-floor fireplace and another, supported on corbels, on the second floor; Fig. 30 shows a large house at Pellestrina, with two substantial ground-floor ranges.

there elaborate structural decoration all in stone – frames, cornices, pediments – but the entire wall surface is veneered with thin stone panels in geometric patterns, and with further embellishment in the form of paterae of rare marbles. However, the nature of this veneer is made very clear: the panels are not structural, but are backed by a robust brick wall and they are even 'book matched' like timber veneers in furniture to emphasise their insubstantiality.

   The use of stone in a more structural way soon followed, though, in the work of Codussi (Palazzo Corner-Spinelli *c.*1497–1500 and Palazzo Vendramin-Calergi *c.*1500–5) and later again in that of Sansovino and Sanmicheli. Codussi's façades are entirely three-dimensional, that is, they are conceived as a classical whole, with superimposed orders of columns and entablatures; however, the rôle of stone on a façade was still not what it appeared to be, and even here Codussi reinforces the stone with brickwork behind. There are very few buildings indeed that have their principal elevations entirely of structural stone: almost all have a brick backing wall, bonded into the stone in the manner described

31 and 32 Chimney-pots: Fig. 31 shows a fine group of traditional Venetian inverted cone chimney pots or *fumaioli*, on the Giudecca, while Fig. 32 shows a more modest collection of *fumaioli* on a row of cottages at Burano.

33 The Cà d'Oro marks the apogee of the elaborately decorated gothic façade, and is entirely faced with Istrian stone and rare marbles.

34 Detail of the façade of S. Maria dei Miracoli; the main features are all finely carved stone, but again the whole wall surface is veneered with thin panels of marble.

by Serlio.[18] Even as a veneer the use of stone for an entire façade was extremely expensive, and only the wealthiest of the noble families could afford such a finish. It is thus not surprising to find that there are no all-stone façades in the smaller lagoon communities; there are two such houses at Chioggia (the Grassi and Lisatti *palazzi*) but none at Murano, even the splendid Trevisan and Giustinian houses having façades that are basically of stuccoed brick, albeit with much stone detailing.

Windows

> One must add here that all of the windows are glazed not with waxed linen or paper, but with beautiful clear white glass, held in frames of wood and kept in position with iron and lead, not only in the palaces and apartment buildings but everywhere else, even in humble places, which causes visitors to marvel, as in this field the city is boundlessly rich, the which riches come forth from the furnaces of Murano[19]

[18] S. Serlio, *The Five Books of Architecture*. All quotations here are from the first English edition (London 1611), and republished in facsimile (New York 1982). '. . . when a man is to mix hard stones & bricks together, which requireth great diligence and Arte: for that bricks are like flesh in a piece of worke, and hard stones like the bones to knit and hold them together: which two things, if they be not well and fastly bound together, they will, in time, decay . . .' Among many recommendations, he states that 'it is requisite, that the hard stones should be set so farre within the wall, that although there were no morter to hold them together, yet they should, of themselves, stand fast in the wall'. In general, Serlio did not approve of the 'veneering' techniques of the Lombardo: 'I would always more commend the worke that is wholy bound in the wall, then that which is ioyned together or covered . . . for that the houses which have beene made so in former time, by ancient workemen, and were covered over with marble and other fine stones, are now seene all without stones before, and nothing but the wall of bricke, that stood behind them, standeth still: but those buildings, where the hard stones are bound and ioyned into, and with the bricks, are yet standing . . .' (*The Five Books*, fourth book, chapter 9, fol. 64) The fourth book was first published in Venice in 1537.
[19] Sansovino, *Venetia Città Nobilissima*, book IX, p. 384.

35 Codussi's Palazzo Vendramin-Calergi: the façade as a classical screen, all of stone.

Sansovino's observation graphically illustrates the status of glass at the time as a very expensive luxury in most cities of Europe and, as he remarks, its use elsewhere was generally confined to the houses of the wealthy.

Windows as a building element exhibit a wider variety of forms in Venetian architecture than any other feature. In the important palaces and other houses, they naturally closely mirror the changing styles of architecture over the centuries, and are often very elaborate, with complex surrounds, mouldings and many lights. In the lesser houses with which this study is largely concerned, they are usually simpler, often single lights, although multi-light windows even in a more modest house always indicate the presence of the main hall or *pòrtego* behind them. Gothic windows which began as a simple pointed arch form developed elaborate profiles with cusped intrados and carved extrados, with trefoils and quatrefoils. Later, too, they often had an outer frame of a narrow band of stone set into the brick wall.

In many of the lesser houses in the city and its satellites, centuries of alteration and modernisation have often meant that the windows are virtually the only surviving feature from the original construction and are thus invaluable for dating purposes. Despite Arslan's important survey of the great gothic *palazzi*, much work remains to be done in analysing the lesser gothic houses in the light of his own conclusions and those of Maretto

The fourth Booke,   The ninth Chapter. Fol.64

36 Illustration from Serlio's *Five Books*, showing the three methods of combining stone façades with structural brickwork. He did not approve of the veneering technique shown on the right.

and Muratori.[20] There are comparatively few examples of complex gothic fenestration in the lesser lagoon villages, although the windows were still the elements usually singled out by the later medieval masons for their finest work.

The arched windows of the Renaissance always have a stone head, often with an emphasised or carved keystone, and this feature sometimes appears on very modest houses indeed. Larger houses naturally incorporated a wider range of Renaissance or classical motifs, with flanking pilasters, columns, friezes, and multi-light windows, often of the *Serliana* type. Square-headed windows remained common in the lesser houses and were nearly always used for the ground storey, whether it was used as a *fòntego* (in a large *palazzo*) or as living accommodation in a more modest house. Simple square or rectangular lights were also almost universally used for the topmost storey. It is thus only on the *piano nobile* or first floor of the *palazzetto* or smaller houses that the more complex window types are found. Even here they were often still quite simple, although taller than those to the other floors, and often with semicircular heads; sometimes they also had balconies (see below). Even in very modest houses, windows were often surrounded with Istrian stone, although in the smallest cottages it was confined to head and sill only. In larger houses the window arrangement and size directly reflect the plan behind them and even in fairly small houses some emphasis is usually given to the central window or windows on the first floor, indicating the position (or at least the vestige) of the traditional *pòrtego*.

The windows themselves consisted of a simple pair of casements, with timber frames;

[20] E. Arslan, *Venezia Gotica*, P. Maretto, *L'Edilizia*, S. Muratori, *Studi per una Operante Storia Urbana di Venezia* (Rome 1959).

37 This and the following illustrations show the development of fenestration styles in the city and its satellites. Fig. 37 shows the reconstructed Veneto-Byzantine colonnade to the *piano nobile* of the Fòntego dei Turchi: stilted arches and elaborate classical capitals.

38 Torcello: Palazzo dell'Archivio – a much simplified late Veneto-Byzantine window, still with a stilted arch, but also with cusped extrados.

39 Burano: detail of the three-light window to the Palazzo del Podestà, a fairly simple version of the trilobate form, probably of the fifteenth century.

41 Burano: detail of the three-light window to the council chamber in the Palazzo Comunale, which may be tentatively dated to the mid-fifteenth century.

40 Murano: detail of a two-light window to a house on Rio dei Vetrai, a more elaborate version of the trilobate window head, crowned by a *fiorone*.

42 Malamocco: three-light window to the council hall in the Palazzo Comunale, with similar detailing to that at Burano (the balcony is later).

glazing in many cases would originally have been with waxed cloth or paper, although bottle glass was used from a fairly early date, at least in the *palazzi*, and later more generally, because of the proximity of Murano's furnaces. It is still very difficult to document the spread of the use of glass for window glazing.[21]

The exterior of the window was protected from the elements by timber shutters; the characteristic Venetian shutter consists of four leaves, two to each side, and hinged so that when open, it could be retained by clips to the outer face of the wall.[22] Other forms of shutter were also used, including those consisting of fixed timber louvres in casements. Once again such refinements were found only in houses of some status, and in the lesser cottages there was no such protection at all.

Balconies

The earliest Venetian houses had no balconies, but often had a carved stone panel or pluteus below the window. True balconies began to be used after the fourteenth century; older ones are therefore detailed in the gothic manner, and usually take the form of a miniature arcade, with pointed arches and small cylindrical columns – balusters – of stone. Later Renaissance balconies are naturally more classical and more robust and they became larger and more pronounced in the baroque era. They are almost always of Istrian stone, from all periods, as are the corbels that support them and also the balustrading.

Balconies are to a large extent a luxury feature and are thus not found at all on the smaller houses. In the slightly larger houses of the *borghesia* they are usually found only to the central windows to the *pòrtego* at first-floor level; it is only in the quite substantial houses and *palazzi* that they are generally found on most or all of the windows to the *piano nobile*. They are hardly ever seen on the lesser storeys such as the top or attic floor.

Doors

Like windows, doors are notable for their considerable variety of treatment; in the great houses, the portico was an important symbolic element, and in all periods and styles was often elaborately carved. In the gothic *palazzi* the landward door of the house usually has a square head with a broad stone surround, often with rope-moulding, dog-tooth or other patterned decoration. The water entrance is usually arched, although both portals are similarly detailed. Very often the landward entrance gave onto a courtyard and then in turn to the house itself. This outer gateway often has an arched head but with a stone transom, and sometimes with a fine carving in the lunette; often, too, the arms of the owner are incorporated above the portal.

In smaller houses portals were naturally simpler, but still always with a stone surround. Their symbolic importance was retained and even in quite modest houses they are more carefully detailed than almost any other element of the façade. As we will see, most lesser

---

[21] But see below, chapter 14 for notes on the glazing to the *palazzi* of Torcello.

[22] Again, we cannot determine with precision the period in which the characteristic four-leaf shutter came into widespread use. Certainly timber shutters were in general use on larger houses by the later fifteenth century. However, topographical views of the seventeenth and eighteenth centuries indicate that by then there was a mixture of shutter types in use, including the four-leaf type.

43 Early 'florid' gothic: a house on Rio della Pietà in Venice, probably of the fourteenth century (see also below, chapter 9).

44 The mature florid gothic style is epitomised by Palazzo Nani at S. Trovaso, probably of the 1460s or 1470s: detail of four-light window to the *piano nobile*.

45 Florid gothic in the lagoon: detail of the fine three-light window to the Bertolini house in Rio dei Vetrai at Murano, also of the later *quattrocento*.

46 Palazzetto Gussoni at S. Lio, sometimes attributed to Pietro Lombardo: typical detailing of the early Lombard Renaissance, probably of the 1470s or 1480s.

houses (other than the very small cottages of the *minuto popolo*) have symmetrical elevations and the entrance is thus in the centre; it is sometimes large, even on the smaller houses. The door itself is of oak, larch or other durable timber and once again, even in quite modest houses is often substantial. Many original doors have been lost over the centuries, but there still remain a small number of fine gothic examples in a few of the larger *palazzi*.

Entrances after about 1500 reflect the influence of the Renaissance and are thereafter almost always surmounted by a semicircular stone arch. In the medium-sized and smaller houses they are usually detailed in a very similar and sometimes identical manner to the first-floor windows, with simple stone surrounds, arched heads, an emphasised keystone and sometimes carved capitals to the imposts, although usually of very simple form. Indeed, in many cases the portal is the only part of the façade where there is any profiled carved stonework at all.

Cornices

The cornices at the roof eaves are usually of stone, and in most cases are integral with the perimeter gutter. The earliest surviving examples, from the fourteenth century, are of brick, in a dog-tooth pattern, but many examples in stone from both the fourteenth and fifteenth centuries may be found, particularly at Murano. They are often carved with

47 Venice: detail of the early Renaissance four-light window to the Palazzetto della Madonna on Rio della Frescada, with characteristic 'shell' decoration to the arches.

48 The Renaissance in the lagoon: four-light window to the second Contarini house on Rio dei Vetrai at Murano, with 'shell' decoration similar to that shown above.

49 Murano: detail of Palazzo Correr-Grimani, with further examples of typical sixteenth-century window detailing.

50 The baroque in the lagoon: the central window to the *salone* of Palazzo Giustinian at Murano, as remodelled by Gaspari: above the pediment are the arms of the family.

abstract patterns, usually of lozenge form, but also occasionally with chevrons or dog-tooth patterns. They are supported on corbels of stone. Similar string-courses at the lower floor levels are also found, particularly in the larger houses, and especially in the fifteenth century. Cornices in later periods mirror the changing styles elsewhere. Renaissance examples are usually simpler in profile than the gothic ones, and the supporting brackets are now of simple classical profile, similar to those that support the balconies.

Barbacani

The term *barbacane* is frequently encountered in Venetian architecture, although the same word is applied to two quite different elements of structure. One form of *barbacane* is what in England is generally called a jetty, that is, a corbel or row of corbels almost always in stone or timber (very rarely in brick) to support an overhanging upper storey. These jetties are very common in the most crowded parts of the city centre, but less common elsewhere; they were expensive to build and were thus only worthwhile where pressure on land for redevelopment was exceptionally high. The extent of the overhang is sometimes considerable and 600 or 700 mm. is not at all uncommon, although the *Provveditori di Comun* did establish a maximum legal projection, and this guidestone can be seen today on a house in Calle della Madonna, near S. Polo.[23]

---

[23] The stone bears the inscription 'per la iuridicion di Barbacani' and the arms of the Gradenigo family. According to Trincanato (*Venezia Minore*), it is of the fifteenth century.

51 Burano: detail of window to a house on Rio dei Assassini; this modest Renaissance detailing is typical of a number of houses of the later sixteenth and seventeenth centuries on the island.

Barbacani of this type are rare outside the city centre; there are a few at Chioggia, although here the preferred solution to the problem of shortage of space was to build an entirely new room on arches above the public *calle*. In both situations, however, the existing right of way had to be left unimpeded below the extension. Cantilevered jetties usually consisted of large timber beams projecting at right angles from the façade; sometimes they were simple continuations of the interior floor beams, but in other cases they were separate timbers spiked to these floor beams. The sections used were usually large, perhaps 250 × 200 mm., since they had to carry the entire load of the upper façade, often two or even three storeys in height. The beam ends are usually left undecorated unlike the timbers used in the other form of *barbacane*.

This other form is as an additional support to reduce the effective span of a large floor beam. The *barbacane* takes the form of a bracket built directly onto a column capital, and extending out perhaps a metre in both directions. The main spanning beam is then placed onto this *barbacane*; if there is a series of such beams (as is often the case) then each main beam has its effective span reduced by about two metres, and the deflection of these beams at mid-span is thus considerably reduced. From an early date these *barbacani* were often elaborately carved and there are many fine examples surviving today, not only in the city centre but also at Murano and Torcello.[24] Perhaps the finest are in the Ducal Palace,

[24] See below, chapters 11 and 14.

52 This and the following illustrations show some examples of doorways and their development in the city and lagoon: portal of the Foscolo-Corner house on Campo S. Margherita, probably of the twelfth or thirteenth century.

where they help to reduce the very large spans of the main council chambers; they are also sumptuously decorated. The size of timber used for this form of *barbacane* is again considerable, and is often the same in section as the beam which it supports, that is about 250 × 200 mm., or occasionally even larger.

53 Gothic portals in the city: doorway to Palazzo Gritti on Campo S. Angelo, from the fifteenth century, and with the arched head more usually found on canal façades.

54 Palazzo Pesaro-Fortuny degli Orfei: portal onto the *campo*, a typical late gothic surround, probably of the 1450s or 1460s.

55 A very rare surviving medieval door: the entrance to Palazzo Soranzo-Van Axel, also of the fifteenth century.

56 Portal to Sanmicheli's Palazzo Grimani at S. Luca: the mature Renaissance at its most monumental.

57 The Renaissance in the lagoon: doorway to the Soranzo villa on Fondamenta S. Giovanni dei Battuti at Murano, probably of the later fifteenth century, and showing some Lombard influence.

58 The Renaissance in the lagoon: the fine west door to the church of S. Pietro Martire at Murano, probably completed in the 1510s.

59 A simple, robust portal of the seventeenth century, on a house on the Zattere. The oval oculi are also typical of the period.

60 A simple classically based portal at Burano, also probably of the seventeenth century; the upper window is detailed in a very similar manner.

61 *Barbacani*: timber jetties are common in the crowded city centre; this is one of the best-known examples, in Calle del Paradiso, near S. Lio.

Quoins

The outer corners of the principal walls, especially of larger houses, were often emphasised by the use of large blocks of Istrian stone; this practice was particularly common in the later fourteenth and fifteenth centuries. The purpose was basically practical – to tie together the front and flank walls of the house and give additional strength to the corner. However, here again a practical detail became elaborated into decoration; the alternate 'header and stretcher' pattern was in itself decorative, but the corner was often further elaborated with rope-moulding or with small attached columns with miniature bases and capitals. Such refinements are not found in the lesser houses, although even here the structural problem remained and we often find a quoin formed of plain blocks of Istrian stone; there are several houses at Murano where this detail may be seen, as well as the Palazzo Comunale at Malamocco and elsewhere.

62 *Barbacani*: the other form of *barbacane* is a bracket supporting a beam – a fine example on a house on Fondamenta Cavour at Murano, probably of the fifteenth century.

Inlays and bas-reliefs

We have already mentioned the important influence of the Lombard masters in introducing decoration to façades in the form of patterns of inlaid *paterae* of precious marbles. However, many other forms of applied decoration may be found all over the city and in all of its satellite communities, applied in a far less formal manner than that of the Lombardo. Indeed there are probably thousands of apparently randomly applied pieces of sculpture, bas-reliefs, pieces of marble, inscriptions and other memorabilia attached to façades of all styles and classes. The oldest are Roman, much-prized fragments that had usually been found in the ruins of Altino, and often with Latin inscriptions; the others are from every century from the tenth to the nineteenth. A vast booty of carvings and other artefacts was brought back to the city after the infamous Fourth Crusade, to be embedded in the façades of noble palaces. Many others, of course, were specially designed and commissioned.

It is quite impossible to make any useful generalised observations about this fascinating but elusive aspect of the adornment of the Venetian house; specific examples of particular interest, however, are noted in chapters 11 to 14.

Crenellation

Merlatura or crenellation is a feature that can still be seen in a number of buildings, chiefly in the city centre, and several further examples survive on the tops of garden and

63 Crenellation: the most famous crenellation or *merlatura* in Venice is that which crowns the Ducal Palace – detail of the top of the Porta della Carta, with the symbolic figure of Justice by the Bon workshop.

64 *Sottopòrteghi* or colonnades: arcade to the Palazzetto Corner on Rio dei Vetrai at Murano.

65 Colonnades: an example from Chioggia, where they are widespread, especially along the banks of the Vena Canal – Palazzo Lisatti, of the early seventeenth century.

courtyard walls. Originally a military feature, crenellation never had any serious military purpose in Venice, although it was often applied to such strategically important buildings as granaries and the Arsenal in an almost entirely symbolic manner. Few private houses that survive today are crenellated, however; the Cà d'Oro is the best-known example and there is a similarly insubstantial *merlatura* to the Ducal Palace. In both cases the detail is all of stone, highly refined and decorated; in this form it is almost certainly of Islamic origin, the result of Venice's close economic ties with all of the great cities of the Middle East. Crenellation to the top of courtyard walls is more widespread and more simply detailed, usually all in brickwork.

Sottopòrteghi

Sottopòrteghi are arcades with living accommodation above them, and were normally built where space was particularly valuable and where it was therefore desired to build over the public street or quay. They are thus most common in the most densely built-up zones of central Venice, and are also widespread in Chioggia. They are fairly rare in the lagoon villages although a number can be seen at Murano and in *sestiere* Busetti, the most built-up part of Pellestrina.

Sottopòrteghi are usually carried on columns of brick or occasionally of stone; there is a simple continuous timber beam along the main façade (sometimes reinforced with *barba-cani*) and the lesser beams or joists supporting the upper room generally span onto this longitudinal beam and onto the inner wall of the building behind. Occasionally the arcade is arched in brickwork and then rendered, but more often it is left unadorned.

In some villages, such as Burano, we find a long, narrow passageway between two or more houses which remains a public right of way but which has been built over completely by first-floor extensions to the houses on either side. At Murano there is also a group of characteristic examples, on Rio dei Vetrai and elsewhere, where houses have been built over the *fondamenta* on arcades, thus allowing the free passage of the villagers below (see chapter 11).

Shopfronts

Purpose-built shopping streets, of which there are a number of very early date in Venice, had a continuous timber beam at first-floor level which was supported on each side of the shopfront by a column of Istrian stone. This allowed the whole shopfront, or as much as was required, to be open to the street, to provide the maximum light and air to the interior. Calle del Paradiso in Castello is the best-known example of such a street, although altered on several later occasions. The smaller villages could rarely support such concentrations of workshops and retail tradesmen, and these blocks of 'shop-workshops' are thus very rare outside the city centre.

Sanitary provisions[25]

These were nearly always situated in or adjacent to the kitchen, where supplies of water were available for cleaning purposes. In the larger houses, the latrine itself usually consisted of a simple raised dado with a circular seat of stone or timber, connected directly to a vertical downpipe, which was usually 200 to 250 mm. in diameter. The pipe was often positioned in the corner of a room, a corner formed by two main walls, so that the downpipe was at least partly built into the thickness of the walls. This basic arrangement dates from at least as early as the sixteenth century, and probably from considerably earlier.

The method of discharge at the bottom of the wall depended on the position of the house in relation to the nearest canal. If there was a canal directly adjacent, then the pipe discharged into it; in other cases it was necessary to take the pipe down to below street level and then run horizontally, with a slight but even fall, to the nearest point of discharge into a canal.

These horizontal drains were thus very shallow, only just below pavement level, and were circular in section, and constructed in two halves. The lower semicircle was of stone, while the upper half was of timber, and could thus be fairly easily taken off to permit access. However, from time to time the timber deteriorated and had to be replaced, and this periodic replacement was a regular feature of life in the city and its major satellites.

In the cases of both direct and indirect drainage the discharge pipe gave into the canal just above median tide level. Cesspits were only rarely used, at least in the city, although

[25] This summary is closely based on Trincanato's useful account (*Venezia Minore*, p. 115).

they were far more common in suburban and rural areas where horizontal runs of drain into the nearest canal were often too long (and expensive) to be practicable.

General disposal of other domestic waste was carried out by providing collecting bins or containers (*scoazzere*) in central locations, often in or adjacent to parish squares, and these were regularly emptied by government employees. Despite this arrangement a large proportion of domestic refuse undoubtedly went straight into the canals – as it does today – and despite many attempts at curbing the practice through legislation and fines, the *Serenissima* found, as the Comune does today, that it is a practice impossible to eradicate.

Wells and water supply

> Around the edge of the roof are gutters of stone, which collect the rainwater, and which is then conducted by pipes into wells; where it is purged of all of the larger impurities; it returns for the benefit of the people, because here there are no rivers, no basins underground where one might find sweet water, and thus cisterns are used, the water of which is purer and better for the digestion than fresh running water. Of which wells the city is most plentifully supplied, both in public places and in private. One may see that in every square or *campo* or courtyard there is a well, built by public expense for the most part, at various times, as for example was done under doge Francesco Foscari in whose time in one particular year there was no rain from November to the following February, and hence the Republic constructed thirty new wells for the benefit of the poor, and also organized the transport of water by boats from the river Brenta, thus rectifying with ingenuity the natural defects of the seasons . . .[26]

The supply of sufficient quantities of fresh water was a constant problem in all of the larger settlements of the lagoon, which is why rainwater from the roofs was so carefully collected for re-use, whereas in most medieval cities it simply discharged into the streets. In Venice and its satellites wells were the only means of ensuring fresh water in all but the most exceptional seasons of drought. Venetian wells are artificial in that they are in fact large underground cisterns collecting rainwater. They are usually situated in public squares or courtyards and consist of a large 'tank' some 5 or 6 metres deep and usually square or rectangular in plan. This large excavation was lined with a thick layer of clay to render it impermeable, and in the centre was the shaft of the well itself, built of brick and usually circular on plan.

The well shaft stood on a large foundation slab of Istrian stone, and there were small holes left in the joints of the brickwork at the base of the shaft. The entire cistern was then filled with silt or river sand which acted as a giant filter for the water. Towards the top surface small caissons were built, with open bases, and the tops of these caissons had small openings (vulgarly known as *pilelle*) to collect the rainwater. The final surface of the entire *campo* was laid to fall to these *pilelle* and thus the whole area of the square – as well as the roofs around it – became the collecting area for rainwater.

The well-head (*vera da pozzo*) is one of the most characteristic features of the urban environment, not only of Venice but of the lesser communities as well. As the focal point of a parish square or of the private courtyard of a *palazzo* it became a work of art in its own

---

[26] Sansovino, *Venetia Città Nobilissima*, book IX, p. 382. The drought was in the winter of 1425–6. Foscari was doge from 1423 to 1457.

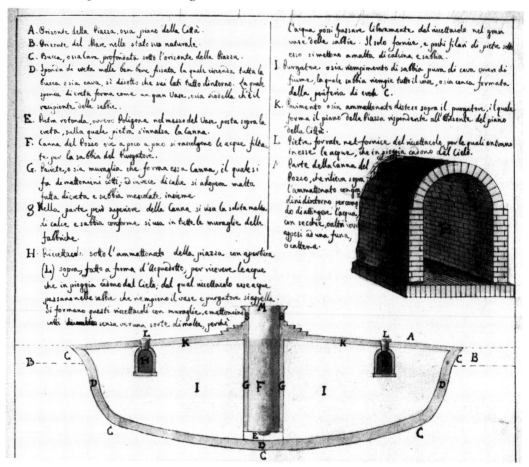

66 Wells and water supply: a sketch section through a typical Venetian well; from Richard Norris *Sketches taken in Italy* (1769) (V.&A. Mus., London; ref. 95.A.17, vol. 1).

right and many examples survive today from all periods from the twelfth century onwards, many of which are elaborately carved and decorated. The Venetian well-heads have justifiably been the subject of several studies in recent years as their 'architecture' closely echoes that of their contemporary palaces and villas.[27]

Quays or *fondamente*: paving in public places

Quays are nearly always constructed of brick or stone or of a mixture of the two materials. Most have been rebuilt over the centuries, although the most important quays, and steps for access to ships, were always of Istrian stone. The public *campi* and *campielli* were originally not paved at all, but left grassed in their natural state. Later, the chief routes across the *campi* were paved with brick and later again, the entire surface was finished in brick, usually laid in herringbone pattern, in squares, the sections being divided by strips of Istrian stone. Several examples of such brick paving may still be seen, and Piazza S.

[27] For some illustrations see Arslan, *Venezia Gotica*. See also bibliog.

67 The Venetian well-head: a fine example of a carved well-head of Istrian stone at Malamocco, in front of the Palazzo Comunale.

68 The cloister of Sant'Apollonia, the only Romanesque cloister in Venice: the brick paving is laid in the traditional herringbone pattern, and the well-head (possibly of the twelfth or thirteenth century and thus contemporary with the cloister) may also be noted.

Marco was also paved in this way until its present pavement of trachite and Istrian stone was laid in 1722. The main shopping streets were also paved from a fairly early date and are still today distinguished by the name *salizzada* (from *selciata*) instead of the usual *calle*. But this paving was also originally of brick, and the widespread use of black trachite from the Euganean Hills, near Padua, was not in general use until the seventeenth or eighteenth centuries.[28]

Bridges

The subject of the bridges of Venice and its satellites is a considerable one, but a very brief note may be useful here to summarise this most characteristic feature of all of the lagoon communities.

   With the exception of the single original spans over the Grand Canals of both Venice and Murano, and perhaps also the two across the Cannaregio Canal, most of the canals of Venice and its surrounding villages are very narrow and shallow, and there was little technical difficulty in bridging them. Many bridges were originally of timber, and a

[28] Of the *campi* still paved with brick we may cite the Misericordia and the Madonna dell'Orto, both in the city. In the lagoon villages, very little, if any, original brick paving survives, and today it is almost all black trachite.

69 Bridges: the majority of bridges in the city and its satellites are simple arches of stone and brick, the stone being used for copings and for the voussoirs of the arch, and brick for the parapets – a typical example near the Arsenal.

70 Bridges: a number of minor bridges in the city and the lagoon are all of timber, like this example at Mazzorbo. They are cheaper to build but require more frequent repair and sometimes replacement.

number can be seen today in the lesser communities as well as several in the city. Cheaper to build initially, they naturally required maintenance, and from time to time complete rebuilding, so that there are no original medieval timber bridges today; however a number of those that we see today, such as the Arsenal bridge or the Castello bridge in Venice or the Pontelungo between Burano and Mazzorbo closely follow medieval patterns in their design.

The majority of bridges, however, were built of brick and stone, and the earliest had inclined ramps with shallow steps to permit horses to cross as well as foot traffic. They were also originally built without parapets as the well-known Ponte del Diavolo at Torcello clearly shows.[29]

In the smaller lagoon villages almost all bridges conformed to this simple pattern. The very few larger spans may be mentioned here individually. The single bridge that spans the Grand Canal of Murano, today known as the Ponte Vivarini, is of iron and timber, but was originally built all of timber and was known as the Pontelungo. Like the bridges of Castello and the Arsenal it consisted of two inclined ramps or ramped steps; it is possible that the central section was removable to permit the passage of larger ships, although de' Barbari does not indicate such a drawbridge. This feature was found, however, on the

[29] Even as late as the eighteenth century, many bridges were still without parapets, as Visentini and others indicate.

original timber Rialto bridge, and that at the Arsenal had a similar section at mid-span to allow the passage of newly completed war galleys.

The long timber footbridge that today connects Burano with Mazzorbo follows a very similar pattern, with two long ramps; although the present bridge is modern it closely follows the design of its predecessors. It is probable, too, that the bridge that once spanned the Mazzorbo Canal, now lost, was again of similar appearance. Such timber bridges were much easier to construct than bridges of stone, which for such long spans would have had to consist of a series of smaller arches like the Ponte di Tre Archi over the Cannaregio Canal in the capital.

The lesser bridges of Murano are all today of the most widespread type, a single stone and brick arch, with brick parapets and stone dressings and copings. At Burano, however, some bridges are of timber and others of masonry, a pattern that seems to have originated in the early eighteenth century, and possibly earlier.

6

The guild system and the building crafts

I Introduction: the guild system

To appreciate the way in which the construction industry was organised in Venice and its satellites, we will first introduce the guild system as a whole. As in all of the other major commercial and manufacturing centres of western Europe, the development of specialised groups of craftsmen and tradesmen evolved at a fairly early date. In the twelfth and thirteenth centuries Venice was a very large city indeed by European standards, with possibly as many as 100,000 inhabitants;[1] in such a great metropolis, with long-established trading links over most of the Middle East, and particularly with Constantinople, we find that the guild system here was possibly more highly developed than in almost any other western city.

The earliest regulations for the Venetian guilds were almost certainly closely modelled on existing practices in Constantinople; despite its long independence, many of the *Serenissima*'s cultural and political roots still lay under the soil of this great city, which remained an important influence on the cultural and economic life of the Republic. Trade associations existed at Constantinople at least as early as the tenth century, functioning in broadly the way that we now understand by the term guild.

The first major legislation in Venice to formally organise similar groups was that effected by doge Sebastiano Ziani in 1173. It is clear, though, that various informal groupings of specialist craftsmen (chiefly formed to protect their interests and ensure continuity of skills) had been in existence for some time already. Ziani appointed *giustizieri* (justices), whose chief tasks were supervision of weights and measures and general 'policing' of the activities of such financially important groups as woolworkers, merchants and the many crafts of the shipbuilding industry. A large number of trade associations thus grew in the later twelfth and thirteenth centuries, some solely concerned with manufacture, and others, associations of dealers or traders. Still others again formed rather different organisations with a strong emphasis on religious instruction and charitable works; these evolved to become the original five *Scuole Grandi*, so named to distinguish them from many lesser groups and from the working guilds or *arti*. With time, some of these groups absorbed some of each other's functions; the *arti*, for example, also took upon themselves charitable functions (chiefly to their own members) and played a prominent part in many Church ceremonies. Such functions were later codified in their statutes.

[1] F. Lane, *Venice*, p. 18.

As these organisations grew, many became more specialised in their membership and thus became true guilds: all of their members now practised the same craft, and the guild itself supervised its members and promoted their interests. The growth of these 'true' guilds was fairly rapid in the first half of the thirteenth century, and by mid-century it was necessary for the government to begin a new system of registration and of control by the Palazzo Ducale over their activities.[2]

In 1261 legislation was passed which indicated not only how numerous these guilds now were, but also how economically powerful and how potentially disruptive to the state if they were not brought under stricter control. It was now necessary for all guildsmen to swear allegiance to the state and, to supervise their activities more closely, the agency of the *Giustizia* was divided into two parts, the *Giustizia Vecchia* and *Nuova* – the former now having exclusive magistracy over the guilds. The *Giustizia Vecchia* had three heads or *capi* who decreed that each major guild was to be headed by a *gastaldo*, elected by the guild members, with a term of office of only one year, and whose appointment had to be ratified by the *Giustizia Vecchia*.

With the basic framework of the *arti* now established, each guild was instructed to codify its regulations, which became known as their *mariegole*. These were submitted to the *Giustizia Vecchia* and, once approved, were the legally binding statutes of the guild. There were many revisions and later additions to the *mariegole* but their original rules remained the basis of the guilds' administration for the next five hundred years. Some principles were universal and were established by the *Giustizia* itself, although many others were naturally unique to a particular trade. In general, for example, it was not permitted to accept any apprentices for training until they were at least twelve years old. Apprenticeships usually lasted for five years, but in some crafts for seven, and were followed by two or three years of practical experience as a probationer or 'journeyman' before one was allowed to set up on one's own with a registered *bottega* or workshop. Each fully qualified craftsman had to pay an annual fee to the guild, as well as a tax to the *Giustizia Vecchia*, the *taglione*.[3]

Each of the working *arti* had its official seat or place of assembly, as well as a registered religious base, the latter usually in the form of an altar or chapel in one of the parish churches. The large number of guilds varied considerably in size, membership and wealth, and hence also in their ability to build suitable premises for themselves.

Nevertheless, the minimum accommodation necessary was a spacious room for assemblies of all the members and for the election of the *gastaldo* and other officials. This hall was the *albergo*, and in the larger, wealthier *arti* was distinct from the other, ancillary accommodation, which included an office for the secretary and often a chapel. All of the guilds were headed by a *gastaldo*; their internal organisation, however, was largely left to

[2] For all of this early period see esp. R. Cessi, *La Politica dei Lavori Pubblici della Repubblica Veneta* (Rome 1925). See also R. Predelli, *Il Liber Comunis detto anche 'Plegiorum' del R. Archivio Generale di Venezia: Regesti* (Venice 1872). There are brief extracts in Zuccolo, *Il Restauro*.
[3] The *mariegole* of all the trade guilds are published as G. Monticolo, ed., *I Capitolari delle Arti Veneziane*: 3 vols. (Rome 1896–1914). See also G. Nepi Scirè *et al.*, *Arti e Mestieri nella Repubblica di Venezia*; R. Mackenney, 'Arti e Stato a Venezia tra medio evo e "600"' in *Studi Veneziani*, V (1981); the same author's 'Guilds and guildsmen in sixteenth-century Venice' in *Bulletin of the Soc. for Renaissance Studies*, Autumn 1984; the most exhaustive modern survey of the trade guilds, however, is R. Mackenney, *Tradesmen and Traders: The World of the Guilds in Venice and Europe c. 1250–c. 1650* (London 1987).

71 The Scuola dei Mureri: this fairly modest structure was the guild-hall of the *arte* of builders or *mureri*, and stands at the corner of Salizzada S. Samuele. The main meeting hall was on the first floor.

the members themselves, and the larger guilds had several other officials, including a treasurer or accountant, a scribe or secretary, and often an inner committee of between six and nine members who collectively administered the guild's affairs. This committee was known as the *Banca* or bench.

The social status of all guildsmen was clearly defined, as was Venetian society as a whole. At the top of the social ladder was the nobility, the oligarchical group forming the government of the Republic. The Senate, the Maggior Consiglio, the Council of Ten, the doge himself – membership of all of these bodies and offices was the exclusive prerogative of the nobility. Membership of the patriciate thus conferred on these few dozen families many privileges but also a great number of obligations; the nobility were the State and the State was the nobility. No other person was permitted to participate in the government of the Republic; all heads of ministries and departments, all ambassadors to foreign states and all supreme justices had to be drawn from this small group of merchant-nobles.

Below the nobility was the citizenry, almost as restricted in membership, although numerically several times larger; the citizenry provided government with all of its senior bureaucrats, secretaries, lawyers and the like, in fact all of its senior civil servants. The citizenry was allowed to engage in trade and commerce (and many did so very successfully indeed) but could not practise any 'mechanical trade'. This was the exclusive sphere of the working guilds, the *arti*. By the time of their reorganisation in 1261 the *arti* numbered several dozen and their number continued to grow. At their peak there were just over a hundred major *arti* and as many again of the lesser, ancillary trades.

Finally, below these numerous *arti* there were the common people, the *minuto popolo*, a class that included many forms of casual manual and unregistered labour, unskilled workers of many kinds, as well as the truly poor, the indigent, beggars, and the un-employable. All of these four classes were fully represented in the city and almost all had at least some representatives in the villages surrounding the *Dominante*.

The social and political rôle of the trade guilds was thus clearly defined by the later thirteenth century. Economically, their members collectively formed a vital element in the wealth of the state; although all international trade was exclusively in the hands of the upper classes of society, the manufacture of goods and artefacts generated huge sums of money both within the state and in the form of foreign earnings. The wool industry, printing and glass production, for example, were all staples of the domestic economy. So, too, was the vast naval dockyard of the Arsenal, the largest industrial complex in western Europe, employing several thousand men and producing ships both mercantile and military in a quantity impossible in any other great port in the western world.

The fortunes of the many trade guilds fluctuated considerably over the centuries. Some declined, others prospered. Some amalgamated with others, while a few became obsolete and disappeared entirely. Their function remained constant, however, to look after the interests of their members, to supervise the training of apprentices, and act as a pressure-group on the government.

They also retained important religious functions, although they remained quite distinct from the *Scuole Grandi*, of which there were eventually seven. These were religious confraternities based directly on the Church, and their membership was open to the nobility as well as the citizenry and others; each was entitled to have up to 600 registered members.

The *Scuole Grandi* were chiefly concerned with charity and religious instruction, but became immensely wealthy, and all built sumptuously decorated *scuole* for themselves. The trade guilds also retained charitable functions, but these were generally confined to their own members and their immediate families.

The basic administration of the *arti* remained in force until a major reorganisation in the early sixteenth century. This began in 1520 with a decree that each guild was thenceforth to be administered by two bodies, one of which was the existing *Banca*, now consisting in most guilds of twelve men known as the *Dodici di Banca*. The other was a new body of a further twelve men, the *Zonta* (*aggiunta* or augmentation) who were to be summoned to all important meetings of the *Dodici* and were to vote with them. The purpose of these *Zonte* was clearly stated: they were an attempt to combat widespread nepotism and other forms of favouritism and vote-rigging among members of the existing *Banche*. For this reason none of the members of a *Zonta* were to be related in any way to the old *Dodici di Banca*.

Two new officials, the *Sindici*, were also appointed to each guild to supervise the accounts. Many of the *arti* had become very wealthy in the two centuries since their registration; they had accumulated property, much of it as a result of bequests by members, and despite their comprehensive codes of conduct, it was clear that this wealth had often led to corruption and other improper practices.[4]

Further reforms were promulgated in the sixteenth century, again applicable to all of the working *arti*. Many were new attempts to reduce nepotism and corruption; a decree of 1537, for example, made it compulsory for the *gastaldi* of the guilds to hand over to their successors all of the moveable property of the guild with an up-to-date statement of its accounts within one month of leaving office. The same measure decreed that any member in receipt of charity was barred from voting for any of the new officials at election time. Increasingly heavy fines were levied on *arte* officers for maladministration or dereliction of duty; in 1596 refusal to accept the office of *guardian* was punishable by a fine of fifty ducats, or twenty in the case of the office of secretary.

Further decrees throughout the seventeenth century attempted to reform the *arti* and improve their administration. Apart from property investments, many guilds also owned works of art, gold, jewellery and reliquaries; a *terminazione* of 1637 made it compulsory for the *arti* to keep inventories of all such items, together with an official declaration of their value. Similar measures were reiterated from time to time. One reform in 1700 co-ordinated the election of all new officials to the *Banca*, now known as the *Banca Nova*; thenceforth all such elections were to take place in October, November or December, so that all new guild officials took up their posts on 1 January of the next year. Fourteen years later, a decree refers yet again to the 'aperti disordini, che sempre più si vanno innoltrando nel Maneggio, e Governo delle Scole di Divozione e altre Fraglie [*arti*]'. Yet again it was decreed that any amendments to the official *mariegole* of the guilds had to obtain government approval before they became valid; the three *Provveditori al Comun* were now the registrars for these statutes.

It was also ordered that the apparently widespread practice of the *gastaldi* keeping some of the more valuable and portable treasures of the *arti* in their own homes was to cease immediately. Thenceforth these treasures were to be kept locked in the coffers of the guild with three different keys, only one of which was to be held by the *gastaldo*, the others by two other senior guild officials. The suspicions of the *Provveditori* as to the propriety of some of these officials could hardly have been expressed more clearly.[5]

Having now outlined some of the more important aspects of the development of the guilds in general, we will now turn to those directly concerned with the building industry.

II The building-trade guilds

The building trades were probably some of the first of the 'mechanical crafts' to have formed themselves into some kind of unofficial or semi-official association; unlike several of the manufacturing guilds, they did not grow to accumulate very great direct commercial power, but as in all heavily urbanised societies, the builders were among the most important of the more 'passive' guilds, not least of all in the direct way in which they transformed the physical appearance of the city itself. As we saw, Venice was a European

---

[4] The reorganisation of 1520 is in a collection of these amendments published by the State in 1746 as *Raccolta di Terminazioni et Ordini de Mag. Eccellentissima de' Provveditori di Comun* (copy in B.M.V. Misc. C. 19447).
[5] See note 4 above.

metropolis by the early part of the thirteenth century, and it is certain that the building crafts were populous.

The chief of them numbered only three: firstly there were the stonemasons (*tagliapietra*, or in dialect usually *taiapiera*), the carpenters (*marangoni* or *falegnami*) and the *muratori* or bricklayers. The first two groups appear to have existed in some form as semi-official guilds by the early thirteenth century; in the reorganisation and registration of the *arti* in 1261, however, all three of these key trades notified the *Giustizia Vecchia* of their existence and of their intention to be formally registered, with their own *mariegole*. The carpenters were the first to do so in 1271, although their *mariegole* were comprehensively revised in 1335. The statutes of the bricklayers or builders were presented only a few days after those of the carpenters in 1271, but they, too, later notified the *Giustizia* of various addenda, in 1277, 1280, and several other years thereafter until 1322. The statutes of the stonemasons, however, were not finally registered until 1307, although the craft itself had been notified as early as 1278.[6]

The stonemasons' guild[7]

The *arte* of the stonemasons was arguably the most important of the three trade guilds, not only in the aesthetic sense, but also because the stonemasons were, or became – in many cases – the real designers and managers of large and important building projects. It is useful, therefore, to summarise some of the more important clauses or *capitolari* of the guild's statutes, since they give considerable insight into the extent of the power of such guilds over their members. The *arte* was administered by three *soprastanti* or supervisors, who, like the *gastaldo* of the guild, retained their posts for only one year. They had many responsibilities, one of which was to regularly inspect all of the officially registered *botteghe* or *curie* (masons' yards or workshops), to examine the type and quality of stone that was being used, and to ensure that the *bottega* was being run 'in good faith', that is, fairly and honestly. The *soprastanti* also had wide powers to fine any of the guild's members for virtually any form of professional malpractice, and for which a fine or *multa* of twenty *soldi* (or more if deemed necessary) would be levied.

The general administration of the *arte* was in the hands of a secretary, together with a committee or *Banca* of nine officials. These nine, together with the *gastaldo*, also had to regularly inspect the workshops of their members, not only to ensure their proper administration, but also to record their own valuations of the stone in stock, and of that currently being worked.

The statutes contain a number of other clauses dealing with the type and quality of stone that could be used, the intention of all of them being to maintain high standards of workmanship and to penalise any member whose craftsmanship or business dealings fell below the standards set by the guild. For example, it was strictly forbidden to use more than one type of stone in any piece of work; if stone was sold to a client direct from the yard, it had to be clearly marked and identified as to its type and quality. Among several other similar clauses, it is instructive to note that the only stone specifically referred to by

---

[6] G. Monticolo, *I Capitolari*.
[7] For the masons' *mariegola* see Monticolo, *I Capitolari*, III, pp. 249 *et seq.*

name is that from Istria, which already comprised the overwhelming majority of all of the stone worked in the city and its satellites. Specific mention is made of the three chief sources of Pola, Parenzo and Rovigno.

A significant part of the guild's income undoubtedly came from a steady flow of fines for various offences and forms of misconduct, but more regular funds were derived from a levy of one *soldo* that was payable by every member of the guild on the occasion of Mass on the third Sunday of every month. Other useful sources of income included an annual fee payable to the *arte* by those who imported stone from abroad, as a form of import fee, amounting to the significant sum of 32 *soldi* per year. (Stone from Istria was not imported as the peninsula was Venetian territory.)

Membership of the guild was strictly limited to those Venetian nationals who had completed the long apprenticeship and satisfied the *soprastanti* as to their competence. However, it was not impossible for foreigners to work at their trade in the city; they had to apply to the guild and provide evidence of their qualifications, in other words, that they were registered at their craft in some other city. If they were approved, they paid an initial registration fee of twenty *soldi*. Apprenticeships in the guild, as in all of the others, began very young, and it was normal practice to begin training between the ages of twelve and fourteen;[8] one was thus normally qualified at about twenty to set up on one's own. Further evidence that this was generally the case is provided by the stipulation in the statutes that no member of the *arte* was to be able to stand for election to office until he was at least fifteen years old. We must finally briefly mention the important charitable obligations that the guild had towards its members and their families. The *soprastanti* were obliged to visit all members if they were sick, and if they found any who were 'indigent or in poverty . . . if there [were] funds available, then the guild may and must give them charitable assistance'. Members of the *arte* also had responsibilities for the care of the dead; they had to keep vigil over the coffin, and give practical aid and comfort to the bereaved. Both of these responsibilities are indicative of the quasi-religious status of all of the working guilds. Although they were clearly not purely religious confraternities like the *Scuole Grandi* and existed primarily to serve the interests of their members, nevertheless the *arti* were very closely bound up with the established Church at almost every level; they all had altars or chapels of devotion in the city's churches and they were all represented at every one of the major religious festivals of the Church's calendar.

The carpenters' guild

The statutes[9] of the other two principal building trades, the carpenters and bricklayers, contain many clauses similar to those of the masons, and in general both *arti* were organised in a similar way. The guild of carpenters or *falegnami* had the longest and most comprehensive list of regulations, amounting to well over fifty clauses; however, this guild had a more complex structure than the other two and was divided into four 'sub-guilds', each covering a more specialised branch of the woodworker's skill: there

---

[8] Palladio, for example, was only 13 when he began his apprenticeship in Padua in 1521 (J. S. Ackerman, *Palladio* [Harmondsworth 1966] p. 20).
[9] Monticolo, *I Capitolari*, II, pp. 180 *et seq.*

were the cabinet and furniture-makers; those who made frames and cornices; those who specialised in marquetry; and finally the building joiners and carpenters. (A fifth, quite separate, guild contained the shipwrights of the Arsenal.)

In the statutes of 1271 the carpenters were described as *magistrorum domorum*, a phrase that indicates their important rôle in the construction of houses. However, the *mariegole* contain surprisingly few clauses of a technical nature, although clause XIIII is of interest since it gives the *gastaldo* the right to select fifteen members to work on the major reconstruction that was in progress on the Ducal Palace in the last two decades of the thirteenth century.

The carpenters were subject to the same sort of general controls as were the masons. All their work had to conform to acceptable standards of workmanship and the prices charged had to be just. No work could be taken from another member without his authority, nor could it be transferred or sub-let without approval. As with the masons, new arrivals in the city wishing to register and set up on their own had to pay an initial fee of 20 *soldi* or 40 *soldi* if they were not yet trained and wished to serve their apprenticeship here. A further clause required a deposit (*sacramentum*) to be left with the *Giustizia Vecchia* for those wishing to work outside the city in the Dogado ('a Grado usque ad Caput-Ageris'); this deposit was fixed at 20 *soldi* in the addenda to the *mariegole* of 1335.

As with the other guilds there was a long list of festival days on which it was forbidden to work; they included 'all of the festivals of S. Maria and of the Holy Cross, the Twelve Apostles, the Feast of S. Marco, the Four Evangelists' and a further eight or nine others. The fine for working on these days was five *soldi*, a significant deterrent. On many of these days, the guild members were required to take part in processions and other rites, again emphasising their important links with the established Church.

The bricklayers' guild

Like the carpenters, the *muratori* compiled a *mariegola*[10] comprehensive in its scope; some of its clauses may be summarised here. A number of them deal with the contractual aspects of the craft and with continuity of work, and thus indirectly indicate the key rôle that the *muratori* had in many contracts as general building contractors.

For example, if work on one project had to be suspended and the builder thus transferred his attention to another contract, this latter work had to be completed within a pre-determined period of time or he would be fined the considerable sum of 100 *soldi*. Such a fine would also be levied if, having completed work on the second contract, the *muratore* did not then immediately return to the first one. It was forbidden to sub-let any work to another *maestro* or to transfer work to him without the consent of the client or building owner on penalty of a fine of ten *lire* (200 *soldi*); it was also forbidden to any *maestro* (and later also to any apprentice) to work on a day-to-day basis unless a clear agreement had been made with the client beforehand.

It is clear from this strong emphasis on such contractual matters, and from the large

[10] Ibid. pp. 283 *et seq.*

fines imposed, that in the cases of many building projects – particularly those that did not require the services of a team of masons under their own *maestro* – the *muratore* was in effect the main contractor of the project, a rôle that we will discuss further below. A further clause in the *mariegole* forbade any work to 'quays, walls or any other works that are adjacent to canals, ponds or public streets without the authority of the *Giustizia Vecchia*'; this was one of a long series of addenda attached to the original *mariegole* in 1313.

The conditions imposed on foreigners wishing to work in the city were almost identical to those of the stonemasons' statutes: the *muratori* were allowed a period of grace of only eight days, after which they had to register with the *gastaldo* of the guild and pay a registration fee of one *lira*, a sum that was increased to three *lire* in about 1286. The funds thus raised were to be distributed among the sick and infirm members of the *arte*.

On completion of his apprenticeship, a newly qualified craftsman had to pay five *soldi* as a registration fee; if the son of a member wished to set up on his own with a workshop either independently or on the death of his father, he would have to pay 30 *denari* (2½ *soldi*) to the guild to be re-registered.

All of these funds were employed in the administration of the guild, in charitable works and sometimes in the acquisition of investments. The charitable obligations were very similar to those of the other building guilds and indeed of the *arti* in general. Among other duties, members had to keep vigils over the deceased until their burial, and funds were to be made available whenever possible for disbursement to members in need of charity.

The lesser guilds

Apart from these three vital trades, there were several other guilds whose members were partly or exclusively concerned with the building industry. Smiths, for example, produced a wide range of accessories, fixtures and fittings, such as hinges, straps and cramps for stone, gates and railings. Many of these fittings were undoubtedly bought 'off the peg' by the *muratore* or carpenter and fitted as necessary. In other cases they were specially ordered, but again were fitted by the main building tradesmen. Only in the very largest *palazzi* do we find extensive use of decorative metalwork for gates and grilles.

The other ancillary trades were the glaziers, plasterers, painters and terrazzo-layers. Plasterers were naturally all employed in the building industry but the guild of painters embraced every type of painting from the simple decoration of wall surfaces to the great fresco works of Tiepolo and the canvases of Titian and Tintoretto, all of whom were members of the *arte* of *pittori*, with their seat at S. Sofia and with S. Luca as their patron. Painters were often called upon to decorate a wide variety of objects and temporary constructions, from saddles to barges, floats and 'machines'.

More strictly confined to building operations were the glaziers and *terrazzieri*. We have discussed window glass earlier; considerable prestige attached to its use generally, but despite its widespread adoption in Venice and the lagoon it was still very difficult to form large panes and these were confined to the houses of the wealthy. In more general use was bullion, consisting of a large number of quite small, round pieces of glass, usually only 10 to 12 cm. in diameter and set into lead cames within a frame of timber. These were far easier to form than flat sheet and comparatively cheap, although their section (with a thick 'knob' in the centre) made their transparency limited. All building glass came from Murano. In very humble houses, however, windows were still filled with heavy waxed paper, which had to be replaced from time to time. Little is known of the details of the spread of glass for windows, although in Venice it was certainly widespread in larger houses by the *quattrocento*.

We have described the work of the *terrazziero* in an earlier chapter. Terrazzo was almost universal in most periods as a finish to the upper floors of all larger houses, but was rare in more modest houses, where simple boards remained the only cover.

III Stonemasons, builders and architects

The detailed development of the building-trade guilds in Venice is a complex matter on which much further research needs to be done; although we are extraordinarily fortunate to still possess so many examples of the skills of the medieval masons, carpenters and bricklayers of the thirteenth and fourteenth centuries, there is an acute shortage of direct documentary information as to the practical aspects of building construction, site organis- ation, delegation of authority and so on, making useful generalisation still very difficult. The rôles of the members of the three key building trades were certainly not always constant in relation to each other, nor were they in relation to the profession of the architect, and these various relationships are very difficult to analyse comprehensively. We may here do no more than make some observations and suggest a few conclusions that appear likely from the small amount of detailed evidence so far discovered and examined. We may begin by discussing the rôle of the master stonemason.[11]

The term *tagliapietra* or *taiapiera* is more difficult to define than may at first be thought. At its most literal, it simply means a cutter of stone although, as we have seen, the training that was necessary before one was allowed to practise as a mason was long, comprehen- sive and arduous. However, in most of the lesser settlements of the lagoon (and on many simpler projects within the city) the mason was only rarely required to produce work any more complex than simple squared ashlar for lintels, steps and thresholds. As we will see, this was because of the overwhelming importance of brick as the basic building material. At the other extreme, a true *maestro* in the craft of masonry was capable of executing works of extraordinary grace, refinement and technical ability, and was a man of great skill and experience, not only in the execution of the work, but also in its initial overall design.

We should thus try and clarify the rôle of the master mason by reference to projects of different sizes and degrees of complexity. A very simple cottage or small house, such as the hundreds at Burano and Pellestrina (and in some of the peripheral zones of Venice itself) would require the services of a mason for only a very short period of time, to cut and provide the few pieces of dressed stone – chiefly lintels and sills – to complete the work. In such extremely simple buildings all of the structural carcase was the responsibility of the

---

[11] For some observations chiefly relevant to practice in England and France in the late *medioevo* see J. M. Harvey, *The Gothic World* (London 1950) and the same author's *The Medieval Architect* (London 1972). A vital source here, though, is S. Connell's unpublished Ph.D. thesis, 'The employment of sculptors and stonemasons in Venice in the fifteenth century' (Warburg Inst., Univ. of London 1976).

72 Detail of the façade of S. Michele in Isola, designed by Mauro Codussi, and completed in *c*. 1475. In this superb example of early Renaissance architecture in Venice the skills of architect, master stonemason and sculptor combine in such a way that the contribution of each is very difficult to define with precision.

muratore and the carpenter. Indeed, there is much evidence to indicate that in most cases the *muratore* fitted these few pieces of stone without recourse to a mason on site at all. The stone would thus have been ordered in advance, cut and worked in the mason's *bottega* (which was almost certainly in the capital) and simply delivered to the village for fixing by the builder.

In larger houses, such as the *case padronali* of Pellestrina and the houses of the *borghesia* in general, the rôle of the mason is less easy to define with precision. With such houses a clear element of overall design was necessary and we must conclude that a single figure was responsible for this design – the layout of the rooms, the composition of the main façade and the detailing of special features such as balconies, gables and the main portal. In many such cases, certainly the majority, the designer was a *muratore*, that is, a master builder, rather than a mason.

We do not yet know enough of the details of the apprenticeships of the two key trades, although in many such fairly substantial houses the amount of worked stone in their construction is still very small and the large majority of the work was the responsibility of the builder and the carpenter. The *muratore* was thus no mere bricklayer but a man quite capable of designing and supervising the construction of a substantial house. He almost certainly approached a mason for the detailed design of such special stone features as balconies, which at least in some cases would also have been installed by the mason. We know that the apprenticeship of the latter involved considerable study of design and proportion and it is almost certain that the *muratore*, too, received similar background instruction. We have only to examine the façades of some of these 'middle rank' houses to become aware that their proportions are carefully composed by men of some skill.

In larger, more grandiose projects, the picture is considerably clearer. Indeed, the more imposing a house was, the better-defined were the rôles of those involved in its construction. A large *palazzo* in the city (or one of the more sumptuous villas of Murano) would require the services of a small team of masons under their own *maestro*; some members of his team would almost always have been apprentices. In charge of the overall design and supervision of the project, the co-ordination of the masons and other craftsmen was another *maestro* and it is he who after about the end of the fifteenth century is often described as the architect. In the case of a large public building for the State or a major church or monastery this 'design *maestro*' or architect was often given the important symbolic title of *proto*, a term difficult to render in English but which approximates to Chief Surveyor or Architect of the Works. Whether employed directly by the government as its own *proto* (as Sansovino was at S. Marco) or by another authority (as Codussi was at S. Zaccaria) the title carried with it considerable prestige, and it was only given to men who had reached the highest levels of technical skill and of public service, and who almost without exception had an important *corpus* of work to their name already.

By the later fifteenth century the term architect was in fairly frequent use in Venice and it was applied in a way not very dissimilar to that in which it is used today, as the overall designer, co-ordinator and supervisor of an important building project. Quite often, however, he was still referred to as *maestro* or *magister*, however, and the two terms – *architetto* and *maestro* – were by no means mutually exclusive. For example, Mauro Codussi was a *magister* when he was employed on the completion of S. Zaccaria in the

1480s although his rôle was clearly that of the architect;[12] a *maestro* like Codussi took full responsibility for the creative aspects of the work, the design decisions, both in general and in detail. It is extremely unlikely that he still engaged in the physical execution of the work, although he worked up designs and details on paper and parchment, often to a large scale, and closely supervised all the execution of his designs. He usually went to the quarries to select the stone and organise its transport to the site.

A *maestro* such as Codussi, therefore, had now ceased to be a master mason in the literal, practical sense and was indeed a true architect. However, he had still had to serve a full seven-year apprenticeship in his youth, followed by three years or so as a 'journeyman' before being allowed to work as a mason on his own account. Codussi was born in about 1440, so he was still fairly young – about 30 – when he began work at S. Michele, the project that established his reputation in the city.

On projects such as S. Zaccaria, which involved a large quantity of specialised stone sculpture, the architect would often personally recommend a sculptor to his employer; the sculptor's work would be executed with the very close co-operation of the master stone-mason, but both were under the overall control of an architect such as Codussi.

Mauro Codussi is a particularly useful example to examine, as he was not only the designer of some of the earliest and finest early Renaissance buildings in Venice, but he is also one of the few architects in this important period – the later fifteenth century – about whom we have useful documentary evidence. The difficulties, indeed the futility of the precise definition of titles such as architect in this key era are illustrated again in Codussi's case; in 1483 he was retained at S. Zaccaria to complete the church begun by Gambello, and was honoured with the title of *proto*, as well as being referred to in correspondence as *magister*; nine years later, however, when appointed to rebuild the nearby parish church of S. Maria Formosa, he was described as 'architetto tajapietra'. Apart from the greater cachet, and possibly artistic freedom, given to a *proto*, though, it is clear that in both cases Codussi's position was indeed that of designer and controller of the construction of the projects, an architect who had first trained and become a master mason.

We may gain a little insight into the social status of a man such as Codussi (under whichever title he was employed) by relating his salary to the economic context of his time. In 1492 he was engaged at the Scuola Grande di S. Marco and his contract for that year specified his salary as six ducats per month for the eight and a half months of the year that he actually worked; for the rest of the year he returned to his native Bergamo. His work at S. Zaccaria nine years earlier had received a similar salary; in June 1483 he had been paid 80 ducats for a full year's service.[13] We know that Codussi lived in a fairly modest manner while in the city, and he seems to have accepted the loss of salary that sometimes resulted directly from his prolonged sojourns in his home town. To try and put his income in its context we may examine a few typical rents for houses and apartments in Venice at about this time. For example, a terrace of fairly large houses near SS Apostoli was rented in 1499 for annual *fitti* (rents) of 24 or 25 ducats each, while a terrace of more modest houses in Riello at S. Geremia could have been rented in 1537 for only 10 or 12

---

[12] See L. Angelini, *Le Opere in Venezia di Mauro Codussi* (Milan 1945). More comprehensive and authoritative is L. Puppi, *Mauro Codussi* (Milan 1977).
[13] Angelini, *Le Opere*, pp. 17 et seq.

73 West façade of the church of S. Zaccaria; the lowest order of the façade (and probably the second) are the work of Antonio Gambello and executed after 1460. The remainder is by Codussi and was begun in 1483.

ducats per year; these latter houses each had five rooms. Further down the social scale again, we find a large development which is today known as Corte S. Marco in Dorsoduro (near the Treponti) consisting of 24 almost identical cottages built around a large private courtyard; in 1515 the cottages rented at only five or six ducats per year.[14] It is clear therefore that Codussi could have afforded to live reasonably comfortably (but by no means luxuriously) in the capital in the 1480s and 1490s; evidence from elsewhere also confirms that a spacious *borghese* house rented in this period for about 20 or 25 ducats per year.[15]

For corroborative evidence of the social status of Codussi, or his successor Sansovino, we may mention one or two other contemporary salaries discussed by Pullan and Lane. By about 1550, half a century after Codussi's death, a typical salary for a building *maestro* (not an architect but a trade master) was about 30 *soldi* per day; in this period it was common for such a man to have been paid only for the days actually worked rather than by monthly salary. If we assume that he worked for 250 days per year, his annual income – with almost complete continuity of work – was about 60 ducats (at 6.4 *lire* per ducat). For comparison we may note Lane's figure of 100 ducats as a typical annual salary for a ship's master at this time.[16] Some time earlier, in 1529, Sansovino had been appointed *proto* of S. Marco, the most prestigious of such posts in the city, but his salary then was still only 80

[14] All three of these examples from G. Gianighian and P. Pavanini, *Dietro*, pp. 72, 84 and 110 respectively.
[15] For example, the house that the *nuncio* (envoy) from Chioggia rented in the capital at this time was 20 ducats (Goy, *Chioggia*, p. 64).
[16] Lane, *Venice*, p. 333; also B. Pullan, *Rich and Poor in Renaissance Venice* (Oxford 1971) *passim*.

ducats, as Codussi's had been several decades earlier. However, it was clear that such a figure was no longer appropriate and it must have fallen significantly behind other salaries. By 1539, ten years later, Sansovino's annual fee had more than doubled to 200 ducats, although this rise may also have been partly due to his increased prestige.

Both Codussi and Sansovino were true masters, however, men acknowledged by their contemporaries as the finest architects of their day; they were thus only employed on projects of major importance, public or private. The extent of involvement of a master mason (rather than architects such as these) was similarly dependent on the size of a project, its prestige and the funds available. The rôle of the architect generally grew quite naturally out of the rôle of the master stonemason largely because stone was the most prestigious building material and the working of stone was the most skilled of the building crafts; stone was also very expensive. There is thus a direct correlation between the size, status and complexity of a project and the development of the modern architect as a 'super-mason' whose special design skills were closely bound up with his skill in the technical use of stone, the most expensive and difficult material available.

However, a large number of substantial projects were designed and built by a master mason who did not carry (or perhaps aspire to) the title of architect. His involvement in many other, rather more modest schemes depended quite simply on the amount of stone used, that is, the amount that could be afforded. After about 1500 most new churches had façades entirely of stone, and the special nature of their construction also ensured that there would often be extensive stonework internally, for piers, pilasters, vaults, column capitals. The same observation applies to the most important public buildings of the government and its agencies. However, in the case of private houses, and particularly those of middle rank (or lower), the use of stone was still confined to major elements of structure and decoration, such as surrounds to doors and windows, cornices and balconies, while all of the basic loadbearing structure of the house remained of brick. As we saw earlier, until the later fifteenth century the façades of even the largest palaces were of brick, albeit with lavish stone detailing, and often with a veneer of plaster. Even later Renaissance palaces that were entirely faced in stone nearly always had a stout brick wall behind to reinforce it, and this composite construction usually followed Serlio's good advice discussed earlier.[17] The distinction between a stone-veneered façade and the rare examples of structural stone façades is an important one, since in almost every case the basic structure was built by the *muratore* or master builder rather than the master mason.

Builders and carpenters

The status of the stonemason in the community was usually that of a skilled craftsman, often the most prestigious of the building team. A mason could rise – if he had sufficient technical skill and design ability – to become a fairly notable public figure in Venetian society, although his social status remained that of a master craftsman, a guildsman. Within the craft, too, there were wide variations in skill, status and hence also in remuneration.

With the *muratore* this range was probably narrower, although there remained signifi-

[17] See note 18 to chapter 5.

cant variations; the *muratore* only rarely rose to the position of *proto* of a major building project, although Andrea Tirali is an example from a later era. Tirali first followed the trade of his *muratore* father Francesco, but in the early 1680s, when he was in his mid-twenties, he began to study architecture seriously and thereafter his rise was remarkably rapid. He was appointed *vice-proto* of the important agency of the *Magistrato alle Acque* only five or six years later.[18]

As a broad generalisation, though, it may be said that the craft of the *muratore* was less prestigious than that of the master mason; to some extent this lack of prestige appears unwarranted as there is little doubt that the master builder was responsible for the design and construction of a large number of substantial buildings in the city and its satellites. Our difficulty today lies in the precise definition of the extent of the *muratore's* responsibilities, and it is almost certain that his contributions in this field – both technical and aesthetic – have been underestimated. Certainly we may state with confidence that he was the most important of the three chief building crafts simply in terms of the volume of work for which he was responsible; Venice is a brick city, and the relationship of the mason to the *muratore* in the most general terms may be described as that between a small and generally somewhat élite group of specialists – the masons – and a considerably larger group of more general craftsmen who were responsible not only for the construction of the majority of the houses in Venice and its neighbours but also for the overall design of many of them as well. Their training was therefore almost certainly broader than that of the masons, encompassing not only significant background learning on proportion, principles and materials, but also on general aspects of building construction and of site and contractual administration, particularly in the co-ordination of ancillary trades, among which the most important was the carpenter-joiner.

Putting aside for a moment the difficult matter of the *muratore's* precise contractual responsibilities, we may mention one example of his technical skills that is often overlooked in general surveys of Venetian architecture, and that is the very long tradition of fine decorative brickwork in the city and lagoon, a tradition that can be traced by surviving examples back to the eleventh and twelfth centuries and which remained important until at least the latter part of the fifteenth century, when it was eclipsed largely by the increased use of decorative stonework. The tradition of elaborate brick decoration reached its apogee in ecclesiastical works rather than private houses; one of the earliest and finest examples of such work is at S. Donato at Murano where some of the brick detailing is more complex than the stonework, and which dates from the twelfth century. Similar but rather less complex work can be seen at S. Fosca on Torcello, and of roughly similar date. The best examples of later gothic brickwork are nearly all in Venice itself, and in particular the great monastic churches of the Frari, SS Giovanni e Paolo and S. Stefano.

It is clear therefore that the *muratore* was no simple bricklayer, even in the early medieval period, but was often a craftsman of great skill and technical ability. In the later medieval period, we may attempt to summarise his rôle in the building process thus: in fairly small projects, and in many that were of some size but which (for various reasons) involved very little stonework, the *muratore* was the overall designer and master builder, who consulted and liaised with the mason where necessary but who remained the 'main

[18] For a summary of Tirali's career see E. Bassi, *Architettura del Sei e Settecento a Venezia* (Venice 1980) pp. 169 *et seq.*

74 The summit of achievement in decorative brickwork in the lagoon: S. Donato at Murano, built *c.* 1100–40.

contractor' in very broadly the sense that we use the term today. In much larger and more prestigious projects the *muratore* would usually be subordinate to the master mason, the *proto* or the architect who assumed the rôle of overall designer of the building and supervised all aspects of its construction. There appears to be no evidence for the existence of a specialised 'sub-guild' responsible for the very specific task of the design and construction of foundations in this unique environment and the pile-drivers were thus probably directly responsible to the *muratore* who designed the footings himself. He thus carried a very heavy burden – literally and metaphorically – for the whole of the structure of a building from piles to roof tiles.

However, there remain many more detailed questions regarding the precise extent of responsibilities on a major building project in the later medieval period, which await further research.[19]

After the *muratore*, the carpenter was the most important of the other building trades. Unlike the former, he dealt almost exclusively with one material, but his involvement in all stages of a large building project was almost as extensive, since timber was used in footings, for all upper floors and for roofs. His work involved a mixture of what we would today call carpentry and joinery, that is, he was responsible for all of the main structural or

[19] See Harvey (1972), *Gothic World*, although again his examples are mostly from northern Europe and should perhaps be used with caution.

carcassing timber and for windows and other fittings that required far more accurate working. Structural timberwork in most houses was fairly straightforward, often involving large sections of wood but sections that were rarely required to be worked to complex profiles. This carcassing consisted chiefly of square or rectangular beams for upper floors, smaller rectangular sections for roof trusses and rafters, and boarding for floors. One of the few elements of structural timber traditionally carved to elaborate profiles were *barbacani*, while the chief elements of joinery were of course doors and windows and their frames and, later, shutters. In larger *palazzi* elements such as ceilings were often elaborately decorated with covings, cornices and frames for paintings but these would mostly have been installed by the specialist groups of cornice-makers. Despite the considerable importance of the carpenter at nearly every stage of the building process, he never achieved the position of eminence of the master builder as far as we can determine, and thus remained subordinate to him.

IV The building trades outside the city centre

We must now travel beyond the six *sestieri* of the crowded metropolis, but the principle of control by the trade guilds remained in force throughout the Dogado. However, outside the city, most villages were too small to have a comprehensive guild structure and Chioggia, the lagoon's second city, was the only community large enough to form an exception to this rule. Here, each of the major guilds had a branch which was affiliated to that of the capital. In the eighteenth century some of them amalgamated to form larger groupings of allied crafts; the Scuola di S. Giuseppe, for example, was the 'umbrella' guild for both carpenters and *muratori*. Here, as in Venice, the *arte* of the stonemasons grew to become the most influential of the building trades, although the carpenters and *muratori* were considerably more numerous.[20]

We may summarise here the very few details that we have as to the numbers of men legally registered in these trades. Chioggia was fairly well provided with trained craftsmen; in the 1766 *Anagrafe*, the first that has survived, there were 28 carpenters, 44 bricklayers (*muratori*), six thatchers and nineteen stonemasons. There were also 43 smiths of various types, and six glassmakers, although in both cases only a small part of their output served the building industry. A little later, in 1784, the Scuola of S. Giuseppe recorded a total of 73 members, both carpenters and *muratori*, so numbers seem to have been fairly stable in this period; there were now 17 masons.[21]

Pellestrina, Chioggia's closest satellite, was always poorly served by resident builders, despite the fact that it expanded rapidly in the period up to about 1740. By the 1784 survey there were 21 bricklayers and four masons here; the surprising number of five glaziers is also recorded.[22]

These two dozen builders must also have been responsible for at least some of the many new houses built at S. Pietro and Porto Secco on the same lido in this period, since no permanently resident builders were recorded in either of these smaller villages. Many of

---

[20] See Goy, *Chioggia*, and esp. statistical appendices.
[21] Ibid. See also Archivio Comunale di Chioggia B. 757.
[22] Archivio Comunale di Chioggia B. 766 b. 13 (also B. 757).

the more specialised tradesmen who built the large settlement of Pellestrina (and in particular the *case padronali* there) had to come from Chioggia to work, or possibly from Venice.

On the Lido of Venice, too, there were very few builders in permanent residence; only two bricklayers were listed in the *Anagrafe* of 1742 which covered the northern half of the littoral. However, both S. Maria and S. Nicolò were within easy reach of the capital whence their builders undoubtedly came.[23]

In the northern lagoon the only settlement large enough to support a permanent community of builders was Burano, although none of the various government surveys provides a detailed breakdown of crafts here; the 1766 survey simply lists a total of 267 'artigiani e manifattori', who included in their number boatbuilders, smiths, tailors and shoemakers.[24] At Murano, as at Burano, all of these crafts are grouped together, with 219 members, although here, as with the Lido, we may safely conclude that all of Murano's more specialised building tradesmen came from Venice to work.[25] Undoubtedly, in both of the larger islands there were sufficient competent local builders to provide the basic needs of the community, while for more complex work (certainly in the case of Murano's villas) specialists were brought from the capital, either commuting, or taking up temporary residence if the work justified it.

It is inconceivable, for example, that the very few masons at Burano were used to any more complicated work than simple door and window surrounds. This conclusion is borne out in a reference of 1692 when restoration work was being undertaken at the Palazzo Comunale of Torcello, and when Bernardo Lavezini was brought from Venice to restore the main façade.[26] Similarly, restoration of Murano's Palazzo Comunale in 1614 required the services of a glazier, *maestro* Gierolemo, who was also brought from Venice, from the parish of S. Canciano.[27] No builders at all were recorded at Torcello or Mazzorbo in any of the *anagrafi*; both hamlets were far too small to have supported such tradesmen alone.

The rôle of the stonemason in these villages was extremely limited. There are very few buildings indeed outside the city centre that were erected by men wealthy enough to have afforded the services of an architect or a true master mason or the elegant and very expensive façades that such men designed and built. The exception to this rule is Murano and its patrician villas; of the more important surviving houses there, it is the earliest survivors – the gothic houses and fragments – that provide evidence of the mason's skill at its most refined, and in particular the work at Palazzo da Mula. This house and that of the Foscari were built in the same way and with the same divisions of responsibility as were their contemporaneous *palazzi* in the city centre.

Of the Renaissance villas at Murano the two Soranzo houses offer examples at which very competent stonework may be seen; however, there is none of the elaborate window tracery of the earlier period, and later Renaissance stonework both here and in the lesser villages is generally fairly simple although often quite refined in its detailing and proportions. The more elaborate work of the baroque and rococo periods is very poorly represented outside the city centre, the only examples being a handful of churches. The mature

---

[23] Ibid. B. 766.   [24] A.S.V. Anagrafe di Tutto lo Stato 1766.   [25] Ibid. 1780 revision.
[26] A.S.V. Milizia da Mar B. 183.   [27] Ibid. B. 210 (Camerlenghi di Murano 1613–14).

baroque is represented by just one large house, the remodelled Palazzo Giustinian at Murano. Despite this paucity of outstanding examples, however, there is competent work of all periods to be found, from the gothic work at Palazzetto Corner in Murano to the simple but honest stonemasonry on the *case padronali* of the seventeenth and eighteenth centuries at Pellestrina.

The stonemason remained a comparatively rarely seen figure in these villages, though, and the large majority of the humdrum building work was undertaken by the *muratore*. In all of the lesser villages he was a general building contractor, and was often called upon to build nothing more complex than a series of structural walls with simple rectangular openings; his key rôle here was not in the field of technical craftsmanship but rather as the designer of the house and its general builder. Like the handful of masons, the *muratori* of these villages remain for us today, almost without exception, anonymous figures who left virtually no written record of their activities, apart from a number of scattered references to work on public buildings, bridges and other communal works. Such men were almost all simply competent local builders, adequately trained and in some cases clearly men with a good sense of scale and proportion in the overall design of a number of the larger houses.

Despite his almost complete anonymity, the *muratore* remains the most important craftsman in the building of these villages, and today several hundred examples of his work still stand, most of them dating from the seventeenth and eighteenth centuries. However modest the appearance of many of them, the fact that so many of these houses remain in fairly sound condition today, after two or three centuries in what is often a very hostile environment, indicates the high standard of competence of their original builders.

7

The economics of building in the lagoon

In all periods of history building has been a labour-intensive traditionally based industry that required the expenditure of considerable capital. Most of the houses in the lagoon communities are small, but so, too, were the incomes of those for whom they were built; even the construction of one of Burano's tiny cottages was a large investment for the subsistence-level fisherman who built it.

The cost of labour was always a large proportion of the total expenditure on any building project. However, building in the lagoon also involved an extra element of cost in the transport of materials to the islands, the unique difficulties of trans-shipment of many goods from the mainland onto barges for delivery to the site. On many occasions these transport costs are detailed separately in accounts, such as the L.3.10 recorded at Mazzorbo in 1586 when various works of restoration to the *osteria* of S. Bartolomeo and the church of S. Piero were required.[1] Transport overheads sometimes amounted to only two or three per cent of the stated costs of a project, although it is certain that other transport charges were 'lost' within the rates quoted. For example, when the Palazzo at Torcello was restored in 1443 the price of bricks was L.7 per thousand and that of roof tiles L.13 per thousand but this was the price delivered to site. The brickworks were probably in the vicinity of Mestre and the price as they left the kiln was undoubtedly less.[2]

Bricks were probably delivered direct from the works to the site if the kilns were accessible by water; many of them were, particularly those in and around Mestre. There were several canals and navigable streams in this area, so that not only bricks, but also lime and sand for mortar could all be delivered with comparative ease, although certainly not without cost.

Methods of delivery of timber to the villages are less easy to establish with certainty. In spring, when the major rivers of the Terraferma were in flood, timber was brought down to Venice in the form of rafts; these were then taken to various quays around the perimeter of the city where they were broken down and deposited at the timber yards, chiefly along the Zattere, the Riva degli Schiavoni, and (later) the Fondamente Nuove. It is certain that most of the timber for the villages followed the same route, and was then trans-shipped in small quantities to the lagoon communities as required. Special arrangements applied to works on public buildings; we have a number of records of timber for a Palazzo Comunale or for repair work to bridges that was specified as having come from the Arsenal, the 'squeri grandi di Castello'. This arrangement pertained because the Arsenal was the state

[1] A.S.V. Podestà di Torcello B.554 b.12 (Cassa della Comunità di Mazzorbo).
[2] Ibid. b.10. See also Appendix II, p. 346.

depository for timber, most of which was naturally for use in the great shipbuilding industry, although public works such as the above (which were supervised after the sixteenth century by the Milizia da Mar) had to use timber from this source. As a typical example of this practice we may cite restoration on the Palazzo of Torcello in 1609 and the 'barca porti il legname da venezia [sic]'.[3]

Because of the very modest nature of most of the lagoon houses, the third major building element, stone, is far less important than the other two. However, almost all building stone came across the gulf from Istria and again was unloaded onto the commercial quays of the city before being trans-shipped by smaller boats to individual stone-masons' yards. From there, after having been worked, it was transported as required, mostly in quite small quantities, to the villages.

We have already discussed the question of water supply and the difficulty in maintaining adequate reserves in the city in times of drought. The problem was even more acute in the lesser communities, many of which had insufficient wells; it was thus often necessary to deliver water by barge, particularly if important building operations coincided with a natural shortage. Thus in 1445 we read that one Ser Domenego provided Torcello with four boat-loads of water which were siphoned into the well of the Palazzo so that work on the *lozeta* (the flour *fòntego*) could proceed; the cost of this service was six *lire*.[4]

It is clear therefore that building operations of all kinds in the lagoon villages faced an added burden of costs in the form of trans-shipment charges applicable to all forms of material from bricks to water. Regarding the more general aspects of building costs we must first make the observation that detailed data on private housebuilding are extremely scarce, and our conclusions must be qualified by the fact that they are based on very limited evidence. In the sphere of public works different criteria applied altogether. The work itself was the responsibility of the podestà and his village council at the local level, and of the Milizia da Mar, a department of central government, for authorisation and funding. Detailed methods of funding varied considerably, however, and sometimes at least part had to be raised locally. Again we have far more detail of public works than private housebuilding; one of our earliest detailed records dates from 1443 when the Palazzo at Torcello underwent major restoration, and there are many estimates and bills from later periods. With the very long time-span covered in this survey, however, few useful comprehensive conclusions can be drawn on building costs since they naturally fluctuated considerably with inflation, costs and standards of living, availability of labour and so on.

However, we may examine one or two of these public records and attempt to relate them to other contemporary costs and incomes. We may begin by examining the Torcello figures for 1443;[5] the total cost of this restoration was L.239.9, of which 86 *lire*, or about 40 per cent of the total, were paid directly to the four craftsmen and three labourers engaged on the work; the latter were paid a further six *lire* to clean up afterwards, and L.1.4 was paid for transport charges for some of the materials. The ratio of labour to material costs of 40:60 per cent remained approximately constant for a long time thereafter.

The restoration was extensive, involving the partial reconstruction of the Palazzo;

---

[3] Ibid. b.12.   [4] Ibid. b.10.   [5] Ibid. See also chapter 14 below, and Appendix II, p. 346.

included in the priced list of materials are 1,700 small bricks and 2,500 standard bricks, as well as 800 roof tiles. However, there is hardly any worked stone in the contract, and so the door and window openings that survive today are, as far as we know, those from the original fourteenth-century building. Most of the work is brickwork and joinery, and we may conclude that it took some months to complete; although not detailed individually, the salaries probably amounted to about 15–18 *lire* for each of the craftsmen and perhaps five *lire* for each of the three labourers. It also seems likely that the two carpenters were brought here from Venice specifically for the work, since they were allowed expenses for food, whereas there is no such allowance for the two *muratori* who thus probably lived on Torcello or commuted from Burano to work.

It is difficult to draw detailed conclusions as to the costs of building materials, although, as we might expect, bricks appear cheap compared with the costs of large beams of timber or pieces of stone. One *lira*, for example, would buy 150 bricks, while a single floor beam cost well in excess of one *lira*; a barrel of lime cost six *soldi* (there were 20 *soldi* per *lira*), the same price as a timber pile for the foundations; a slab of stone for a balcony cost rather more than one *lira*.

We have very few other detailed accounts from this period, and no rent-rolls for the islands have survived until the later sixteenth century; however, we have a couple of contemporary salaries to afford a comparison. The salary of the parish priest of Mazzorbo at this time was 16 *soldi* per month, or about ten *lire* per year, so the building craftsmen seem to have been reasonably well paid although we do not know how long they took to complete their work; for another roughly contemporary comparison, the two treasurers of the *comune* of Torcello in 1415 received salaries of 14 *lire* per year.

The *muratori* and carpenters thus had a fairly good income compared to a fairly senior local official.[6] One or two further comparative figures for the same period are the sum of L.25, which was the rent for a large orchard in the 1450s,[7] and the rent of L.40.12.6, which was paid in 1454 by Girolamo Barbier to Lorenzo da Lezze, a noble, for his house, which was almost certainly of some size.[8]

There seems little doubt that a skilled craftsman such as a joiner or builder could earn an acceptable income even in these smaller communities, certainly by comparison with the low and often highly erratic seasonal incomes of the poor fishermen and *ortolani* who comprised the majority of the working population in these villages. Indeed, the only residents of some of these communities who earned good and comparatively secure incomes (at least for their term of office) were the public officials, the priests and their organists. The exceptions to this general rule were the more important landowners of Pellestrina and the successful glassmakers of Murano.

We have a few other records of building operations in the later fifteenth century, almost all in the field of public works, and we may cite a couple here. At Torcello, the flour *fòntego* (which stands adjacent to the Palazzo) was also restored at about the same time; the *fòntego* is considerably older than the Palazzo (see chapter 14) and was already well over a hundred years old by now. The work was mostly concerned with finishing trades, and includes the large sum of L.48.16 paid to Master Zorza, a painter. Such a sum suggests

[6] Ibid.   [7] Ibid. (Conto della Massaria) (before 1456).   [8] Ibid. b.11.

elaborate finishes, possibly frescoes, which have been lost long ago. Further interesting items include a boat-load of water for the works (indicating more shortages) and waxed cloth for the windows of both the Palazzo and the *fòntego* (or *lozeta*), the latter at a cost of about one *lira* for each building.[9]

It is not until the late sixteenth century that we have rent-rolls to add to our knowledge of lagunar economics. In particular the *catastico* or land register of 1581 gives full rent-rolls for all of these villages, although there is still very little documentation on building costs. By that date a small cottage at Burano rented for ten or twelve *lire* per year, while the two shops owned by the *comune* brought in 20 lire each in rent; a larger house (of which there were very few) rented for about the same sum.[10]

These rents are all very low. Torcello in the same year spent L.200 on routine mainten-ance to the hamlet's few bridges and quays, and Torcello was a very small, poor com-munity.[11] Only a few years later, L.53 were spent on replacing a few structural timbers in Torcello's Palazzo and repointing the brickwork; this modest sum thus represented five years' rent on a Burano cottage.[12]

An even clearer indication of the general poverty of Burano can be gained by comparing rents here with those in the capital. A large number of rents on (mostly speculative) property in the city have been recently published and we may cite a few here. A development of cottages in Castello is a typical indication of rent levels in a zone of the city that has always been poor, and traditionally occupied by sailors and labourers from the nearby Arsenal. These two terraces in Corte dei Preti (off the present Via Garibaldi) were rented in 1564 for a total of 280.12 ducats; there were 39 different tenancies, most of them cottages or small apartments of two or three rooms, and thus similar in size to a typical Burano cottage. The average rent was thus about 6½ ducats (that is, around L.35 to 40), figures that are notably higher than those at Burano, even in this modest and remote zone of the city.[13]

A second example is a small development of six apartments in Calle Lanza at S. Gregorio in Dorsoduro. Again they were comparable in size to a Burano cottage, each flat consisting of two rooms; in 1581 they were rented for a total of 18 ducats, or three ducats each (about 20 *lire*). Here again, the rents charged were about double those at Burano at about the same time. The little block in Calle Lanza is a very simple building indeed, with three flats on the ground floor and three above, built in the form of a 'C' around a tiny private courtyard. They are slightly better built than the cottages at Pellestrina and Burano, but devoid of decoration, and it is clear that in these lesser communities it was quite uneconomical to build to any standard higher than the barest, simplest minimum. When houses were built for rent in these villages the returns were so modest that no expense on any form of decoration could have been economically justified.[14]

By their nature, therefore, almost all of the cottages at Burano and elsewhere were very small and simple; only a minimum of proficiency in bricklaying and carpentry was necessary for their construction. Rents were, and remained, very low indeed. With such a

[9] Ibid. b.10. See also Appendix II, p. 326.
[10] A.S.V. Dieci Savii sopra le Decime B. 549 b. 83, *et seq.*   [11] Ibid.
[12] A.S.V. Podestà di Torcello B. 554 b. 12 – in 1593 and 1609 respectively.
[13] Gianighian and Pavanini, *Dietro*, p. 68.   [14] Ibid. p. 70.

basically subsistence-level population there was little possibility of large-scale speculative development and there was no market at all for larger, more expensive houses that might have commanded higher rents. Almost all of the development that took place here, therefore, was carried out by local people for the immediate needs of themselves and their families.

In considering the many tiny cottages of Burano, there is one aspect of the building process that should not be overlooked and which has been touched upon elsewhere.[15] This was the practice of taking materials from abandoned houses, particularly at Torcello and Mazzorbo, for re-use at Burano. The practice was widespread, particularly in the seventeenth century, and indicates the sharp contrast between poor, crowded and expanding Burano and its two small and declining neighbours. The Buranelli had always had a reputation for their wayward and frequently illegal behaviour; they were notorious smugglers and very reluctant tax-payers, and despite a series of government edicts the pattern of 're-cycling' building materials continued unabated. Such materials were far too valuable to be left to the mercy of the elements when a Torcello house was finally abandoned and its owner moved to the capital. Brick and timber could be easily re-used; marble, too, was valuable for lintels and steps. These materials undoubtedly formed a significant proportion of the total that was necessary to build the large number of new cottages at Burano in the later seventeenth and eighteenth centuries. If a Buranello was caught with a boat full of timber one moonless night in the Mazzorbo channel the punishments (theoretically at least) were severe indeed, but they did little to reduce the nocturnal traffic. Even the monasteries of Torcello were so efficiently pillaged after their closure by Napoleon that after a few years all that remained of these once impressive structures was a flat, weed-covered site and a few large pieces of stone, too heavy to be moved.

Although Burano is better-served than the other villages with surviving rent-rolls, to a large extent our observations also apply to the other islands. Torcello and Mazzorbo were both mere hamlets, too small to be self-sufficient and completely dependent on Burano and Venice for their builders and for all other supplies and services. Murano also contained a significant number of poor *ortolani* and fishermen, whose cottages closely resembled those of Burano, and here some of the same economic conditions pertained. The two *lidi* of Venice and Pellestrina were rather different; here the ownership of farmland played a major rôle in determining the social and economic structure of the communities and on both *lidi* (but notably at Pellestrina) there was an important social group whose wealth was based on the land and on income from it. They were thus rural or semi-rural economies rather than the essentially landless economies of both Murano and Burano.[16]

We have a number of accounts of public building works from the last decades of the sixteenth century, and we may compare the prices of a few basic building materials with those noted earlier. Bricks, for example, had cost L.7 per thousand at Torcello in 1443; in 1593 when the *fòntego* or *loggia* in the same village was repaired, they then cost L.20.16 per thousand. The price of a barrel of lime, six *soldi* in 1443, had now risen to one *lira* and two *soldi*; it is difficult to compare timber prices as the dimensions of beams are never stated, although a plank of larch cost about eight *soldi* in 1443 and the 'tole d'albero' required in

[15] Goy, *Chioggia*, p. 194.   [16] Ibid. Part II generally.

1593 were only slightly more expensive at ten *soldi* each. It must be stressed that these are random examples and that few comprehensive accounts have survived from the intervening period, so that we can draw few firm conclusions as to the detailed pattern of cost increases, although in some cases it is clearly considerable.[17]

The general economic circumstances that had determined building development in the sixteenth century broadly continued to apply throughout the following century. In communities such as Burano the overall economic status of the population changed comparatively little, although there were sometimes sharp fluctuations – often notable increases – in numbers. However, such increases, while they provided the incentive for much small-scale housebuilding activity, did very little to alter the basic socio-economic structure of the village as a whole. Torcello and Mazzorbo continued their long, slow decline; Murano, too, experienced a considerable change in its fortunes that also led to decline, a path that brought its own social structure closer and closer to that of Burano, its hitherto much poorer neighbour to the north. Murano's fall was principally the result of the rapidly diminishing interest in the island by the nobility as they turned to their great new estates on the Terraferma.[18]

Pellestrina remained a special case; its vineyard- and orchard-owners grew to become a significant class of moderately prosperous farmers. After recovery from the disastrous 1630 plague, population increased steadily, not only in Venice but throughout the Terraferma Empire, and with it the demand for the high-quality market-gardening produce of the *lidi* and the flatlands south of Chioggia. These market gardeners (or at least some of them) profited accordingly, and the *case padronali* of Pellestrina are the direct result of this comparative confidence and affluence in the latter part of the seventeenth and early eighteenth centuries.

The second government land register of 1661 allows us to examine the rents of property once again; if we return to Burano we find that the average rent for a tiny single-roomed cottage was now between four and six ducats (L.25 to L.38), rising to around seven or eight ducats (L.44 to L.50) for a two-roomed cottage and to nine or ten ducats (L.56 to L.62) for one of three rooms. These rents are between two and three times those recorded in the first survey of 1581.[19] If we now go to the capital, we may again compare Burano's rents with one or two examples there; a long terrace of houses in Borgoloco S. Lorenzo, owned by the eponymous monastery, was divided into small units, each of which was let in 1668 for an average annual rent of only 12 ducats. However, the last decades of the century marked a period of significant increases in rents, and when part of this terrace was rebuilt and replaced with a smaller number of larger units (ten instead of 18), the rents in 1711 had risen to an average of 36 ducats.[20] Further up the social scale, we find a group of substantial middle-rank houses in Calle Pasqualigo at S. Stefano, which were let in the early 1670s for between 40 and 60 ducats.[21] Again it is clear that despite notable increases, rents in the villages remained at very low levels compared to those in the capital, with no incentive for any large-scale speculative developments, such as we find in this time in the city centre.

---

[17] A.S.V. Podestà di Torcello B. 554 b. 11.

[18] For ample documentary evidence of Murano's decline, see esp. A.S.V. Milizia da Mar B. 206–214 (Camerlenghi di Murano).   [19] A.S.V. Dieci Savii B. 461.   [20] Gianighian and Pavanini, *Dietro*, p. 76.

[21] Ibid. p. 74.

A rare case of a private housebuilding operation recorded in detail in 1691 has survived from Burano; it is recorded because the owner, Piero Costantini, wanted permission to build a *sottopòrtego* across a public quay, and thus required the approval of the village council. He submitted a lengthy description of his plan, clearly intended to impress the councillors with the quality of materials he proposed to use, including a row of columns of Istrian stone supporting the *solaio* (upper floor) and a new chimney to serve two new fireplaces, although he prudently decided to re-use the old roof tiles. His builder, Maestro Minio, estimated the work to cost 110 ducats, and it took nine months to complete, from June 1691 to March 1692; after a series of interim payments a final account of 102 ducats was agreed by Minio.[22] This was still an expensive operation; with annual rents of only 8 or 9 ducats, it would have taken Piero many years to recoup his outlay if he had put the house on the market to rent. However, it is unlikely that this is what he did. The Costantini were a numerous but poor family with ten branches, all living one branch to each tiny cottage, and Piero almost certainly extended the house to shelter his own family, although 100 ducats was a very large sum for a Buranello to raise, and a *sottopòrtego* an expensive form of construction. The fruits of Minio's labour may perhaps be seen today in a house on Rio di Terranova near the church, where we see one of the very few porticoed houses in Burano.

There are many surviving records of public works in the later seventeenth and eighteenth centuries, but very few of private housebuilding activity although we know it was considerable. Even for public projects, however, it was often difficult to obtain funds, particularly from central government. Nevertheless, the public *palazzi* of the villages were all restored at least once (and in some cases several times) simply to keep their already ancient fabric standing.

By now the usual procedure for such work was for a village council to obtain an estimate from a builder, which was divided into materials, labour and transport charges. This was then debated by the council and accepted or rejected; in the latter case a lower figure was negotiated. There is very little evidence of competitive tendering, and an example of this more usual negotiated method is given in 1704, in a tender for a new bishops' house at Torcello, for which a long priced schedule of work survives (see Appendix II).[23] The first estimate in the large sum of L.18,187 was reduced to L.13,337 before it was acceptable to the Procurators. The estimate gives us a comprehensive picture of building costs at the time; most of the work is priced in the ancient (and almost universal) method of the linear foot or the square *passo*[24] depending on the nature of the trade. The largest item of work is the construction of the main walls and footings; this was all billed together at 12 *lire* per square *passo*. Covering the roof was a slightly cheaper operation at 10 *lire* per *passo*, while finishing the floors with terrazzo, a fairly labour-intensive and time-consuming task, was priced at 12 *lire*, the same rate as the walls.

The house was to be large, built on two floors, each with an area of about 60 square *passi* (163 sq. m.). Thirty-three windows were specified, each with a stone sill, and each of the latter cost eight *lire* to carve and install. The windows were all fully glazed and sixteen of

[22] A.S.V. Podestà di Torcello B. 552 b. 10.
[23] A.S.V. Milizia da Mar B. 186. See Appendix II, p. 347.
[24] The Ventian *passo* was divided into five feet, *piedi*. The *passo* measured approx. 1.74 m. and the *piede* thus about 348 mm.

them (probably those to the *piano nobile*) were fitted with timber shutters at the considerable cost of 48 *lire* each. A notable feature of the 'Bill of Quantities' is the comparatively high cost of timber, even compared with the stonework. Most of the latter was no doubt simple in profile, and generally cost about one *lira* per linear foot for sills, steps and balconies, while timber for the beams to the first floor was over twice as expensive at 44 *soldi* per foot, and floorboarding cost five *lire* per *passo* of area. Even the *sorzoni* of larch (possibly the planks forming the *zattaron* for the foundations) cost over one *lira* each, and the window shutters were by far the most expensive items in the whole house. The reasons for these high timber prices may be sought in the political context of the time; throughout the first years of the century much of the territory from which the Republic obtained its timber – the Friuli, Veronese and Vicentino – was subject to numerous military incursions by both French and Imperial armies, against both of which the *Serene Republic* attempted a policy of armed neutrality. Nevertheless, it is certain that timber supplies were disrupted by this bellicose activity, with consequent shortages and price rises.

There was further significant inflation as well as shortages over the long period up to the next government land register of 1741, naturally affecting housebuilding and the cost of public works. Once again we may return to Burano to examine some new typical domestic rents; by now a small cottage cost seven or eight ducats per year, about half as much again as the rents in the 1660s. A larger house now rented for 15 ducats, while a retail shop with living accommodation cost 25, 30 or even 50 ducats per year.[25] We may again compare these rents with examples in the capital; a terrace development of two-storey cottages in Rio delle Burchielle (S. Croce), and built in the *seicento*, was rented in 1711 with average *affitti* of 30 to 36 ducats.[26] These houses compared with the rather larger Burano cottages in size and so rents in Venice were thus still more than double those in the lagoon village, even in a zone never considered very *signorile* and certainly not very central. A second example is the terrace of cottages in Corte dei Preti discussed earlier; in the 1770s the cottages all consisted of two or three rooms and were thus directly comparable in size to those at Burano (they were later altered). At that time rents ranged from 9 to 20 ducats, figures which Gianighian and Pavanini rightly regard as 'extremely low for the latter part of the *settecento* and comparable with those requested in Amore Dei houses', that is, in subsidised charitable almshouses.[27] Even so the rents are broadly similar to those at Burano. Clearly there had been little change in the overall economic condition of a village like Burano in the later *settecento* and the population remained generally very poor with rents still low.[28]

We may conclude this brief survey by remaining at Burano and citing a handful of small-scale public works, which give an overall impression of the modest scale of such works and the limited skills necessary for executing them. The first was the repair of the public granary in 1725, which cost L.46.8 and required only the services of a single bricklayer and a carpenter; half of that sum was the cost of their labour.[29] Four years later the first of a series of repairs to the village's bridges was recorded; again only a bricklayer

[25] A.S.V. Dieci Savii B. 472.   [26] Gianighian and Pavanini, *Dietro*, p. 144.
[27] Ibid. p. 69.   [28] A.S.V. Milizia da Mar B. 187.   [29] Ibid.

and carpenter were needed, the whole operation costing 103 ducats. This was a significant sum, chiefly because of the more expensive materials used. The main structure was of timber, formed of large beams, while the steps were of stone; these were worked elsewhere and fixed by the *muratore*. In most building operations materials accounted for 40–50 per cent of the total cost but here the use of stone meant that they accounted for three-quarters of the total bill.[30] Repairs to the bridge over Rio Piccolo the following year cost nearly 200 lire (about 40 ducats); again only a bricklayer and a carpenter were employed.[31]

A few decades later an outside architect was appointed by the village council to survey all the public works of the community and report on their condition; in September of 1780, Bernardo Macanizzi (possibly a *proto* of the Milizia da Mar) advised that four bridges needed urgent repair, and that a new standard was required for the Piazza, as well as a new bell for the parish church. Maistro Comello was employed to carry out the work,[32] although his first tender was reduced by 20 per cent before it was accepted by the council. Three years later yet another bridge was in need of repair, and a frame was also now necessary on which to hang the new bell (acquired from Malamocco, where it was considered 'of no practical use'), and on this occasion the Milizia da Mar ordered that competitive tenders should be obtained. Three local builders submitted prices (of L.1059, L.993 and L.968) after which further negotiations produced a new bid of L.900 from the man who had submitted the highest original bid. Giovanni-Antonio Costantini was paid in three instalments, one third in advance to buy materials, one third when the work was half complete, and the rest on completion. It was quite unrealistic for Costantini to find L.300 for materials since such a sum probably represented several months' income to him.[33]

These modest local works all took place only a few years before the fall of the Republic. We can see that the position and income of building craftsmen in the villages did not undergo any significant changes even in the long period that we have outlined above. In any trade there are always men who are more skilled and successful than others and it may be that our examples are indeed these more successful men. With that caveat, however, we may conclude that building craftsmen enjoyed some degree of status in their communities and many received incomes notably higher than those of their neighbours, although none could compare with their counterparts in the capital in income or in prestige.

Within this small lagunar world, housebuilding almost always took place simply when and where it was required by the villagers themselves. Speculative development barely existed outside the city centre and nearly every one of the houses of Burano and Pellestrina (and most of those at Murano) was built directly or indirectly by and for its owner-occupier. In periods of rapid population growth a number of villagers built houses for rent by others but only on a very limited scale and only when there was such overcrowding that an immediate tenancy on completion was almost certain. Such very

---

[30] Ibid.   [31] Ibid., and also B. 188.   [32] Ibid. B. 188.   [33] Ibid.

small-scale 'speculative' development, with its low building costs but equally low returns, was of no interest at all to the major private and institutional property owners of the capital, who in these same periods of rapid population increase could realise far higher returns by development in Venice than would ever be possible beyond the six *sestieri*.

Part II

Housing typology

INTRODUCTORY NOTE

In this central section of the book we briefly outline the evolution of the most characteristic building typology of the city of Venice – the *palazzo-fòntego* of the nobility – and summarise the great influence that this typology has had on many lesser forms of housing both in the city and in the lagoon villages. Indeed, a basic appreciation of this key form of building is almost essential to understand most of these lesser typologies. We will also identify and give examples of the comparatively few house types that do not conform to this basic layout – the tiny, cellular cottages and the speculative terraces, both of which may be found in the city itself as well as in its satellite communities.

8

The city *Palazzo-Fòntego*: its structure and appearance

In general it can be said that many of the later forms of domestic architecture that evolved in Venice and its satellites after about the fourteenth century derived to a very large extent from that most characteristic of Venetian building forms, the *palazzo-fòntego* of the merchant-aristocrat. This form has its origins in the early medieval period, although unfortunately very little evidence has survived today of these earliest *fònteghi*. Nevertheless, the *fòntego* as it evolved became the archetypal city building, combining the functions of trade and commerce – on which the Republic depended for its existence – with the living quarters of the merchants who conducted this trade. The unique nature of Venetian government, with its comparatively small oligarchy of noble families, and the complete fusion of these families into the commercial structure of the Republic's economy, meant that the *fònteghi* became power-bases, both in the commercial sense as the seat of a family's wealth and business empire, and also as the city base of a noble clan which was an essential element in the government of the state.

The *palazzo-fòntego* thus has great symbolic importance, as well as great importance as an influence on other and lesser building forms. Its two most notable characteristics are its distinctive plan and the equally distinctive principal elevation, which is almost always symmetrical and usually (universally until the sixteenth century) clearly expressing the spatial structure behind it.

> The Halls (i.e. the *pòrteghi*) were built by the Ancients in a cross shape, that is, in the form of a 'T', which gave rise to an ill-proportioned edifice, but this custom was modified so that they ran from one façade of the house to the other, and the openings of the windows were thus opposite each other. The same was true of the portals and of the windows to the flanking rooms in such a manner that with each opening in correct proportion, not only was the result pleasing, but . . . the rooms were all clear and full of sunlight . . .
>
> In the composition of the palaces, the windows to the Hall are placed in the centre of the façade so that the position of the Hall is clear to the passer-by . . .
>
> Among the façades, some of them had a *loggia* at ground floor level, with columns and vaults, although these were on the same plane as the rest of the façade. And it was done in this manner by the Ancients because when the merchandise was taken to the house, it was unloaded in the *loggia*, on either side of which were the rooms for storing it. The portals are tall and square, and each house that is built on the water has two of them, one of which serves as a quay, and the other is the landward entrance. Each substantial palace has a courtyard with a well in the centre.[1]

---

[1] Sansovino, *Venetia, Città Nobilissima*, book IX, p. 384.

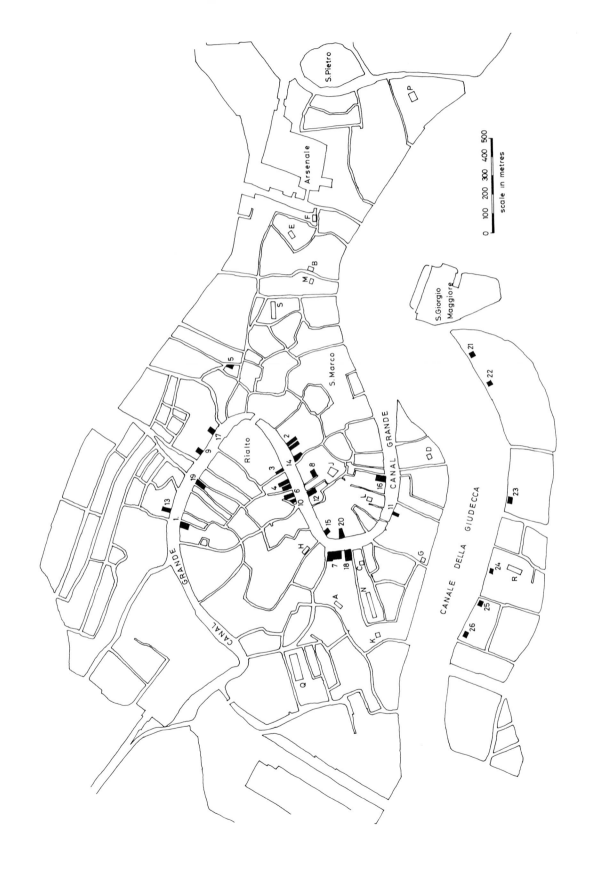

S.Pietro

P

Arsenale

E
F

M
B

S

5

S.Marco

Rialto

17
9
2
19
3
14
8
4
10 6 J
12
16
15
7
20
18
H
A
D
L
11
G
N
C
13
1

CANAL GRANDE

CANAL GRANDE

Q
K

S.Giorgio Maggiore

CANALE DELLA GIUDECCA

21
22
23
24
R
25
26

0 100 200 300 400 500

scale in metres

75 Venice: Location of the *palazzi* discussed in Chapter 8 and the lesser houses discussed in Chapter 9

 1 Fòntego dei Turchi
 2 Cà Loredan and Cà Farsetti
 3 Cà Businello
 4 Palazzo Donà and Donà della Madonetta
 5 Palazzo Soranzo-Van Axel
 6 Cà Bernardo at S. Polo
 7 Cà Foscari and the two Giustinian *palazzi*
 8 Palazzo Pesaro Fortuny degli Orfei
 9 Cà d'Oro
10 Palazzo Grimani at S. Polo
11 Palazzo Contarini dal Zaffo
12 Palazzo Corner-Spinelli
13 Palazzo Vendramin-Calergi
14 Palazzo Grimani at S. Luca
15 Palazzo Contarini delle Figure
16 Cà Corner della Cà Grande
17 Palazzo Michiel delle Colonne
18 Cà Rezzonico
19 Cà Pesaro
20 Palazzo Grassi

Renaissance villas on the Giudecca
21 Villa Mocenigo
22 Palazzo Minelli-da Ponte
23 Villa Visconti
24 Accademia dei Nobili
25 Palazzo Emo-Donà
26 Palazzo Vendramin

Location of houses and developments discussed in Chapter 9
A Casa Corner and other houses in Campo S. Margherita
B House in Rio della Pietà
C House in Calle del Traghetto at S. Barnaba
D Palazzetto Costantini on Rio Terrà Catecumeni
E Houses on Campo dei Due Pozzi, Castello
F Renaissance *palazzetti* adjacent to the Arsenal
G Renaissance house on the Zattere
H Renaissance *palazzetti* on Rio della Frescada at S. Tomà
J House on Campo S. Angelo
K Campo dell' Avogaria at Angelo Raffaele
L Campo Pisani at S. Stefano
M Cottages near S. Giorgio dei Greci
N Calle Lunga at S. Barnaba
P Paludo S. Antonio in Castello
Q Terrace developments at S. Maria Maggiore on Rio Terrà dei Pensieri
R Corte dei Cordami on the Giudecca
S Terrace in Borgoloco S. Lorenzo

1 The Veneto-Byzantine *Fòntego*

The earliest *fònteghi* were certainly very 'Byzantine' in appearance and the modern historian usually has to resort to the example of the much-restored and rebuilt Fòntego dei Turchi, and to attempt extrapolations from it, in order to evoke an image of the Grand Canal as it was in the thirteenth century. In fact the Fòntego remains a useful building with which to begin this survey, despite its virtual reconstruction in the later nineteenth century. The building is extremely distinctive in appearance and has a number of features that were later to completely disappear with the great gothic palaces of the following centuries. Despite considerable speculation, its original builder is unknown, although at the time of the War of Chioggia in 1379 it was owned by the Venetian government, which donated it to the Dukes of Ferrara in 1381, and in whose hands it remained for more than two centuries. It then passed to the Priuli family, Venetian patricians, then to the Pesaro, and in 1621 it became the base for the Turkish trading community in the city, which it remained until 1838. Today it is the city's Museum of Natural History.

The Fòntego was originally built as the palace-warehouse of one of the 'merchant princes' of the Republic. It is constructed on two chief storeys, of which the lower was exclusively given over to trade and commerce, while the upper contained the living quarters of the family. In its principal elevation, the Fòntego has a long ground floor *loggia* on ten arches, surmounted by an upper *loggia* of 18 smaller arches. The two corners are defined by three-storey towers or *torreselle*, the design of which is attributed by many writers to the survival of an older tradition of fortification. In fact, the city was so securely surrounded by its own natural moat, the lagoon, that one of the most notable features of its domestic architecture of all periods was (as we noted earlier) the lack of any element of defensive design at all. Even the Ducal Palace itself, when rebuilt in the fourteenth century, was constructed with a completely open arcade at ground level and *logge* above, just like the much earlier Fòntego. The two *torreselle* on the latter are thus entirely decorative, with spacious *logge* on each of the three floors. The broad central wing, too, is surmounted by a complex crenellation which again, like that of the Palazzo Ducale, is purely decorative and of similarly insubstantial construction.[2]

The plan of the Fòntego is symmetrical, but the most important element is the broad *loggia* with its axis along the front façade; behind this is a narrower central hall or *androne* at right angles to it. The two elements together thus form the T-shape described by Sansovino above. The light, airy, ground-floor *loggia* is a feature of most early Veneto-Byzantine palaces, and can also be clearly seen at Cà Loredan, Cà Farsetti and elsewhere. The latter house has a ground-floor arcade which extends for the full width of the façade with only minor modifications at each end to mark the last traces of the traditional *torreselle*. Cà Loredan also has a broad, central *loggia*, but here the corners are more strongly emphasised, although only at ground-floor level. Like the Fòntego, both houses originally only had two storeys, and in both of them the principal private accommodation on the first floor is denoted on the façade by a continuous and almost undifferentiated arcade for the full width of the elevation. At Cà Loredan we can see again the faint traces of the *torreselle* in the two small, square corner rooms, divided by paired columns from the central hall, but

[2] A. Sagredo, *Il Fondaco dei Turchi in Venezia* (Milan 1860).

76 Cà Loredan (nearest camera) and Cà Farsetti, on the Grand Canal at Rialto, both examples of Veneto-Byzantine palaces, although both much restored over the centuries. The second storeys of both houses are later.

at Cà Farsetti the lateral hall extends for the full width of the house. Both *palazzi* thus still had an essentially T-shaped plan, with ancillary rooms on either side of the longitudinal hall that lay behind the lateral portico.

The T-shaped plan is common to nearly all Veneto-Byzantine houses; it can be seen again at Cà Businello at S. Silvestro, almost opposite Cà Farsetti. Here the plan again retains the two small corner rooms at each end of the transverse loggia, as at Cà Loredan. Structurally, the T-plan has one important difference from the plans of the more mature gothic houses: with a *loggia* that extends for the full width (or most of the width) of the façade, the first floor transverse hall is supported on beams orthogonal to the main façade, and this façade thus carries a considerable load, although it is often supported on arches of remarkably slender proportions. Behind this transverse *loggia* the inner hall or *androne* lay at right angles to it, and hence the beams spanned in the other direction, parallel to the façade and supported on spine walls within the house.

The 'pure' Veneto-Byzantine form of plan, as represented by Cà Loredan, thus has a structural arrangement that logically follows the T-plan. In some later houses, such as Cà Businello and Palazzo Donà, the width of the central *loggia* is reduced and the two corner rooms once again increase in prominence, both structurally and in elevation. Indeed, in both of these examples, the tripartite division of the façade is clearly established in the form that was to survive in principle throughout the next three or four centuries. In this earlier period, however, the central *loggia* was still significantly wider than the *androne*

77 Cà Businello at S. Silvestro: façade to the Grand Canal.

behind it and hence the essential T-plan is retained. The continuing importance of this *loggia* is reflected in a prominent central multi-light window on the *piano nobile*, which often has five lights (as at Palazzo Donà), six (as at Cà Businello) or even seven, as at Cà Loredan.[3]

At Cà Businello, however, the central *loggia* has been considerably reduced in width, and at Palazzo Donà it has effectively disappeared, so that the central multi-light window now gives directly onto the longitudinal hall or *pòrtego*. The façade is now divided into three parts each of equal or almost equal width; the central one-third is a direct expression of the long *pòrtego*, the main axis of the house, while the outer two-thirds represent the two rows of ancillary rooms on each side of this axis. The often considerable depth of the *pòrtego* required the retention of the large multi-light windows for light and air, but the lateral rooms were much smaller, and hence on the main façade each of them is lit by two tall single-light windows inserted into a large area of solid masonry forming the two side wings of the façade. These elements provide all of the essential features of the mature Venetian tripartite plan and elevation, which was to survive in principle (with only comparatively minor modifications) for all of the remaining long life of the Republic.

Structurally, the plan of the house had thus been rationalised to produce three zones of equal width, and a high degree of standardisation of structural elements (especially floor beams) was now possible. Aesthetically, the tripartite plan was clearly expressed in the divisions of the main façade, and the symmetrical A–B–A elevation was almost uni-

[3] For analyses of these Veneto-Byzantine plans, and for floor plans of most of the houses discussed here, see Maretto, *L'Edilizia*, pp. 48, *et seq.*

78 Palazzo Donà: façade to the Grand Canal.

versally established. In this arrangement we can still see the echo of the ancient *torreselle*: a spacious central multi-light window is balanced on both sides by more solid (almost tower-like) elements into which individual lights are inserted. While clearly expressing the plan behind the façade, the massing of the elevation also assists the structural stability of the whole; aesthetically, too, it provides a balanced composition of solids and voids.

2 The great gothic *palazzi*

The large number of gothic palaces that survive in the city centre were built over the long period of time – almost two full centuries – from the late Veneto-Byzantine houses of around 1300 (such as Palazzo Vitturi at S. Maria Formosa) to the fully mature and imposing *palazzi* such as that of Francesco Foscari of the 1440s and the Pesaro-Fortuny of the very late fifteenth century. Before identifying some of the more notable features of this most important phase in the development of the *palazzo-fòntego*, we may make a few general observations on their evolution.[4]

The Veneto-Byzantine houses were all originally built on only two storeys, with a simple division of function between commerce on the ground floor and domestic quarters above. However, by the early fourteenth century Venice had already grown to become a

[4] The bibliography on these great houses is naturally extensive; see the selected bibliog. to the present volume, and also the useful bibliog. in G. Lorenzetti, *Venice and its Lagoon* (Trieste 1975); E. Arslan, *Venezia Gotica* (Milan 1970); G. Perocco and A. Salvadori, *Civiltà di Venezia*, 3 vols. (Venice 1973–6).

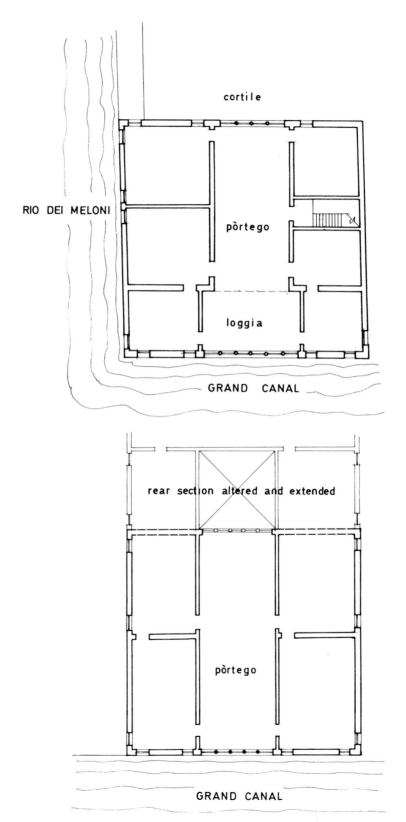

79 Comparative plans of two Veneto-Byzantine houses: Cà Businello (above) and Palazzo Donà (below).

great city and a commercial capital of international importance; many of its clans of merchant-nobles were now extremely wealthy, while the city itself had now become one of the largest urban centres in western Europe. Major sites for new development, especially in the period prior to the great plague, the 'Black Death' of 1348, were becoming more and more scarce. One of the chief features of this period, therefore, is that houses were now built higher, almost always on three storeys and sometimes on four, especially on the most valuable sites along the Grand Canal. The great houses thus not only became larger, but their plans became more complex and specialised.

In the overall planning of the house, the chief feature is the universal adoption of the tripartite plan. The vestige of the central *loggia* remained in the form of a great multi-light window, usually extending for the full width of the *pòrtego*, the central one-third of the façade; behind it, the *pòrtego* itself ran back for the full depth of the house, with all of the other accommodation leading directly from it. At ground-floor level, the central *androne* (directly below the *pòrtego*) was the chief warehouse for goods and place of business for the merchant-noble, and on either side of it, the smaller rooms were used for storing goods and for offices for administering the owner's trading empire. In many cases the *androne* was built sufficiently high to allow the insertion of a mezzanine floor (*mezà*) down either side, thus doubling the area of ancillary accommodation. Towards the rear of the house a gap was left on one side of the *androne* to form a small square courtyard which permitted the entry of light and air, and in which a well was often located. If the site was deep enough there was also a larger, more 'public' courtyard at the rear of the house; the landward approach to the *palazzo* was through this *cortile*, in which there was also usually a well. In many cases, too, a fine open stair rose from this *cortile* so that the upper apartments could be reached without entering the business and commercial parts of the house. The *androne* was usually terminated on the waterfront façade with a modest *loggia*, or more often simply with a single large portal with an arched head.

All of the principal family rooms were located on the *piano nobile*, including those for receiving and entertaining guests. The plan precisely echoed that of the ground floor, with the *pòrtego* or great hall directly above the *androne*. The hall was the focal axis for the entire household and was often very large indeed; however, since it was usually still very long in proportion to its width, it was lit at both ends by full-height and full-width windows, each in the form of a group containing between four and seven lights.

On either side of the *pòrtego* the two other important rooms were those at the front overlooking the canal, and these nearly always retained the two tall single-light windows that we saw in the later Veneto-Byzantine houses. Structurally, most of the great gothic *palazzi* are very simple and rational: as in the later thirteenth century houses, they basically consist of four parallel structural walls, all orthogonal to the façade, and all of the floor-beams spanned onto these four walls. The main façade thus carried no direct floor loads at all (although it usually carried part of the roof load) and hence it remained feasible to introduce such large multi-light windows into the centre of the elevation. And again, as with the Veneto-Byzantine houses, the mass of more solid masonry near the corners assisted the overall stability of the structure.[5]

---

[5] However, problems of differential settlement over the centuries have still been widespread. For a recent comprehensive survey, Zuccolo, *Il Restauro*, is indispensable.

80 Palazzo Bernardo at S. Polo: façade to the Grand Canal.

There are a number of variations of this basic plan, but they do not invalidate its general principles. For example, the position of the main light well or *cortile* varies considerably: in some cases it is on the left side and in others on the right. Sometimes it is at the rear of the house producing an overall L-shaped plan, while in its more usual position halfway down one side the plan has a C-form. These variations have been analysed by Maretto in great detail, but they are all essentially variations of a common theme. Sometimes a site of particularly irregular shape gave rise to special arrangements of the plan, and Palazzo Soranzo-Van Axel is a good example on its awkward and very irregular site.[6]

Above the *piano nobile* there was at least one further storey of private accommodation consisting of bedrooms, other family rooms and the kitchen. In the largest houses there were two further storeys, one of which consisted almost entirely of family rooms and bedrooms, while the uppermost storey was occupied by servants, kitchens and storage facilities.

In considering this vertical zoning, we may mention another variant of the basic arrangement, in which we find two *piani nobili*, one above the other, and both of equal importance. There are several such houses, and in most cases it appears that each of the two floors was occupied by a quite separate apartment, each belonging to a different branch of the same family. Cà Bernardo is a fine example of such a house, where ingenious

[6] For plans of the *palazzo* see Maretto, *L'Edilizia*, p. 100.

81 One of the two contiguous Giustinian palaces on the Grand Canal next to Cà Foscari.

82 Cà Foscari: façade to the Grand Canal.

planning produced not only two separate apartments, but each had its own private *cortile* at the rear of the house and each its own water entrance on the Grand Canal.[7]

The hub of all of these houses was the *pòrtego*, the great hall or *salone*. In the large palaces these halls are of imposing dimensions; that at Cà Foscari was probably originally 25 m. long, while those of the two adjacent Giustinian houses are both more than 30 m. long. The largest of all of these great later gothic palaces is Palazzo Pesaro degli Orfei, which covers an entire city block at S. Beneto, and has a central hall no less than 42 m. long. Its plan is complex, and contains two private courtyards and there are two *piani nobili* together with three lesser storeys; each floor has an area in excess of 1,000 square metres.[8]

Apart from the irregular plans that had to be adopted by necessity on sites of irregular form, the only other major departure from the tripartite plan is that which we find on sites of very restricted width (but adequate depth) and where there was simply no space for a centralised symmetrical plan. In such cases the solution was simply to omit one of the two side wings, so that there is a bipartite plan, consisting of the *pòrtego* and a series of ancillary rooms on one side only; Palazzo Erizzo and Palazzo Sagredo may be cited as examples of such a plan. Once again, however, the plan allows for the insertion of a private *cortile* to produce an L-shaped or C-shaped overall form.

Despite these examples of irregular forms, though, the great majority of *palazzi* and of middle-rank houses adopted the tripartite form. Although there are naturally many minor

[7] Ibid. pp. 86 and 89.   [8] Ibid. p. 98.

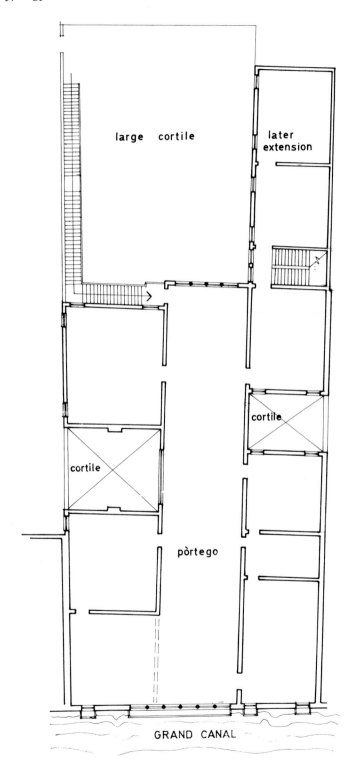

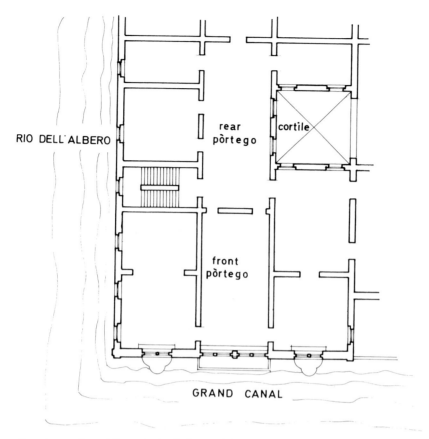

83 Comparative plans: plan of the principal *piano nobile* of the gothic Palazzo Giustinian II (left) and plan of the *piano nobile* of Codussi's Palazzo Corner-Spinelli (above).

variations of detail, of sculpture, of decoration, there is nevertheless a strong 'family resemblance' among many of these great (and not so great) houses. The basic Venetian house plan was now universally established, and it was to have thousands of derivations in the city and its satellites over the next three centuries; indeed, this seminal form produced many descendants in the *Serenissima*'s Terraferma Empire after the permanent acquisition of most of the present-day Veneto in the early part of the *quattrocento*.

3 The early Renaissance *palazzi*

There are naturally important philosophical and stylistic differences between the late gothic *palazzi* and the first fully fledged Renaissance examples, but before briefly discussing these differences, a note on the planning and function of these houses is appropriate. In general, the principles of the plan remained largely unchanged from the later gothic era. Most early Renaissance *palazzi* have traditional tripartite plans, with a long central axis and ancillary rooms on either side. The plan thus remains axial and symmetrical; the distribution of fenestration on the main façade therefore also remains

84 Three illustrations from the first English edition of Serlio's *Five Books*: fols. 30, 31 and 53 respectively, all from the Fourth Book. All three are palace façades, and clearly intended to be models for palaces on Venice's Grand Canal. Serlio's influence on his contemporaries such as Sansovino was considerable, and we may compare his heavily rusticated lower storeys with Sansovino's Cà Corner della Cà Grande.

traditional (despite the few notable exceptions discussed below), with a central multi-light window flanked on each side by a pair of single lights.[9]

We may cite one particularly fine example of an early Renaissance *palazzo* which embodies all of these traditional elements and yet makes full use of the new architectural language of the time: Palazzo Grimani at S. Polo was built in the very first years of the sixteenth century, possibly by the Lombardo or Buora families, although there have also been attributions to Codussi. It is by no means a large or imposing house, although the proportions are extremely fine, the whole façade being richly decorated and clad with Istrian stone. There are three storeys; the lowest still fulfils many of the functions of the later gothic *fòntego*, and is fairly spacious, with a central portal and four large windows to light the flanking rooms. These windows have classical surrounds and are surmounted by triangular pediments. Above the ground storey there are two *piani nobili* of almost equal importance; the first has slightly more prominence than the second, but in both cases the *pòrtego* is lit by an elegant three-light window, while the two flanking single lights on either side echo the fenestration of the ground floor.

The architectural language used throughout is fully classical, with no vestige of gothic; the proportions are refined and the detailing of extremely high quality. However, the overall composition of the façade is entirely traditional as is the plan of the house behind; we see here, therefore, the gothic *palazzo* transformed into the Renaissance *palazzo* but with no significant reappraisal of the form and function of the house. There was clearly no need; the Venetian house had evolved over the previous three centuries to fulfil a number of specialised functions in a unique environment, and had developed an equally unique solution to these requirements. The two aspects of Renaissance design that are most noteworthy at Palazzo Grimani are not its plan, but firstly the mature use of the classical vocabulary at what was still a fairly early date in Venice, and secondly the extensive use of fine stonework to achieve a result that is not impressive in scale but in its richness and refinement.[10]

Other early Renaissance *palazzi* such as the Contarini dal Zaffo[11] exhibit many similar features to the Grimani, and it is almost certain that a number of the same architects and master masons were involved at least to some extent on several of these houses: Codussi, Buora and Lombardo have been linked with the Contarini house, while Codussi's own more clearly individualistic approach is seen at the Corner-Spinelli and Vendramin-Calergi palaces.[12] In the former house, a new and quite different pattern of fenestration is used, and instead of the traditional central multi-light window flanked by *monofore* (single lights), here only one window type is used throughout. It consists of a two-light window surmounted by a semicircular arch, into which a small oculus is inserted. This one type is used singly to define the lesser rooms on either side of the *pòrtego*, and in pairs to indicate the *pòrtego* itself, on both first and second floors. We see here a significant departure from

---

[9] For a very useful survey of Renaissance *palazzi* of the sixteenth to eighteenth centuries, see E. Bassi, *Palazzi di Venezia* (Venice 1976). It also contains numerous elevations and plans from *Admiranda Urbis Venetae* by Antonio Visentini.

[10] Bassi, *Palazzi*, pp. 418, *et seq.* As she notes, many attributions have been made to the Lombardo family, although Paoletti favours Buora as the most likely author. See above.

[11] Ibid. p. 94.

[12] For bibliog. on Codussi, see bibliog. to the present volume, and also the bibliog. in Bassi, *Palazzi*, Lorenzetti, *Venice* and Perocco and Salvadori, *Civiltà*; see also Angelini, *Le Opere*.

85 Palazzo Grimani at S. Polo: the recently cleaned façade to the Grand Canal.

86 Palazzo Grimani: detail of the lower part of the façade. The treatment is fully Renaissance in style but the fenestration pattern is entirely traditional.

87 Palazzo Corner-Spinelli: façade to the Grand Canal.

traditional forms of fenestration, and Codussi's use of a more truly classical unit of fenestration (together with a much more powerful use of the ancient vocabulary) renders the Corner-Spinelli a far more classical and yet a far more original house than the Grimani, with its close links to its gothic heritage.

Behind this revolutionary and imposing façade, however, the plan of Palazzo Corner-Spinelli remains, like the Grimani, very conventional indeed. In a number of these early sixteenth-century palaces, restrictions of the site led to a plan that is virtually square (although in some cases a corner is still 'cut out' to form a small *cortile*) and this square is divided into the three traditional equal parts, with a central *pòrtego*. At Codussi's second major palace, however, a further decisive step is taken along the path towards a fully mature and fully developed Venetian Renaissance *palazzo*.

The Vendramin-Calergi house (Fig. 35) is not only by far the largest of these early examples, but is far more truly 'Roman' in its scale and conception than any of the others. The façade is a great screen, all of stone, and with three equal orders; no special prominence is given to the first *piano nobile*, which is now simply one of the three tiers of classical orders that comprise the façade. The basic unit of fenestration, the coupled window with oculus above, first used at the Corner-Spinelli house, is again the sole motif of fenestration here. At the Vendramin palace, however, the long central *pòrtego* is widened out at the end to form a *loggia*, echoing those of the much earlier Veneto-Byzantine palaces, and this *loggia* in turn gives rise to a central grouping of three of the coupled windows. Only one such unit lights each of the two flanking rooms and the pattern of fenestration is thus 1–3–1, a rhythm which is identical on both first and second floors. On the ground floor the central double light is simply replaced by a large single portal.

The palace at S. Marcuola in several respects thus marks the most radical departure from traditional forms yet seen in the city, not because of its modified plan (which is in fact only a minor adaptation of traditional forms) but in its scale, in the robust 'Roman-ness' of its detailing, and above all in the subjection of the various functions within the house to the overall discipline of the powerful superimposed orders of its great façade. Codussi's other major contribution to the internal planning of the Venetian *palazzo* was the re-positioning of the main stair in the body of the house, giving off the *androne*, as we discussed in an earlier chapter.

The Vendramin-Calergi palace marked an apogee, albeit an early one, in the development of the Renaissance *palazzo* in the city. Of its time it was quite without peers, but it set an important precedent, a monumental standard for others to follow. And it was indeed emulated, chiefly by Sansovino and Sanmicheli in the middle decades of the *cinquecento*, and by Scamozzi a little later.

4 The mature and later Renaissance palaces

The origins of the majestic façades of Sanmicheli and Sansovino lay not in the very early Lombard Renaissance forms of the Buora and Lombardo families, but rather in the more truly classical forms of the Roman and Florentine Renaissance. As such they represent the expression not only of the strongly individualistic nature of their architects but, in a wider sense, of the imposition of what were essentially foreign, that is classically inspired forms, onto the traditional structure of the Venetian *palazzo*.[13] It is thus not so surprising to find that during the later sixteenth and seventeenth centuries many of the new palaces built in the city reverted in their composition to more clearly recognisable, traditional Venetian motifs. This is not to say that they were not fully Renaissance in character, but rather that the Renaissance elements were incorporated into façades that once again clearly expressed the traditional tripartite plan that lay behind them. Many such palaces returned to the 'gothic' pattern of fenestration with a large multi-light window to the *pòrtego* and two pairs of single windows on either side, a traditional arrangement that had never really

[13] Sansovino, of course, was a Florentine who spent much of his early life in Rome. He went to Venice in 1527 at the age of 41, having been in Rome for the previous ten years. Although Sanmicheli was from the north (b. Verona 1484) he, too, spent much of his early years in and around Rome, and also moved to Venice after the sack of the former city in 1527.

88 Palazzo Grimani at S. Luca, Sanmicheli's great work of the early 1560s.

89 Palazzo Contarini delle Figure near S. Samuele: façade to the Grand Canal.

been lost. Such a pattern can be discerned not only in the earliest Renaissance palaces of clearly Lombard origin (Palazzo Grimani, Palazzo Contarini dal Zaffo) but also in many others from the middle and later sixteenth century.

We may cite two mid-century examples to illustrate these two clearly divergent attitudes towards the development of the composition of the façade. The first, Palazzo Grimani at S. Luca, is Sanmicheli's masterwork, and was designed in *c*. 1556–9. It exemplifies very clearly the noble, massive, Roman approach to the mature Renaissance, with its superimposed classical orders of columns and powerful cornices.[14] There is still a significant degree of centralisation in the façade, chiefly evinced by the great portico and its two flanking arches, but on the upper storeys only the paired columns on either side of the central *loggia* suggest the plan that lies behind the façade; as at Codussi's Vendramin palace, the entire elevation has become a great classical sculptured screen.

Roughly contemporary with the Grimani *palazzo* is that of the Contarini 'delle Figure', next to the group of Mocenigo houses at S. Samuele.[15] Here the concept is much less monumental; the façade is far lighter in its detailing, with decorative motifs that are Lombard rather than Roman or Florentine in origin. There have been attributions to Scarpagnino, although it has also been suggested that the house was partly the work of

[14] Bassi, *Palazzi*, pp. 146, *et seq*. See also G. Boschieri, 'Il Palazzo Grimani a S. Luca' in *Rivista Veneta* (1931); R. Gallo, *Michele Sanmicheli a Venezia* (Verona 1960); E. Langeskiöld, *Michele Sanmicheli the architect of Verona* (Uppsala 1938).

[15] Bassi, *Palazzi*, pp. 382, *et seq*. She also outlines Palladio's very close connections with the house; he was a close friend of Jacopo Contarini, who owned the palace in the 1570s, and where Andrea frequently stayed when he was in the city.

90 Cà Corner della Cà Grande: elevation to the Grand Canal, drawn by Visentini (R.I.B.A. F.6 [160]).

Codussi, or of 'Codussian' inspiration; since Codussi died in *c.* 1504 the attribution must be indirect. The chief unusual feature of the façade is the triangular tympanum above the four-light window to the *pòrtego*; in most other respects the principal elevation is of traditional origin in the disposition of its elements and in the clear expression of the structural form behind the façade.

We may thus discern two well-defined paths of development in the mid- and later sixteenth century. One is that followed by Sansovino and Sanmicheli, which later led to the monumental Baroque of Longhena, and which may be summarised as the adaptation of the monumentally classical forms of the Romano-Florentine Renaissance, as promulgated by Sansovino himself and by Serlio. The other course is the less monumental one, consisting of a far more restrained, measured route of development, which retains elements of the Lombard Renaissance in the composition of façades and in the much lighter detailing of their chief elements. This latter course also retains the traditionally Venetian clear expression of the internal structure in the composition of the main elevation.

Although a full century separates the construction of the great mid-sixteenth-century houses (such as Sansovino's Cà Corner della Cà Grande) from the mature baroque palaces of Longhena (Cà Pesaro and Cà Rezzonico), the latter are clearly derived in scale and spirit from the *palazzi* of Sanmicheli and Sansovino. Cà Corner della Cà Grande is perhaps the most closely proto-baroque of these *cinquecento* palaces, and here Sansovino used further elements that were foreign to the Venetian tradition. For example, the plan incorporates a grandiose internal courtyard, placed at the end of the axis formed by the *androne*. On the main façade there are certain elements clearly derived from Serlio, particularly the rusticated ground storey and the great three-arched central portal. However, on the *piano nobile* we see a façade treatment quite foreign to the lagunar tradition – a continuous row of seven bays of almost equally spaced windows, all identical and all divided by paired columns. These orders are repeated on the second *piano nobile* and above it there is a row of oval *oculi* to the low attic storey. There is virtually no central emphasis on these upper floors, no grouping of lights to indicate the *pòrtego* behind, but simply a solid, powerful rhythm of fenestration much closer in spirit to that found on contemporary palaces in Rome (such as the Lateran and Farnese) than to other houses in Venice. Here the whole façade, like those of the Vendramin and Grimani palaces, is once again treated as a richly modelled screen, but with considerable depth and far more three-dimensional sculptural form than could be found on any contemporary Roman palace. It is this strong modelling perhaps more than any other individual feature that illustrates Sansovino's appreciation of the unique qualities of the Venetian environment, its light and the effect of the reflections of water on these rich façades.[16]

The path of development of Sanmicheli and Sansovino was followed by Longhena at Cà Pesaro and Cà Rezzonico, but by few others in the city. Architects of their stature were naturally few, but the other reason for the scarcity of examples of such rich monumentality in the later sixteenth and seventeenth centuries is more mundane – the cost. Palaces of this size and degree of sculptural elaboration were enormously expensive, particularly so given the unique difficulties of building in a city where all materials had to be transported

[16] Ibid. pp. 88, *et seq.* See also D. Howard, *Jacopo Sansovino* (Yale 1975); new edn. 1987.

91 Cà Corner della Cà Grande: perspective view of the façade, again by Visentini, after a painting by Canaletto (first published in *Prospectus Magni Canalis Venetiarum* 1742, Part II Pl. 10).

92 Cà Pesaro: another detail of one of Visentini's engravings from the same series as Fig. 91.

by barge. The examples just discussed – the Grimani, Corner, Vendramin and Corner-Spinelli palaces – were all faced entirely with stone, and thus represented the development of the Venetian *palazzo* at its most refined, luxurious and expensive. These great monuments to the taste and affluence of the wealthiest of all the Venetian patriciate were naturally the prerogative of only a very few, and it is in the much larger numbers of less monumental houses of the seventeenth century that we see the continuation of many elements of the traditional *palazzo* form. Nevertheless, one of the most notable effects of these Renaissance palaces on the appearance of the Venetian house was the use of stone for all of the principal façade whenever funds permitted it.

Many later sixteenth- and seventeeth-century palaces reverted to the clear expression of the tripartite plan in the composition of their main façades. The *pòrtego* was often lit by a large and complex *Serliana*, while the flanking rooms are usually lit by two pairs of single light windows once again, in the pattern developed more than three centuries earlier. We may cite Palazzo Giustinian-Lolin at S. Vidal as an example of such a façade, probably of the 1620s, while Palazzo Michiel delle Colonne,[17] despite its unusual ground-floor colonnade, has both *piani nobili* lit in what may now be described as the revised traditional manner – that is, with a central *Serliana* and flanking pairs of single-light windows, all surmounted by triangular pediments.

5 The baroque

For the reasons noted above, examples of large-scale baroque *palazzi* in the city are very much scarcer than examples of more modest forms; the apogee of this period is undoubtedly the work of Longhena at Cà Rezzonico and Cà Pesaro, the two largest and most opulent houses built in the city for more than a hundred years. Cà Rezzonico was built for the Bon family and was begun in 1667; by this period many noble families had invested truly vast sums of money in extensive mainland estates and some were now landowners on an almost regal scale. These huge estates were managed from equally imposing villas, hundreds of which could now be found in all parts of the present-day Veneto and Friuli, the *Serenissima*'s Terraferma empire.

The city-centre *palazzo* had thus now become a power-base of a rather different sort from its original function as a *palazzo-fòntego*. It still served as the focal point of a large extended family, but now its principal purpose was for social life and entertainment, the direct if superficial expression of the wealth and social position of its owner. In the case of Cà Rezzonico, Longhena died before the house was completed and work was continued by Gaspari. However, the Bon family found it impossible to complete this huge and costly edifice and sold it to Giambattista Rezzonico in 1750. It was finally completed by Massari in about 1756 for its new owner, and two years later his son Carlo was elected to the pontificate. The palace has a visual unity that belies its long, erratic building programme, and Massari closely followed Longhena's original grand conception when adding the second *piano nobile*.[18]

[17] Bassi, *Palazzi* pp. 104 and 57 respectively. See also the same author's *Architettura del Sei e Settecento a Venezia* (Venice 1980), pp. 86, 123, 150, 178, 198; see also pp. 28, 248 and 266 for Pal. Michiel.

[18] Bassi (1976), p. 114; see also Bassi (1980), pp. 83, *et seq.*; G. Lorenzetti, *Cà Rezzonico* (Venice 1936); G. Semenzato, *L'Architettura di Baldassare Longhena* (Padua 1954); and bibliog. to the present book.

93 Cà Rezzonico: façade to the Grand Canal.

The *palazzo* is very imposing indeed, although a number of aspects of its form are still traditional; the most notable new feature is the impressive monumental rear staircase giving access to the huge first-floor ballroom, the largest such room in a private house in the entire city, and a room that clearly epitomises the overwhelming importance of the palace as a centre of entertainment and culture rather than of commerce. The remainder of the house has a basically conventional plan although it is grandiose in scale; the first-floor *pòrtego* is 10 metres wide and 25 metres long, while the ballroom is the same length but half as wide again.

The main façade to the Grand Canal is powerfully modelled and articulated, although its derivation from such houses as Cà Corner della Cà Grande is clear, particularly in the seven equal bays of the upper storeys and the row of oculi to the attic floor. The ground storey is perhaps the most impressive of the three, with its heavy rustication and a massive three-part central portal of truly Piranesian grandeur.

Cà Rezzonico and Cà Pesaro have much in common;[19] the latter house was begun in

[19] See note 18 above, and also E. Bassi, 'Palazzo Pesaro' in *Critica d'Arte* (1959).

1628, although here, too, progress was very slow and in 1652 it was still in hand when Giovanni Pesaro (who was doge in 1658–9) left the house to his nephew Leonardo, exhorting him to ensure the completion of this great work. By 1682 the first *piano nobile* was finished but the second was not added until 1709; the original design has always been attributed to Longhena although no conclusive documentary evidence has been found. The upper *piano nobile* was added by Gaspari, continuing the design of the first floor, in much the same way that Cà Rezzonico was completed.

In both palaces we see the maturation of the Venetian baroque at its most ornate, grandiose and self-assured; in both houses the main façade, like that of the much earlier Vendramin-Calergi *palazzo*, is treated as a great decorative screen of superimposed orders of columns and with very strong modelling. While this powerful effect of three-dimensionality and *chiaroscuro* clearly evolved to a significant degree as a response to the unique environment of the lagunar capital, it is equally clear that the composition of such façades is now only tenuously connected with the 'mainstream' development of the façade of the Venetian *palazzo*; they are *tours de force* in their own right, and these tenuous vestiges are confined solely to the monumental central portal and to some modest indication of the tripartite structure that still lies behind these façades, often by the use of paired columns between the windows to the *pòrtego* and those to the flanking rooms. Such a device is still used at Cà Pesaro, but at Cà Rezzonico even this minor centralising feature is gone, and we see seven identically treated bays.

These two palaces effectively mark the final peak, and the end of the development of the great city *palazzo*. It is true that several important houses were built later, but with the exception of a very few examples, such as Massari's Palazzo Grassi of the 1750s, their general composition was based in plan on traditional tripartite forms, and their elevational treatment, whether baroque (although never as robust as the work of Longhena) or neo-classical, usually respects the ancient tradition in the pattern of fenestration.

Palazzo Grassi is a fine but very late and atypical example of a luxurious Grand Canal palace, with a number of unusual and un-Venetian features.[20] In its external appearance it is refined but restrained, with a main façade of almost neo-classical simplicity. The modelling is far less pronounced than in Longhena's work, and in some respects Palazzo Grassi is an early example of proto-classicism. The site is slightly irregular on plan but with a very broad frontage to the Grand Canal, and this has allowed for the insertion of a spacious transverse *loggia* at ground level, and an equally large *salone* on the *piano nobile* above it. Behind the *loggia* is a short colonnaded *androne* which leads to a large square courtyard forming the hub of the whole house. This axial progression is terminated at the far side of the *cortile* with a monumental stair to the *piano nobile*. Massari took full advantage of the immense wealth of his clients and of the unusually spacious site to produce a house which probably comes closer to the Renaissance ideal of the classical Roman city palace than any other work in the Venetian Republic since Palladio's proposals for the Palazzo Iseppo Porta at Vicenza, to which Palazzo Grassi has several similarities. This house therefore marks the final flowering of the great city *palazzo* in a truly classical form and it was completed only a few years before the fall of the Republic.

[20] Bassi (1980), *Architettura*, pp. 324, *et seq.*

We may now summarise the essential elements in the development of the city-centre *palazzo-fòntego*. The tripartite form which had already evolved in the early gothic period was to remain the most fundamental basis of house-planning throughout the city and its lagunar satellites. This tripartite plan is itself logical and rational: it allows for the planning of houses of fairly restricted width but of a depth that would be determined by that of the individual site. On most sites it was possible to build such a house that was three rooms in width, that is, with a central axis and two side wings. However, on very narrow sites, one of the side wings could simply be omitted, to produce an asymmetrical plan, but still retaining the axis of the *pòrtego*. The structural form of the house was equally simple and logical; in most cases the *pòrtego* was the same width as the flanking rooms, leading to a very high degree of standardisation of timber sizes for the floor beams, as well as ensuring the best possible distribution of loads onto the four parallel structural walls. The inner or spine walls carried higher floor loads than the outer, flank walls although the latter carried a higher proportion of the load of the roof.

The plan that thus developed was remarkably flexible and adaptable given the restraints imposed by these four parallel walls. For example, it was possible to insert mezzanine floors above the ground storey; it was possible to leave out a part of the plan to form a small courtyard in almost any position within the overall envelope of the house; it was possible to subdivide the two side wings to produce a large number of different combinations of ancillary rooms of various sizes; the stair could be located in either of the side wings and as far forward or back on the plan as was desired; it was possible to build two *piani nobili* if required – one above the other – or two attics, or any of several other combinations of major storeys and subsidiary floors.

But it is in the tripartite division of the principal façade that this classic plan had its most lasting and universal effect. This arrangement, and in particular the presence of the central axis (*androne* and *pòrtego*) gave rise to the A–B–A rhythm of bays, a pattern that was so deeply entrenched that when the principles of Renaissance design were absorbed here, almost all Renaissance *palazzi*, despite the new vocabulary of their detailing, still respect this tripartite rhythm, in sharp contrast to the mature Renaissance palaces of Florence and Rome, with their regular, uninterrupted rhythms of fenestration.

9

Derivations from the *palazzo-fòntego* in the city

Having outlined the chief features in the development of the great *palazzo-fòntego*, we may consider the enormous influence of this typology on the characteristic lesser forms of development within the city's historic centre. The *palazzo-fòntego*, representing the wealth and power of the merchant aristocrats who ruled the city-state, represented the apogee of Venetian domestic architecture in every period from the Veneto-Byzantine to the baroque and neo-classicism. However, the city and its satellites naturally contained many more members of the lesser strata of society than this small, precisely defined oligarchy, and these lesser houses, particularly those of the *cittadinanza* (the citizen class) closely reflect the achievements and aspirations of that key social group, many of whose members aspired to – and a few achieved – that ultimate symbol of self-advancement in the Republic of San Marco, elevation to those exclusive ranks of the nobility and an entry in the *Libro d'Oro*.

There are no great palaces in any of the smaller settlements of the lagoon with the exception of the important handful of villas at Murano, but there are a number of substantial houses variously described as villas, *case coloniche* or *case padronali*, that are of considerable architectural importance and often closely resemble the city houses of the *cittadinanza*. We may now examine a representative handful of these latter houses which represent a key typological link between the great *palazzo-fòntego* and the rural or sub-urban villa of the smaller lagoon communities.

Like the great palaces, the *palazzetti* of the citizenry were naturally built over a long period of time, and they are similarly found in all parts of the city. The two most important features that they have in common with the *palazzi* are their interior planning and the symmetrical tripartite arrangement of their façades. In many respects, therefore, they are simply scaled-down versions of the *palazzo-fòntego*. This general observation is true of the later Renaissance houses as well as the earlier gothic *palazzetti* such as the example at S. Barnaba cited below. One notable difference, however, particularly in the period up to the later fifteenth century, is the number of storeys on which they are built; the later medieval houses of the *cittadinanza* are almost all built on only two storeys (sometimes with an attic), although increased pressure for redevelopment on the rapidly dwindling amount of available land meant that most citizens' houses of the sixteenth and seventeenth centuries were built on three floors. In all cases, as we might expect, the detailing is more robust and less refined here than on the great palaces, and there was no question of any citizen's house being faced entirely with stone: it was far too expensive.

Nevertheless, some of the houses of the *cittadinanza* – from all periods – are quite

94 Gothic houses in Campo S. Margherita.

substantial, and in many cases the overall proportions of their principal rooms (as we see below) did not differ appreciably from those of the *palazzi* of the patriciate, whom the citizenry – as always – wished to emulate. Floor spans, for example, often fell within the range of from five to six metres in both nobles' houses and in those of the citizenry, simply because such spans were the most economical to build, and produced rooms of adequate width for most purposes. With the almost universal use of the tripartite plan, we therefore find many such *palazzetti* that are three spans in width, producing a façade of 16 to 18 metres across, a width very similar indeed to that of many notable palaces on the Grand Canal. Storey heights, too, were often similar, although, as we noted, there was usually only one full storey (the *piano nobile*) above the ground floor, and this arrangement produced a façade with considerably more horizontal emphasis than that found in the noble *palazzi*.

Our first example is somewhat difficult to analyse, although architecturally important, forming part of a small group of gothic houses on Campo S. Margherita. Casa Corner is the most notable house, although the two adjacent gothic houses are more useful in this study, as they have several points of similarity with houses in the lagoon, particularly those of Murano.[1]

The development of this group is complex and it is probable that the original structure of the two gothic houses is considerably earlier than the fifteenth century, the date of their main façades. They were possibly built as early as the thirteenth century, and Trincanato has identified several features suggesting such a date, including the long narrow *androne* (effectively only a wide corridor) in the left-hand house, and the unusual main entrance to

[1] For illustrations and sketch plans see E. R. Trincanato, *Venezia Minore* (Milan 1948) pp. 256, *et seq.*; also Arslan, *Venezia Gotica*, pp. 28 and 33.

95 Casa Corner in Campo S. Margherita: general view of the façade.

96 Casa Corner: detail of façade showing the irregular fenestration pattern and the prominent projecting roof.

the contiguous Casa Corner. However, despite the probable survival of these and perhaps other elements, the present appearance of the houses, as remodelled in the fifteenth century, has much in common with the Corner and Obizzi houses at Murano.

Both of the two contiguous houses have a low ground storey occupied by shops and workshops, and only one spacious *piano nobile* above. In the centre of both façades is a gothic three-light window with a balcony; at both ends of these combined façades are two single-light windows, lighting the rooms ancillary to the *pòrtego* in the traditional manner. The houses are typical of their class in their scale, in the disposition of the major elements and in the pronounced horizontality of their façades. Particularly notable is the wide spacing between the secondary windows; the multi-light windows are large and rise for the full height of the *piano nobile*, again a typical feature of such houses.

Casa Corner, or Foscolo-Corner, also contains certain elements suggesting an early original construction, later modified. It has a very irregular plan, built around a central *cortile*, with shops (possibly original) onto the square. The rooms on the *piano nobile* are reached by an open stair in the *cortile*, in the manner of the great *palazzi*, while the main façade reflects the irregular plan behind it. The entrance is to one side, and on the first floor the main hall or *pòrtego* lies parallel with the main elevation, rather than orthogonal to it; it is lit by a four-light gothic window. This plan is a survival of the Veneto-Byzantine form, the most prominent feature of which (as we have seen) was the lateral *loggia* along the front elevation. As with the other two houses, the façade is broad, with wide gaps between the windows, and a strong horizontality rendered more prominent by the over-sailing roof, which projects a considerable distance from the wall face in the 'Florentine' manner; a similar roof is found on another nearby gothic house at Dorsoduro 2958. All of these houses are very similar in size and proportions to those of the Obizzi, Sodeci and Corner at Murano; among these similarities we may also note the very informal fenestration pattern. To a degree, this reflects the irregular plans behind these façades but to some extent it appears merely capricious. For example, at Casa Corner at S. Margherita only one window has its sill at floor level, while the others all have quite different sill heights – in fact only two are the same. A similar informality is seen at the same family's house at Murano; here sill heights are constant but the spacing between the windows is irregular and the windows themselves are of several different widths.

This asymmetry and informality is only partly explained by the fact that some of these houses (but not all) were remodellings of a pre-existing structure; this accounts for the asymmetrical position of the multi-light window to the *pòrtego*, but does not explain the different sizes and sill heights of the other windows. We may cite another example of a medium-sized gothic house in Rio della Pietà (see below) where it would have been quite possible to produce a fully symmetrical façade but where again the fenestration pattern is irregular.

We thus have a small group of houses of the *cittadinanza* from the medieval period some of which contain elements of the seminal tripartite plan (and in some cases modified to suit the shape of the site or the structural constraints of an existing building) but which also form a distinct sub-category of their own. The chief features of the group are strong horizontality and very asymmetrical façades; they are all built on only two floors and closely resemble a small but important group of houses at Murano. In all cases, too, the

97 Gothic house on Rio della Pietà: façade from the canal.

ground floor was almost certainly originally occupied by shops or workshops, with a single spacious apartment on the *piano nobile*.

Our second example, in Rio della Pietà (Castello 3616) is larger than the houses at S. Margherita; it also follows the tripartite plan much more closely. Again there are only two storeys but here the ground floor is of more importance and probably formed the original *fòntego* of the house. Maretto has suggested a date of construction of about the middle of the fourteenth century, and it appears to be considerably earlier than our third example, the house at S. Barnaba. The plan is trapezoidal, following the shape of the site, with the main façade onto the *rio*; the house itself has an L-shaped plan with an open *cortile* in the internal angle, from which the stair almost certainly originally rose (the east wing is a later extension). The *androne* is narrow and off-centre, the left wing of the house being notably narrower than the right; the latter is occupied by a single large room, with two windows onto the canal. The corresponding room in the left wing has a single window. The house is similar in size to that at S. Barnaba and is a fairly typical example of the genre – a spacious but not luxuriously appointed *palazzetto* built by a reasonably prosperous *cittadino*. The construction on only two floors again produces strong horizontality in the façade, and although the fenestration is still irregular the lights are more standardised than those in our first example. However, there is still no attempt to impose the rigid symmetry and discipline that we find in the great *palazzi* of this period.[2]

Such strict symmetry can be seen in our third example, a house in Calle del Traghetto at S. Barnaba (Dorsoduro 2786), a useful example of a substantial citizen's house probably of the early or middle part of the fifteenth century. The ground floor is fairly modest, but is surmounted by a particularly spacious *piano nobile*; the plan is tripartite and entirely conventional, with the left wing extended to the rear and thus partly enclosing the *cortile* that occupies the rest of the site and gives access to the *rio* at the back. The internal planning is regular and identical in principle to that of many contemporaneous *palazzi*;

[2] See also Maretto, *L'Edilizia*, p. 82.

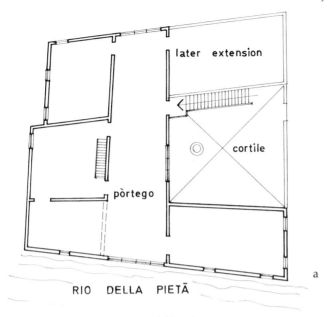

later extension

cortile

pòrtego

RIO DELLA PIETĀ

a

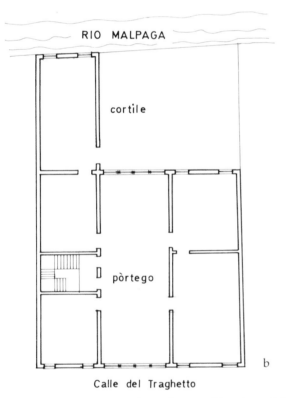

RIO MALPAGA

cortile

pòrtego

b

Calle del Traghetto

98a and b Comparative plans of two gothic *palazzetti*: house in Rio della Pietà and house in Calle del Traghetto at S. Barnaba. The former has an irregular tripartite plan partly (but not entirely) as a result of the shape of the site; the other house has a classically regular plan.

99 Façade of a gothic house in Campo dietro il Cimitero, at Angelo Raffaele, a fine example of the symmetrical tripartite form on a medium-sized *palazzetto*.

four rooms lead off the *androne*, one in each corner, while the stair rises in two flights halfway down the left wing. Each element of the tripartite plan is of almost exactly equal width; the large *pòrtego* measures 5 metres in width, 4.2 metres in height and 14 metres in length. This hall is thus not much smaller than many such halls found in the houses of the nobility.[3]

The main façade directly echoes the regular plan behind it, with a large four-light window to the *pòrtego* and a pair of single lights to each flanking room; the windows to the ground floor are very simple, as is the portal. We see here, therefore, a very clear attempt to emulate the rigid formality and symmetry of the great palaces, but although the principal rooms are indeed all quite spacious, the detailing throughout is very simple, with no elaborately carved stonework, no balconies, traceried window-heads or rope mouldings. All of the builder's efforts were expended on the construction of a solid and sizeable house, but with no superfluous expenditure on 'unnecessary' decoration. Such an approach might be said to epitomise the class for whom such houses were built – successful *cittadini* who earned their money carefully and spent it wisely. There are a few examples of such houses elsewhere in the lagoon, chiefly at Murano, but they are rare in the other villages, simply because the class itself was rare or non-existent.

[3] Ibid. p. 116 (with a plan of the zone).

We may finally consider a fourth medieval example, which has an important similarity to a small group of houses also at Murano, Palazzetto Costantini on Rio Terrà Catecumeni (Dorsoduro 74). It was built in the fifteenth century and faced a narrow *rio*, later reclaimed; its long ground-floor colonnade thus originally stood at the water's edge and the first floor spanned the quay, as we see at the Corner, Obizzi and other houses at Murano. Like them, too, it is built on only two storeys; the plan is simple, symmetrical and tripartite, although the house was built in a zone of the city that was not densely developed and hence also resembled the suburban nature of Murano. There was even space for a *cortile* at the side of the house and a large garden at the rear, both of which have survived today.[4]

1 The smaller medieval houses

The more modest houses of the fourteenth and fifteenth centuries contain some of the features of the *palazzetti* noted above, but they were often built on cramped or difficult-shaped sites. Their scale is thus reduced and there is usually very little external decoration. These houses broadly represent the lesser citizenry and the members of the working guilds (the 'mechanical trades') as well as shopkeepers of many kinds.

There are comparatively few examples of such houses in the central zones of the city; inexorably increasing pressures for redevelopment, particularly in the sixteenth and seventeenth centuries, meant that many of them were demolished and replaced by larger houses or apartment blocks, to gain space by building on four or five storeys. As we might expect, these earlier smaller houses, like the larger *palazzetti* just discussed, were usually built on only two storeys, or occasionally on three. They are chiefly distinguishable from the *palazzetti* by their very simple detailing and their often asymmetrical plans. In many cases the only feature on the façade with any modelling is the two- or three-light window to the main living room on the first floor, which is a scaled-down version of the traditional *pòrtego*. In most examples the ground floor was given over to a retail shop or the *bottega* of the owner who lived above.

In many cases, too, sites were too narrow for a tripartite plan and so often one of the side wings was omitted completely. Where space permitted, however, a symmetrical plan was adopted, as in our first example below. Even here, though, the central *pòrtego* is no longer a spacious hall for entertaining, but has been reduced in scale to become the all-purpose living room of the house. This first example is at the north end of Campo dei Due Pozzi in Castello, and is on two storeys with a central gable added later. Although the door is off-centre the plan inside is symmetrical, with a central *pòrtego*, a room at each corner and the stair rising directly out of one room. A two-light gothic window denotes the *pòrtego*, with single lights to the flanking rooms. De'Barbari shows the house with a full second floor, which was later removed and the present gable added.[5]

An adjacent house in the same square is of roughly similar date and also on three storeys; economic pressures for redevelopment of land were rather higher here than in other peripheral zones of the city because of the proximity of the Arsenal and the need to

---

[4] See also Trincanato, *Venezia Minore*, pp. 269, *et seq.* (with sketch plan).
[5] Muratori, *Studi per una Operante Storia*, p. 106.

100 A small two-storey gothic house in Campo dei Due Pozzi, of basically symmetrical form.

101 A compact three-storey gothic house on the same square as Fig. 100.

house several thousand dock workers within easy reach of its gates. This house was probably originally built as two units and it is likely that the ground-floor shop is original. The building is a useful example of a very compact plan-form, developed in response to the requirements of a specialised neighbourhood. The later descendants of such modest houses can be found in all parts of the city and the lagoon, and we will discuss these derivations further in chapter 10.

2 Renaissance *palazzetti*

As in the case of the great *palazzo-fòntego*, the replacement of gothic forms of detailing by those of the Renaissance in the latter part of the *quattrocento* did not lead to any significant re-appraisal of the overall form of the lesser houses and *palazzetti*. Once again continuity is the most dominant feature of these smaller houses, and we find many examples from the period from about 1480 to 1520 in which a mixture of the two styles can be seen.

In essence, therefore, there is very little difference between later gothic houses such as that at S. Barnaba, transitional houses such as that of the *provveditore* of the Arsenal (noted below) and houses slightly later again, that are fully Renaissance in character. Many of these *palazzetti*, like their predecessors, were built on only two storeys, again indicating the fairly modest status of their owners. The ground floor is still given over either to the trade or *fòntego* of the owner, or it may have been sub-let as retail shops or a *bottega* for another craftsman. The first floor thus once again consists of a single fairly spacious apartment; in houses of this size the *pòrtego* formed a practical living room as well as circulation space, giving access to the adjacent bedrooms. Often there were two or three additional rooms in the roof, one of which may have been the kitchen, and the others probably servants' rooms.

The dimensions of these Renaissance *palazzetti* closely followed those of their gothic predecessors; some of these houses are quite generous in size and resemble some of the villas at Murano. Exterior detailing is usually simple but often refined, with finely carved stone to the entrance and the three- or four-light window to the *pòrtego*, as well as the roof cornice.

An example of such a house is no. 2427 in Castello, a few metres from the land-gate of the Arsenal. It was probably built to house one of the *provveditori* of the naval base and its front façade effectively forms part of the enclosing wall of the Arsenal. Built on two storeys, it has a conventional tripartite plan, with central *pòrtego*, and is approached by its own bridge spanning the narrow Riello dell'Arsenale. It is likely that the house was originally built in the gothic style, as de'Barbari appears to show it, and hence the Renaissance windows flanking the *pòrtego* are later insertions, possibly executed shortly after the completion of the adjacent land-gate of the Arsenal itself, built by Gambello in *c*. 1460 in a fully Renaissance style.

The house is one of a small group, with its neighbours, all on two storeys and all probably built for a similar purpose; it thus represents the type of accommodation that then befitted a *cittadino* in a fairly important public post. We may briefly mention another example of the early Renaissance *palazzetto* in its transitional phase: this is a house on the

102 Early Renaissance *palazzetti* built as accommodation for the *provveditori* of the Arsenal; one has a mixture of gothic and Renaissance detailing.

Zattere at no. 929, which is built on an arcade, with columns of Istrian stone and large carved timber *barbacani* supporting the first floor.[6] The house is originally of the fifteenth century, as can be seen in the gothic windows to the flank walls, and the main façade was modernised during the sixteenth century. Like the house in Rio Terrà Catecumeni, there is a strong suggestion of suburbia in its horizontal proportions, and the large garden, which has again survived today, reinforces this impression.

For two final examples of fully Renaissance *palazzetti* only a few metres apart, we may consider nos. 2901 and 2925, in the *sestiere* of S. Polo, and both on Rio della Frescada. The earlier of the two is probably Palazzetto della Madonna, faced in brickwork, and so called from a small bas-relief set into the façade. The house has a broad, spacious elevation, with a four-light window to the *pòrtego* and two single windows to each of the flanking rooms. The ground floor has been altered, but originally contained either the *fòntego* of the owner or *botteghe* for rent. Its planning is entirely conventional, and again the two-storey form

---

[6] Trincanato, *Venezia Minore*, pp. 276, *et seq.*

103 Palazzetto della Madonna on Rio della Frescada, a substantial early Renaissance *palazzetto* with a particularly broad plan.

104 House at no. 2925 also on Rio della Frescada, probably of slightly later date than the first.

105 House on Campo S. Angelo, probably of the seventeenth century.

produces a façade of strong horizontality. The nearby house is slightly later in date, and is rather smaller and less refined in its detailing. Again the ground floor is occupied by ancillary and commercial uses, although part of it is a public right of way which passes under the house as the Sottopòrtego Gaspare Gozzi. The *piano nobile*, however, is completely traditional in its plan and fenestration pattern, the *pòrtego* being lit by a three-light window with a very prominent stone balcony. The two houses are rather unusual in having only two storeys in what was, and remains, a densely developed zone in the centre of the city; directly opposite the first *palazzetto* is Palazzo della Frescada, a classic gothic patrician palace, massive in volume and built on four substantial storeys.[7]

Later examples of Renaissance *palazzetti* are numerous and may be found in most parts of the city. Many of them closely resemble the above examples, being built on two storeys, often with a spacious first-floor apartment, and sometimes with refined stonework to the main openings, balconies and other details. In scale, volume and proportions they may be closely compared with the few remaining patrician villas at Murano and the handful on the Giudecca.

Many other later Renaissance houses are considerably more modest in size and in the

[7] Maretto, *L'Edilizia*, p. 106; see also Muratori, *Studi per una Operante Storia*, p. 91.

quality of their construction. These may be loosely described as the houses of the lower citizenry and the many trade guild members, and are the natural development of houses such as that on Campo dei Due Pozzi noted above. The appearance of these houses is very simple, with only limited use of stonework. One typical example may be cited out of hundreds; this is a house on the south side of Campo S. Angelo, recently restored.[8]

It has a slightly irregular plan as it abuts the little Oratory of the Annunciation although the façade is symmetrical and conventional. The house is on three storeys, the lowest of which is occupied by shops and may also originally have been so used. The upper floors are very simply detailed, with only a modest balcony to the central window of the second floor *pòrtego*. The façade is surmounted by a large gable with a triangular tympanum and flanked by simple volutes; such detailing is very similar indeed to that on a large number of seventeenth- and early eighteenth-century houses in the lagoon villages, notably at Pellestrina (see pp. 286–313).

An even more modest example of such a house type may be found in Campo dell'Avogaria at Angelo Raffaele (Dorsoduro 1618).[9] Once again it is built on three storeys with an attic; however, there are no ground-floor shops here, and the whole building is residential. The symmetrical façade is very simple indeed, and virtually devoid of decoration, with the exception of the modest balconies to the central windows at both first and second floors, and the very simple gable with its equally simple crowning pediment. The house is probably of the eighteenth century, and like that noted above, it has dozens of equivalents – symmetrical but very plainly detailed – in almost all of the lesser lagoon villages and also at Chioggia.

3 Cottages

This summary of the most characteristic types of Venetian housing is intended to identify examples of the house typologies in the city which have close affinities to the typical forms in the lesser lagunar settlements. In these latter communities no house form is more widespread than the small, simple cellular cottage. However, it is not surprising to find that this house type is now extremely rare in the central zones of Venice. Commercial pressures on land for re-development here have been extraordinarily high for centuries and, as we have seen, the high density apartment block, built on four or even five storeys, evolved at an early date to satisfy the acute demand for the maximum accommodation on each available site. Such high-density speculative developments were particularly widespread in the sixteenth and seventeenth centuries[10] and it is only in a small number of tiny pockets of 'leftover' land in these central districts that it is still possible to find a few examples of such artisans' cottages.

They are naturally more numerous in the peripheral zones but even here they are rarely found extensively, but rather in scattered groups and on patches of land between larger and more densely developed sites. The examples noted hereunder are taken quite at random, and serve simply to indicate that this humble house form does indeed exist in the

[8] For analysis of the parish and the *campo*, see Maretto, *L'Edilizia*, pp. 123, *et seq.*
[9] For notes on the development of the zone see Muratori, *Studi per una Operante Storia*, pp. 96, *et seq.*
[10] For many examples, see Trincanato, *Venezia Minore*, and also Gianighian and Pavanini, *Dietro*.

106 Tiny cottage adjacent to Palazzo Pisani at S. Stefano.

107 Two single-storey cottages in a courtyard near S. Giorgio dei Greci. This type is now very rare in the city.

city itself despite the overwhelming predominance of the great *palazzi*, apartment blocks and other large-scale developments. In a number of cases such cottages seem to have been built on the edge of a site owned by an important patrician family; such a family would have its headquarters in a great palace on the Grand Canal or other major waterway, but behind it there was often a deep, narrow site containing their private courtyard and at the far end of which may be found an accretion of minor, ancillary accommodation possibly

108 A short terrace of two-storey cottages in Cortesella della Vita at S. Barnaba.

109 Corte Tagliapietra at S. Barnaba contains a mixture of small houses and cottages.

originally occupied by servants or old-established tenants, and here we sometimes find such cottages.[11]

Our first examples are two small houses in Campo Pisani at S. Stefano that are dwarfed by the enormous bulk of the adjacent Palazzo Pisani,[12] one of the largest and most imposing in the city. Both cottages are typical simple cellular constructions, and virtually identical to the large numbers of such houses at Burano and Pellestrina. Both have now become a part of the complex of accommodation that fills this side of the *campiello*; the smaller of the two still has a traditional Venetian chimney, and both are very simply detailed. The larger house has a symmetrical façade with a central doorway despite its very restricted width, and the door is flanked by typically seventeenth century *oculi*.

Our second example comprises two cottages that flank a semi-private courtyard near S. Giorgio dei Greci, at Castello no. 3663. They are both built on a single storey and are very similar indeed to a small group of surviving examples at Pellestrina both in their form and in their extremely simple detailing. Such cottages are now rare in all parts of the lagoon; few of the major villages did not at one time or another experience notable increases in population and hence in the demand for land for redevelopment. Burano once almost certainly contained many such cottages but they were almost all rebuilt on two or three storeys during the eighteenth century or were extended by the addition of an upper floor.[13]

[11] G. Bellavitis, 'Rediscovering the Palazzo' in *Architectural Review* (London, May 1971) pp. 290, *et seq.*
[12] For the *palazzo* itself see Bassi (1976), pp. 360, *et seq.*
[13] See chapters 12 and 13 below.

These two *casette* have a long narrow plan, basically consisting of a single fairly large room, although this was probably originally subdivided into two parts either by a partition or else simply by function, one end being used for sleeping and the other for cooking and eating. The entrance in most of these cottages was positioned halfway down one of the long side walls, as it is in both of these examples. If the cottage was slightly larger there were probably two clearly defined rooms, with the entrance giving directly onto the kitchen-living room and the bedroom reached from it. The construction of these *casette* is extremely simple, the roof consisting of a double-pitch bearing onto the two long walls, although in other examples a monopitch is found. Decoration is minimal: only one of the cottages has a single feature that might be described as decorative, and that is the stone gutter supported on a row of stone corbels, although even this apparently rather extravagant feature is purely functional in origin.

The Campo dei Due Pozzi, in which we saw two examples of small-scale medieval housing, also contains some smaller houses from later periods, both in the square and in its immediate environs.[14] In the south-west corner of the *campo* are two cottages; that on the right has been altered but in some respects it remains a typical example of the narrow-plan cottage most frequently found at Burano and Pellestrina. This type often has the chimney in the centre of the façade, as we see here. The first floor is more spacious than usual, however, with storey-height windows. The more simple structure on the left is typical of a very large number of such plain, undecorated, two-storey cottages and the ground-floor shop may be original – the *campo* has always been a local social and retail focus.[15]

Another zone that contains a number of smaller houses and cottages is the western part of the islet of S. Barnaba, and particularly the series of *calli* and *corti* on either side of the Calle Lunga; this pattern continues onto the adjacent islet towards S. Sebastiano. Cortesella della Vita contains a short terrace of small two-storey cottages very similar to many examples at Burano, while Corte Tagliapietra, a few metres away, also contains a mixture of small houses and cottages, all very humble in appearance and ranging from tall, narrow houses on four storeys to one isolated example of a two-storey cottage. Like those in Cortesella della Vita, it is a cellular unit of the very simplest type, with no decoration whatsoever apart from the prominent stone cornice-gutter.

Our last example was examined by Trincanato[16] and it lies in the easternmost zone of the city, at S. Antonio. It is a row of very small two-storey cottages in Calle delle Furlane (Castello nos. 1094–8), the most prominent features of which are their large robust chimneys. Each cottage contains two rooms on the ground floor and two on the first, but they were built as two separate little apartments, with the entrances to the upper floors on one *calle* and those to the ground floor on the other side of the block. It is rare to find such an arrangement in cottages of this very modest size although such arrangements were more common in the larger speculative developments of apartments for rent. These cottages are in all other respects very simple indeed, typical of the homes of the humblest

---

[14] See note 8 above.
[15] For many other examples see Trincanato, *Venezia Minore*, pp. 127, *et seq.* (for the *sestiere* of Castello) and pp. 251, *et seq.* for Dorsoduro.
[16] Ibid. pp. 223–4.

of all Venetian citizens: their occupants were probably fishermen since this is a zone remote from the city centre but well positioned for access to the lagoon and to the open sea by the Porto di Lido, and this was for centuries a traditional quarter for fishermen.

This group of examples serves to indicate that in many parts of the city, particularly the peripheral zones, we can identify all of the chief typologies of small houses and cottages that we will find later in the lagoon villages.

4 Terrace developments

There are a number of examples of large-scale terrace developments in the city centre whose accommodation varies from the small two-storey cottages that we have just examined to substantial developments of apartment blocks, built to let on the open market, and whose tenants in many cases were *cittadini* of some substance. Many of these latter buildings date from the sixteenth and seventeenth centuries, and several have recently been analysed by Gianighian and Pavanini.[17] It is not appropriate to discuss these larger developments here, however, since they are only found in the inner zones of the city and there are no similar examples in any of the lesser lagoon settlements. Such major blocks of apartments typically contain a mixture of accommodation, usually on three or four floors (occasionally on five) and are often ingeniously planned to provide each apartment with its own street entrance; the floor plans are often complex and interlocking, as are the staircases. Such developments are truly metropolitan in their scale, density and sophistication; their tenants were often well-to-do businessmen, tradesmen or *maestri* in the specialist guilds. Some were nobles or notable citizens. The developers of such buildings were usually either wealthy patricians or institutions – the *scuole*, or more particularly the Scuole Grandi, or the many wealthy religious houses.

Speculative developments on a more modest scale are of greater relevance here, however, since those for whom such projects were built were chiefly small traders or craftsmen, a class with at least some representatives in all of the larger lagoon villages. We can thus see close similarities linking such developments in the city with those in its satellite communities.

As with the smallest cottages, land shortages in the city centre (particularly the *sestieri* of S. Marco and S. Polo) rendered small-scale terrace development prohibitive, as the sites were so expensive. Such terraces are thus again only found in significant numbers in the peripheral zones – the assembly of sufficient land in the centre to build a large terrace was a difficult, if not impossible task, and the return in rent would not justify such an effort. A glance at de'Barbari's survey of 1500 indicates the zones that were ripe for such de-velopment at the turn of the new century. There were few left, although one was the extensive marshy area owned by S. Maria Maggiore in the western part of Dorsoduro. It was still a marsh in 1500 but was drained and developed for the first time in the *cinquecento*;[18] we may cite here one or two examples of small-scale terraces built along the banks of Rio (now Rio Terrà) dei Pensieri.

In this zone, so far from the city centre, land values remained much lower, and it was

---

[17] G. Gianighian and P. Pavanini, *Dietro i Palazzi*, pp. 45–57, with many illustrations.
[18] Ibid.

110 and 111 Two examples of speculative terrace building in the peripheral zones of the city. Fig. 110 is a short terrace built in the 1670s by the noble Antonio Bernardo on Rio Terrà dei Pensieri. Fig. 111 is a rather larger development next to it, and probably of the very early nineteenth century.

still economical here to build on only two storeys. Terraced cottages were in any case a fairly efficient building form, even when we consider the low yields in rent; with only two floors, foundations could be very modest indeed while the smaller rooms required reduced timber sizes for beams and roof trusses. A long terrace would allow almost complete standardisation of such dry elements of construction as carpentry, windows and doors, and could thus be built very rapidly. Standardisation reduced construction time and thus provided the developer with a quicker return on his original investment. If the terrace was built on three storeys, as a number of them were, it was also possible to achieve high densities, as open space was usually limited to very small private courtyards or simply a broad private *calle* (usually known as a *corte*) down the rear of the terrace.

There are three developments in Rio Terrà dei Pensieri that may be noted here (the *rio* was reclaimed in the nineteenth century). The first is a row of two-storey cottages, recently restored, on the west side; Gianighian and Pavanini have identified the site as the property of the noble Procurator Antonio Bernardo in the 1670s, together with a large adjacent site facing Rio delle Burchielle. The development consisted of a row of eleven cottages on this adjacent site and five on the smaller one; this work was virtually complete by 1678, when the cottages were already being rented out at 20 ducats per year. The short terrace is in many ways typical of such speculative schemes; the houses are small, although the plans are not all regular and have been much altered since they were built. The cottages have a simple, double-pitch roof which is continuous over the whole terrace, and is punctuated only by a single small dormer to each house. The complex rhythm of the façade is the result of using alternate, 'handed' plans, and it is further broken up by the four prominent chimneys with their characteristic profile. The detailing is generally very spare, as we might expect, and the door and window openings are all simple rectangles with stone heads and sills, but no other form of decoration.

The second terrace is on the east side of the *rio terrà*, a little further north. The site was occupied by a wax-making factory until the mid-seventeenth century, but the first cottages were replaced by the present long terrace of twelve cottages in *c.* 1696; an adjacent site in the same ownership, that of the noble Nicolò Corner, was also redeveloped in around 1708. This latter site fronted Rio della Cazziola and when redeveloped comprised 'six cottages at ground floor level . . . rented at 10 ducats each . . . and a further six at first floor above the aforementioned, and these [were] rented at 12 ducats each'.[19] Rents for the long terrace of twelve cottages varied considerably, and in 1711 the rent-roll shows incomes of between twelve and thirty ducats.

These cottages, like the first example, are all on two storeys, but with very irregular plans and consequently with accommodation that ranges from small two-roomed apartments to houses of four or five rooms. The external appearance of the terrace, however, is simple in principle, its variety deriving solely from the irregular spacing of the elements, which include a number of prominent chimneys. Doors and windows again all have simple stone surrounds, and the only other feature is the heavy stone gutter along the whole length of the terrace, supported on stone corbels.

For a final example of speculative terrace development in the city we may turn to

[19] Ibid. pp. 144, *et seq.*

112 A large terrace in Borgoloco S. Lorenzo in Castello, redeveloped by the monastery of that name in 1665; a good example of the simple, repetitive terrace built for rent, and virtually devoid of architectural features.

Borgoloco S. Lorenzo, a long straight *calle* bounded on both sides by land in the ownership of the eponymous monastery. This house owned a considerable amount of property in the district; in a register of 1648 this property totalled 106 'stabili o case', both on the Borgoloco island and on the adjacent island of the church itself. The block on the south side of the Borgoloco consists of a long terrace of three-storey houses; they were built later than the north side, and a stone plaque records their 'restoration' (in fact, a reconstruction) in 1665. The terrace is of ten houses very simple in both plan and appearance; although on three floors they were not intended for horizontal subdivision into apartments, as was often the case, but were built as individual houses, each one consisting of an entrance and a single stair giving access to three rooms on each of the upper storeys. The house plan is thus very similar indeed to the standard small English terrace house plan of the later eighteenth century. At the rear of each house was a very small private courtyard. All ten were identically planned and their façades are also identical; there is no external decoration whatsoever other than that provided by the stone corbels supporting the cornice-gutter. This was a speculative development of the simplest, most rational type, and the overall configuration of the block may be compared with the terrace on Rio di S. Mauro at Burano, with which it has very many similarities, despite the fact that two centuries separate their construction dates.

Recent research into the S. Lorenzo development has shown that the monastery received a large increase in rent from this reconstruction; the total income from the whole terrace doubled from 223 to 448 ducats when it was re-let in the 1660s.[20]

[20] Ibid. pp. 76 and 136.

As an example of such developments, S. Lorenzo is one among many, both in the city itself and also outside, at Murano, Burano and on the Giudecca. Their design was so simple and devoid of decoration that it remained unchanged for a long time; aesthetic considerations formed virtually no part of the design of these projects, and they were built purely to maximise returns in income. Like their counterparts in the lagoon, those in the city were generally built in periods of sharp population growth and of rising prices, in order to take full advantage of the guaranteed market as soon as they were complete.

10

Housing typology in the lagoon villages: an introduction

Many of the housing types in the lagoon villages derive either from the great *palazzo-fòntego* of the city centre or from the much smaller houses of the citizenry and the *minuto popolo*. In those parts of the lagoon where we find a strong and continuing historical presence of the nobility, particularly at Murano and the Giudecca (and for a time also at Torcello and Mazzorbo) there is evidence of the adaptation of the city *palazzo* to form houses variously described as villas, *case coloniche*, *case padronali* and *casoni*. Whatever the precise practical function of such a house was, its *signorile* origins are usually fairly clear and are expressed in its form and composition; it has a symmetrical plan with a central hall or *androne* and an elevational treatment which, like the city *palazzo*, clearly expresses the spatial structure behind the façade. Naturally, the quality of workmanship (often more lavish inside than on the façade) was also much higher than that on the fishermen's houses by which these *casoni* were often surrounded.

At the lesser social levels we find very close similarities between the houses of successful craftsmen in these villages and those of their peers in the capital, although they are often influenced by the villas to which they are sometimes adjacent, particularly at Murano. In general, the scale is as modest as we might expect from this class, the only exceptions being the group of *case padronali* at Pellestrina that represent a unique social group in the lagoon, a reasonably well-off class of farmers, many with estates beyond the confines of the lagoon.

We may summarise here the chief housing types in the lagoon, and this classification can be divided into five major groups; there are many houses that are not easy to classify, however, and over a long period of time many also experienced changes in ownership and in patterns of use. Many *case coloniche*, for example, later became simple working farm-houses, and a number of Murano's villas were similarly 'demoted' after the nobility had virtually deserted the island by the eighteenth century. A summary of these main groups, however, may assist in forming a basis for the more detailed descriptions in Part III.

1 Villas

The patrician villa is the simplest house to define as it was built by a small, finite group of families and usually for a specific purpose quite different from the *raison d'être* of the other four groups of houses. The two islands most closely associated with the nobles' villas are Murano and the Giudecca; the latter island really lies outside the scope of our detailed survey since it is part of Venice itself, but the development of both islands as places of

113 The patrician villa: engraving by Luca Carlevarijs (*c.* 1703) of the Vendramin villa on the Giudecca. The house was built in the late *quattrocento* and had a famous and extensive garden.

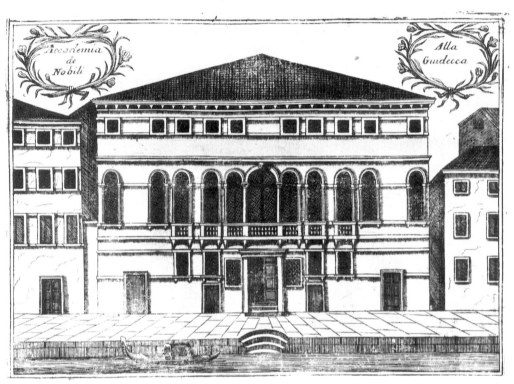

114 The Accademia dei Nobili, also on the Giudecca: an example of the adaptation of the form of the Renaissance villa for other uses, in this case to educate the sons of the patriciate. Engraving by Coronelli in *Palazzi di Venezia* (1709) (B.C.V. Stampe G. 5).

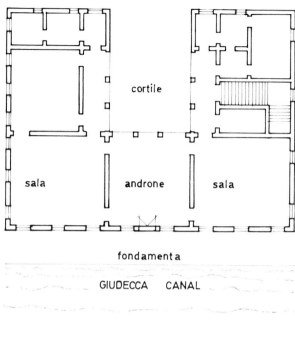

cortile

sala   androne   sala

fondamenta

GIUDECCA   CANAL

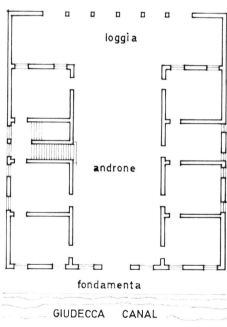

loggia

androne

fondamenta

GIUDECCA   CANAL

115 Comparative plans of two patrician villas, those of the Mocenigo (above) and the Vendramin (below), both on the Giudecca. The Mocenigo villa survives but is much altered. In both cases the relationship of the plan to the garden at the rear is a key element in their design.

resort for wealthy nobles is so similar that all general observations on Murano are equally applicable to the Giudecca.

The chief feature that differentiates the villa from the larger houses of the citizenry is its function; it was not built as a main or permanent residence but as a place of resort, of pleasure, and as such was only occupied for a part of the year, usually the summer months. These villas were built to escape from the pressures of public life and commerce and hence, unlike the city *palazzi*, they had no commercial function to fulfil. There was no need for a ground-floor *fòntego* or for shipping to be moored to the quay outside. Their planning reflected this purely social function and the villas were often built on only two storeys, with a spacious, broad plan, and often with a *loggia* at the rear giving onto the extensive garden. The villa may thus be defined as a house built by and for the nobility and whose function was to serve as a temporary retreat from the owner's permanent residence in the city centre. The patrician villa survives in the lagoon today only at Murano and the Giudecca; in both islands many of these houses have been lost, although we will examine the few important houses that survive at Murano, and the way in which they were developed, in a later chapter.

2 *Case coloniche* and *case padronali*

Our second group is less easy to define than the first; a useful, if slightly narrow definition of a *casa colonica* would be a house built by the nobility but used on only fairly rare occasions, and usually situated further from the city than Murano and the Giudecca – hence the adjective *colonica*. As we will see, however, some of the houses thus described are in fact quite small, similar in size to a spacious farmhouse, and on occasion difficult to distinguish from such a house built by a reasonably prosperous local farmer. Such a distinction would be very difficult to draw at Pellestrina were it not for the information in the government land-registers, from which we know that, despite the substantial size of some of these houses, they were all built by local farmers for their own use. They are thus *case padronali*, since their owners were indeed the *padroni* of their communities. The patrician houses in the lesser islands must have been chiefly used as bases for hunting and fishing, and the few examples that survive can only be tentatively identified as such by their rather more refined detailing and the quality of their construction.

The houses built by local *padroni* can themselves be subdivided very broadly into two groups: those that are quite large but still architecturally very simple working farmhouses, and those that have a significant amount of architectural pretension and were built as a family seat, often with the use of classical detailing, prominent entrance porticoes, stone balconies and so on. Those at Pellestrina form the largest group of examples of the latter type, several of which clearly had aspirations to be regarded as villas. All of the houses in both sub-groups, however, are similar in size and function; they were farmhouses, and the headquarters of a large, extended family. They are usually solidly built, often square or nearly square on plan and usually on two storeys, although occasionally (particularly at Pellestrina) on three. Their plans and elevations are symmetrical and tripartite, and hence their derivation from the classic city *palazzo* form can be clearly seen. The closer re-

116 The *casa padronale* or farmer's villa: a fine example on the waterfront at S. Vio, Pellestrina.

semblance, however, is with the houses of the citizenry in the city centre, with which they have much in common, notably in size and in their detailing.

All of the *case padronali* and *case coloniche*, whether built by the patriciate or local farmers, were in fact working farmhouses. Although some of the *case coloniche* were only in use by the owners for a few weeks every year, they were maintained by local residents, and usually had a farm, or at least some orchards and vineyards attached to them. Like the houses of the islanders, therefore, they were surrounded by outbuildings, stores and a *cavanna* for storing a boat. Another feature common to almost all of these houses is that they were built as detached structures, rather than elements in an urban or suburban fabric. They stood on a sizeable plot of land, facing a navigable watercourse, and the fact that they were freestanding provides a link with some of the more modest villas of the nearby Terraferma. Certainly a few of the larger *case padronali* at Pellestrina have more in common with these villas than they do with houses of comparable size in the city centre. The Terraferma villas were also working farmhouses, of course, and usually compact structures detached from any others. In this sense, too, these lagunar farmhouses differed from the villas of Murano and the Giudecca, which were usually built next to each other on a fairly crowded waterfront in a suburban environment; when these two islands were fully developed in the later sixteenth century, their villas formed an almost continuous wall of development along the quays of Murano's Grand Canal and the Giudecca Canal.

3 Houses of the *Piccola Borghesia*

The third group of houses is also fairly easy to identify since it represented a well-defined class, that of the skilled craftsmen or modestly successful small retailer. These houses stand on the next rung of the social ladder, immediately below those of the wealthier traders (usually *cittadini*) and landowners. Whereas the *case padronali* of Pellestrina and the *case coloniche* of the nobility directly express the status of their owners – or at least their aspirations – these lesser houses are notable chiefly for their extreme modesty. This is not to say that they are devoid of architectural interest or quality, but rather that here we do not find the conscious effort to make a 'public impression' that we see very clearly in the *case padronali* on the *lidi*. In the latter houses it was important to incorporate certain features to express the status or ambition of their owners, and to emphasise their position in the social order of the island; this next group of houses represents a social group that was not as wealthy and perhaps by nature more cautious.

There are only examples of such houses in communities that were large and stable enough to have developed a significant class of modestly successful small tradesmen; thus we find a small but identifiable group of them at Burano, where the archives clearly show the emergence of such a social group in the later sixteenth and seventeenth centuries, mostly consisting of shopkeepers and boatbuilders. We also find such a group at Murano, where the fairly complex social structure, and in particular the presence of the nobility in some numbers, led inevitably to the rise of a 'service class' of shopkeepers and tradesmen, as well as examples of moderately successful glassmakers.

In the smaller, more rural communities, such a class barely existed, and it is very difficult to identify houses of this type at Mazzorbo, Malamocco or Torcello. However, there are significant numbers at Pellestrina, most of them in the central part of the village itself, where almost all retail trade on the *lido* was concentrated – there are very few such houses at S. Pietro or Porto Secco.

The chief features of these houses are their generally symmetrical appearance and modest, although sometimes quite refined, detailing to doors and windows. Many of them are five bays wide, with a central doorway and a larger window above it. Often the door and this window have semicircular heads, while the other windows do not. The houses are almost all on two floors, although occasionally with a central gable or aedicule to light the attic. The main elevation is often well-proportioned, with a horizontal emphasis as a result of the fairly wide frontage, usually approximating to the width of two or two and a half smaller cottages. Plans are usually rigorously conventional, with a central hallway and four rooms to each floor. The interior finishes are simple, as befit the status of the owner, and there is rarely very much decoration to walls or ceilings.

This is the smallest type of house in the lagoon villages that still retains features that are clearly descended from the great *palazzo-fòntego* of the lagunar capital. Naturally, the

117 The houses of the tradesman class: an example on Rio Pontinello at Burano, probably of the seventeenth century.

building materials used are similar, but we can still see clear echoes of the city *palazzo* in the strong desire for symmetry, in the emphasis on the vestigial first-floor *pòrtego* (often little more than a spacious corridor) and in the important central entrance; we can also see these echoes in the proportions of the windows and in the spacing between them. Such houses were certainly not designed by architects, but they were built by masons and *muratori* of some skill and sensibility in matters of proportion and clearly aware of the tradition of which they were a continuing part.

4 Artisans' cottages

By contrast, the numerous small cottages of the lagoon islands were mostly built with no architectural features at all. There are more houses in this broad category – far more – than in all the others together and, as we might expect, these cottages vary considerably in size, shape and disposition of rooms. Nevertheless, with this group of houses we have finally left behind the extraordinarily strong influence of the *palazzo-fòntego* and its characteristic features. The cottages of the thousands of fishermen, lacemakers, glassworkers and farmhands of these communities have no classical plan, no *androne* or *pòrtego* and no *piano nobile*. Only rarely is there symmetry in their appearance although this is still sometimes achieved, even in the modest houses of Burano.

118 The artisan's cottage: the simple cellular cottage is the most numerous of the basic house types in the lagoon – a particularly modest example on Rio Mandracchio at Burano.

There are so many of these small cottages that we may attempt to distinguish between some of the sub-types, which vary in number considerably from one settlement to another; all will be examined in more detail in chapters 11–14.

At Burano, for example, a large tightly packed village, we find that most of the houses are on two or three storeys; they usually have only one or two rooms to each floor, and the front door and stairs are often positioned to one side. This arrangement gave rise to the development of a narrow but comparatively deep plan-form, which was the most efficient way of providing as many houses as possible with direct waterfront access.

At Pellestrina there are several types of cottage plan. In the most densely built-up areas, the Burano plan is the most common, with two rooms to each floor and again often on three or even four storeys. Elsewhere houses often have a slightly wider plan and a symmetrical elevation. At Murano, too, there are several different plan types and in all of the larger villages we can still see a few examples of the smallest cottage of all, either consisting of a single room on each of two floors or even, in a few rare cases, of a simple single room, with a small sleeping 'deck' in the roof space.

In hardly any of these cottages can we find any significant architectural detail at all, any decoration beyond what was strictly functionally necessary. The use of expensive stone was very limited, and usually confined simply to door heads and the heads and sills of windows, sometimes, too, to the cornice-gutter at the eaves.

Such a broad category of house types naturally embraces a large proportion of the villagers of these communities, and the occupations of these many villagers varied from place to place. At Burano almost every cottage was occupied by a fisherman, and only a very few by artisans or tradesmen. At Murano the cottages were occupied by lagoon fishermen (Murano never had a significant sea-fishing fleet), by farmhands who worked on nearby Sant' Erasmo, and by unskilled workers in the glass industry.

At Pellestrina and its two smaller satellites (S. Pietro and Porto Secco) most of the small cottages were occupied by market-gardeners and vineyard workers, although here, too, there were some lagoon fishermen. In the smaller, more truly rural communities, the smallest cottages were again occupied by farmhands or were rented by them from landowners, either local or absentee.

These cottages were built over a long period of time; we cannot establish when the oldest surviving cottages were built, but at Burano (for example) there were already several hundred by the later sixteenth century. In most villages it is probable that the present cottages of brick and tile were slowly built to replace the very earliest cottages which were of timber, probably with roofs thatched with osier. A number of timber cottages survived at Burano until the end of the sixteenth century when we may safely assume they were replaced by houses of brick. We can draw some general conclusions as to the date of construction of many surviving cottages by analysis of government land registers, although these hardly ever allow us to identify individual buildings. However, the two major periods of expansion common to almost all of these villages were the latter part of the sixteenth and the early seventeenth centuries, and the long period of growth from about 1670 to the mid-eighteenth century. We can certainly consign virtually all of the small cottages to these two periods, with the exception of a few others built in the nineteenth century. More accurate dating is very difficult and rendered more so by the fact that the simple practical design of the cottages is almost 'timeless'.

One important characteristic of these cottages is that they were nearly all built individually, in a slow, organic, piecemeal way, each one being built onto the gable wall of a pre-existing house. In general the pattern of growth follows the principles that I established in *Chioggia*, and large-scale speculative development is very rare, as we will now see.

5 Speculative terraces

Large-scale speculative development, common in the capital, was rare in the lagoon. The few examples that do exist are mostly of the nineteenth century, and there are very few indeed from the era of the Serene Republic, most of them from the eighteenth century.

119 The speculative terrace: a fairly late example of this genre in Calle Briati at Murano. The cottages also have a slightly broader plan than was usually the case; detailing is minimally simple.

The later terraces were all built to alleviate the acute overcrowding in some of the villages, chiefly at Burano and Pellestrina.

Speculative development was rare for two reasons, both noted earlier. Firstly, the owners of much of the land were themselves only very modest landowners and simply had insufficient funds of their own (or were not considered credit-worthy enough by others) to embark on such a venture, especially since the rents that could be obtained on completion were so low. The second reason is that, even if an owner did possess sufficient funds, he could only embark on such a scheme at a time of numerical expansion, when population pressures were such that he could be assured of finding tenants immediately on completion. In several periods, notably after the two great plagues of 1575 and 1630, there was simply insufficient demand to make such projects feasible. Thus we can see that the few speculative developments that were undertaken all date from the mid-eighteenth century or from considerably later, the middle and later decades of the nineteenth century.

A speculative terrace had to be built cheaply and quickly and, as in the city, such developments are thus very simple indeed, with virtually no superfluous expenditure on 'Architecture'. The most straightforward type of development was a simple long, straight row of houses, of two or three storeys, with the greatest possible standardisation of plan and detailing, in order to take maximum advantage of the economies of scale that such a scheme provided. However, to build such an economical project the terrace really had to consist of perhaps ten, twelve or fourteen houses, and naturally such a scheme was only feasible if a site of sufficient size was available. To some extent the 'natural' pattern of urban development in the lagoon lent itself to such projects. The traditional subdivision of the land into long, narrow plots, all at right angles to the waterfront meant that, in theory, the owner of a house on this quay, with a suitable-sized plot behind it, could redevelop the whole site with a row of houses for rent. Access to the terrace would be gained via one of the many secondary *calli* or *carrizzade* that already gave access to the backland smallholdings.

Such developments remained rare, though, as we have already seen. Nevertheless, a few were built; there is a handful at Pellestrina, two or three at Burano and some also at Murano. The long, standardised rows are easily identifiable, although there are many more examples of rather more modest speculative developments consisting of perhaps only four or five houses. These are far less easy to identify today, especially if the houses were altered later, but there are several such short terraces at Burano.

In most village examples the terraces consist simply of a row of small, individual houses, almost always on two floors. This is in contrast to the many schemes in the city that were usually on three or even four storeys and often contained a mixture of apartments of different sizes. These different forms are partly a simple reflection of different land values, but lagunar terraces also reflect the strong tradition here of 'one family, one house'. In the city the tradition of apartment-dwelling was equally strong and, as we have seen, even some of the medieval noble *palazzi* were originally designed to contain individual apartments on different floors. The lagunar tradition was quite different and in all of the villages the single family house was universal; it was only significantly varied in times of sharp population increase when we often find two branches of a family sharing one house. However, this sharing often resulted in considerable overcrowding and was always accompanied by an increase in housebuilding to reduce the number of such families. We can thus clearly see the social context in which these terraces should be put, a context in which the single nuclear family was the basic social unit and hence the small family house was the basic unit of accommodation, whether built individually (as most of them were) or built in the form of a terrace by a rare entrepreneurial villager.

Part III

The architecture of the lagoon: an illustrated survey

INTRODUCTORY NOTE

In the last part of the book we survey the architecture of the lagoon communities. The survey is essentially a description of the houses that survive today, and does not dwell at length on the numerous lost villas of Murano or the long-gone *casini* of Torcello. The approach is thus basically descriptive and in a way practical, although I have also attempted to summarise the socio-economic context in which the houses were built. Although not intended as a guide book in the literal sense, it is hoped that these four chapters will provide a reference list of all of the notable houses and house types in the lagoon. I have made considerable use of the various land registry surveys undertaken by the *Serenissima* from the later sixteenth century onwards in drawing conclusions as to the approximate dates of construction of most of the lesser houses. In the case of Murano further detailed research needs to be undertaken into the investments of the patriciate in the latter *quattrocento* and *cinquecento*, and my conclusions here remain provisional. General background material on the island may be found in Zanetti, and more particular primary material in the still rather inadequate archives of the *podestà* in the Archivio di Stato.

11

Murano

Introductory note

Murano is physically the closest of all the lagoon islands to Venice and historically, too, it has been far more closely connected with the lagunar capital than any of the other villages. Murano had a far more complex social structure than Burano or Pellestrina and this structure is still evinced to some extent today in the variety of houses that may be found there.

There were two chief spheres of activity in which Murano and Venice were inseparably tied together. One was the famous glass industry, which was transferred here in 1292 and became the economic staple of the community throughout the following centuries, up to our own day. The other was the proprietary interest of the patriciate and the use of Murano as a weekend retreat, an island on which to build villas, lay out gardens and orchards, and to which the nobility transferred much of their social life during the summer.

The glass industry naturally required furnaces, and at its peak there were several dozen of them, mostly very small, and almost all of them on the lands adjacent to Rio dei Vetrai. The industry led to the development of an entire hierarchy of social life, which also manifested itself in the built fabric of the community. Some glassmakers became very wealthy, and the most important families developed a 'clan' structure similar to, and consciously modelled on, that of the nobles who governed the state. They became an élite citizenry with many rights and privileges: the right to several tax exemptions; the right to bear arms; the right to form an official register of citizens with their *Libro d'Argento* modelled on the nobles' *Libro d'Oro*. The community itself was given the highly unusual privilege of minting its own coinage once a year. The citizens were even given the right on occasion to marry into the nobility. The important glassmaking clans were naturally supported by lesser, more humble workers in allied trades and service industries, all of them represented by a rich variety of housing types.[1]

1 The medieval legacy

Fourteenth-century Murano was a substantial, populous and important community; its wealth was based chiefly on glass production, and by now a complex social order had

---

[1] There is scope for considerable further research on Murano's social and economic history. The only useful guide is V. Zanetti, *Guida di Murano* (1st edn Venice 1866; new facsimile edn Venice 1984), from which the following notes are taken. Zanetti has much contemporary and anecdotal detail of the glass industry.

185

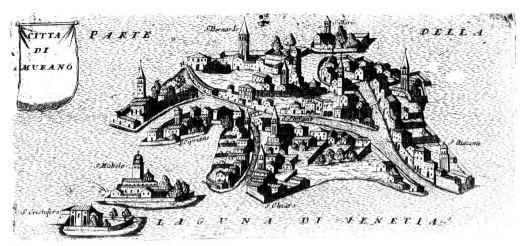

120 Murano: an anonymous sixteenth-century view of the island (Museo Civico Correr, Venice; M.12667).

evolved, nearly as wide in its range as that of the capital less than a mile away across the lagoon.

Murano was governed by a *podestà*, one of the four governorships of the lagoon; like the others he was always a noble, appointed directly by the Signoria. As elsewhere he presided over the island's own council which met in the Palazzo Comunale.

The *palazzo* is lost to us, although we know something of its history and appearance. It was built in 1334 under the governorship of Nicolò Minio and stood until 1555 when it was badly damaged by fire. It was restored on a larger scale and reached its final form in 1595; an illustration of it by Coronelli survives in the Biblioteca Marciana. It was largely of Renaissance appearance, and was on three floors with a spacious arcade at ground level. It stood on the south side of Campo S. Donato facing the canal; the ground floor was of rusticated stone, while the upper floors had a symmetrical façade with a central *Serliana* to both storeys. It thus closely resembled the contemporaneous *palazzi* of the nobility and survived in this form until its demolition in 1815.

Although it was not until the latter part of the fifteenth century that Murano began to be developed by the nobility as a place of resort, the patriciate had had close proprietary connections with the island from a considerably earlier date. Much of Murano was owned by the Church,[2] but of the rest of the land, a number of wealthy noble clans had for a long time owned property here, land that was not fully developed until the sixteenth century. but which in this earlier period was occupied by a number of smaller gothic houses as well as some larger *palazzi*.

Although Murano is richer in gothic houses than any other lagoon village, many more have been lost over the centuries and it is not easy to reconstruct the appearance of the island in the fourteenth century. It was probably developed to much the same extent as Torcello and Mazzorbo were in their period of maximum population and prosperity; the

2 For historical notes on the churches see F. Corner, *Notizie Storiche delle Chiese e Monasteri di Venezia e Torcello* (Padua 1758). See also Zanetti, *Guida di Murano*.

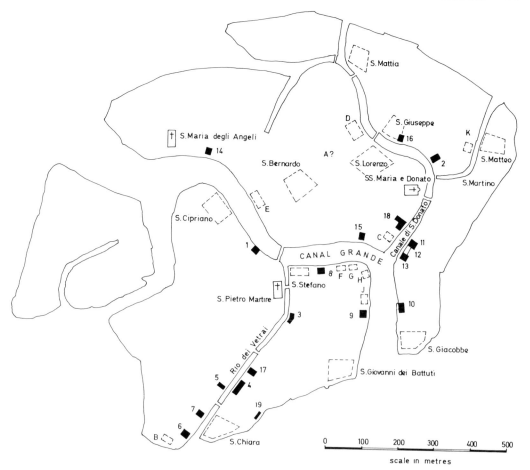

121 Murano: sketch map of the island showing the location of the principal villas and churches. Lost religious houses and villas are indicated by a broken rectangle

Key to surviving villas and houses
  1 Palazzo Da Mula
  2 Palazzo Foscari
  3 Palazzetto Corner
  4 Houses of the Obizzi and Sodeci
  5 Palazzo Bertolini
  6 Palazzo Contarini-Mazzolà I
  7 Palazzo Contarini-Mazzolà II
  8 Palazzo Soranzo I
  9 Palazzo Soranzo II
 10 Palazzo Navagero
 11 Palazzo Trevisan
 12 Palazzo Pesaro
 13 Palazzo Cappello
 14 Palazzo Correr-Grimani
 15 Palazzo Manolesso-Seguso
 16 Palazzo Marcello
 17 Palazzo Miotti-Seguso
 18 Palazzo Giustinian
 19 Casino Mocenigo

Key to approximate location of lost villas
  A Palazzo Vendramin
  B Palazzo Balbi
  C Palazzo Benzon-Manin
  D Palazzo Corner I
  E Palazzo Corner II
  F Palazzo Corner III
  G Palazzo Giustinian at S. Giovanni
  H Palazzo Grimani
  J Palazzo Morosini
  K Palazzo Giustinian at S. Matteo

quays of the main canals were highly developed but it is probable that considerable open space remained behind this zone, chiefly cultivated with vines and orchards.

Before the island received the determined attention of the patriciate at the end of the fifteenth century, most of the houses lining Murano's waterfronts were smaller, more suburban versions of the houses in the city centre. Pressures for land redevelopment here were very similar to those in the outlying parts of the capital – northern Cannaregio, Dorsoduro and the Giudecca. With two notable exceptions, therefore, the gothic houses that survive at Murano today are small or medium-sized *palazzetti*, all built on only two storeys. That there were other houses of this period of more imposing and even palatial appearance we know from the survival of just two of them today – Palazzo Foscari and Palazzo da Mula – and there were several similar *palazzi*, now gone, that compared closely in size, scale and appearance with their contemporaries on Venice's own Grand Canal. However, these *palazzi* were still less numerous than the smaller houses, several of which are described below.

Pressures for development were not equal throughout the island, and the most powerful families acquired sites on Murano's Grand Canal, where their villas were later to rise. The Rio dei Vetrai was the most densely built-up zone, however, forming the retail axis of the island as well as the centre of the glass industry.[3] Here too, though, several notable patrician clans owned land from an early date, and several medieval houses and fragments may be seen here.

Palazzo Da Mula and Palazzo Foscari

Palazzo Da Mula: Fondamenta Da Mula 153 (Grand Canal, s. side)
Palazzo Foscari: Fondamenta Santi 11 (Canale di S. Donato, n. side)

We may consider these two *palazzi* together since although both have been altered and adapted over the centuries, the present appearance of both of them is largely that of a substantial late medieval palace. Of the two, the da Mula house is undoubtedly the more important, and is the finest medieval house on Murano. Much of the principal façade is of the later fifteenth century, and Arslan has suggested a date of around 1480 for the splendid first-floor windows, by which time some Renaissance elements can be identified. However, the original house is considerably older;[4] there are traces of twelfth- or thirteenth-century work in the wall and entrance to the rear garden, and the two small windows on either side of the main entrance portal are also almost certainly of thirteenth-century date. Palazzo da Mula is often cited as a house built for the *villeggiatura* but this is clearly not the case and a palace of some size already stood here two centuries or more before the transformations of the late fifteenth century produced the house that we see today.[5] However, it is probable that these transformations were executed with this new rôle in mind; soon after the work was completed, de' Barbari shows that there were a further three or four houses of similar size and appearance in this part of the island.

[3] Originally all the glassworks stood adjacent to Rio dei Vetrai. The parish church of S. Stefano (destr.) was the glassmakers' own church, where their *arte* was registered.
[4] Arslan, *Venezia Gotica*, p. 16 and Zanetti, *Guida di Murano*, p. 91. See also F. Forlati, 'Restauri di architettura minore nel Veneto' in *Architettura* 1926–7, pp. 49, *et seq.*
[5] Arslan, *Venezia Gotica*, p. 331. As he notes, the capitals to the columns of the central multi-light window are more Renaissance than gothic.

122 Murano: Palazzo Da Mula – principal façade onto the Grand Canal.

123 Murano: Palazzo Da Mula – detail of the *piano nobile* with four-light window to the *pòrtego* and elaborate late fifteenth-century tracery to the flanking windows.

124 Murano: Palazzo Da Mula – detail of left side of façade showing decorative inlaid *paterae* of various dates, and two of the four finely carved stone *oculi*.

Palazzo da Mula has far more in common with the Venetian city *palazzo* than with the later villas both here and on the Giudecca; indeed, it is not dissimilar to the da Mula family's own city house at S. Vio on the Grand Canal. The plan and chief elements of the façade are all of the traditional tripartite type; the plan is symmetrical, with a central *androne* and *pòrtego* above it. Since the house was originally built as a *casa-fòntego* there is a particularly high, spacious ground storey given over to the storage of goods and associated ancillary accommodation. The modernisation of the late fifteenth century involved the rebuilding of much of the façade above first-floor level; most of the finest work is on this *piano nobile*, where there is a central four-light window with fine stonework lighting the *pòrtego*. Even more elaborate are the two large windows to the flanking rooms, with their complex traceried heads, quatrefoils and pendants, reminiscent of the Cà d'Oro of

125 Murano: Palazzo Foscari – main façade to the Canale di S. Donato (recently restored) showing a mixture of gothic and simple Renaissance forms in the detailing of the openings.

three or four decades earlier. Similarly complex and refined carving can be seen in the four *oculi* at high level, each of which has different tracery, and was clearly intended to be a *tour de force* by the mason concerned. Above this elaborate *piano nobile* is a very modest second storey with four simple, square windows devoid of decoration. The façade is further embellished, however, with a series of *paterae*, some in the form of bas-relief panels of Istrian stone, and others of inset panels of rare marbles; the first-floor windows are also surrounded by a typically fifteenth-century narrow outer frame of stone. Finally, in the centre of the façade is a niche containing a statue of the Virgin, the whole with a mixture of gothic and Renaissance motifs.

Palazzo da Mula is an almost unique survivor of a substantial medieval *palazzo* at Murano; the only other example is the much less elaborate Palazzo Foscari. By the end of the fifteenth century there were about eight or nine such houses, most of them similar to, but rather smaller than, their contemporaries on Venice's own Grand Canal. All provided evidence of Murano's rôle as a major satellite of the capital; these *palazzi* had not been built for the *villeggiatura* but by branches of patrician clans to serve the same function as those in the capital – as a family seat and a headquarters for trade and commerce. Only later were these houses adapted for more leisurely uses, and in some cases their original pattern of use probably continued for some considerable time.

The Foscari house, like the da Mula, appears to have had a complex history; according to Zanetti it was originally built in the twelfth century, although there is little, if any, surviving evidence for such an early date in the present structure.[6] The principal medieval

⁶ Zanetti, *Guida di Murano*, p. 166.

126 Murano: Palazzo Foscari – detail of the central part of the façade. The trilobate heads to the *piano nobile* windows suggest a construction date of the later fourteenth century.

features, the central two-light window to the first-floor *pòrtego* and the two small windows that flank it, all appear to be of the later fourteenth century as they are of the trilobate type with cusped intrados and extrados. In addition to its earlier restorations, the house has received two later major refurbishments, one in 1864 and one recently.

Palazzo Foscari is built on three storeys and is very restrained, even severe in appearance; the *piano nobile* is on the second floor with two storeys of ancillary accommodation below it, in the manner of some of the city *palazzi*. The domestic quarters thus consist simply of one spacious apartment, with some minor service rooms in the roof. The façade shows a mixture of gothic and Renaissance motifs; the medieval work is chiefly on the *piano nobile*, while the large ground-floor entrance portal is of simple Renaissance design. It is surmounted by the arms of the Foscari, one of the most powerful of the ancient noble clans of the Republic. The windows to the lower floors are of very simple design and may be contemporary with the portal.

In its proportions, Palazzo Foscari closely resembles many contemporary city *palazzi*, although smaller in size. Its volume is almost an exact cube, and hence the façade is very nearly square; together with the da Mula house it offers an important example of the city *casa-fòntego* transferred to its closest satellite. Most of the other remaining medieval houses at Murano, as we will see below, are either much-altered fragments or they are much smaller, two-storey 'suburban' houses, to which latter examples we will now turn.

The gothic palazzetti

Palazzetto Corner: Fondamenta Manin 71 (Rio dei Vetrai, e. side)
Case degli Obizzi e Sodeci: Fondamenta Manin 6–7 (do.)
House at no. 36 Fondamenta Cavour (Grand Canal, n. side)
Casa Tiepolo: Fondamenta Giustinian 2a (Canale di S. Donato, w. side)

These four houses are all medieval in origin, although the later two were partly rebuilt later, and have much that is of Renaissance character in their façades today. However, the chief feature that all four have in common is that they were built with a ground-floor colonnade that spanned the quay and supported the main accommodation on the first floor. In all cases, too, the timber *barbacani* appear to have survived these later restorations.

Palazzetto Corner is the finest of the four, and was built in the fourteenth century; it has much in common with the Obizzi house further down the same quay. Both have a continuous arcade for the full width of the façade and only one floor of apartments above; the Corner house is built on an arcade of seven stone columns with a continuous timber beam carrying the first floor. The main elevation is asymmetrical in appearance, with a gothic three-light window denoting the *pòrtego*, which is off-centre, and there are two windows on one side and three on the other. All of the windows have detailing characteristic of the houses of the later fourteenth century,[7] and which spread throughout Venetian territory after about 1400. This makes precise dating difficult, although the later *trecento* seems the probable period of construction of both the Corner and Obizzi houses.

The partial asymmetry of the plan of Palazzetto Corner is exaggerated by the use of two quite different sizes of windows and by the irregular spacing between all of them. The façade may thus be closely compared with the house of the same family in Campo S. Margherita which we discussed in Chapter 9: both are fairly modest structures with a strong horizontal emphasis to their façades provided by the broad frontage. Palazzetto Corner, like the Obizzi house, has a strongly suburban scale and much greater informality than its contemporaneous city *palazzi*; in a sense, the house forms a link between the urban *palazzo* and the more properly rural houses such as the two surviving medieval *case coloniche* at Mazzorbo, with which it is also roughly contemporary.

The Corner family had a number of proprietary interests at Murano from an early date (see below); this house may have been the residence of one branch of the clan or it may have been let to a Muranese resident. It is quite possible that the ground floor was intended to be used as a workshop associated with the glass industry.

The Case degli Obizzi e Sodeci are the names traditionally given to a pair of houses on the same *fondamenta*; the first, that of the Sodeci, is very simple in appearance with a single apartment above the ground-floor colonnade. This latter consists of square stone columns supporting some fine timber *barbacani*, very similar in profile to those on the Obizzi house.

The first-floor windows are simple rectangles, with no carved stonework. The adjacent *palazzetto* of the Obizzi is more important and slightly larger; it is also built on only two floors, with another colonnade of stone columns and timber *barbacani* supporting a very

[7] Arslan, *Venezia Gotica*, p. 153. Zanetti (*Guida di Murano*, p. 71) states that Pal. Corner is the mutilated remains of one of the finest palaces on Murano. It is impossible now to reconstruct its original form, and its history is undoubtedly complex. Arslan considers that the columns to the colonnade are not original but later replacements.

127 Murano: Palazzetto Corner on Rio dei Vetrai – general view of the façade with ground-floor colonnade. The first-floor windows are of similar date to those at Palazzo Foscari.

128 Murano: Palazzetto Corner – detail of the fine three-light window to the first-floor *salone*, and adjacent *monofora*.

129 Murano: houses of the Obizzi and Sodeci on Rio dei Vetrai; the Sodeci is in the foreground. Illustration taken just prior to their restoration in 1985–6.

large timber beam carrying the first floor. This *piano nobile* is very similar to that of the Corner house, with its strong horizontality and very informal, irregular pattern of fenestration. This consists of one small three-light window, two further small single windows and a single much larger light. They all have heads of similar profile to those of the Palazzetto Corner and are thus roughly similar in date.[8]

We have thus established the existence at Murano of a small group of these houses, all of which have elements in common with the group at S. Margherita. All are of two floors, and have very unorthodox fenestration patterns reflecting their asymmetrical plans. In addition, all of those at Murano have a continuous ground-floor colonnade; this house type is rare in the lagoon and there are no examples at Burano, Mazzorbo or Torcello, although there is a further small handful in Venice itself, as well as two further lesser examples here at Murano. Colonnades or *sottopòrteghi* were frequently built in the crowded city centre because of land shortages, but these same shortages (especially in the fifteenth century) led to the building of houses of increased height – of three, four or even five storeys rather than the two floors of the Murano group. It appears to be the case that the construction of the Corner and Obizzi houses led to the growth of a small local tradition of such houses; as well as the two noted below, de' Barbari illustrates a further three such houses (all now lost) on Rio dei Vetrai, as well as the 'house of Andrea Navagero' on the Canale di S. Giovanni. Occasionally larger *palazzi* were treated in the same way, and de' Barbari also records a substantial house opposite Palazzo da Mula which has two *piani nobili* above the quayside colonnade.

The two surviving lesser examples of such a form are at no. 36 Fondamenta Cavour and 2a Fondamenta Giustinian. The former is the more noteworthy and we know that it is of

---

[8] That is, probably of the late fourteenth century. Lorenzetti (*Venezia*, p. 815) and Arslan (*Venezia Gotica*, p. 173 n. 153) both agree with this date.

130 Murano: detail of the façade of the Obizzi house, with timber *barbacani* reinforcing the colonnade, and trilobate gothic windows, probably of the fourteenth century.

medieval origin although its present appearance is largely the result of an early-sixteenth-century remodelling. The ground floor has a full-width arcade of five bays supported on tour round columns of pink marble and two square stone corner piers; above them is another fine timber *barbacane*. Again there is only a single upper floor, with early Renaissance windows; a three-light group indicates the *pòrtego*, with two single lights on either side. De' Barbari shows the house before its modernisation, with the same fenestration pattern but with gothic detailing. The *pòrtego* is off-centre and so here again we have an asymmetrical façade which was originally very similar to the Corner and Obizzi houses. The profiles of the *barbacani* here are also similar to the other houses, again suggesting a similar date of construction.

Our fourth example of such a house type is very small, a fragment of a house on Fond. Giustinian sometimes referred to as the Casa Tiepolo, and generally accepted as the much-altered remains of that family's Murano villa.[9] The present house consists solely of a modest two-storey wing onto the quay, of which the ground floor is an open colonnade of medieval origin. It supports a single upper floor containing one larger room and an ancillary room; the fenestration here is probably of the seventeenth century, although the façade is crowned by a stone cornice gutter that is certainly medieval, like the arcade. There is a rear wing behind the screen wall, but the house has been subjected to so much later alteration that no conclusions may be drawn as to its original configuration.

We may conclude this section by mention of a fine arcaded house, but one whose

[9] Zanetti, *Guida di Murano*, p. 120.

131 Murano: house at no. 36 Fond. Cavour: façade to the Grand Canal. The house is gothic in origin, with a colonnade closely resembling those to the Corner and Obizzi houses. The windows were remodelled in the early sixteenth century.

132 Murano: house at no. 2a Fond. Giustinian, another much altered medieval house on a colonnade. The original stone cornice is still visible.

133 Murano: the 'house of Andrea Navagero', a villa with a long, complex history of alteration and adaptation. Photograph taken before its major restoration in 1984–5.

history is even more difficult to deduce than those discussed above. This is the large house at no. 60–2 Fondamenta Navagero and often referred to as the villa of Andrea Navagero, the famous scholar, writer and humanist, whom we will meet again a little later.[10] Navagero was born in Venice in 1483 of a patrician family and had an important political career (he was at one time ambassador to Spain), as well as being a major influence on an entire generation of scholars. Navagero certainly owned a fine villa in this locality although there is no direct evidence that this house was indeed his. Navagero's villa was noted for its garden and arboretum which, like those of the nearby Trevisan and Pesaro villas, ran down to the edge of the open lagoon.

The house at no. 60 has recently been comprehensively restored (1984–5). Prior to this it had deteriorated considerably and the ground-floor arcade has been rebuilt using some of the original materials. The *palazzo* is on two storeys with a broad façade and a small central dormer in the roof flanked by volutes of rendered brick. The ground floor has a full-width colonnade of seven bays, with semicircular brick arches on stone columns. On the *piano nobile* there is a slightly asymmetrical arrangement of seven windows, all with semi-circular heads, and two of which have small balconies. It has been suggested that the house is of early medieval origin, and it has certainly undergone various alterations over

[10] However, Zanetti does not agree with this location and consigns the Navagero house to a site roughly opposite S. Donato in the parish of S. Martino (ibid. p. 155).

the centuries. De' Barbari shows the house in a very simplified form; until its recent restoration some of the arches to the arcade were of gothic, pointed profile, and it is thus very difficult to determine the original date of construction of this colonnade – the first-floor windows seem to be sixteenth-century adaptations of earlier (presumably gothic) windows.

The overall form of the house thus has features that link it not only with the local tradition of two-storey houses with arcades but also with the larger, later houses such as the nearby Pesaro and Cappello villas. These two both have a strong horizontal emphasis to their façades, like the 'Navagero' house and all three are characterised by a series of well-spaced single-light windows, features that are at variance with the 'mainstream' *palazzo-fòntego* tradition.

In all three houses there is a distinct lack of emphasis on the central *androne* and *pòrtego* and hence very little centralisation of the façade; the only central features on the 'Navagero' house is the small roof dormer, while the Pesaro villa has only a stone balcony to indicate the position of the *pòrtego* within.

Other medieval houses and fragments

There are half a dozen or so smaller medieval houses at Murano as well as a handful that retain some slight evidence of their medieval origins. The most noteworthy of the former is the house known as Palazzo Bertolini or Andreotta, at no. 37 Fondamenta Vetrai. It can be dated with reasonable confidence to the middle or latter part of the fifteenth century; the Bertolini were a glassmaking clan and Zanetti, writing in 1866, described the house then as still being in their ownership.

The *palazzo* today is only two storeys high, and was either never completed or was later modified and the upper storey or storeys removed. Above the *piano nobile* is a double-pitched roof where there was clearly intended to be another floor or floors. On the quay there is a large and imposing square gothic portal, which also suggests a completed *palazzo* of some size; there is also a second medieval doorway on the left side of the façade. On the *piano nobile* there is a very fine central three-light window to the *pòrtego* and two pairs of single lights, all surrounded by the narrow frame of stone characteristic of the later fifteenth century; the window heads, too, have stone *fioroni* typical of the period. When completed the house would have been similar in size to the Foscari, and was thus a third example of the mature gothic *palazzo* of the city-centre type, and possibly built on four storeys.

While the Bertolini house is a *palazzo* of some importance, the remaining gothic examples are all far more modest and give some idea of the social range that could be found here during the fourteenth and fifteenth centuries. Two of these lesser houses are also on Rio dei Vetrai; the first, at no. 14–15, is a three-storey house much restored in later periods. The chief gothic features that survive are a three-light window to the first floor with a balcony, and a two-light window adjacent to it; all of the other windows are much later restorations. This was a compact town house with an asymmetrical plan as a result of its narrow site; there was only room for one of the side wings to the *pòrtego*. The only other surviving medieval detail is the typical diamond-pattern stone cornice.

134 Murano: Palazzo Bertolini or Andreotta on Rio dei Vetrai; detail of the façade. A very fine house of the fifteenth century, with a characteristic square portal, and three-light window to the first-floor *pòrtego*.

Further down the *rio*, on the other side, is a rare example of a small medieval house, although again much restored. This is at no. 61 Fondamenta Manin, and is on two floors, the lower of which is a shop. The upper storey retains two well-preserved gothic windows, trilobate in style and thus probably of the fifteenth century. It was possibly built by one of the less wealthy glass families and may be compared with the other medieval cottage on Fondamenta S. Martino. This latter house is slightly larger; again it is on only two floors but the plan is broader, with three gothic lights to the first floor and a central entrance below. We see here, therefore, a symmetrical house of very modest overall dimensions, examples of which are rare in the villages.

Our penultimate medieval house was not built as a private dwelling but as a hospice dedicated to SS Pietro e Paolo;[11] it stands at no. 15–16 Fondamenta Cavour and was founded in 1348 by Nicolò Condulmer and Paolo Signol as a shelter for the poor and

[11] Ibid. p. 44.

135 Murano: houses at nos. 14–15 and 17–26 Fond. dei Vetrai. That on the left is a much restored *palazzetto* of the later fourteenth or fifteenth century.

136 Murano: group of small houses on Fond. S. Martino. That on the right is a rare survivor, a small medieval house.

137 Murano: house at no. 15–16 Fond. Cavour, originally a hospice dedicated to SS Pietro e Paolo. Three medieval windows and the cornice have survived later alterations.

destitute of the island.[12] It has been greatly altered over the centuries and it is not easy to reconstruct its original form; the ground floor is at present a shop, while the first-floor chapel is now an apartment. The only notable medieval features remaining on the exterior are three gothic windows, two on the front façade and one on the side.

Finally, we have a house on Fondamenta Navagero, at no. 51, a few metres from the 'Navagero' house, the last to show clear evidence of its medieval origins. It may be described as a *palazzetto* since, although in poor condition, it was significantly larger than the houses just discussed. It is built on two floors, of which the lower has been much altered; however, there is a fine five-light gothic window to the first floor, and an adjacent single light.[13] The house represents what was probably a fairly typical residence of the Murano *borghesia* in the fourteenth and fifteenth centuries, although today it is an almost unique survivor of the genre.

This surviving handful of medieval houses at Murano is particularly valuable since there are so few houses of the period in any other lagoon community. They do not allow us to paint a detailed picture of medieval Murano, but merely to sketch the outline of this sizeable and flourishing community in the period before it was transformed by the Venetian nobility into their own 'garden suburb'.

---

[12] Ibid, p. 117.
[13] Arslan (*Venezia Gotica*, p. 153) is inclined to date this house, like those of the Corner and Sodeci, to the fourteenth century. All of the first-floor windows have trilobate heads similar to those of the former house.

138 Murano: house at no. 51 Fond. Navagero, a modest *palazzetto* with an asymmetrical plan, but a fine five-light window to the *piano nobile*.

2 The continuing villa tradition

Patrician interest in Murano as a place in which to build a villa – a retreat from the pressures of political life of S. Marco – seems to have begun towards the end of the fifteenth century, although we cannot document its origin with accuracy because of the many close proprietary ties that had already bound the two communities together before this new-found interest. Zanetti mentions, for example, that as early as 1317 Bianca Dolfin and the Donà family both owned property here, the latter with a number of houses and an orchard at S. Donato. Some decades later the Giustinian and Boldù clans also had lands at Murano and in 1411 the Amadi owned a fine palace with a garden which in that year was given over for the use of a group of monks who had fled from the war zone between the *Serenissima* and the Hungarians.[14]

By the last decades of the fifteenth century there were several fine houses here, although still *palazzi* in character rather than villas, and still gothic in style. By the early sixteenth century, though, the island had become highly favoured for the purpose of the *villeggiatura* and this popularity was largely retained for the rest of the century.[15] Indeed, by 1600 there was hardly a major site undeveloped on any of the quays along the Grand Canal, which was now lined with fine villas, many with extensive gardens behind them.

[14] Zanetti, *Guida di Murano*, pp. 278, *et seq.*
[15] For details of the landed interests at Murano the essential sources are the registers of the *Dieci Savii sopra le Decime*, and esp. the following: A.S.V. Dieci Savii B. 459 (for the Estimo of 1581), B. 461 (for the Redecima of 1661), and B. 472 for that of 1740.

Unfortunately, Murano's later history, its decline in the seventeenth century and complete stagnation and decay in the eighteenth and nineteenth centuries mean that many of these villas have now been lost, and we thus have to attempt a reconstruction of the island's appearance at its peak of patrician popularity from only a small number of surviving examples.

Although Murano is very close to Venice, it was not really feasible for the nobility to live there permanently and commute to S. Marco. The unique character of Venetian government meant that every adult male noble was (at least theoretically) obliged to take some part in the government process, even if it amounted to no more than nominal attendances of the Maggior Consiglio. Many, of course, particularly those with serious political ambition, were at the Palazzo Ducale almost every day, serving on various committees, the Senate or the Council of Ten. Almost all government departments were either in the Palazzo itself, in the buildings around the Piazza or at Rialto; it was thus essential that the nobles lived within easy travelling distance of the city centre.

However, it became the practice for a number of committees and agencies to suspend their sessions for some weeks in the summer, and this gave the opportunity for patricians to leave S. Marco, sometimes for just a few days, sometimes for a month at a time, and apart from the Giudecca, the closest place to which they could escape was Murano. It had many advantages, chiefly convenience, coupled with the fact that the island was not yet developed to any degree approaching the density in the city centre. One might have thought that the presence of several dozen glassworks was a deterrent to such colonisation, but they were mostly very small, and although economically very important, they only occupied a minor part of the island. Naturally, the patricians had the wealth and influence to develop Murano much as they wished, since apart from the glass community, the only other important inhabitants were the monks of several large monasteries.[16]

These latter institutions, however, undoubtedly added to the attractions of Murano, since they were havens of peace and tranquillity away from the noisy, crowded city, and with their cloisters and herb gardens provided an ideal companion setting for the noble villas and their own gardens and orchards. So it was that in the last two or three decades of the fifteenth century the nobility invested more and more money and effort in developing Murano as a weekend and summer retreat. The da Mula and Foscari *palazzi* are today the only survivors from the earlier period of patrician house-building, although several

[16] Marin Sanudo gives a list of these extensive Church interests at the beginning of the sixteenth century, which is worth quoting in full:

    Santa Chiara, monache de San Francesco osservante
    San Piero martire, frati di San Domenego osservanti
    San Steffano preti
    San Ciprian abbatia in vita, frati
    Santa Maria di Anzoli, monastero osservante, viveno d'intrada; de berretin
    San Bernardo, monasterio conventual di monache
    San Donado, chiesa cathedral, ha do corpi santi
    San Mathia, frati di San M(ichele), ordine camaldulense
    San Mafio, monasterio conventual de San Benedetto
    San Giacomo, monasterio osservante de San Benedetto
    San Zuanne, una scuola di battudi
    San Salvador (—)
    San Martin, parocchia, monasterio observante
    San Marco e Santa Margarita monasterio osservante di (—)
    (Codice Correr, Cicogna 970, published in *La Città di Venetia*, A. C. Aricò ed., Milan 1980; pp. 201–2).

written sources, as well as de' Barbari's illustration, indicate that there were about a dozen or so large *palazzi* by the end of the century, most of them on the Grand Canal and the Canale di S. Giovanni.

Most of these houses still closely resembled those in the city centre, albeit on a slightly more modest scale. They were compact, foursquare houses, usually on three storeys and with quite conventional tripartite patterns of planning and fenestration. This is not at all surprising since the concept of such a villa was still a very new one and it was natural that for a time traditional urban *palazzo* forms should be closely followed.

Already, then, by the 1480s and 1490s Murano was acquiring its reputation as an oasis of verdure and tranquillity. However, the houses and gardens that were developed there in ever larger numbers in the new century were not intended purely for indolence and relaxation; the builders of several of these villas were men of exceptional intellectual ability, and Murano's gardens rapidly became meeting-places for writers, philosophers and humanists, who made the island an important centre of academic and intellectual life.

Nicolò Priuli's house was described in 1495 as being 'Paradise on Earth by reason of the purity of the air and its fine prospect . . . a place of nymphs and demigods . . .'.[17] Among those who frequented this particular oasis were Cornelio Gastaldi and Caio Licinio but the house and garden of Andrea Navagero was perhaps the most famous of all. Navagero himself was one of the most influential writers of the early sixteenth century, responsible, as Sansovino noted, for 'ten works of history in Latin' as well as numerous essays and epic poems.[18] He composed funeral orations on the deaths of such notable figures as Caterina Cornaro, Queen of Cyprus, and among his official duties Navagero was guardian of the Nicene Library and the state-appointed historian of the Republic. He made this small island one of the most important centres of intellectual life in western Europe for some years until his premature death in 1529. In 1500 Navagero founded a classical academy with Pietro Bembo and others, giving active support to Aldo Manuzio, whose world-famous printing press and publishing house became the chief centre for the dissemination of classical texts in the first decades of the sixteenth century.[19]

Murano's considerable importance in this period was thus manifested not solely in the physical environment of villas and rapidly developing gardens, but also in the intangible sphere of intellectual achievement. The two fields were closely complementary: Navagero's interest in botany and his development of a serious analytical study of horticulture is only one of the many facets of the intellectual climate of the time, expressed in a widespread desire for understanding the natural order and for the classification and rationalisation of natural phenomena. This same approach led to a fuller appreciation of the ways in which man's own immediate environment could be controlled, shaped and improved; hence not only the great importance of the garden here at Murano, but also the only slightly later attempts to develop a better integration of villa and garden, one as a natural extension of the other, and both of them decorated and ornamented with *logge*, statuary, bowers, 'temples' and other visual delights and devices. Some of these gardens

---

[17] Zanetti, *Guida di Murano*, p. 280.

[18] *Venetia Città Nobilissima* . . . book XIII, p. 594.

[19] Zanetti, *Guida di Murano*, pp. 155, 281 and 285. For Manuzio's rôle in *quattrocento* Venetian humanism, see V. Branca, 'Ermolao Barbaro and late *quattrocento* Venetian humanism' in *Renaissance Venice*, J. R. Hale ed. (London 1973) pp. 218, *et seq.*

were already well established by the end of the fifteenth century; Pietro Casola, writing in 1494, describes the 'many things that one can say about this place (Murano), and of its beauty and amenity, surrounded by water and with so many beautiful gardens . . .'.[20]

Among the other noble clans already well established here in the new century was the Grimani family; they owned two houses at Murano by the 1520s, one next to the nunnery of S. Chiara on the east side of Rio dei Vetrai, and the other nearby, later owned by the Obizzi. Both had notable gardens, and the former *casino* was owned by Cardinal Domenico Grimani, who died in 1523 leaving his extensive collection of bronzes and marble statuary (much of it Roman) to the adjacent nunnery, from which the collection was later dispersed. The Grimani villa later passed to the Mocenigo and in Zanetti's day was still standing.

But probably the most notable patrician clan represented at Murano was the Corner or Cornaro, who owned no less than four substantial houses, two of which were sumptuous villas. One of them stood at S. Salvatore, a little west of S. Donato, and probably faced the northern reach of the Canale di S. Donato in a zone of the island that was far more important then than it is today.[21] It was owned by the S. Maurizio branch of this numerous clan and stood until about 1808 when it was demolished. Zanetti's description of this and the second Corner villa is succinct and useful:

> The place of resort of the Cornaro family, as is well known, was the house of the Queen of Cyprus and was truly splendid. It was in the form of two magnificent structures, each one of which alone formed a sumptuous palace fit for a prince. These two buildings were about a quarter of a mile distant from each other; and they were united by means of a great long gallery, ornately decorated, which was built on an arcade of majestic arches. The first of these palaces, built in a fine Roman [i.e., Renaissance] style, was remodelled in 1605 by Scamozzi, and the appearance of which has been preserved by Coronelli . . .

Scamozzi's remodelling produced a villa in the Palladian 'temple' manner, on three storeys, with a low ground floor, a spacious *piano nobile* and an attic. In the centre of the symmetrical façade was a classical portico two storeys high, and with hexastyle columns probably of the Corinthian order, surmounted by a triangular pediment. The whole façade was rusticated and the general appearance similar to Scamozzi's surviving Villa Molin near Padua.

Zanetti continues:

> [the villa] stood on the outer point of the parish of S. Salvatore, exactly opposite the monastery of S. Mattia; the other [villa] stood on the Grand Canal on the quay of S. Maria degli Angeli, having on the opposite bank on the left side the notable form of Palazzo da Mula and on the right the ancient abbey of S. Cipriano. The gallery from the *palazzo* at S. Salvatore thus ran along the left wall of the monastery and church of S. Bernardo, crossing the campo of that name; and following the edge of the lagoon on the right, finally connected with the other palace . . .
>
>   The area where the game of football was played was flanked by an ornate terrace for the spectators, a great fountain with 24 jets of sweet water, a grand triumphal arch, a statue that was almost lifelike, representing the Queen of Cyprus crowned and with her sceptre, and another statue opposite representing Marco Cornaro, father of Caterina . . . [of the two houses] the *palazzo* of S. Salvatore was the most notable and the greatest.

---

[20] Zanetti, *Guida di Murano*, p. 282
[21] See De' Barbari, who shows several large houses in the zone beyond S. Donato. See also Goy, *Chioggia*, p. 242.

This latter villa was almost abandoned when Temanza described it in 1778 and Zanetti states that it was demolished in about 1800 after having been used as a barracks by French troops. The house at S. Maria degli Angeli was lost a few years later. Caterina Cornaro had returned to the capital from Cyprus in 1489, and spent some time here before her sadly enforced permanent exile at Asolo. It has been said that she was a notable patron of the arts and intellectual life; although her direct contribution is debatable it is certain that her presence at Murano acted as an additional catalyst to Murano's development for the *villeggiatura*, as her move to Asolo similarly affected that town; Pietro Bembo, for example, was a regular visitor to both places.[22]

The S. Salvatore house was still in active use a century later when Scamozzi remodelled it, and described it as a 'casa molto honorevole riformata da noi con giardini per delitie . . .'.[23] Albrizzi, writing in 1740, also confirmed that the 'palazzi Cornaro di Murano con la galleria di circa mezzo miglio furono innalzate dal cav. Giovanni Cornaro . . .'[24]

We may summarise here a few of the other lost sixteenth-century villas of the island, although the list is almost certainly not exhaustive. Bartolomeo Moro had a villa adjacent to the Pontelongo, and several other clans owned houses at S. Stefano nearby, including the Lippomano, Badoer, Grimani and Querini. The Erizzo and Mocenigo built villas at S. Maria degli Angeli and the Morosini, Gussoni and Barbo had properties in various other parts of the island, all of them long disappeared and some impossible to locate with precision. Notes on a few of these houses may be found in Appendix I.

As we suggested above, the famous gardens of Murano served two functions: one was simply to provide an attractive setting conducive to entertainment and intellectual gathering, and thus to a significant extent expressive of the environmental philosophies of the time; the other was for scientific botanical research. Andrea Navagero was by no means the only Venetian to devote considerable energy to such investigation and to the collection of rare plants from many parts of the world. Pietro and Francesco Morosini similarly formed important collections of foreign flora and Zanetti notes that when Alfonso d'Este established his own arboretum (which some have claimed to have been the first in Italy) he was advised to go to Murano to the orchards of Cornaro and Morosini for advice and assistance. Marco Cornaro sent plant specimens back from many parts of the Middle East, while Navagero acquired species from as far as India.

When we examine the villas themselves, we find that so many have been lost that it is sadly very difficult today to reconstruct the appearance of the island in detail even at the end of the sixteenth century and more difficult still to picture Murano in the first decades of this key century. Today we are left with a small random collection of surviving houses, some quite atypical of the genre; any general conclusions on their stylistic development must thus be made with considerable caution. The villas that remain vary considerably in their massing, scale and proportions; some have compact 'urban' plans and are thus *palazzetti* rather than villas. Others, of similar size, have quite different proportions, far more linear and 'suburban' in their appearance, while others again fall somewhere between these two forms.

---

[22] Bembo was Caterina's nephew. See Zanetti, *Guida di Murano*
[23] V. Scamozzi, *Idea dell'Architettura Universale* (Venice 1615) part I, book III, chapter 14, p. 280.
[24] Zanetti, *Guida di Murano*, p. 284.

Stylistically the Murano villa of the very late fifteenth and sixteenth centuries has several features that place it apart from the other substantial Renaissance houses elsewhere in the lagoon. These villas were built by the nobility, in many cases by the wealthiest and most intellectually sophisticated members of the Republic's ruling oligarchy; they thus represented the most advanced artistic tastes of the time. By contrast, the *case padronali* of Pellestrina, some of which are similar in size to Murano's villas, were built by successful farmers, whose aesthetic sensibilities (though not lacking) were far removed from those of the Corner or Morosini.

Murano's position as a garden suburb of the capital thus ensured that there would be no time delay between the development of Renaissance theories of architecture in Venice itself and their enthusiastic adoption here. By the middle of the sixteenth century most of Murano was a fiefdom of the nobility, the villas representing the development of Renaissance design from the light elegant detailing of the Soranzo house (clearly of Lombard inspiration, and built at the turn of the century) to the mature and classical monumentality of the Trevisan palace of the late 1550s.[25]

The earliest fully Renaissance houses that survive today are probably the first of the two Soranzo houses (on the Canale di S. Giovanni) and the two Contarini villas, both on Rio dei Vetrai. The first dates from around 1500 and shows features that are typically mature – although chronologically quite early – examples of the Lombard Renaissance. However, here and elsewhere, despite the clarity and maturity of the new classical detailing, the framework of the villa still closely follows the ancient *palazzo-fòntego* tradition of the capital. Amost all of the surviving sixteenth-century houses, with the notable exception of the Trevisan, employ entirely traditional tripartite plans, and their façades, too, are firmly based on historical models in their pattern of fenestration.

The different rôle of the Murano villa, compared with that of the city *palazzo*, is expressed in ways other than a major reappraisal of the form of the house. The *palazzo-fòntego* had already served as a model for all of the upper levels of society for well over 200 years and it was clearly capable of adaptation to more leisurely functions, leaving the plan virtually unchanged. It is in the number of storeys, in the overall proportions and in the pattern of use of the rooms that the different function of the suburban villa is expressed. For example, many villas were built on only two storeys and the proportions of the façade are thus quite different from those of the city *palazzo*, by this time usually built on three or four storeys. A city palace thus has a façade that is usually square or nearly square, whereas at Murano proportions are often in the order of $1\frac{1}{2}$ to 1 and there are even a few examples of villas (such as the Mocenigo on the Giudecca) of more pronounced horizontality, which approaches $2\frac{1}{2}$ to 1.

The suburban Renaissance villa clearly had no need of a ground floor devoted to trade and commerce as did the city *palazzo*; when built on two storeys, therefore, in most cases the lower consisted of the main hall and rooms for entertaining, while the first floor contained the family's apartments. This is a partial reversal of the traditional *palazzo* arrangement, where the first floor, the *piano nobile*, was the storey for 'public' and social

[25] Most of our observations on Murano also apply to the Giudecca, as we noted above. For further notes on the latter island see Goy, *Chioggia*, pp. 235, *et seq*. See also Bassi, *Palazzi* (1976) pp. 520 and 524, for the Vendramin and Mocenigo villas there.

use. The chief reason for siting the main hall and dining rooms of the villas on the ground floor, of course, was ease of access to the garden, which was often approached by an open *loggia*, a colonnade or some other device that formed a transitional space between inside and outside. With such importance attached to the garden, the rear façade was designed with as much care as that to the canal in front, and in a few examples a first-floor *loggia* was built on top of the lower one so that views of the garden could be obtained from the private apartments.

This two-storey arrangement was not universal, however. There are several sixteenth-century houses built on three floors, and where traditional planning is retained. Here the ground floor remains of lesser importance and is still occupied by ancillary and service accommodation, or even, in a few cases, by retail shops. (This was not uncommon practice in the city, where a *palazzo* may have had its landward façade onto a busy shopping street.) The first floor thus remained the traditional *piano nobile* while the second contained bedrooms for the family. This arrangement naturally gave no direct access to the garden from the *piano nobile* and it is probable that such houses did not have extensive gardens; there was certainly little room for them on either side of Rio dei Vetrai, the most densely built-up zone in Murano.

Other surviving villas do not fall easily into either of these two broad categories; the Pisani house, for example, is a modest three-storey villa certainly of noble origin but very simple in appearance. A different type again is the house at no. 31 Fond. Navagero, which is on only two floors but has a long principal façade of seven bays and is closer in spirit to one of the lesser villas along the Brenta Canal than to almost any in the lagoon. Palazzo Pesaro, on the same quay, is different again, with a broad, high façade on three floors and a long row of single-light windows.

We can see, therefore, that the surviving larger houses at Murano form a disparate collection about which generalisation is extremely difficult; we will examine them in more detail below.

3 The early Renaissance villas

The Contarini houses on Rio dei Vetrai
(Nos. 4–6 and 27–28 Fondamenta dei Vetrai, w. side)

The first of these two houses has recently been restored and is at present (1986) the headquarters of a glassworks. It stands at the southernmost end of the canal in a prominent position and with fine views across the lagoon to S. Michele and Venice. The villa is an important example of the Lombard Renaissance style and can probably be dated to the first couple of decades of the sixteenth century. It may indeed have been built by the Contarini and was certainly intended as a *casa di delizie*; it later passed to the Mazzolà, a wealthy glassmaking clan specialising in crystal and mirrors. A plaque with the Mazzolà arms can be seen on the right side of the façade.

The house has a broad, spacious façade on three floors, and symmetrical fenestration. In the centre of the *piano nobile* is a tall, five-light window surrounded by a frame of stone and, directly above, a similar window lights the second floor. Here is an example of a suburban villa that still follows the traditional city *palazzo* model in its vertical zoning, and

139 Murano: Palazzo Contarini on Rio dei Vetrai. A fine early sixteenth-century villa, recently restored. Despite its suburban site, it closely resembles contemporaneous city *palazzi*.

the ground floor is still occupied by ancillary accommodation. (It is regrettable that the recent restoration did not include the opening-up of some of the windows that at an earlier time had been filled in.)

The antecedents of this villa are the great city palaces and the tripartite form is rigorously followed here; however, the broad plan and the wide spacing of the fenestration produce a façade with far more horizontal emphasis than is usual in the city *palazzi*, and with overall proportions of more than 1½ to 1. It may be compared with the Soranzo villa on Fondamenta Colleoni, with which it is roughly contemporary and has a façade of similar proportions, although the latter house lacks the second storey.

140 Murano: the second Palazzo Contarini, later Mazzolà, also on Rio dei Vetrai. Similar to the first, it has two subsidiary floors below the *piano nobile*, and string-courses accentuate its horizontality.

The second Contarini house is frequently confused with the first in several guides to the island. Zanetti and Lorenzetti[26] both claim the same pattern of ownership for this house as for the first villa, that is, it was built by the Contarini and later acquired by the Mazzolà. The house has been considerably altered, however, and is at present the headquarters of Barovier e Toso, another important glassmaking company. Zanetti records that at one time a large stone shield with the arms of either the Contarini or the Mazzolà could be seen on the façade; today a small *scudo* shows the device of the Barovier family.

Like the first villa it was built in the early years of the sixteenth century in the Lombard Renaissance style; it is on four floors with two subsidiary storeys (ground and first), a *piano nobile* at second floor and a very modest attic above. The façade is generally simple and

[26] Lorenzetti, *Venezia*, p. 815.

141 Murano: detail of the façade of the second Contarini house. The decorative panels in low relief are below the sill of the *pòrtego* window and are characteristic of early Renaissance carving in the manner of the Lombardo.

restrained, all of the windows having plain rectangular surrounds with the exception of those to the *piano nobile* where there is a four-light central window and two pairs of flanking lights, all with semicircular heads. Again traditional arrangements are closely followed although the construction on four floors produces a very 'urban' quality in the house, and renders it a *palazzetto* rather than a villa.

As we have seen, the Rio dei Vetrai was the most densely developed part of Murano even in the medieval period, and by the early sixteenth century a few metres of frontage to the quay here were of considerable value. When de' Barbari recorded the appearance of the island in 1500 (before the present house was built) the west side of the *rio* was lined with a mixture of one-, two- and three-storey houses, but many of the smaller ones were replaced in the early decades of the new century by houses such as this one and those at nos. 35 and 39 (see below). All are evidence of notably increased density of development in the first half of the sixteenth century. There was little room here for more spacious villas such as we find being built in this period on Murano's Grand Canal, and most of the houses are compact in form. Only our first example, the Contarini house, has the appearance of a true villa, but this was the last house on the quay and had the advantage of an unusually large plot on which to be built.

The elements that both Contarini (and both Soranzo) houses have in common are the detailing of the windows, particularly those to the *piano nobile*. In all cases this detailing is Lombard in origin, that is, it derives at least to some extent from the motifs used by Codussi, the Lombardo and Buora families in the last decades of the previous century. The columns between the multi-light windows to the *pòrtego* all have capitals of a simplified Corinthian form, and the semicircular heads to the windows in this case also have a narrow, refined profile with characteristic 'shell' decoration.[27] The second Conta-

[27] Cf. the window heads at S. Maria dei Miracoli and esp. at S. Michele in Isola.

142 Murano: Villa Soranzo on the Grand Canal. Recently restored, this is perhaps the finest of the surviving sixteenth-century villas on the island.

rini house has a further element of such Lombard decoration in the form of a row of stone pilasters below the *pòrtego* windows; these panels are decorated with shallow relief carving typical of such work.[28]

The Soranzo villas

Fondamenta Colleoni 15–16 (Grand Canal, s. side)
Fondamenta S. Giovanni 7–8 (Canale di S. Giovanni, w. side)
The first of the two Soranzo villas, that on Fondamenta Colleoni, probably represents the sixteenth-century Murano villa in its purest form. It has recently been comprehensively restored, and was described by Zanetti as 'a *palazzo* in the Lombard style, of imposing construction, all built on arches in the Roman manner . . . in this house the family that built it sought refuge from the terrors of the plague. This palace, with its beautiful and extensive orchards, formerly the original gardens, was still owned by the patrician family until a few years ago . . .'.[29]

The restoration has made it possible once again to appreciate the fine proportions of this elegant house. Built on two storeys, it has a wide, spacious façade slightly asymmetrical in its fenestration. It conforms in general to the traditional tripartite form, although the prominent string courses and cornice give the façade a strong horizontal emphasis. The *pòrtego* is lit by a four-light window with a robust stone balcony, while the central portal has a square head and is flanked by two large square windows with their original fine

[28] Again, see the work of the Lombardo at S. Maria dei Miracoli.
[29] Zanetti, *Guida di Murano*, p. 65.

143 Murano: the second Soranzo villa, on Fond. S. Giovanni. It is probably slightly earlier in date than the other, and has two gothic windows in the attic. The façade is in very poor condition but was originally rendered in imitation of stonework, with prominent 'rustication'.

144 Murano: detail of the four-light window to the *piano nobile* of the second Soranzo villa. Although badly altered the refined Lombard detailing and proportions are still discernible.

wrought-iron grilles. The classical detailing is generally more 'Roman', more substantial than that to the other Soranzo villa or the two Contarini houses.

Of the two storeys, the *piano nobile* is the more important; the ground floor is chiefly given over to secondary accommodation, while the first floor contains an airy, light and spacious *salone* with its adjacent ante-rooms. The arrangement is a little surprising in that it offers no direct access from this *salone* to the garden, although a similar pattern of use is found at both the Pesaro and Cappello villas, and all three had gardens of some note. It is possible that the villa was only used for comparatively short sojourns and the ancillary accommodation was fairly limited.

In its appearance the Soranzo house is one of a small, well-defined group which includes the other Soranzo house nearby, as well as the Minelli and Mocenigo villas on the Giudecca; although the fenestration pattern on the last two examples is rather different, all three are distinguished by a close similarity of scale and proportion, by a strong horizontal emphasis and by their arrangement on only two storeys. In all cases the *piano nobile* remains in its traditional position on the first floor.

The second Soranzo house appears to be of slightly earlier date than the first, and stands not far from it. It probably dates from the last decade or so of the fifteenth century, and can be tentatively, but not positively, identified on de' Barbari's view of the island. The house has similar dimensions to the first Soranzo villa; again there are only two storeys although here there is also a dormer in the roof in which are inserted two very late gothic windows – the rest of the façade is fully Renaissance in character. The ground floor is entirely clad with Istrian stone (now in very poor condition) while the upper part of the façade is of brick, originally rendered in imitation of stonework, with prominent rustication. The elevation is symmetrical, apart from the later insertion of an additional doorway, and follows the tripartite form. As in the other Soranzo house a fine four-light window denotes the *pòrtego*, although it has been badly altered and the two outer lights filled in. Like the Contarini houses described above, the Soranzo shows the clear influence of the Lombard 'school' in its stone detailing, particularly in this originally very elegant four-light window and the fine surround to the main portal. The latter has a simple square head but the flanking pilasters have the rectangular fielding and central roundel motif, as well as the florid capitals, typical of the works of Lombardo, Codussi and their immediate followers.

Of the two Soranzo houses this one appears to have been the most important for pastoral escape from the city. Zanetti records that Jacopo Soranzo, senator and Captain of the Republic, passed the last years of his life here, and that the main hall was decorated with portraits of the most illustrious members of the family, all by leading artists of the day. The family apparently ceased using the villa in the seventeenth century, when they began renting it to local families.

In the early sixteenth century, however, the section of waterfront adjacent to the two Soranzo houses was one of the two most favoured zones of Murano for patricians to build their villas, the other being the Fondamenta Navagero. Between the Soranzo houses also once stood those of the Grimani, Morosini and Giustinian, all now lost.

4 The later-sixteenth-century villas: introductory note

The surviving later-sixteenth-century houses form a diffuse group that is difficult to classify. The group includes the monumental Palazzo Trevisan, a unique building not only to Murano but without peer throughout the lesser lagoon communities; other houses of the period include two other noble villas so much altered over the centuries that their original form is no longer clearly discernible. In the case of the Pesaro house there are traces of a gothic predecessor; in the Cappello, its medieval origins are fairly clear, although little in its outward appearance today either indicates its origin or its sixteenth-century modernisation. There are also several more typically late-sixteenth-century houses, however, that may be compared with their contemporaries in the city centre; among them are the Correr-Grimani house and that at no. 39 Fondamenta dei Vetrai.

5 Palazzo Trevisan

While the *palazzo* of the Da Mula is indisputably the finest gothic house at Murano, the Trevisan is undoubtedly the most important house of the Renaissance. It is correctly described as a *palazzo* rather than a villa because although it was specifically designed and built for the *villeggiatura* it is in appearance quintessentially an urban building, a palace of monumental presence and great architectural importance.

A brief outline of the history of this notable house may be summarised here;[30] Camillo Trevisan was born in 1515, the son of Bernardo, who was from a branch of the clan that had been excluded from the nobility in the famous *Serrata* of 1297; Camillo thus had the status of a citizen, although this in no way detracted from the extremely high regard in which he was held by his contemporaries. He was a brilliant advocate and one of the finest orators of his generation; Francesco Sansovino, his contemporary, referred to him as 'riverito per lo vostro valore, amato per la vostra bontà, et lodato per l'affabil vostra maniera da tutte le genti'.

In 1555, at the age of 40, Camillo inherited the site at Murano from his aunt Orsa; on the site was 'una corte cum alcune casette'[31] which he cleared so that he could immediately begin work on the *palazzo* that we see today. It was probably completed quite rapidly, within three years or so, and in around 1558 Camillo took up residence there, where he entertained many notable guests until his somewhat premature death in October 1564. The house then passed to his sister Maria, who leased it to some of the wealthiest of the noble clans of the Republic, including the Donà and Da Lezze; all of them further enriched what was already a remarkable house, and also further developed the large landscaped garden that extended to the edge of the lagoon.

The design of the *palazzo* has been a matter of scholarly debate almost continuously since soon after its completion four centuries ago. There have been attributions variously to Palladio, to Daniele Barbaro, Sansovino, Rusconi and Sanmicheli, although detailed examination still suggests that of these men, the first two were the most likely authors,

---

[30] Bassi, *Palazzi* (1976) pp. 528, *et seq.* See also G. M. Urbani de' Gheltof, *Il Palazzo di Camillo Trevisan a Murano* (Venice 1890); L. Olivato, 'Antonio Visentini su Palazzo Trevisan a Murano' in Bollettino C.I.S.A. (Vicenza 1972); A. Caiani, 'Un Palazzo Veronese a Murano' in *Arte Veneta* 1968.

[31] The ownership is recorded in A.S.V. *Dieci Savii, Estimo* of 1537 B. 58. See also Bassi, *Palazzi* (1976).

145 Murano: Palazzo Trevisan – main façade onto the Canale di S. Donato. The monumental elevation today has a much more severe appearance than originally intended, when much of its surface was frescoed.

146 Murano: Palazzo Trevisan – detail of the central part of the façade with the great *Serliana* to the first-floor hall.

possibly in collaboration, and with the close involvement of Veronese and Vittoria, both of whom are known to have worked on the house.

In 1890 De' Gheltof observed that

> Palladio had a number of followers, mostly of poor imagination . . . among the best of these was Daniele Barbaro . . . who trained in the Faculty of Arts at the university in Padua . . . a mathematician, philosopher, antiquarian, who wrote a Commentary on the Rhetoric of Aristotle, a Treatise on Perspective and had an outstanding interest in architecture, having also written a Commentary on Vitruvius.

Barbaro was a notable Renaissance scholar and humanist, whose own direct involvement in the decorative arts reached its highest expression in the magnificent villa built for him and his brother by Palladio at Maser, and which was also decorated with elaborate stucco work by Vittoria, while all of the principal rooms were frescoed by Veronese.

The debate over the design of Palazzo Trevisan centres chiefly on the possible degree of involvement of Palladio himself, and the extent to which the design may have been a collaboration between Palladio and Barbaro; despite his other accomplishments there is no indication that Trevisan himself had any gifts in this sphere. De' Gheltof inclined to the conclusion that Palladio may well have furnished some initial ideas or sketches, perhaps preliminary plans, which were then 'worked up' by another hand, possibly that of

Barbaro.[32] Palladio was engaged on Barbaro's villa at Maser in about 1555–7, and the villa was substantially complete by 1558; the Trevisan house was thus built at almost exactly the same time, and when Francesco Sansovino described it in 1562 it had been complete for about three or four years. It is probable that the basic structure was finished by 1557 or 1558 but that the decorative internal finishes continued for a further year or two thereafter. It thus seems likely that both Veronese and Vittoria transferred their attentions here almost immediately after their work at Maser was completed, although Veronese's work at Murano was by no means as extensive or important as his great cycle of frescoes at the Villa Barbaro.[33]

Apart from the close personal connections between a number of these important figures in the period from about 1555 to 1559, however, the physical evidence of Palladio's involvement at Murano is circumstantial; there is no documentary evidence, although there are two aspects of the palace's design that have suggested his hand, one general and one more particular.

The more general aspect is the overall plan of the house and specifically the use of a transverse hall in the centre of the plan, with its semicircular 'apsidal' ends. Such a hall is not a traditional Venetian feature and there are no precedents for it in the noble palaces of the city centre. Although there is no such hall at Maser, Palladio used such a device in a number of projects, some of them completed buildings and others simply sketches, preliminary designs that were never executed. Of the completed works, the most prominent example is Palazzo Chiericati at Vicenza, begun in 1550, and in which the main *salone* of the house has its long axis parallel to the main façade, behind the broad *loggia*, and is also given apsidal ends. Palazzo Valmarana (begun in *c.* 1565) also has a transverse *loggia* giving onto the central *cortile*, only the front half of which was ever completed.[34] In this case the *loggia* has square ends, but there are several other projects which include such a transverse space with twin apses, either as a *loggia* giving directly onto a *cortile* or as a room integrated within the body of the house;[35] among these we may cite the design for Palazzo Trissino as well as at least two sketches in the RIBA collection. One of these latter is attributable to the period around 1554 and would thus be chronologically suitable as a basis for the development of such a form here at Murano.

Palladio's known attempts to develop a *palazzo* design specifically for the Venetian environment are comparatively few, and none was executed to these designs. The best known is the project for a house (presumably on the Grand Canal) on page 72 of the second of the *Quattro Libri*. The proposal is noteworthy for the comparatively few concessions that it makes to the Venetian palace tradition of equal tripartite forms and fenestration patterns. It may be usefully compared with Serlio's proposals for the composition of Venetian palace façades in which these traditional forms are carefully taken into

32 Zanetti, *Guida di Murano*: ' . . . this beautiful structure built to the design of Andrea Palladio, or at least of his school . . .'
33 Bassi, *Palazzi* (1976) pp. 530, 538. Villa Barbaro is illustrated (not very accurately) by Palladio in the *Quattro Libri*, book II, p. 51. See general bibliog. to the present volume, and also G. Mazzariol, *Palladio a Maser* (Venice 1965). The best modern survey of his work is undoubtedly L. Puppi, *Andrea Palladio* (Milan 1977; new edn Milan 1986).
34 *Quattro Libri*, book II, pp. 6 and 16.
35 There are similar rooms in several unexecuted projects; see, for example, pp. 26 and 44 in book II of the *Quattro Libri*; see also Puppi, *Andrea Palladio*.

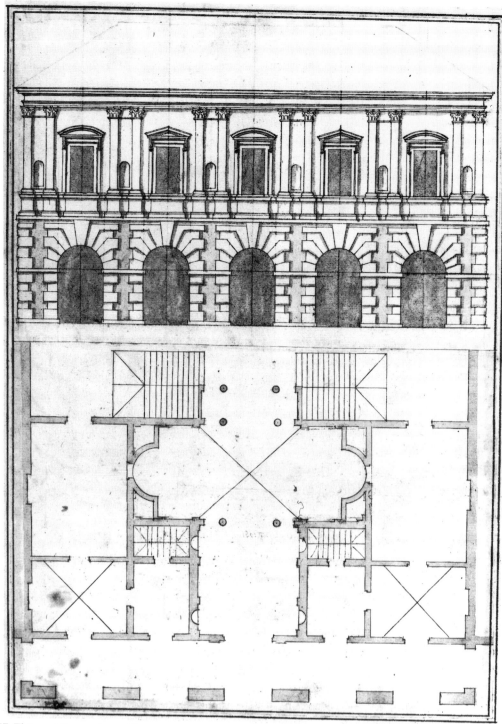

147 This and the next two illustrations show Palladio's development of the transverse hall or *loggia* as a key central element in planning houses and villas: plan and façade, possibly a preparatory drawing for Palazzo Civena Trissino at Vicenza. The *palazzo* was built after 1540. The most notable features of the plan are the continuous arcade along the street frontage and the large transverse central hall, with apsidal ends. The rear *loggia* is also slightly reminiscent of that at Murano (R.I.B.A., XVII.14).

220   *The architecture of the lagoon*

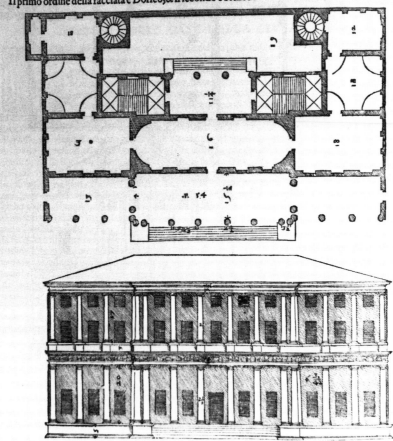

IN VICENZA ſopra la piazza, che uolgarméte ſi dice l'Iſola; ha fabricato ſecondo la inuen
tione,che ſegue,il Conte Valerio Chiericato,cauallier & gentil'huomo honorato di quella citta.Ha
queſta fabrica nella parte di ſotto una loggia dauanti, che piglia tutta la facciata : il pauimento del
primo ordine s'alza da terra cinque piedi:il che è ſtato fatto ſi per ponerui ſotto le cantine,& altri luo
ghi appartenenti al commodo della caſa, iquali non ſariano riuſciti ſe foſſero ſtati fatti del tutto ſot
terra ; percioche il fiume non è molto diſcoſto ; ſi anche acciocche gli ordini di ſopra meglio godeſ-
ſero del bel ſito dinanzi. Le ſtanze maggiori hanno i uolti loro alti ſecondo il primo modo dell'altez
ze de' uolti:le mediocri ſono inuoltate à lunette ; & hanno i uolti tanto alti quanto ſono quelli delle
maggiori. I camerini ſono ancor esſi in uolto, e ſono amezati.Sono tutti queſti uolti ornati di com-
partimenti di ſtucco eccellentiſſimi di mano di Meſſer Bartolameo Ridolfi Scultore Veroneſe; & di
pitture di mano di Meſſer Domenico Rizzo, & di Meſſer Battiſta Venetiano, huomini ſingolari in
queſte profesſioni. La ſala è di ſopra nel mezo della facciata : & occupa della loggia di ſotto la parte di mezo. La ſua altezza è fin ſotto il tetto : e perche eſce alquanto in fuori ; ha ſotto gli Angoli le
colonne doppie, dall'una e l'altra parte di queſta ſala ui ſono due loggie,cioè una per banda;lequali
hanno i ſoffitti loro , ouer lacunari ornati di belliſſimi quadri di pittura , e fanno belliſſima uiſta.
Il primo ordine della facciata è Dorico,& il ſecondo è Ionico.

SEGVE il diſegno di parte della facciata in forma maggiore.

148 Palladio: plan and principal façade of Palazzo Chiericati at Vicenza, from the *Quattro Libri* (Book 2, p. 6). The house has a broad but very shallow plan, and was built after 1550. The plan turns the traditional Venetian *androne* through 90°, and the hall (again with apsidal ends) lies parallel with the main façade. Again, beyond the hall is a narrower *loggia* giving onto the garden.

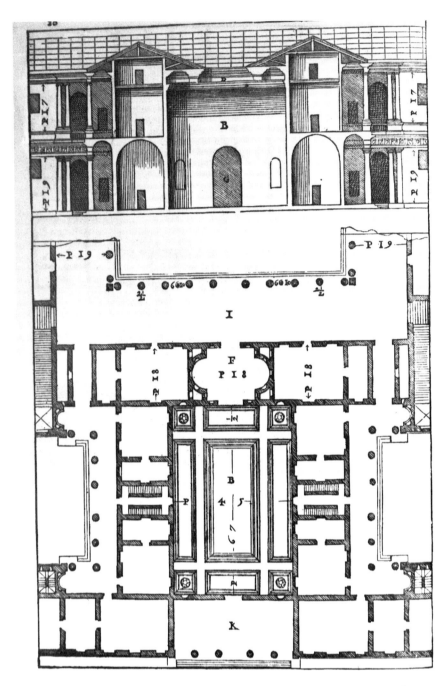

149 Palladio: the 'atrio Toscano', again from the *Quattro Libri* (Book 2 p. 26). Here the transverse hall is quite small and forms a lobby between the main hall and a spacious rear colonnade; again it has semicircular ends.

150 Murano: Palazzo Trevisan – drawing of the front façade by Visentini. The illustration is not entirely accurate, as he omits the rusticated quoins and the cornice is simplified (R.I.B.A. F.4 [22]).

consideration. Palladio's scheme has a deep, narrow plan but there is no long, central *androne*; instead we have a spacious entrance *loggia* to the canal, nearly square on plan and with four internal columns; beyond this there is a central hall from which the stairs and a small *cortile* are reached. At the rear is a larger *cortile* with colonnades at either end. Although the central axis of the *palazzo-fòntego* is retained, therefore, it is considerably modified and becomes a sequence of spaces – a notable Palladian device – rather than a simple *androne*. The façade, too, owes little to traditional types and the fenestration to the upper floors consists of a row of single lights, emphasis at the centre being provided by a projecting bay with a triangular tympanum. A slightly later project for a *palazzo* in the city (for which we have the façade only) has been dated by Ackerman to about 1570; in spirit it is more monumental and more akin to Sanmicheli's and Sansovino's great works than to any earlier local tradition. Grand and formal in concept, it has a rusticated ground floor and a giant order of applied columns to the two upper storeys. A giant order is another motif quite foreign to the Venetian tradition and was never used here by either Sansovino or Sanmicheli despite their foreign background and influences. However, Palladio respects the tripartite tradition here to the extent that the central *pòrtego* is denoted by a *Serliana* with symmetrical flanking wings. We may conclude, therefore, that Palladio made only limited concessions to the local tradition of façade composition and was clearly prepared to introduce elements which, although he had already used them on the Terraferma, were still alien to the lagunar vernacular.

Several aspects of the more detailed design of the Palazzo Trevisan also suggest links with Palladio. One of these is the frieze of stucco *paterae* on the rear *loggia* of the Murano house; these are very similar indeed to those on the Convento della Carità (now the Accademia) executed by Palladio in about 1561. Here they are in terracotta rather than stucco and may be seen above the ground-floor colonnade to the main *cortile*.[36] We may also note that the Tuscan capitals that support these two friezes are virtually identical. A further similarity of detailing is the balustrading to the first-floor windows at the Carità which again is very similar indeed to that on the great *Serliana* at Murano, and is of a profile that was only rarely used by Palladio himself. Despite these significant details, however, we have no direct or contractual evidence linking him with Murano, and so we may only speculate that he may have provided some preliminary designs, details or motifs, that were then adapted or incorporated by another.

Palazzo Trevisan has a compact plan and a similarly compact façade which is almost square.[37] Its appearance today is noble, grand and more than a little severe; however it must be recorded that much of the façade was originally decorated with frescoes by Prospero Bresciano and thus had a far lighter, more colourful appearance. Considerable imagination is therefore needed today to reconstruct this original elevation, although there is a watercolour (probably of the eighteenth century) in the Museo Correr that shows a reconstruction of Bresciano's scheme for the façade.[38] The fenestration is generally very simple with the exception of the great, lofty *Serliana* that lights the hall on the *piano nobile*. Below this window is a heavy stone balcony supported by extremely large, ponderous stone corbels. The main entrance is simple in appearance and modest in size; the only other notable features on the façade today are the rusticated stone quoins and the truly monumental roof cornice with its elaborate classical profile and considerable projection. All of the lesser windows have simple stone frames and sills, with no other decoration.

---

[36] The frieze is above the *loggia* on the garden façade.
[37] See esp. drawing nos. XVII 2v and XXII 20 in the R.I.B.A. collection. In both cases the transverse *loggia* occupies a similar position in the plan to that at Murano.
[38] See drawing no. C1.III,7377 in Museo Correr for the reconstruction of its original appearance. See also Bassi, *Palazzi* (1976) p. 536.

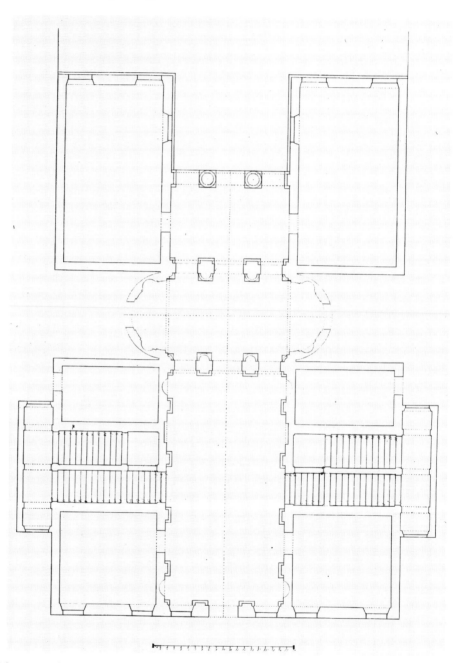

151 Murano: Palazzo Trevisan – ground-floor plan of the house, also by Visentini (R.I.B.A. F.4 [22]).

The façade is tripartite with three equal zones and the central *Serliana* is flanked on both sides by pairs of single windows positioned in the traditional Venetian manner, near the corners of the rooms behind them. Despite this noble simplicity, the fine proportions of the façade and in particular the monumental *Serliana* and the roof cornice indicate that this

152 Murano: Palazzo Trevisan – longitudinal section, again by Visentini. The main façade is to the right; the heavily rusticated columns to the *androne* are clearly shown, as is the apsidal end to the transverse hall, with a similar hall above it. To the left of these two halls are the superimposed *logge* facing the garden (R.I.B.A. F.4 [22]).

is by no means a typical mid-sixteenth century Venetian *palazzo*; the scale, too, is far more imposing than that of any other Murano house, and it quite dominates the waterfront and the adjacent substantial villas of the Pesaro and Cappello. It is a true *palazzo* transposed to the suburban quays of Murano and still today appears a little incongruous, too noble for its setting.

Even in its present poor condition, the interior confirms this first impression. The portal gives onto a central hall, with flanking rooms and the stair beyond, to the right. But this is not the long, narrow *androne* of the typical Venetian *palazzo*, as halfway down its length the transverse hall is inserted; beyond it again the *androne* terminates in an open *loggia* giving access to the garden. However, this *loggia* itself is deeply recessed from the plane of the rear elevation, with two large rooms projecting beyond it on either side, thus forming a central space which acts as a transitional zone between the house and the first large *cortile* of the garden beyond. We thus have a carefully contrived series of spaces which culminate in the garden and, at its far end, the open lagoon. The recessed rear *loggia* is a device that can be found elsewhere, for example at Villa Mocenigo on the Giudecca where the *androne* is shortened even more, to become a simple square hall, beyond which is a spacious *cortile*, colonnaded on three sides and with the fourth open to the garden.[39]

[39] The Mocenigo house may have been influenced by the plan of Pal. Trevisan as the former was probably not completed until the end of the sixteenth century.

Palazzo Trevisan has two principal storeys, both of equal height and importance, although this arrangement is not clear from the façade; above them is a lesser attic storey. This equality of importance of ground and first floor is in contrast to the traditional hierarchy of spaces in most palaces and villas; here, the ground floor is effectively the *piano nobile* since the main rooms for receiving and entertaining guests are located here, with direct access to the all-important garden. The plan of the first floor is almost identical to the ground floor and was occupied by Camillo's richly decorated and furnished private apartments.

The original elaborate interior finishes have been much altered over the centuries; many fine decorative features have been lost completely, and the general condition of the interior is very poor, although it is still possible to effect a comprehensive restoration programme, which is essential if further deterioration is to be prevented. The *androne* is framed by robust stone pilasters and flanked by doorway and niches originally containing statues. The ceiling is of coffered timber, although all of the original decoration is now lost. The *androne* gives onto the apsed transverse hall; again there are four niches that originally held statues and here again there is a fine timber ceiling, in this case a barrel-vault much of the decoration of which (by Zelotti) has survived intact. The Doric pilasters of this hall are repeated in the atrium beyond it, in which we find the terracotta frieze with the Palladian motifs noted above. The stuccoed relief panels at high-level in the atrium are by Vittoria and largely undamaged. In the room to the right was a fireplace of red Verona marble, also designed by Vittoria and executed by Francesco da Salò in 1557; the walls of this room were all originally frescoed by Veronese and were described by his contemporaries as a *capolavoro*, a masterwork; all are now gone. The room opposite was decorated by Zelotti and only faint traces of this work have survived today.

The first floor is reached by an imposing stair from the *androne*; the large *pòrtego* directly above it gives access to the upper apsed hall, also directly above the lower; this was the other room originally decorated by Veronese. The walls have been whitewashed but it is possible that the remains of these frescoes still lie beneath, as it was said that they did in the nineteenth century. The floors of both this room and the *androne* are both decorated with geometric designs in terracotta; the upper colonnade has been partly bricked-up as have two windows in the main hall.

Many more fine works of craftsmanship have been lost or dispersed. Trevisan had a rich collection of arms, tapestries, silks, damasks, framed pictures and other works, all of them long disappeared. The later history of the house shows its long, slow decline to its present deplorable condition. On the death of Maria Trevisan, it passed to Alessandro in 1608 and then to Marcantonio, who owned it at the time of the *Redecima* of 1661. In that year it was rented to Ludovico Widmann for 118 ducats per year; it remained the property of the Trevisan, however, until the middle of the eighteenth century. In 1740 the house passed to abbot Camillo Gaetano, who was the last male of the line; it then became the property of his sister, wife of Nicolo Donà, and when he died, it passed to the Maffetti and then to the Errera. While it remained in Trevisan hands it appears to have been well-maintained, but thereafter the condition of the *palazzo* deteriorated. It later passed to a private company and in 1848–9 was used as a barracks; thereafter its decline was very rapid.[40]

[40] Bassi, *Palazzi* and De' Gheltof, *Il Palazzo*.

Today it is owned by a glassmaking consortium; it is still structurally sound but much of the remaining decoration is in poor condition. The garden is now completely lost, its fountains and statuary broken or removed; much of its site is today occupied by glassmaking factories and sheds.

The frescoes that originally decorated the main façade of the house were already fading by the later seventeenth century and by the mid-eighteenth had virtually disappeared. It is to be hoped that the value of this fine house is appreciated by the authorities and that a comprehensive restoration is soon undertaken. Palazzo Trevisan is unquestionably the most important Renaissance house at Murano and its condition is a matter for considerable concern; its value lies not simply in the quality of its detailing and the nobility of its proportions, but as the finest surviving villa on the island it epitomises the most important era of Murano's history, when the island was a centre of the cultural and intellectual life of the Serenissima.

6 The later-sixteenth-century houses: a general survey

Immediately adjacent to the Trevisan *palazzo* are two other houses originally owned by the patriciate, but both of which have been much altered over the last four centuries. Their present appearance, however, is chiefly the result of sixteenth-century modifications and hence we may describe them here. The later history of both houses may be said to epitomise Murano's own decline and fall from prosperity.

Palazzo Pesaro stands next to the Trevisan house; it is probable that the present structure, which is largely of the sixteenth century, was remodelled from an earlier, medieval *palazzo*. There appears to have been a gothic house on the site in the first years of the *cinquecento*, although there are no medieval elements in the façade today. The villa is on three storeys and has a broad façade with no less than ten single-light windows to the *piano nobile*. These are not regularly spaced, however, and three of them are joined by a continuous robust stone balcony indicating the location of the main *salone* behind. This hall is not central on plan, and hence there are three windows on one side and four on the other. Both ground and second floors are of little importance; they both have simple square windows and even the portal to the quay is very modest.

The form of the house indicates a history of adaptation and modification, as does the structure of the roof, which suggests a later extension on one side. Nevertheless, the house is substantial and was of considerable importance in the sixteenth century; it is less imposing today chiefly because of the very poor condition of the main façade. However, we can see similarities in its proportions to the Mocenigo villa on the Giudecca and also with the country villa of the same family at Oriago, both of which houses have very broad façades with a large number of single-light windows. Such an arrangement remains rare in the lagoon, however, and it is a clear departure from the 'mainstream' of the Venetian tradition.

The detailed history of the Pesaro house is far from clear. Nonetheless, Zanetti claimed that it was originally 'decorated both inside and outside by the most celebrated painters of the sixteenth century; in particular the great hall was especially highly reputed'.[41] When

[41] Zanetti, *Guida di Murano*, p. 159.

153 Murano: Palazzo Pesaro on the Canale di S. Donato, next to Palazzo Trevisan. The façade is in poor condition but is still impressive by its size.

Zanetti wrote, all that remained of the decoration to the ceiling of this *salone* was a single oil painting, although traces of fresco were still visible behind the whitewash to the walls. The house also had a notable garden extending to the edge of the lagoon, like that of the adjacent Trevisan house. The villa declined with the general loss of interest in Murano by the patriciate in the later seventeenth and eighteenth centuries, and there is little in the appearance of the house today, other than its size, to indicate its earlier more illustrious history.

Palazzo Cappello stands next to the Pesaro house again; unfortunately, it has suffered even more than the former villa from alteration, deterioration and neglect, although its present condition is fairly sound. It was also originally a gothic house, and several traces of the medieval fabric may still be found; on the main façade we may note the survival of the stone roof cornice, the corbels that support the first-floor balcony, and the door surround. Zanetti states that the whole of the front façade was rebuilt, however (presumably reusing these elements), and that the original façade was built on the water's edge with a spacious colonnade.

In addition to the reused medieval elements on the front elevation, there are further gothic elements within the building, including walled-up arches in the *androne*; the remains of a fine marble stair were also visible in the mid-nineteenth century, and at the rear are further medieval traces including a three-light window and an oculus with quatrefoil. It appears, therefore, that much of the body of the original house survived the rebuilding of the waterfront façade although, as we see, the new front elevation was very

154 Palazzo Mocenigo on the Giudecca: drawing by Visentini. Although the proportions are not accurate, he clearly shows the regular seven-bay fenestration (R.I.B.A. AF.3 [173]).

modest and unassuming. However, we may gauge some idea of the social importance of the Cappello house in the sixteenth century by the fact that Bianca Cappello was brought here as a child by her father Bartolomeo, for the *villeggiatura*; in 1574 King Henry II of France was lodged here while on his state visit to Venice. He arrived at Murano on 17 July of that year and Bartolomeo was his host; the king was conducted on a tour of inspection of the glassworks of the island, and according to Zanetti 1,976 *lire* and 11 *soldi* were spent on his entertainment. The rest of his visit to Venice was marked by extraordinary displays of lavish festivity, which were later recorded in the histories as a great event in the story of the Serene Republic; at the rather more parochial Muranese level, however, his visit was commemorated by the striking of a special *osello* (the Muranese coin), valued at 300 *zecchini*, with a view of the Cappello house on one side and a portrait of the king on the other.

If we remain on Fondamenta Navagero, but proceed towards S. Donato, we arrive at the fourth and last major house on the quay. This is at no. 31 and is a substantial villa on two floors and with a very broad façade with strong horizontal emphasis. Very little is known of the house's history, and its patrician ownership has not yet been traced; nevertheless, it is a house of some note, and despite alterations at ground level the essential elements of its form can be clearly identified. The first-floor *pòrtego* is lit by a prominent *Serliana* with a balcony and further central emphasis is provided by the

155 Venice: house on Rio del Gaffaro (Dorsoduro 3532), which closely resembles that on Fond. Navagero at Murano, and also the Michiel-Deste villa at Burano.

pedimented gable above it. On either side of the *pòrtego* are three single windows, thus producing a long, seven-bay façade. The house cannot be dated with certainty, but it is probably of the very late sixteenth or early seventeenth century; there is little ornamentation to assist more accurate dating, although the triangular pediment is rare in the lagoon until the seventeenth century, and the two small oval oculi flanking the portal are also typical of the period and may be seen in a number of houses of the *seicento* at Pellestrina as well as the Michiel-Deste house at Burano. This latter is the only house outside Venice that closely resembles the Murano villa; both have unusually long façades with pedimented gables and many single-light windows. Both are slightly later developments of houses such as the Pesaro noted above or the Mocenigo villa on the Giudecca, all characterised by a broad, spacious façade and only two storeys of accommodation. There are also similarities to one or two villas on the nearby Terraferma; we may cite the Cappello at Stra, a rather more elaborate house but of broadly similar proportions.

156 Murano: Palazzo Correr-Grimani on Fondamenta Venier. General view of the restored façade – a Renaissance city *palazzo* transposed to the suburban quays of Murano.

It, too, has a central emphasis and three flanking bays on each side like the Murano villa. Another very similar example is in Venice itself, on Rio del Gaffaro, of similar date to the villa at Murano and with very similar detailing. Again there is a central *Serliana* surmounted by a pediment, as well as two very broad side wings, one of four bays and the other of six.[42]

There are only two further important later-sixteenth-century houses at Murano, and both are *palazzi* in character rather than villas; they have compact plans and both rise to four storeys. The two houses are the Correr-Grimani at no. 44 Fond. Venier and the house at no. 39 Rio dei Vetrai, the ownership of which has not yet been traced. The former is an imposing house standing on the Grand Canal near S. Maria degli Angeli. It follows the precedent of many of the larger city *palazzi* in having the *piano nobile* on the second floor above two storeys of ancillary accommodation; above the *piano nobile* is a simple attic storey. The façade is typical of the latter part of the *cinquecento*; all of the windows have

[42] At Dorsoduro no. 3532. See also Goy, *Chioggia*, p. 245, fig. 87.

157 Murano: *palazzo* at no. 39–42 Fondamenta dei Vetrai. Roughly contemporary with the Correr house, it is unusual for Murano in having two superimposed *piani nobili*.

158 Murano: detail of the two four-light windows to the house in Fig. 157; the lower order has Ionic capitals, while the upper has modified Doric capitals.

plain rectangular frames apart from those to the *piano nobile*, which have semicircular heads. Two of these are coupled and share a large stone balcony, indicating the *pòrtego* within. Like the second house, the Correr-Grimani has a conventional tripartite plan and façade, the only unusual feature on the latter being the two chimneys that rise up in the centre of each side wing. Such an arrangement is unique among the larger surviving houses at Murano, and appears to have been original.

The house was probably built by the Correr, and despite its urban appearance, was undoubtedly intended for the *villeggiatura*; its overall form can be simply attributed to the fact that by the later *cinquecento* sites on the Grand Canal were very difficult to find, and hence the necessity to build on four floors. The *palazzo* later passed to the Grimani, who enriched the interior further; the main hall was decorated with frescoes, and there was an adjacent ballroom of imposing size, also decorated with frescoes by Tiepolo. The house suffered the fate of many such villas in the eighteenth and nineteenth centuries, however, and deteriorated rapidly. The ballroom is now entirely lost, and many of the paintings in the rest of the house had already deteriorated badly when Zanetti wrote.[43] At the end of the Second World War it was acquired by the Zaniol family, since which time it has been restored and well-maintained.

The second house, on Rio dei Vetrai, is very similar in size and planning to the Correr;

[43] Zanetti, *Guida di Murano*, p. 98.

159 Murano: the *casino* of the Pisani on the Grand Canal, a modest but well-proportioned house, once far more opulently decorated inside than its appearance suggests.

here, though, there are two *piani nobili*, at first and second floors, with ancillary rooms at ground- and third-floor levels. The plan is conventional, but both main halls here are lit by large four-light windows of typically late-sixteenth-century appearance. The house was in very poor condition until its restoration in 1985, and both balconies to the *pòrtego* windows have been lost. The house is another rather late example of one built for the *villeggiatura*, but which again takes a more 'urban' form than some of the earlier *cinquecento* houses. By the later decades of the century sites on the crowded Rio dei Vetrai must have been very rarely available; indeed, by the century's end there were virtually no waterfront sites left undeveloped anywhere in Murano. The larger houses of the later *cinquecento* and *seicento* are thus nearly always fairly narrow in plan and commonly rise to three or four storeys. This particular house is only unusual in that there are two *piani nobili* of equal prominence, with Ionic columns to the lower order and modified Doric capitals to the upper one.

Two other houses of the sixteenth century are worthy of note here, although both are special cases; the first is a villa of very modest appearance, suggesting the family house of a reasonably prosperous glassmaker, as its detailing is so simple and its size by no means imposing. However, no. 10 Fondamenta Cavour is said to be the much modified remains of the famous *casino* of the Pisani family, a noble clan of great power and wealth. The house is on three storeys, with a simple paired light to the first floor; it appears to have undergone considerable alteration in this last century, and Zanetti's description bears little resemblance to its present unassuming appearance. Very little is known of the detailed history of this once notable house.

160 Murano: detail of the façade of the *casino* of the Mocenigo, facing the lagoon near Fondamenta Manin. The fine Palladian windows are roughly contemporary with the more monumental Palazzo Trevisan, both of the 1550s.

Finally, in this section, we turn to the *casa di delizie* of the immensely wealthy Mocenigo family, which stands on the edge of the lagoon behind Fondamenta Manin, facing San Michele and Venice. The structure of this once elegant pavilion survives nearly intact although today it is almost entirely surrounded by glassworks, and quite inaccessible to the public; the lagoon façade, however, may be clearly seen from the *vaporetto* between the Faro and Colonna landing-stages. The pavilion is built on a single storey, all of brickwork, and is finely detailed in the Palladian manner, with a rusticated base, an applied order of Doric columns on tall bases (all of brick) and with a strong cornice. The large windows are surmounted by pediments of alternately curved and triangular profile, and were clearly designed to take full advantage of the magnificent views across the lagoon towards the city. The interior of the *casino* consists of three spacious rooms, the ceilings of which are all decorated with frescoes in the style of Veronese. Each room has a distinct theme depicted in these paintings. That of the first room is music, and the ceiling painting has a figure of Apollo in the centre surrounded by the nine Muses, each of whom is depicted with a musical instrument. The second room is dedicated to poetry, and is decorated with the figures of sixteen poets, among whom are Petrarch and Tasso. The third room is dedicated to Love; here the figure of Love is in the centre of the fresco, and is surrounded by the twelve months of the year, between which are depicted twelve of the classical gods, including Bacchus, Pan, Mars and Apollo.[44]

[44] Such iconography is typical of the later *cinquecento*; we may again cite the work of Veronese at Maser.

Zanetti concluded that the paintings were the work of various hands, and mentions Bracazzo, 'an almost unknown artist' who worked with Veronese on the Hall of the Council of Ten in the Ducal Palace in 1553–4. He also records that the walls were also originally frescoed in *chiaroscuro* and with landscapes but that these were whitewashed over some time before the 1860s.

Despite its inaccessibility, the Mocenigo *casino*, even in its present condition, offers a rare and important example of such a structure, a pavilion intended purely for pleasure, a true *casa di delizie*. The pavilion formerly had an extensive garden on the landward side, which was still well-maintained in Zanetti's day but is now almost entirely gone. There were several such *casini* at Murano in the later *cinquecento*, structures that were not intended for permanent residence or even for a prolonged *villeggiatura* but simply for use as pavilions for entertainment and intellectual discourse. Palazzo Trevisan formerly had a broad *loggia* in the garden that served a similar purpose, and there are still a few examples of these *casini* in the outlying districts of Venice. In these latter cases they were built in conjunction with a substantial house (like Palazzo Trevisan) and usually stood at the far end of the private garden or *cortile*, facing the back of the *palazzo*. It was only possible to execute such an arrangement where a spacious site was available and this was out of the question in the central zones of the city. However, on the periphery, particularly in northern Cannaregio and the Giudecca, a number of these *logge* or *casini* were built in the later *cinquecento* and *seicento*. They contained no service or ancillary accommodation, all of which was in the main house; the Mocenigo *casino* was very similar to these city examples, and was thus probably only used for 'day trips' from the capital.[45]

7 *Palazzi* of the seventeenth century

There are only three important Murano houses that survive from the *seicento*; our final, fourth example, the imposing Palazzo Giustinian, also has the appearance of a seventeenth-century *palazzo*, although in fact it was a major remodelling of an existing gothic house.

Of these first three, Palazzo Manolesso-Seguso (Fondamenta Cavour no. 47) is probably the earliest, and may be of the very late *cinquecento*. It is another *palazzo* rather than a villa, rising to four floors and of imposing height. The *piano nobile* is once again on the second floor, like that of the rather earlier Correr house; the façade, however, is asymmetrical, and one side wing was either never built or was later demolished. Zanetti inclined to the latter conclusion although, as we know, a number of Venetian palaces were built with asymmetrical plans if the site was restricted in width. The house thus consists of the central wing (the *pòrtego* of which is lit by a large three-light window) and the east wing. If completed, the house would have been one of the largest *palazzi* in Murano, and faced a similarly impressive group of villas on the opposite bank of the Grand Canal.

The house was built by the noble Manolesso clan for the *villeggiatura* and originally had extensive gardens at the rear, all now occupied by glass factories; it later passed to the

---

[45] Of the few such pavilions that survive in Venice today, we may mention that of Pal. Da Lezze at the Misericordia. The *palazzo* was built by Longhena after 1645, and the *casino* probably in the 1660s. Like the Mocenigo it is on one storey with applied columns to both façades, one of which gives onto a large private *cortile*, and the other onto Rio della Sensa. See Bassi, *Palazzi* (1976) pp. 308, 320, 444.

161 Murano: Palazzo Manolesso-Seguso – a fairly typical example of a seventeenth-century city *palazzo*, although in this case with an asymmetrical plan.

162 Murano: Palazzo Marcello on the Canale di S. Donato, also of the seventeenth century, but in poor condition and much altered over the centuries.

Seguso, a family of glassmakers who owned property in several places at Murano, including the banks of Rio dei Vetrai. The present condition of the house is poor and the windows to the *piano nobile* have been partly walled-in; however it remains a good example of one of the later noble houses to be built here, at a time when many patricians had already turned their attentions to the Terraferma for their *villeggiatura*.

Our second example is also quite imposing, but is a house built in a zone remote from the modern centre of Murano. Palazzo Marcello stands on the Canale di S. Donato beyond the church and is surrounded by far more modest dwellings. The history of the house is complex and it has suffered considerably from alterations and adaptation to other uses. Built for the noble Marcello in the very late sixteenth or early seventeenth century, it was acquired in 1737 from the family by the Procurators of S. Marco, Alvise Contarini and Marcantonio Giustinian, and offered to a group of Carmelite nuns;[46] it was thus adapted for use as a nunnery until 1810 when the order was suppressed; eighteen years later it was restored and reoccupied by Augustinians. For a short time it also served as the local parish church and was only finally reconverted to residential use at the beginning of this century.

Not surprisingly, these vicissitudes have resulted in many alterations to the house; the main hall or *pòrtego* had been used as a chapel for the religious orders and its very prominent *Serliana* window much modified. Despite the poor condition of the fabric, however, we can still identify the main features of a once imposing late Renaissance

[46] Zanetti, *Guida di Murano*, p. 167.

163 Murano: Palazzo Miotti on Rio dei Vetrai, of the later seventeenth century, and one of the very last major houses built here.

palazzo of the traditional type. The *piano nobile* is raised above a very lofty ground floor which may originally have consisted of two separate storeys; above the spacious *piano nobile* is a modest attic floor. The entrance is large but very simple, and above it the *Serliana* had a stone balcony, long disappeared.

   Our third house in this group is the last to have been built: Palazzo Miotti stands on the east bank of Rio dei Vetrai (at no. 24) and is of the later seventeenth century. It is on four storeys, two of which – the first and second – are detailed as *piani nobili*, each with a paired central window and a prominent balcony. On the top floor there is also a central *pòrtego*, lit by another two-light window, which extends above the roofline to form an aedicule, flanked by volutes and capped by a curved pediment. These latter features are typical of the late seventeenth or very early eighteenth century, and may be closely compared with such details on the *case padronali* of Pellestrina. The house is much taller than its immediate neighbours, and was possibly intended to have been used as separate apartments; the Miotti[47] were a glassmaking clan, as were the Seguso, another family associated with the

[47] The Miotti, like the Seguso, were both listed on Murano's register of 'original citizens' in 1605 (Zanetti, *Guida di Murano*, p. 210).

164 Murano: Palazzo Giustinian – principal façade on the Rio di S. Donato, the result of Gaspari's remodelling of the original late medieval house of the Cappello.

house, so that it may not ever have been intended for use for the *villeggiatura*; by the time of its construction, Murano's great era of noble prosperity was over.

Palazzo Giustinian (Fondamenta Giustinian no. 8)

Our final Murano villa is the largest and in some respects the most prominent house on the island; it is also the best-known to the visitor as it has been the seat of Murano's glass museum since 1861. This impressive structure has a more complex history than its façade indicates; it was originally a medieval *palazzo*, the property of the noble Cappello family, who also owned the house diagonally opposite across the canal. When the bishopric of Torcello was finally transferred to Murano in 1659 the house became the episcopal residence, and when Marco Giustinian succeeded to the see he bought the house outright in 1707 and began a major programme of modernisation. At the end of this work the *palazzo* had been transformed from a large gothic house into an imposing baroque palace,

165 Murano: detail of the ceiling to the main *salone* of the house, a fresco of the Apotheosis of S. Lorenzo Giustinian by Francesco Zugno.

the only such example in Murano. The modernisation was the work of Antonio Gaspari; one of his drawings for the work has survived in the Correr collection. Gaspari retained most of the basic structure, but replaced all of the windows on the main façade with new openings in a typically robust, classical style. The portico was also remodelled, while the large seven-light gothic window to the first-floor hall was transformed into a central three-light window flanked by two pairs of two-light windows, all with stone heads and prominent balconies.

The house is on three storeys, a fairly high ground floor (now faced with rusticated stone up to sill level), an extremely lofty, spacious *piano nobile* and a simple but unusually generous second floor. Gaspari's modernisation of the façade also included the incorporation of the remains of an adjacent house on the left side, and the necessity to retain the basic structural elements of the original house led to an asymmetrical spacing of all of the principal windows. The plan is thus also asymmetrical: the main first-floor hall is off-centre and is unusual in that it now has its longer axis parallel to the façade rather than orthogonal to it. At quay level, the entrance leads directly into the *androne* which retains the dimensions of the original entrance hall. To the right a stone stair rises to the *piano nobile*, and directly beyond the *androne* is a rear wing of the original house, which is largely unaltered and encloses a large private *cortile*. This rear wing is supported on an elegant colonnade with stone arches that are early Renaissance in character, although the windows above are all florid gothic in style. We may thus date this wing to the latter part of the *quattrocento*, and it is very likely from examining Gaspari's drawing (which shows the

166 Murano: the *cortile* at the rear of Palazzo Giustinian with late gothic fenestration and a very early Renaissance arcade.

original fenestration to the main façade) that the whole house originally dated from the 1460s or 1470s.[48]

The plan of the upper floors echoes the L-shape of the ground storey. The main *salone* on the first floor is a fine, impressive room; the large fresco painting on the ceiling is by Francesco Zugno, and depicts the Apotheosis of S. Lorenzo Giustinian, the first Patriarch of Venice.

Palazzo Giustinian is thus the only large baroque house on Murano; Gaspari's work in Venice is fairly extensive and includes the Zenobio and Albrizzi palaces. However, the difficulties of modernising the existing structure here at Murano have resulted in a house that is imposing in scale but somewhat mechanical and repetitious in detail; the main windows are strongly modelled, though, and the tympanum above the *pòrtego* window is surmounted by a very large florid coat of arms of the Giustinian family which is more expressive of the baroque spirit than any other part of the façade.

The palace remained the seat of the bishops until 1805 when it passed to the Patriarchs of Venice; in 1840 it was acquired by the Municipality of Murano (then a separate *comune*) and in 1861 the Glass Museum was founded here by Murano's leading historian, Vincenzo Zanetti.[49]

[48] We may attempt a slightly more accurate dating of the original house by reference to a city palace, the Soranzo-Van Axel, which can be dated to the years 1473–9 (Arslan, *Venezia Gotica*, p. 322 and note 37). This house is also predominantly florid late gothic but it has a *loggia* in the *cortile* with an early Renaissance arcade very similar indeed to that at Murano; in fact the capitals are almost identical. This suggests a very similar date for the Murano villa.

[49] Zanetti *Guida di Murano* has a comprehensive description of the palace in 1866, five years after he himself had founded the glass museum there.

8 The houses of the citizenry

The patricians and the leading glassmaking families were by far the most important groups in the development of Murano's domestic architecture. The latter group embraced a wide socio-economic range, however, from the heads of some of the most famous glassmaking clans, *maestri* of great skill and sometimes of considerable wealth, down to the humblest apprentices. The group could also be extended to include those ancillary workers who serviced the industry by supplying charcoal, sand and other materials, and provided transport for completed goods.

The social picture of the island is completed by a small but still significant group of fishermen, as well as retail tradesmen of various kinds and market gardeners, many of whom probably worked the extensive orchards of nearby Sant'Erasmo. Each of these social groups is represented by at least some surviving examples of vernacular housing. For clarity we may attempt to define the lesser houses of Murano as follows.

Firstly, there are the houses of the major glassmaking families. These often resemble the smaller villas of the nobility, although their function was naturally different and they were in use all year round, as conventional family homes. In many cases the ground floors were occupied by shops or workshops associated with the glass industry, and there were usually two floors of accommodation above. As we would expect, few of these houses had extensive gardens for relaxation and recreation. In later periods, notably the 18th century, when the nobles' direct interest in Murano had virtually ceased, many of their villas were acquired or rented by these glass families and thus became family houses, often being divided into apartments or otherwise adapted to less noble functions.

Secondly there are the smaller, more modest houses of the lesser Muranesi; these were built either by the less affluent glass families or by shopkeepers, craftsmen and other small-scale entrepreneurs. These houses are very similar indeed to their counterparts elsewhere, the handful at Burano, for example, and many in the outlying districts of the capital. Generally they are simple and sober in appearance, usually symmetrical but with little decoration or ornamental detail.

Thirdly there are the tiny cottages of Murano's underclass, the fishermen and market-gardeners, and of the 'floating population' of casual labourers and seasonal workers. These are the simple cellular cottages of which there are so many at Burano, and a representative number may also be seen in all parts of Murano today.

Murano's leading glassmaking families had the status of citizens, but that of all of the other Muranesi was simply the *minuto popolo*, the common people. The glass industry had always been concentrated on the banks of the Rio dei Vetrai, and so here, sandwiched between the rather larger houses already mentioned, there was a dense mixture of lesser houses varying in size from fairly substantial glassworkers' houses to smaller houses belonging to those in the lesser crafts and in retailing. Murano's popularity among the patriciate in the 16th century also brought increased prosperity to those in the service crafts, the indigenous Muranesi, while at the same time increasing the value of land and pressure for its redevelopment. Several glassmaking clans redeveloped land on Rio dei Vetrai that had been in their possession for some time prior to this new noble popularity, and to maximise space, most of these new houses were built on three or four floors. We

167 Murano: house at no. 83–5 Fondamenta dei Vetrai – an example of the comparatively small number of more modest Renaissance houses of the sixteenth century.

may cite here two examples of sites built up in this way during the *cinquecento*, both on the west bank of the *rio*, at nos. 31 and 35. The first stands next to the Contarini-Mazzolà house and was on a site wide enough to permit the traditional tripartite plan, on three storeys. A simple paired light with a balcony indicates the *pòrtego*, but the façade is very simply detailed, although crowned by a stone cornice of typically sixteenth century profile. Almost next door, at no. 35, is another house of the *cinquecento*, but built on a narrower site and with an asymmetrical plan with only one side wing; in compensation for this restricted width, the house rises to four storeys. The detailing of the façade is again very simple and typical of the period, the roof cornice being almost identical to that at no. 31; there is also a small bas-relief of St John the Baptist set into the façade, which is probably contemporary with the house.

168 Murano: the Vendramin house at 21 Fondamenta S. Lorenzo. Much altered, it was built in the sixteenth century; the adjacent house was part of the original *palazzo*.

169 Murano: house at the corner of Rio dei Vetrai and the Grand Canal, with typical seventeenth-century pedimented gable and volutes. Behind is the early Renaissance campanile of S. Pietro, begun in 1498.

A third substantial *cinquecento* house, but rather later in date, is that at no. 83 on the same quay. It may be described as a *palazzetto*, and was the family seat of the Ballarin, one of the most notable of the glassmaking clans, and famous since the 15th century. It is a large broad-fronted house with a conventional tripartite plan and on three storeys together with an attic, represented by a large central dormer with a triangular pediment. The house epitomises the social position of these leading glass families; in size it is very simply detailed with little superfluous ornament and the stone modelling is very restrained.

We may continue this brief general survey by mention of a further few houses that illustrate the fairly broad range of these smaller *palazzetti* and *borghese* houses. The Vendramin house at 21 Fondamenta S. Lorenzo is an unusual building, much altered both within and without. In 1615 it was the residence of Cardinal Francesco Vendramin, as is evinced by a carved inscription on a fine ornate fireplace of red Verona marble which survives in one of the rooms. The house has been converted into two separate buildings of which the left part still bears traces of its former appearance in the form of four very tall windows to the original *piano nobile*.

With the Vendramin house we enter the *seicento* and there are several fairly substantial houses of this period; two large structures at the very northern end of Rio dei Vetrai again provide vestigial evidence of Murano's former fame as a suburb of the nobility. The houses at nos. 136–8 and 139 are contiguous; the first is large, built on three storeys and

170 Murano: house at no. 7 Fondamenta Santi, an unusual construction of the *seicento*. The octagonal *oculi* at the ground floor are rare, as is the fenestration pattern.

with a conventional tripartite plan, the simple façade somewhat enlivened by the baroque detailing of the balcony and the volutes to the roof gable. The other house is of earlier date but has been extensively altered; Zanetti states that the house (or houses) on this site are the remains of the great *palazzo* of the Giustinian that formerly stood on this important site in the very centre of Murano. The family had owned a large house here from the later medieval period, and we know of a letter written by Bernardo Giustinian in 1441 when the house already stood.[50] Indeed, it can be identified on de' Barbari, immediately adjacent to the Pontelungo. The present house seems to have retained the original stone cornice, of characteristic fifteenth-century profile, although the rest of the present façade is of the late *cinquecento* or *seicento*.

(Bernardo's letter indicates his appreciation of the verdant delights of Murano some decades before the large-scale patrician colonisation of the island; he refers to the 'loci

[50] Ibid. p. 90. The main body of the house was apparently standing until major alterations in 1819; by then it had passed to the Morelli, a Murano family. It is clearly shown in a painting by Giuseppe Heintz the Younger, in the Correr Museum, entitled *Corso nel Canal Grande di Murano*. It shows a large villa, with a prominent row of windows to the *piano nobile*. The original medieval palace thus appears to have been remodelled twice, once in the *seicento*, and again in the first years of the nineteenth century. Bernardo's will states: 'Item I leave to Lorenzo my son and executor the palace situated in Murano in the zone of S. Stefano with its garden and the cottage of the gardener [*ortolano*] and this must be passed down the generations to the sons of Lorenzo my son, who is to keep the palace well-maintained and the garden well tended.'

jucunditas, et, ut ita dicam, rusticana amoenitas'. When he died, his will left specific instructions to his son to keep the garden well-maintained.)

Our two final examples of substantial middle-rank houses are quite different in character, and are also in quite different parts of the island. The first is a two-storey house at no. 7 Fond. Santi near S. Donato, and in recent times the property of the Barovier, an important glass family. It is probably of the seventeenth century, although little is known of its history, and its appearance is unconventional; there is a low ground storey with a square portal at each end of the façade as well as two oval oculi. Above, there is a lofty *piano nobile* with four tall, round-headed windows, each with a stone balcony. It is possible that the building was originally a hospital or religious foundation, but this has not been established with certainty.

Our last example is more conventional and stands at no. 16 Fondamenta dei Vetrai, near the Contarini house. This is a rare example of a mature Baroque *palazzetto* of the eighteenth century, built on a narrow site and three storeys high. Despite the narrow site, the tripartite form is still followed, with paired lights to the *pòrtego* at both first and second floors. The semicircular window heads have keystones in the form of human heads, and above the second floor is an attic with aedicule in a characteristically vigorous eighteenth-century style, with flanking volutes and applied columns with Corinthian capitals.

9 Smaller houses and cottages

The broad range and variety of the houses of the nobility and citizenry of Murano is reflected, although naturally to a more modest extent, in the lesser houses, those of the fishermen and artisans. There are a number of examples of the very smallest 'Burano' type of cellular cottage and there are also slightly larger houses, some on three storeys. There are also a few speculative terrace developments. All of these lesser types are found in all parts of the island; the only zone where there are comparatively few very small cottages is along Rio dei Vetrai where land scarcity led to high densities and where the major glass families were the chief landowners. There are also few such cottages on the Grand Canal, where the nobility had 'squeezed out' the lower social orders by the latter part of the sixteenth century. Such smaller houses are thus found on the lesser canals and in the hinterland of Murano, along the minor *calli* and *campi*; many were destroyed by the large-scale nineteenth-century redevelopment of the glassworks, but some remain, and the selection that follows is arbitrary, although representative of the remaining variety that can be seen.

Our first example is a group of three houses on the north side of Campo S. Donato; they were probably built as a terrace, as they share a common cornice of stone, although they have all been altered later. They are on three storeys, with a narrow frontage, and resemble many such houses at Pellestrina and Burano. Here the second floor takes the form of a large gable, which is almost the full width of the house and is surmounted by a triangular tympanum; all three gables are slightly different, however, suggesting their later rebuilding. The houses are probably of the eighteenth century, although the detailing is very simple and does not allow more accurate dating. As is usual in such narrow

171 Murano: a group of small houses on Campo S. Donato, probably of the later seventeenth or early eighteenth century.

172 Murano: houses on Fondamenta Santi. Those on the right form a short terrace of three identical cottages.

173 Murano: a small cottage on Fondamenta dei Vetrai, bearing the date 1749 in the stone panel on the façade. Pedimented gables are unusual on such modest houses.

houses, the façades and plan are asymmetrical, with the entrance and stairs to one side, again like many such houses elsewhere in the lagoon.

Just around the corner, at no. 2 Fondamenta S. Lorenzo, is a smaller, two-storey cottage very similar indeed to the archetypal cellular 'Burano' house, but with a slightly wider, three-bay façade. Similar examples may be seen nearby, opposite S. Donato and at no. 10 Fondamenta Santi. This zone contains several further smaller houses and cottages, and we may mention another group on Rio di S. Matteo, at nos. 38 and 39, next to the little gothic houses noted earlier. These are on two floors, with a small, simple roof dormer flanked by volutes.

The row of houses opposite the apse of S. Donato also contains a mixture of two- and three-storey houses, all of very simple appearance. Most are of two bays with asymmetrical plans, although one is of three floors and has a symmetrical form, with two oculi flanking the central entrance.[51]

If we now return to Rio dei Vetrai, we find few cottages on the *rio* itself for the reasons described above, although one small house is worthy of note, that at no. 87 on the west side. It is a modest but symmetrical eighteenth-century house, with a small dormer complete with tympanum and volutes that seem a little incongruous on such a small cottage; a stone panel set into the façade bears the date 1749.

Very close by is the Campo della Pescaria, on which stand two larger houses, both probably also of the eighteenth century and with the broad plan characteristic of the larger

[51] Goy, *Chioggia*, p. 244, fig. 85.

174 Murano: house on Campo della Pescaria, today divided into two, but originally one fairly large house, similar to many of the eighteenth century at Pellestrina.

houses at Pellestrina. Both are on two storeys with a central pedimented gable and a symmetrical form; they were built either as fairly spacious family houses or possibly intended to contain two separate apartments.

Crossing Rio dei Vetrai, and walking down Viale Garibaldi, there are several further examples of these smaller house types. At nos. 41 and 42 there is a pair of very simple two-storey cottages, both modified, but both with first-floor windows spanned by semi-circular brick arches, a comparatively rare detail in such cottages, and more typical of speculative developments in Venice itself, particularly in the *cinquecento*.[52]

10 Terrace developments

The few larger terraces at Murano mostly date from the nineteenth-century modernisation of the glass industry. However, we may illustrate the genre by reference to two or three examples, one of which is a little further down Viale Garibaldi. This terrace occupies the north side of Calle Briati, and consists of seven houses, all of two storeys and with wider façades than was usual in such developments. They are of three bays but with the entrance to one side, allowing for the provision of an entrance hall to one side of the front parlour. In all other respects the cottages are quite conventional and very sparsely detailed; they are probably of the later eighteenth century.

[52] See, for example, Gianighian and Pavanini, *Dietro*, pp. 68, 70, etc.; there are also examples in Trincanato, *Venezia Minore*.

175 Murano: façade of the oratory of the Ospedale Briati, near Viale Garibaldi – a rare and delightful example of the Baroque at Murano. The central plaque records the date of construction, 1752.

176 Murano: long terrace of cottages in Calle Barovier, near S. Maria degli Angeli. All are three bays wide, and almost certainly of the early nineteenth century.

While in Viale Garibaldi, we may mention another development which does not strictly fall within the terms of reference of this book but is an example of the adaptation of the cellular cottage form to other uses. This is the Ospedale Briati, built by Giuseppe Briati in 1752, as a block of charitable almshouses for the widows of former glassworkers. The building is in the form of a rectangle, with a small central *cortile*, and with the accommodation for twelve women in apartments ranged around the *cortile* on two storeys. In the centre of the main façade is the delightful little baroque oratory, entirely faced with Istrian stone and surmounted by an ornate pediment. The rest of the block is very simply detailed, and has the appearance of a terrace of cottages; the only stonework is that to the cornice and the window surrounds.

Our third terrace is more typical, occupying the whole of the south side of Calle Barovier, near Palazzo Grimani on Fondamenta Venier. The houses are probably of the nineteenth century, built to house workers for the large new glass factories nearby; they consist of a single row of eleven cottages, all of two storeys, and extremely simple in appearance. Like the terrace in Calle Briati, the houses are three bays wide, but asymmetrical in plan, and with two rooms to each floor. Each cottage also had a tiny backyard. Apart from the moulded cornice, the front façade is entirely devoid of decoration.

12

Burano: a village of fishermen's cottages

1 A medieval introduction: the Palazzo Comunale and the Palazzo del Podestà

Burano is unique among all of the islands in the further northern lagoon in that it has survived today as a large, populous and reasonably thriving village. It is also unique in its social structure, and has been so for as far back into its history as records allow us to go. Since the early sixteenth century, and probably for a good deal longer, Burano has been a community of fishermen, with a simple one-class social structure that is directly reflected in its appearance today, and specifically in its housing. Its two neighbours, Torcello and Mazzorbo, both formerly had a more complex social order, with much of their land owned by the Church or the Venetian nobility, and with a stratified society again originally reflected in a wide range of housing types. Most of the private houses of these two communities disappeared centuries ago, however, as both islands slowly declined from their peak of medieval importance and their wealthier citizens all moved to the lagunar capital.

Burano also once contained two monasteries, and a small part of the lay population of the village must have consisted of a form of service community, supplying various goods and services not only to these two large monastic houses but also to the two adjacent more affluent neighbours. Burano's several hundred fishermen provided much of their food, while those Buranelli who did not attempt to make a living from the sea provided such services as boatbuilding and repairing. Some of them also undoubtedly worked the land on Mazzorbo and Torcello while others again represented the 'mechanical trades' – smiths, carpenters, shoemakers and others.

With the exception of the two gothic structures in the main square of the village, there are no surviving medieval buildings at Burano, and any conclusions as to the appearance of the village in this period must remain highly speculative. However, we may begin our survey with these two buildings, the only guides that we have to fourteenth- and fifteenth-century Burano.

Medieval Burano was subject to the authority of the *podestà* or governor of the northern lagoon, resident on nearby Torcello. The village contributed funds towards the maintenance of the canals, bridges and quays of the three communities of the locality, although each of the three had their own village council, all of which were presided over by the *podestà* when in session. Burano's Palazzo Comunale is a fairly small building on the west side of Piazza Galuppi, the large square that forms the civic focus of the village. The building is on two storeys and built of brick, with stone detailing; it has recently been

177 Burano: Palazzo Comunale – general view from Piazza Galuppi. The ground floor has been considerably modified, although the *piano nobile* largely retains its medieval appearance. The three-light window indicates the position of the council hall.

178 Burano: Palazzo Comunale – detail of first floor, with single-light window and typical *quattrocento* diamond-pattern cornice-gutter. The large bas-relief panel is a very battered winged lion of S. Marco.

restored. The façade is asymmetrical and has been altered on more than one occasion. At ground level there are two square doorways, probably original, but there are also four larger openings that were inserted later, in the eighteenth century. On the first floor the position of the council chamber is denoted by a fine gothic three-light window, the profile

179 Burano: the Palazzo del Podestà, probably of the later fourteenth or early fifteenth century.

of which suggests a date of construction of the early or middle part of the *quattrocento*; to the left the ante-room and stairs are lit by two single windows, both with gothic heads. There is also a cornice-gutter of stone, supported on corbels, and with diamond-pattern decoration again typical of the *quattrocento*. The façade is further decorated with several paterae and stone panels of various dates.

The Palazzo has a broad façade and its general appearance very closely resembles the contemporaneous smaller gothic *palazzetti* in Venice; the three-light window that lights the council hall here corresponds to similar windows that light the *pòrtego* of a private house. Indeed, were it not for the larger openings at street-level, Burano's Palazzo Comunale could easily be mistaken for a private house of the asymmetrical type, that is, with central axis and only one side wing. These larger arches were formed in the 1750s, partly to allow the insertion of two small shops, which were then rented out by the council to raise revenue. (They let for 20 ducats per year, one being used for the sale of beef and the other for 'castrado'.) The rest of the ground floor was used for the storage and sale of flour to the villagers.

The interior of the Palazzo is fairly simple, the council hall occupying most of the upper floor, while the ante-room is approached by an open stair from the ground floor. The floor of the ante-room is supported by a large timber beam reinforced by *barbacani*, and these in turn are supported by two stone columns.

The only other medieval building in Burano today is the house immediately adjacent to the Palazzo on the east side. It is today occupied by the offices of the *comune*, and is

180 Burano: Palazzo del Podestà, today the village council offices. Detail of the medieval portal on the right of the façade, with two trilobate *monofore* to the first floor. The profiles of the sills and window heads are typical of many houses of this period in Venice and also at Murano.

sometimes referred to as the house of the *podestà*. There is some evidence that it was indeed used for this purpose, although the governors of the northern lagoon did not permanently transfer their base from Torcello to Burano until the eighteenth century. However, it is possible that in earlier periods at least a part of the house was used by village officials, for whom there was clearly little room in the Palazzo Comunale.

The 'Palazzo del Podestà' is a substantial house on three storeys, each of equal height, although the first floor is more elaborately detailed than the others. The ground floor has a fine but simple gothic portal in the centre of the façade and a second, of identical appearance, on the right; both have rope-moulding decoration typical of the later *trecento* and *quattrocento*. The building has been considerably restored and altered over the centuries, and it is difficult today to reconstruct the original interior arrangement, although in principle the plan is tripartite, with a central axis and two side wings. The main portal gives onto a central *androne*, while the right one gives access to a second hall, which

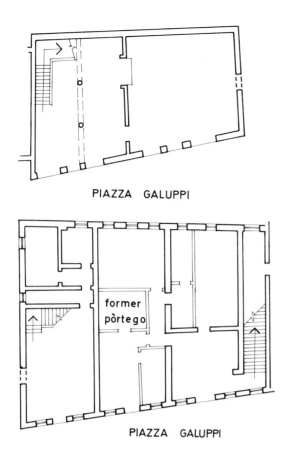

PIAZZA GALUPPI

former pòrtego

PIAZZA GALUPPI

181 a Ground-floor plan of the Palazzo Comunale
b Ground-floor plan of the Palazzo del Podestà. This has been considerably altered internally.

perhaps originally gave onto a stair to the second floor. Such an arrangement was not unknown in Venice, and thus provided two quite separate living quarters, a self-contained flat at second floor and a larger maisonette on ground and first floor. The plans of the upper floors were thus basically tripartite and conventional, as the windows to the façade suggest. All of those to the first floor have gothic detailing, with trilobate heads and stone sills on lion's head corbels, again details typical of the later fourteenth and early fifteenth centuries. The *pòrtego* is lit by a three-light window, the balcony of which has been lost; the side wings are lit by pairs of single windows in the traditional manner. The detailing to the second floor is much simpler, although all of the original carved sills survive. The stone profiles are all virtually identical to those on the Corner and Obizzi houses at Murano, and we may thus conclude that the house was probably built in the late fourteenth century. The rest of the façade is very simple in appearance, although again the medieval stone cornice has survived.

These two modest civic buildings are our only physical link with medieval Burano. It is not until well over a hundred years after their construction, that is, the later sixteenth century, that we can begin to sketch the appearance of the village as a whole. Even in the later *cinquecento* all of the villagers were very poor indeed, and despite the fact that numbers were rapidly increasing, Burano's inhabitants almost all lived in small cottages of the simplest cellular type. A number of these cottages were still of timber in this period, with roofs of osier thatch, although the majority were now of brick, with tiled roofs.

2 The housing

Most of the hundreds of small cottages that today comprise the village of Burano were built in two periods of notable population growth, the first dating from recovery from the 1575 plague and continuing until the next severe outbreak in 1630; the second was a much longer period of growth from about the 1660s to the middle of the following century. A third significant period of change came much later again, in the middle of the nineteenth century. The houses of Burano are mostly extremely difficult to date individually, however, since they are almost all architecturally very simple; only a few have any features of style or ornamentation that make such dating possible with any confidence. However, we may draw a few general conclusions in this field a little later.[1]

Burano's population increased significantly during the sixteenth century; it was a large village of fishermen, who had good direct access to the sea by the wide, deep channel of the Burano Canal and the Canale di Treporti. The ebb and flow of these waters also ensured that malaria was never a major problem here, as it was at nearby Torcello. Our first detailed picture of Burano dates from the land-registry of 1580–1, and by now the village's social structure – and hence its housing pattern – was well-established in the pattern that was to continue almost to our own day. Most Buranelli lived in tiny one- or two-roomed cottages, with only a very small number of larger houses. Many more cottages were built and many others enlarged in the last decades of the sixteenth century and the first three of the seventeenth, until the 1630 epidemic. Numbers were probably regained by the 1650s, and a long era of steadily accelerating expansion began; a significant proportion of the cottages that survive today date from this second long period of growth until about the 1740s, by which time Burano was a very highly developed and crowded community indeed.

The island's one-class social order is directly reflected in the very limited range of house types and sizes. The number of larger houses, belonging to that tiny group of inhabitants forming Burano's 'citizenry', is so small that we may discuss almost all of them individually. Well over 90 per cent of Burano's housing thus consisted, and consists, of small two-storey cottages, with one or two rooms to each floor. There are also a number of three-storey houses, indicative of rising pressures for redevelopment of the very limited amount of available land, particularly in the eighteenth century. Most of the cottages were built piecemeal, individually, by simply adding on to the gable end of an existing cottage or row of cottages. Speculative terraces or groups of houses are very rare for the reasons

[1] For the sake of brevity, the chief surveys and land-registers that form the basis of the conclusions in this chapter regarding housebuilding activities are all summarised thus: A.S.V. Dieci Savii B. 459 (survey of 1580); B. 461 (that of 1661); B. 472 (that of 1741); A.S.V. Anagrafe di Tutto lo Stato 1766. See also A.S.V. Podestà di Torcello B. 433, 434, 541, 551; A.S.V. Milizia da Mar B. 187–9; A.S.V. Catastico Napoleonico Lib. 8.

discussed in chapter 7; the two larger examples here both date from the nineteenth century, and earlier development was almost all cellular and organic in character.

There are about ten or a dozen slightly larger houses, those of the 'citizenry' (technically still the 'common people' – there were no *cittadini* at Burano) although hardly any are large enough to be called *case padronali*. Indeed, there was no land at Burano to allow the growth of a class of landowning *padroni*, since the island is so small; these few larger houses were built by slightly more successful local craftsmen, fishermen and boatbuilders. There is a much narrower range of wealth here than in any other community in the lagoon, and even these few 'citizens' were still very modest in their standard of living. Their houses are chiefly notable for their wider, symmetrical façades but they are still fairly small and their decorative features extremely limited.

We may examine the houses of Burano, however, by starting at the top of the social scale and considering a house that is unique on the island, and a villa without peer elsewhere in the northern lagoon.

3 The Michiel-Deste house

This large villa stands on the bank of Rio della Zuecca (Giudecca) at no. 386, adjacent to the timber bridge. It is the largest private house in Burano, and appears to have been built by the Michiel family in the early seventeenth century. The earliest land registry survey, that of 1581, does not locate houses or provide details of size, but merely lists the rents paid on them. Although two very high rents are listed here (one of 80 and one of 84 *lire*), they cannot be identified with this house with certainty, and the villa's appearance is certainly more indicative of the seventeenth century than the later sixteenth.

The second survey of 1661 is more useful, as it lists rents and also provides detail of house and apartment sizes. Four properties are listed with ten or eleven rooms, and two are the property of Francesco Michiel, although at the time both were let to Buranelli. Of the other two, one was the property of Carlo di Carli, the wealthiest local villager, although it, and the fourth large property, are both lost to us today. Examination of the plan of the villa on Rio della Zuecca shows that there are about ten rooms on each of the two principal floors, and hence we may be fairly sure that this is the Michiel villa.

When we examine the third land register survey, that of 1741, we see that the Michiel had retained their two large properties. Our conclusion appears to be correct, since they are the first two entries in the Burano register, and the first was listed as the property of Lorenzo Michiel ('for his own use') and the second was 'for the use of Andrea', clearly a brother, son or other close relative. There are now no other houses of comparable size listed on the register. The villa appears to have remained the property of the noble Michiel until the later eighteenth century; by the time of the Napoleonic survey of 1808 the house can be positively identified as in the ownership of the Deste family, a numerous Burano clan with several separate branches. Its owner in that year was Santo Deste, and it is almost certain that by now it was divided into smaller apartments (as it is today), possibly for several branches of the clan. It was clearly far too large to have survived as a single family house.

182 Burano: the Michiel-Deste villa – general view of the main façade onto the Rio della Zuecca (giudecca).

183 Burano: the Michiel-Deste villa – detail of the central bay of the façade. A simple but impressive seventeenth-century villa.

The villa is built on two principal storeys, and its main elevation faces Rio della Zuecca. It is nine bays long, with one main central doorway and two subsidiary ones towards each end of this long façade. The main portico is all of stone with a semicircular head and prominent keystone; on either side are two unusually elaborate stone oculi, which suggest the construction date as the early seventeenth century. These are flanked by two single lights, then by the secondary doorways and then by two further single windows.

At first-floor level, there is a single large window to the *pòrtego*, directly above the doorway (with a stone balcony) and four single-light windows on each side, all with square heads. At second-floor level there is a large central gable with two windows, surmounted by a triangular pediment. The ground floor is clad with stone up to dado height and the rest of the façade is of rendered brickwork.

The Michiel-Deste house is thus a very substantial villa surrounded by tiny fishermen's cottages and this sharp contrast increases the effect of what is in any case an impressive house. In overall form, it resembles the villa at no. 31 Fondamenta Navagero at Murano, although in several respects it is more impressive in appearance and more satisfactory in its proportions. However, it has few peers, and in character is more akin to some of the Terraferma villas of the early *seicento* than to any other houses in the lagoon, although it may have had similarities to some of the lost villas of Murano. There is some affinity with the Mocenigo villa on the Giudecca although the latter lacks the prominent central emphasis of the Burano house, and has eight equal bays.

Even on the nearby Terrafirma there are few villas with such a broad, generous plan; one of the few is the Cappello house at Stra, which has similar overall proportions, although here the *pòrtego* is emphasised by a group of three lights and the *pòrtego* itself is raised above the flanking accommodation to form a notable central feature, again capped by a large triangular pediment. The Villa Cappello has three bays on each side of the central axis, compared to the Michiel house and its four bays. Of the few other Terraferma villas of similar appearance we may mention the Morosini house at Polesella; like the Michiel and Cappello villas it has a broad plan on only two storeys and is more imposing than the other two chiefly because there is a spacious *piano nobile* above a low ground storey, which is approached by a great flight of steps. It, too, has a wide façade of nine bays, of which the central three form the external expression of the *pòrtego* within, and are capped by a large pediment. Despite these few somewhat similar examples, the Michiel-Deste villa remains a special case within the lagoon, and certainly unique to Burano.

The internal planning of the house is basically conventional, with a broadly symmetrical plan and a *pòrtego* extending for the full depth of the house, forming the main axis. However, the considerable width of the villa allows not just for a single set of rooms on each side of the *pòrtego*, but for two groups on each side, as the plan indicates. The house has been considerably altered inside (as was suggested above) and divided into several smaller apartments; at least one and possibly two additional stairs have also been inserted. It is probable, though, that the outermost rooms formed secondary or ancillary accommodation serving the principal rooms that gave directly off the *pòrtego*. The main stair is in its traditional position, halfway down one side of the *pòrtego*, while there was probably at least one further service stair. It is difficult to draw any further detailed

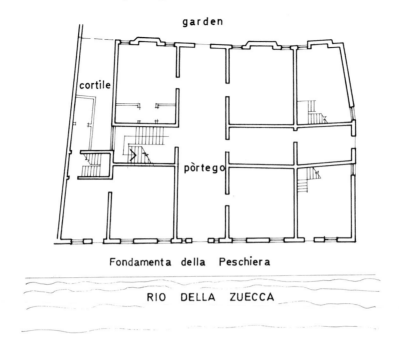

garden

cortile

pòrtego

Fondamenta della Peschiera

RIO DELLA ZUECCA

184 Burano: the Michiel-Deste villa – plan at ground-floor level, showing how the traditional Venetian tripartite plan is here expanded to five main structural bays, while retaining the central axis, the *pòrtego*.

conclusions as to the original use of the rest of the house; including further service accommodation in the roof, there were possibly more than twenty-five rooms.

4 The houses of the 'citizenry'

Most of the small number of larger houses on the island were built in the later sixteenth and early seventeenth centuries as the result of the emergence of a group of moderately successful tradesmen and boatbuilders. By the time of the 1661 survey this group was fairly numerous and about thirty houses in the survey may be ascribed to this small class; it is probable that this 'citizenry' was responsible for the smaller number of such houses that we see surviving today. However, the group never represented more than a very few per cent of the total population of the village, and almost all of the rest were very poor indeed.

These houses form a small, well-defined group today, about ten in all. They are fairly easily distinguishable from the hundreds of smaller cottages, not merely by their size but because most of them have architectural features absent from the simple cellular cottages. They have a wide plan, usually about double the width of a cottage, and there is nearly always a symmetrical front elevation of five bays, although there are a few asymmetrical four-bay examples.

There is considerable difficulty in establishing precisely when these surviving examples were built. We can only deduce house sizes from the 1581 survey by the amounts of rent paid; there were only a handful of such larger houses recorded, on which rents of 30 to 40 *lire* were paid, instead of the 12 to 15 *lire* for a small cottage. By 1661 there were nearly 20 houses listed with six or more rooms and so some of these twenty almost certainly correspond to the houses standing today. Most of them were thus built in the period prior to 1575 or in the couple of decades before the 1661 land registry survey, as serious outbreaks of plague almost certainly ruled out their construction at any other time. The detailed appearance of one or two of the houses suggests the earlier of the two periods, the mid-sixteenth century, although most are probably of the *seicento*. These larger houses listed in 1661 are scattered in all parts of the island, with no concentrations, for example, on the main axis, the Rio di Burano (which was later reclaimed). By then the average rent for such a house was twenty ducats or more, compared to five or six for a smaller, much more typical cottage.

During the long period of continuing expansion in the later seventeenth and early eighteenth centuries, it seems that this small *borghesia* expanded (as indeed did the population generally) and even to some modest extent prospered. Their houses that survive today have a refinement of proportion and of detail that is a little surprising when we consider the very humble social context in which they were built. But they were clearly constructed by men with a degree of aesthetic sensibility and an awareness of proportion that suggests at least some links, however tenuous, with developments in the capital. They are by no means *palazzi* or even *palazzetti* but nor are they crude, simple cottages. Several of them are very similar indeed to a small group of houses at Murano of roughly similar date, and it is likely that the builders of the Burano houses were not native Buranelli but men 'imported' from Murano or even from Venice itself specifically for the task of building these larger, more refined houses.

They are still simple in appearance, however, with very little applied ornament; their attractive appearance is based chiefly on the balance and symmetry of their façades and on the modest emphasis given to the central doorway. This nearly always has a semicircular head of stone, with a keystone and pilasters with very simple classical capitals. The window to the *pòrtego*, directly above the door, is also given some slight emphasis, either by an arched head or a stone balcony or occasionally by both. In a few examples a further degree of dignity is added by a central *abbaino*, with a triangular pediment and sometimes with flanking volutes. Such houses are closely linked in style with the *case padronali* of Pellestrina, although they are slightly smaller and less 'villa-like' in appearance, chiefly because they were not built as freestanding structures but as elements in a densely built-up urban context, usually simply as façades in a terrace. Apart from their broader plans, the Burano houses generally retain the same storey heights and window sizes as those of the cottages by which they are surrounded.

With the exception of the doorways and the central first-floor windows, all the windows are simple rectangular openings, just like those of their smaller neighbours. The plans, though, are naturally more spacious; the symmetrical façade is reflected in a centralised, tripartite plan, with the hall giving access to the rooms on either side. This hall is simply a fairly spacious corridor in most cases rather than the *androne* of the larger houses, and usually gives access to four rooms, one in each corner of the plan. The staircase sometimes

185 Burano: house on Piazza Galuppi, at no. 189; typical of the small group of larger houses on Burano, most of them built in the later seventeenth century, and nearly all with five-bay façades.

186 Burano: house at no. 171 Piazza Galuppi, another example of the *borghese* Burano house, here with a heavy stone balcony.

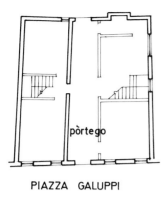

PIAZZA GALUPPI

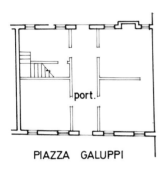

PIAZZA GALUPPI

187 Burano: ground-floor plans of the two houses on Piazza Galuppi, nos. 171 and 189, both with the traditional tripartite form.

rises directly out of one of these rooms, usually one of the two at the rear; in other cases it is positioned halfway down the length of the hall (as it is in the much larger *palazzi*) between the front and rear rooms.

We may summarise here the appearance of the more noteworthy of these houses, three of which stand on Piazza Galuppi, the hub of the community. The house at no. 189 is next to the medieval Palazzo Comunale and in most ways epitomises the genre. It is symmetrical in plan and elevation, with five bays; the portico is central and has a simple square doorway directly above which is the *pòrtego* window, with a semi-circular head and a balcony with a wrought-iron balustrade. Several such houses have similar balconies formed in stone but with iron railings in order to save on construction costs since stone balusters were expensive. The house has a prominent stone cornice-gutter with flanking volutes of rendered brick. All of the stonework is extremely simple, with no carved profiles or keystones.

The other two houses are also on the west side of the Piazza, and abut one another at nos. 171 and 175. The first has the five bays typical of these houses and closely resembles our first example, the chief differences being that the first-floor balcony is all of stone and

188 Burano: a house on Rio della Zuecca near the Deste villa, a spacious but simply detailed example of the *borghese* Burano house.

189 Burano: house on Rio dei Assassini at no. 402, built over a pre-existing right of way (Calle del Squero). The upper part is of the five-bay type.

190 Burano: central part of the façade of a five-bay house on Rio Pontinello. Detailing is very simple except that to the doorway and the *pòrtego* window.

the doorway has a semicircular head with a carved keystone. The detailing generally is rather more complex than the first house, and all the window heads are surmounted by labels or hoodmoulds of carved stone, a most unusual feature in such a modest house. The central dormer in the roof is crowned by the triangular pediment formed in stuccoed brickwork typical of these houses.

The adjacent rather smaller house is somewhat unusual in being only four bays wide, and is thus asymmetrical in both elevation and plan. Despite its unifying cornice and central dormer it appears possible that it was built as two separate houses and is thus a fairly rare example of such a semi-detached pair.

Our other examples of these *borghese* houses are scattered throughout the island. One of them stands on the Rio della Zuecca, a few metres from the Michiel-Deste house, at no. 262. It has an unusually spacious plan of five bays, but in most other respects is typical of the group; the doorway and *pòrtego* window both have semicircular heads, with carved keystones and with similar imposts to both openings. Unusually, there is no stone cornice-gutter (it may have been lost), nor is there any central dormer in the roof. The plan is symmetrical and traditional, despite various modifications at the rear, and the stair rises halfway down the length of the hall in the traditional manner.

Another such house stands on Rio Pontinello at no. 213; again only the doorway and *pòrtego* window have any worked stone, all of the other windows being simple rectangular openings. A similar house can be seen further down the same quay; here the *pòrtego* window is simply detailed but has a prominent stone balcony with an iron balustrade.

One final example is a house on Rio dei Assassini, at no. 402. It has a typical five-bay façade but is unique in this group in that it was built over an existing *calle*, which divides the building in two at street level and is bridged to form a *sottopòrtego*. In most other respects the house conforms to the general pattern, with a prominent stone balcony in the centre of the façade and a dormer with triangular tympanum.

We can see from these brief notes that these houses have a number of features in common, in addition to their overall plans and façade arrangements. The use of expensive worked stone is kept to a minimum and generally confined to entrance doors, cornices and balconies. Occasionally we find a carved keystone (usually classical but sometimes in the form of a mask) while more complex carving is confined to the balustrade of the first-floor balcony.

5 The Burano cottage

Far more typical of the village than this handful of *borghese* houses is the humble Burano cottage, usually with no architectural pretensions at all, although sometimes it, too, has a pedimented gable or a symmetrical façade. The smallest and still most typical cottage is very simple to describe indeed: it is built of brick, rendered externally and with a double-pitch tiled roof, although the very smallest cottages (with only one room on each floor) often have an even simpler monopitch roof. The front door and windows have prominent heads and sills, usually of Istrian stone, which sometimes, but by no means always, lines the jambs (see below). The windows today are also always fitted with the typical Venetian four-leaved timber shutter. There is usually no external decoration other than that provided fortuitously by the row of corbels supporting the stone gutter. In the few cottages that do have further decoration, this generally consists of a simple string-course at first-floor level or a small dormer in the roof with a triangular pedimented gable.

Since Burano consists of several hundred of such modest houses it might be assumed that the village's appearance is very uniform. This is far from the case, however, partly because of the many bright colours that adorn the façades of most of the cottages, but chiefly because of the large variety of minor variations of these basic units of accommodation, variations of plan, of orientation, of size and proportion of windows, of storey heights, of direction and pitch of roofs. There is a great richness and variety in the urban fabric of the village despite the even and consistent 'grain' of nearly all of its housing. The urban scale is consistent throughout the island; there is only one major public square – Piazza Galuppi – and all of the axes of the village consist of narrow canals with a *fondamenta* down both sides. The minor axes of growth, the narrow, parallel *calli*, are all orthogonal to these canals. Most of the *calli* are very narrow and in several places have been built over

191 Burano: house at no. 103 on Piazza Galuppi. We occasionally find architectural flourishes such as this gable even on very small houses.

192 Burano: a section of the waterfront on Rio di Terranova, with a typical group of two- and three-storey houses. Many minor variations ensure that every house is slightly different, although all conform to the overall scale of the quayside.

CORTE TERRANOVA

D

A

B

LAGUNA

193 Burano: plan of part of the island of Terranova, indicating the typical urban 'grain' of the island and with a representative selection of house-plan types.

194 Burano: a block of houses adjacent to Rio della Zuecca, and with a characteristic group of chimneys.

with first-floor rooms to form long, dark *sottopòrteghi* beneath them. There are a very few single-storey cottages remaining at Burano, although almost all of the village's cottages today have two or three floors; unlike Pellestrina there are no houses here on four storeys. Although the amount of building land here was very limited (particularly in the eighteenth century) there was not the same high concentration of development along a couple of hundred metres of waterfront that we see in parts of Pellestrina. Most of the cottages originally built at Burano, however, were of only one or two floors and so the many three-storey houses were either rebuilt in their present form in the eighteenth century or had an extra storey added in that period, as numbers increased and land became more scarce.

The very smallest Burano cottage consists simply of one medium-sized room, about four or five metres square, although there is often a very small *abbaino* fitted under the roof, which is a simple monopitch. The most typical cottage, however, has two floors and may contain either a single room or two rooms to each storey. A slightly larger cottage again will have two storeys but also a dormer in the roof indicating the presence of a small attic. The largest cottages have three full floors, with two rooms on each, and in these cases there is hardly ever any further attic accommodation in the roof-space.

We can see, therefore, that the Burano cottages vary in size from a single room up to a maximum of six rooms. However, regardless of the total number, houses of these types are always only one room in width, that is, about four metres, or a single bay. The spans of all the floors were thus quite small and could easily be constructed using very modest beam sizes, an important consideration since, as we have seen, large sections of timber

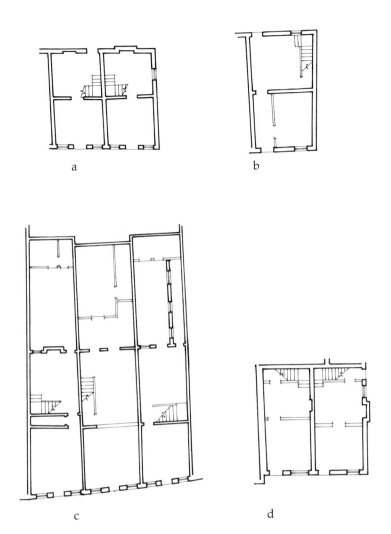

a

b

c

d

195 Burano: examples of plans of cottages all of which are two rooms deep (some with later extensions). Most have symmetrical façades; in all cases the stair rises out of the rear room: a. pair of cottages in Cao di Rio Sinistra, b. cottage in Rio di Mandracchio, c. three cottages in Cao di Rio, d. pair of cottages in Via Galuppi.

were expensive. It is this uniformity of width, the standard room or 'cell' size, that more than any other single factor gives such a cohesiveness and consistency of scale to the village. Regardless of whether a row of houses has two or three floors (or usually some of each) the rhythm of the façades produced by this regularity gives a high degree of consistency while also allowing for almost limitless minor variations of detail.

Although there are indeed many such variations, the façades of the cottages are of two basic types, the symmetrical and the asymmetrical. The symmetrical façade has a central doorway flanked by a window on each side, while on the first floor (and the second if there is one) there are two windows directly above those of the ground floor. The asymmetrical elevation has the entrance at one side adjacent to the party wall, and with usually two, but

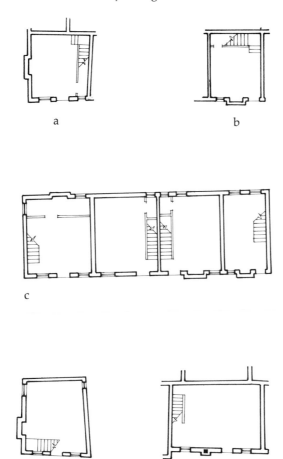

196 Burano: examples of plans of 'single-cell' cottages, with only one room to each floor: a. cottage in Rio Pontinello, b. cottage in Rio di Cao Sinistra, c. terrace of four cottages in Cao di Rio, d. another cottage in Cao di Rio, e. cottage with an unusually broad plan, again in Cao di Rio.

sometimes only one, window at the side. On the upper floor or floors the window positions directly correspond with the openings below; thus if there are two ground-floor windows, there are three on the upper floors, one being directly over the doorway.

Almost all of Burano's several hundred cottages fall into one of these two groups, the façades of which correspond to the plan arrangements inside (see above). There are other elements, however, that provide further variety to the street scene, and one is the dormer window or gable. Dormers are usually small and simple, and nearly always have a double-pitch roof which is expressed on the façade as a triangular pediment, or at least the faint suggestion of one. The dormers almost always contain just one small window.

The other element sometimes expressed on the front façade is the chimney. In many cases the fireplace is on the flank or party wall between two cottages and thus rises within the building until it emerges above the roof. However, it is not uncommon to find the fireplace on the front façade and hence there is a prominent projection up the elevation

197 Burano: house on Rio Pontinello, with a three-bay façade. Where the site was wide enough, such an arrangement provided the symmetry that was an important consideration in the design of even these modest cottages.

198 Burano: another three-bay cottage, possibly of the nineteenth century, whose modest dignity has been enhanced by hood-moulds and an ornamental frieze just below the cornice. This example is on Rio di S. Mauro.

199 Burano: two further examples of the symmetrical façade on very modest cottages.

200 Burano: house on Rio di Terranova with an asymmetrical façade. Space has been gained by building over the *calle* at first floor.

formed by the chimney, and terminating some distance above the roof with a *comignolo*. The chimneys at Burano are always square or rectangular in section and terminate in a simple square *comignolo* usually capped with a tiny, tile-covered, double-pitched roof. Occasionally we find the larger traditional Venetian inverted pyramid shape for the *comignolo*, but it is comparatively rare here, and the even larger, elaborate inverted cone is not seen here at all – it was far too much of a luxury for the poor fishermen of Burano. In houses where the chimney is visible on the front façade, the rest of the elevation clearly has to be asymmetrical, and in these cases the door is on one side with the fireplace in the centre and a single window on the other side. Sometimes the chimney is offset above ground level and is set within the house so that the wall surface outside is flush; more often, however, it is taken down to the ground as a projection, and it broadens out on the lower floor to indicate the position of the fireplace or range inside. This characteristic tapered form is typical of many Burano cottages, and there are often projecting string-courses to further accentuate the shape of the chimney.

201 Burano: small cottage on Rio della Zuecca, with a prominent chimney of rather unusual form.

The form of the roof of the cottages varies considerably, which may appear surprising when we consider how small most of them are. However, some are one room deep, while others have two rooms to each floor, and some are within a terrace while others are in small blocks or at the end of a terrace. We therefore see a variety of roofs to cover these different conditions. The smallest cottages usually have a simple monopitch; more common is a double pitch, falling towards the front and back of the house. This is the usual type for houses within a terrace, where it facilitated drainage. It is not uncommon, however, to find four-way pitched roofs, particularly on slightly larger houses and houses that are or were free-standing. We also find hipped gables, particularly on end-of-terrace houses where it was clear that there could be no further development onto the end of the block for reasons of space. The fact that most Burano cottages were built individually means that there is rarely continuity of roofs over more than one house, and each one is thus roofed individually, with little regard for the height of its neighbour.

The cottages of Burano have very few decorative features indeed. We have mentioned one, the dormer window, which is occasionally singled out for embellishment with a

202 Burano: a very small cottage on Rio di Terranova. Symmetry was impossible on such a narrow site, and the detailing is extremely simple.

203 Burano: house on Rio di Mandracchio, built over the public quay with a *sottopòrtego*; these are very rare at Burano because of their cost. This may be the house of Piero Costantini discussed in an earlier chapter.

204 Burano: decorative detailing is occasionally found on such tiny cottages as this – pediment on a house in Rio Pontinello.

small triangular pediment, but there are few other such features. Occasionally we find a moulded cornice at the roof eaves, formed in render on a base of two or three courses of corbelled brickwork; sometimes, too, the stone gutters are supported on rows of stone corbels which are purely functional although they also serve to add to the dignity of the house. In a number of cases these corbels are in fact rendered brick, often painted white to match the very few pieces of worked stone elsewhere on the façade.

The wall surface generally is entirely flat and plain, with no adornments or features at all, simply painted rendered brickwork. In recent years the traditional render protecting the soft red bricks has been painted in a very wide variety of colours, many of them extremely bright. These highly artificial paint colours have replaced the traditional range of more muted natural pigments, which can still be seen in rather more general use at Pellestrina.

The only decorative feature (if it can be so described) common to every one of Burano's cottages is the treatment of the door and window surrounds. These are invariably lined with a bold white frame, often of Istrian stone and usually very simple in profile; these frames, like the uniform bay width of the houses, form another unifying feature that 'ties together' the appearance of the whole village. The colours of the houses themselves vary from ochre and russet through to bright blues and greens, but all of the houses, with barely a single exception, have every one of their door and window openings framed in white. In a number of cottages this frame is a little deceptive, however; closer inspection shows that only the window head and sill are of stone, and that the two side reveals have been painted white to give the appearance of an entire frame, although they are merely painted render. On occasion, even the head is not of stone but is formed by a shallow brick arch, again rendered and painted, and leaving only the sill of stone. Sometimes the entrance is a similar 'deceit' but here, too, the threshold is usually of stone. In almost all cases the stone has a simple rectangular section, only the window sill having a slight projection and a fall to throw off rainwater.

We can see another modest deceit in the painting of the wall surface where very often the lowest part of the wall, up to the level of the ground-floor window sill, is painted a different colour from the rest of the house and sometimes projects slightly further forward. This treatment is a faint echo of that found in the larger houses in Venice where this lowest section of wall is built of coursed stone or of brick faced with stone up to the sill level, where there is a stringcourse also of stone. Here we see a simple rustic version of the plinth, using the most basic of materials, simply a different colour of paint.

Even in humble Burano, therefore, the principle of emulating one's superiors is seen expressed in a number of simple ways, in modest deceptions such as painting render in imitation of stone, and also in more significant ways, chiefly in the over-riding importance given to symmetry in the façade, wherever this was feasible; symmetry in even a tiny cottage gives it more dignity and presence.

6 The cottage and the way of life

For most of Burano's history over the last four centuries nearly all Buranelli lived in considerable poverty, hardship and overcrowding; the present attractive appearance of the cottages should not obscure the fact that most are extremely small and until the notable reduction in population in the last two or three decades many of them sheltered an entire family in only one or two small rooms. Mains plumbing and electricity are also both very recent improvements to the Buranelli's way of life.

In the smallest cottages of all, those with just a single room and a tiny attic or loft, all functions were carried out in this one all-purpose space, the loft usually serving as a bedroom. The single ground-floor room, perhaps 4 or 5 metres square, was a combined kitchen, dining and living room, and the fireplace not only heated the cottage but also served as a cooking range. At its simplest level the Buranello's diet consisted of fish and polenta, occasionally supplemented by vegetables from nearby Mazzorbo or Torcello. The fish were simply grilled on a rack over the fire, while the polenta was mixed in a large pot or cauldron and cooked over the same fire.

Even in the more typical cottage, that with two rooms, there was considerable over-crowding, and in the past – just as today – many domestic activities were conducted out of doors. Cooking today is often conducted outside on a small portable barbecue, but even before this recent and most useful addition to the Buranello's kitchen equipment, many aspects of village life took place outside. The men of Burano, nearly all fishermen, made use of the quay next to their cottage for sorting and cleaning the catch, for mending nets and maintaining their smaller lagoon boats, their skiffs and *sandoli*; many of the women practised lacemaking, as is well known, and for which good light is essential. During the summer, and for as much of the year as the weather permitted, therefore, this activity was also conducted out of doors, usually on the front step, but sometimes in one of the many small semi-private courtyards with a group of neighbours. Many of the older women of Burano continue this traditional activity although naturally the arrival of the electric light has meant that lace can be made indoors throughout the year.

In the past some of the cottages had a small private courtyard attached to them; many of these courtyards were lost in the great period of expansion in the later seventeenth and eighteenth centuries, when they were built over, and very few remain today. Most of them lie around the perimeter of the island; in the more central zones, all of the land that is not built-up is in the ownership of the *comune* and paved, lit and maintained by it. This land is thus the property of all and the property of none, and is used by the villagers as common land. Washing is strung across *corti* and *calli*, meals are eaten outside in summer, and in many places plant pots are set outside on the quays; in short, the cottages generally overflow into the streets outside. The few Buranelli fortunate enough to have a small private garden maintain it with the same care that is given to the cottages themselves, and the gardens are planted with oleanders, azaleas and other colourful shrubs.

As we have seen, historically the village was always poor and public facilities were rudimentary. There was only one major well for the entire community, in the centre of the Piazza (with a very large 'tank' below it) and the only drainage for the domestic effluent and refuse consisted of Burano's canals. The *rii* were shallow and very prone to silting; they required, but only rarely got, regular maintenance and re-excavation, and there is little doubt that until the recent post-war period Burano was a very poor deprived community indeed.

The Rio di Burano and the Piazza at one end of it have always together formed the main axis and nucleus of the village. Until the eighteenth-century expansion there were very few shops, and virtually all communal facilities were concentrated on the Piazza. Not only was the well here, but on one side stood the parish church and the house of the priest; on the other side was the village council hall, the house of the governor and the official outlet for the sale of flour. Later, there were also two meat shops as well as central shops for the sale of wine and oil. During the eighteenth century the Rio di Burano developed as the retail axis of the village, and by mid-century there were about 20 shops here.

However, the average Buranello remained poor, eking out a living fishing – mostly at sea, rather than in the lagoon. The little *sandoli* that the villagers used for general communications within the lagoon were often used to row over to Torcello and scavenge for building materials among the abandoned *casini* there, especially in the eighteenth century, and again after the dissolution of the monasteries in the early nineteenth century.

The Burano cottage is inseparable from the quay of the canal. These narrow *rii* are still the essential 'streets' of the community and the cottages of the island cannot be considered on their own in isolation from their aquatic life-line; all of the *rii* are lined with *sandoli*, moored in front of their owner's house just as a horse would have been tethered in a mainland village or a car parked in a modern one. Within the cottages themselves the last few decades have brought many changes and improvements; all houses now have fresh piped water and electricity, although there is no piped gas, and bottled gas is widely used for cooking and heating. Many houses have washing machines; almost all have a television. However, it is still not unusual to see washing being done in a large tub and scrubbed out over the canal in the timeless, universal manner.

7 Terrace developments

Speculative developments are very rare at Burano for the reasons discussed in earlier chapters. The Buranelli have always been extremely poor, and hardly any accrued or had access to sufficient capital to even consider any large-scale development in housing for sale or rent. Even in the period of notable expansion from about 1670 to 1740 when many new cottages were built, they were developed individually.

There is a handful of small terraces, however, probably dating from the mid-eighteenth century, and almost certainly built on the site of a small garden or orchard. Such groups of houses usually number only four or five, and even this modest scale of development was beyond the capabilities of most villagers; examples of such small-scale developments as this are still very few.

There are only two larger, more ambitious terraces in the whole village and both of them date from the early nineteenth century, after the fall of the Republic.

The first is a row of eight houses on the west side of Corte Comare. It is not recorded on the Napoleonic survey of 1808 but it was complete by the time of the 1848 survey; despite their comparatively late date, the cottages are traditional in appearance. They are all on two storeys with symmetrical façades, and each house has a small central dormer in the roof with a triangular pediment. The accommodation provided was quite modest: the central door to each house leads directly into a single ground-floor room, from which the stair rises up one side to another single room at first-floor level; there is a small attic room in the roof. The very restricted space inside is somewhat ameliorated by the fact that the terrace overlooks an extensive 'village green' where there is ample space for the activities referred to earlier.

The second large terrace is fairly close to Corte Comare, on Fondamenta Cao Molecca, on the east side of Rio di S. Mauro. It is of even later date than the first terrace, since the site was still undeveloped in the land survey of 1848, and thus dates from the second half of the nineteenth century. It consists of a long block of ten houses, all on three storeys, and very simple indeed in its design and detailing. In character it is unique on Burano although there are many such larger terraces of this period in the outlying districts of Venice.

The houses are all identical, and the entire block is covered by a simple double-pitch roof with no attics or dormers. Each house has a symmetrical façade with a central

205 Burano: terrace developments – the long row of eight cottages in Corte Comare, built in the early 1800s in traditional style. The mechanical repetition of detailing clearly shows their origin as a single development.

206 Burano: terrace developments – the largest speculative development in Burano is this long row of ten houses on Cao Molecca, built in the mid-nineteenth century. Despite recent redecoration, its monolithic nature remains quite out of scale with the village in general.

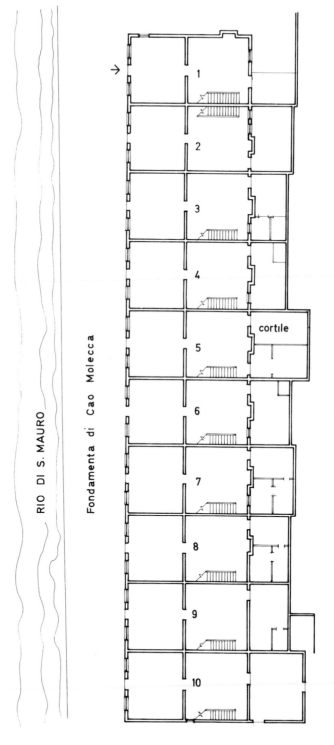

RIO DI S. MAURO

Fondamenta di Cao Molecca

1

2

3

4

cortile

5

6

7

8

9

10

207 Burano: plan of the ground floor of the terrace on Cao Molecca – ten identical houses, each with a tiny *cortile* at the rear. The upper floors precisely repeat the ground floor.

208 Burano: there are a number of small, less conspicuous terraces in the village, such as this block of five cottages on Rio di Terranova, probably of the later eighteenth century.

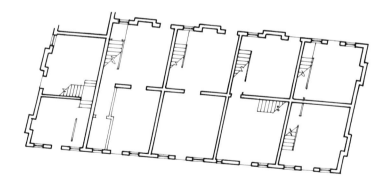

209 Burano: plan of the ground floor of the terrace in Rio di Terranova.

210 Burano: the central block of a group of three cottages in Corte Comare, where additional dignity is given to the group by this large central pediment. The houses have been altered since they were built.

doorway and a window on either side; the upper floors each have two windows and all of the fireplaces and chimneys are at the rear of the block, thus producing a completely flat, unmodelled front elevation. Apart from a small cornice at the eaves this façade is devoid of decoration.

The interior planning of the houses is very simple: the front door gives onto a single square room, and a door at the rear gives access to the kitchen, with the range in the centre of the rear wall. The stairs rise directly out of the kitchen up to the rear first-floor room, and this plan is repeated at second-floor level. There are thus six rooms in all, two to each floor. Each house also has a very small backyard in which there is a toilet and a shed for storage. The terrace is typical of such speculative nineteenth-century developments, built to produce the maximum accommodation (and rent) from the minimum of initial construction cost. The architectural features, such as they are, conform in general to the lagunar vernacular, but the overall appearance of the block is quite atypical of the smaller 'grain' of the village as a whole.

In addition to these two larger terraces, there are several smaller rows in all parts of the island. They vary in size from groups of only three cottages up to maxima of perhaps five or six. Some of these smaller groups are quite difficult to identify today as they have been adapted, enlarged and otherwise modified so that it is not always easy to establish their original arrangement. A group of houses on Rio di Terranova has survived largely intact externally, although alterations have been made to the plans inside. As we would expect, the basic arrangement here is simple and rational, each cottage having two rooms on each of the two storeys. As in the Cao Molecca terrace, the stair to the first floor rises directly from the kitchen. The plans of the five houses were identical with the exception of the cottage at one end which has two fireplaces and two chimneys. Other smaller terraces are less clearly identifiable: a group of three houses again in Corte Comare was probably built as a short terrace, although the central one has an additional storey and a large central gable to give some distinction to the group, which occupies a fairly prominent site. The houses are probably of the nineteenth century and have been significantly altered later.

13

Pellestrina

1 The village and its people

Pellestrina is a *lido*, a long, narrow ribbon of land between the lagoon and the sea, and on which are situated three separate settlements. Pellestrina village itself lies at the southern end of the *lido*, and is effectively a satellite community of Chioggia, as indeed it has been for all of its recorded history. It is much the largest of the *lido*'s three villages, with a population of about 5,500, roughly the same as that of Burano. The other two villages, S. Pietro in Volta and Porto Secco, are much smaller with about 1,800 inhabitants together; both of these hamlets lie towards the northern end of the littoral.

Although fishing has always had a certain importance in the life of the islanders, they are predominantly agricultural workers, and traditionally the *lido* has been cultivated with vines, maize and vegetable crops for the markets of Rialto; this rural economy gave rise to a significant number of fairly substantial farmhouses. There was never the important direct interest in the *lido* by the Church or the nobility that we find at Torcello and Mazzorbo, and the social structure that evolved here (and which is evinced in its housing) was thus based purely on the ownership of land. The island is small, however, and its cultivable area very restricted, so that ownership of land on the *lido* alone would have generated only a very narrow range of social classes and of wealth. However, many Pellestrina families have had very close ties with Chioggia for several centuries, and many of them owned considerable tracts of land on the mainland south of that town. These interests led to large disparities of wealth between the major landowners on Pellestrina – with interests elsewhere – and those who were merely local tenants or *mezzadri*, and this fact in turn led to the development of a fairly wide range of house types reflecting this broad social spectrum. There are tiny cottages here, like those of Burano, but there are also substantial farmhouses, a number of which have been described as *case padronali*, indicating the status of their owners as *padroni* (masters or landlords) of the community. Such houses have similarities to the villas of Murano and the Giudecca, on a slightly more humble scale, and even with some of the more modest patrician villas on the nearby mainland.

Pellestrina's urban development has much in common with that of the other lagoon villages such as Burano – slow expansion in the period until the great plague epidemic of 1575, consolidation and further expansion until the second severe plague of 1630, followed by a much longer period of growth for about a hundred years until the mid-eighteenth century, an expansion which, in essence, has produced the village that we see

286

today. The littoral has a more complex urban form than the other villages in this survey, and its development has consisted not of the growth of a single urban nucleus like Burano, but of a larger linear village (Pellestrina itself), which was originally divided into four zones or *sestieri*, together with the two quite separate nuclei further north. With time and expansion, the two northern hamlets tended to merge together, although we can still identify the two original nuclei; the four southern zones of Pellestrina itself were established after the Venetians' war with Genoa in 1379, and were recolonised by four of the leading families of Chioggia. These four names are still retained today to identify the zones, although they, too, have expanded so that there are now only quite small areas of open space between each *sestiere*.[1]

We thus have a series of local nuclei, each of which has its focal point in the form of the parish church: from south to north, there is firstly the *sestiere* of Busetti and then that of Vianello, the two most densely developed parts of the island, with the church of Ognissanti as the social and spiritual focus; a little further north is the votive temple of S. Vio and then the *sestiere* of Zennari. The northernmost *sestiere*, that of Scarpa, has its church of S. Antonio, which has now given its name to this part of the littoral.

North again, there is a long undeveloped zone formerly owned by the Canons of S. Marco, and beyond it we come to Porto Secco, named after the reclaimed *porto* that formerly divided the *lido* in two. The small village focuses on the church of S. Stefano, while finally, at the northern end of the *lido* is S. Pietro in Volta, with its homonymous church.

Urban development is far from uniform in these various built-up zones of the island and in many cases is still confined to a strip of housing along the waterfront, with vines, orchards and smallholdings behind them. Only in a few places is there significant development of the backland, and the most densely built-up zone is the part of Pellestrina closest to Chioggia. Here, in Busetti, there is virtually no open space left at all, and adjacent Vianello is also densely developed.

Buildings on the littoral that date from before the end of the sixteenth century are probably very few, if indeed they survive at all. There are no medieval buildings on the *lido*, and even as late as the last years of the *cinquecento* Pellestrina remained only a straggling hamlet of about fifty houses. As elsewhere in the lagoon, it is difficult to date most of the houses here with precision, although at least a few of the *case padronali* were built in the period immediately before the 1630 plague; however, it is only after about the 1660s that the island's major period of growth began.

We may divide the houses of the island very broadly into four chief types, the main characteristics of which may be summarised as follows.

[1] Once again, for convenience (as with the previous chapter), the chief archival sources for the conclusions as to Pellestrina's urban development are summarised thus: Archivio Comunale di Chioggia (A.C.) 23 to 34; various refs. scattered among the records of the meetings of Chioggia's Maggior Consiglio; further misc. records in the series Ducali, in A.C. 10 to 18.
   The main population and land register information is found in: A.S.V. Dieci Savii B.458 and 473, as well as the 1766 Anagrafe di Tutto lo Stato. Further local surveys ordered by the podestà in Chioggia are in A.C. 900 (Reg. dei Beni e Livelli) and A.C. 757 (Diversi) and A. C. 766. Further material may also be found in A.S.V. Milizia da Mar B. 239.

Firstly, there are the *case padronali*, all substantial farmhouses with significant architectural features. They were all built as detached houses and many are on two storeys although often with rooms in the roof. They all have symmetrical façades with central doorways and regular fenestration. They all face the lagoon shore, with their 'backs' to the sea, since the quay here forms the lifeline for all essential communications. They all have one or a number of features that clearly indicate their aspirations to be regarded as villas rather than simple working farmhouses; these features may include stone balconies, corbels and gutters, dormers with pediments, volutes and scrolls, and prominent main doorways. The *case padronali* tend to be older than many of the lesser houses, and most date from *c.* 1610 to 1630 and from about 1690 to 1730 or 1740.

Secondly, there are the houses representing the next stage down the social ladder from the group represented by the *case padronali*. These are the houses of the Pellestrina farm workers who owned comparatively little land, and possibly none at all. There are more of this type than any other, although they vary considerably in their size and form. In general, though, they are notably larger than the typical fishermen's cottages of Burano and are often on three or even four storeys. This higher density is again the result of notable shortages of waterfront sites in the southern part of Pellestrina village, where several of the larger *case padronali* had already accounted for much of the most attractive land here by the early part of the eighteenth century. Only a few of these numerous smaller houses have many decorative embellishments, but there is considerable variety in their plans and elevational arrangements.

Thirdly, there are the speculative terraces of houses, built on a single plot of land, for rent or for sale. Speculative building was as risky a venture here as elsewhere; at least some of the few examples date from the middle decades of the eighteenth century, when numbers were rapidly increasing and the developer was virtually assured of a tenant or a sale on completion. Again most examples of these developments are in the more crowded zones of Busetti and Vianello.

Fourthly, there are the very smallest houses, the tiny one- and two-roomed cottages almost identical to those of Burano. Once again they have no decorative features of any kind, and are also difficult to date with accuracy; since they are the most simple houses required for warmth and shelter, those built in 1560 are almost exactly the same in appearance as those built in 1760.

2 The *Case Padronali*: an introduction

The *padroni* of Pellestrina were the descendants – or some of the descendants – of the original four clans of Chioggia who had recolonised the littoral after the Genoese War of 1379–80, that is, the Scarpa, Vianello, Busetti and Zennari. As we saw above, some branches of some of these clans had accumulated large estates on the Terraferma between Chioggia and the traditional southern boundary of the Dogado. Not all branches of the four clans were wealthy, however, since at Pellestrina the normal pattern of inheritance was that land was divided equally between the sons of a marriage. With population growth, therefore, all holdings tended to become smaller. Nevertheless, there was a small élite of these *padroni* who also took advantage of the rapidly increasing population growth (particularly in the early eighteenth century) and built new houses to sell or rent and thus further increased their income. The remainder of the land on the littoral was in the hands of absentee ecclesiastical owners, and worked by the islanders as tenants or *mezzadri*. It is not surprising, therefore, to find that the *padroni* invested much of their income not only in property to let to others, but also by building suitable *case padronali* for themselves and their families.

Some of these houses are fairly small, unpretentious, but solidly built farmhouses, with the barest minimum of sober decoration. Others were more ornate, their principal façades clearly designed to impress on the community the status and aspirations of their owners. Most of these *case padronali* are thus a fusion of two basic approaches to house design: one is the general vernacular of the lagoon, with its modest-sized rooms, simple but strong detailing, clay-tiled roofs and rendering to protect the soft brickwork from the elements in this particularly exposed location. Such an approach employs easily available local (or comparatively local) materials and a minimum of specialised craftsmanship. The other approach to the design of these houses comes from the other social direction, that is, downwards from the patrician *palazzi* of Venice and more particularly from the villas that the nobility were building in very large numbers in the seventeenth and early eighteenth centuries on the Terraferma, but especially along the banks of the Brenta Canal.

The *padroni* of the lido – even the richest of them – did not inhabit the same social or economic world as the Pisani or Mocenigo, but the inevitable process of looking to such great families for direction in matters of style and taste led to the construction of a number of these 'farmers' villas' on the littoral. Indeed, a handful seem to have been modelled quite closely on the smaller Terraferma villas of the patriciate. These 'model' villas are compact, freestanding houses with none of the elaborate arcades, pavilions and *barchesse* of the larger villas of Palladio and his followers. They are often square on plan, solid in appearance and usually on two (occasionally three) storeys. Examples of this type are the Pisani villa at Noventa Padovana, the Manzoni nearby, the Levi at Mira and the Venier at Mira Vecchia.

The other chief characteristic shared by such villas and the *case padronali* of Pellestrina is the centralised, symmetrical, tripartite plan, always reflected in the elevation, which has a large window or group of windows to the *pòrtego* and nearly always a central dormer or aedicule in the roof.

The farmers' villas are distributed fairly evenly down the Pellestrina littoral, with a slight preponderance in the south, in the four *sestieri* of the main settlement. The total number of such houses is perhaps twenty-five or thirty, although at the more modest end of the scale, the distinction between them and the more ordinary farmhouse cannot be made with precision. The *case padronali* always have some element of pure decoration, however, that helps to distinguish between the two types; even a small *casa padronale* will often have an elaborate pedimented gable. At the upper end of the scale there are two or three houses such as the fine one at S. Vio (now the village police station) that can bear direct comparison with the smaller patrician villas on the nearby mainland.

All of the farmers' villas are built on or immediately adjacent to the lagunar waterfront, facing west, and this is their only important elevation. The back faced a small garden or orchard, with the open sea just beyond, and this rear façade is always very simple and

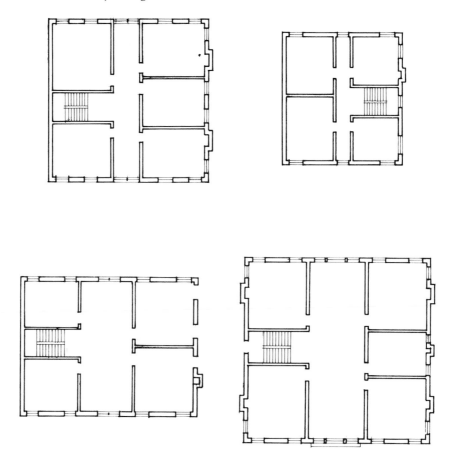

211 Comparative plans of some *case padronali* on the *lido* of Pellestrina: these four houses are no. 95 S. Antonio, no. 161 S. Vio, no. 231 S. Vio and no. 30 at Pellestrina. Apart from some significant differences in size, the plans are all very similar indeed: all conform to the tripartite form. In the larger examples the *pòrtego* forms a spacious all-purpose living room, while in the smaller ones it is simply an access corridor.

severe, with small windows to maximise protection against winter storm and flood. The houses are thus virtually one-directional and all important rooms faced west. Since the *padroni* owned more land than most other villagers they could afford to build houses with a comparatively broad plan, which also gave the opportunity to design a more spacious principal façade, rather in the manner of some of the villas of Murano.

The planning of the houses here differs little in essence from that of the smaller *palazzi* of the city centre, or the villas of Murano. Plans are almost without exception of the classic tripartite type, with a central *androne* on the ground floor and the *pòrtego* directly above it. Depending on the width of the house, this central axis is sometimes simply a spacious corridor and sometimes it is wide enough to form a central *salone* like those of the great *palazzi*, with a width of four or five metres. On the ground floor there are usually four rooms, one in each corner of the plan; the staircase sometimes rises directly out of one of the rear rooms, or in the slightly larger houses it is positioned halfway down one side of the *androne*, as in the larger city *palazzi*. The first-floor plan precisely echoes that of the lower floor, and there are usually two smaller rooms or one large one in the attic, lit by a window in the centre of the façade, and surrounded by an aedicule.

There is comparatively little variation in the overall size of these houses; the chief differences lie between those farmers' villas built on only two storeys (and an attic) and those on three full floors, also often with an attic. There are roughly equal numbers of each type; we may conclude that the two-storey houses were probably generally built for a single, nuclear family whereas at least some of the larger houses were almost certainly built for bigger, more extended families which may well have included two heads of household (often brothers or cousins) together with their respective wives and children. A three-storey house thus allowed for the possibility of some horizontal subdivision as well as perhaps some shared facilities such as the kitchen. A two-storey house would contain a total of seven to ten rooms, while a three-storey house could provide as many as eleven or twelve rooms.

Such conclusions are supported by analysis of the two government land-registry surveys of 1661 and 1741. Not only was there a notable expansion of population in this period (in which most of the *case padronali* were built) but we also see that whereas in the earlier survey many houses were indeed shared by more than one branch of a family, by the latter date the practice was almost extinct. We thus see that most of the larger houses are somewhat older than the two-storey houses and that the construction of these smaller, later houses to some extent at least ameliorated earlier overcrowding. Pellestrina families were indeed large, and by 1766 average family size was nine, the highest figure recorded in the lagoon villages. We may safely assume that a number of these *case padronali* sheltered large families of perhaps a dozen or more members, many of them young children.

The pattern of use of these farmers' villas is fairly simple to establish. The kitchen occupied one of the two rear rooms on the ground floor and in it was a large open fire or range, which in some cases incorporated an oven. The rest of the ground floor was occupied by general living accommodation and probably a general store for oil, grain and other bulk goods as well. All of the first floor (and the second if there was one) was occupied by bedrooms, of which there were three or four to each full storey. In some of the three-storey houses it is probable that the two upper floors were each used as a separate apartment, in the manner of some city *palazzi*, and in these cases probably all of the ground floor was given over to storage of goods, foodstuffs and materials, again closely echoing the pattern of use in the traditional city *palazzo-fòntego*.

The tripartite plan is almost universal in these houses, and the façade always reflects this plan. It is thus symmetrical and often shows considerable refinement in the proportions of its fenestration and the disposition of the elements. Window detailing is usually very simple, as is the main portal, and the quite imposing effect of a number of these houses is due less to the complexity of their detailing than to the overall proportions of the façade. In general the details are a somewhat simplified version of the typical seventeenth- and eighteenth-century work in Venice itself. There is significant use of stone, but never as an overall facing material – it was far too expensive – although it is often seen fairly extensively in door and window surrounds, balconies, cornices, corbels and dado-rails, and as copings to gables.

The central doorway usually has a semicircular stone head, with a keystone and sometimes with carved imposts; windows frequently have a projecting stone head or hood-mould and a similarly profiled stone sill. There is usually a prominent cornice at eaves level, often of classical profile, and in many cases a paired window on the first floor indicates the position of the *pòrtego*. Directly above it a gable or aedicule in the roof is almost universal and forms the single most distinctive feature of these houses. It usually frames a pair of lights and is surmounted by a pediment. The aedicule is more carefully detailed than any other feature on the façade; often there are flanking volutes of rendered brick, and with a number of different profiles. The crowning pediment is usually triangular but a few are semicircular or ogival and one or two have complex profiles of a truly baroque character, albeit on a very modest scale.

Windows are generally rectangular, with simple surrounds of stone and render, although those to the central *pòrtego* often have a small stone balcony with a balustrade of stone or iron. Occasionally, too, the central light has a semicircular stone head to add greater emphasis and centralisation to the façade. Above the prominent cornice the tiled roof nearly always has a four-way pitch, as the plan of the house is usually square or close to a square. Chimneys are often a prominent feature; a few are of the inverted conical type, but most are square with an inverted pyramidal pot. In the larger houses there are several fireplaces; as well as the kitchen range, there were often fireplaces in each of the main rooms, so that we see four prominent vertical features, one to each quarter of the plan. As in the city *palazzi*, the central hall was unheated, receiving only indirect heat from the rooms on either side.

Despite the strong family resemblance between many of the *case padronali* there is considerable variety of detail, and it is difficult to devise sub-groups for further analysis of the genre. We may now summarise the more important of these houses and note their chief distinguishing features. For purely topographical convenience I have grouped the houses according to their location on the littoral; the reference numbers for each house are those of the land registry of the Comune of Venice, since these are the most authoritative for purposes of identification.

3 The *Case Padronali* of Pellestrina village

This section of the *lido* extends from Ognissanti church at the very southern end of the inhabited littoral as far north as the votive temple of S. Vio. It includes all the most densely built-up zones of the village where the social and economic life of the island is concentrated.

The finest house in the village is that at no. 30, mentioned above, and at present the village police station. It has several features in common with some of the smaller mainland villas: there are two storeys and a large central dormer in the roof, the façade is symmetrical and tripartite, as is the plan inside; the central portal has an arched head and is flanked by small square windows each with a prominent hood-mould. The main feature of

212 *Casa padronale* at no. 30 in Pellestrina, one of the most imposing of the farmers' villas; see floor plan in Fig. 211.

the *piano nobile* is the large central *Serliana*, the only one to be found on the island's farmers' villas, with its robust stone balcony. It is flanked by four simple rectangular lights, and directly above it is the pedimented gable, also lit by a smaller *Serliana*, and flanked by attached columns and volutes; the gable is crowned by a radiused pediment. The house also has three prominent traditional Venetian chimneys, one conical and the other two pyramidal.

The house was clearly built for one of the most important *padroni* of the island and equally clearly intended to impress his fellow landowners. The detailing is very generous by the standards of the *lido,* with considerable use of worked stone, although not all of it is refined in execution and in some respects the proportions are less satisfactory, for example, than those of the smaller house at no. 6 (see below). Nevertheless, it is one of the handful of the most important houses on the lido; it may also be one of the earliest, since the detailing suggests the seventeenth rather than the eighteenth century, although we cannot be certain of its date of construction.

The house at no. 6 has several similarities to no. 30. It is also on two storeys with a prominent central gable, and is also five bays wide. It may also be one of the earliest of this group of houses; it is not shown on the survey of 1640 but may well have been built soon afterwards. The ground floor is detailed in a very similar way to no. 30, but at first floor there is an elegant two-light window to the *pòrtego* instead of a *Serliana*; it, too, has a

213 Detail of the façade of no. 30 Pellestrina; the modelling of the elevation is robust but a little unsophisticated.

balcony all of stone. The large central gable has two small simple windows, and is again capped by a curved pediment. The detailing is generally less robust and more refined than that of no. 30, although both houses are clearly farmers' villas rather than simple farmhouses and were built by men of some skill. Both have a spacious *piano nobile* above a more modest ground floor, and it seems likely that the main family rooms were on this first floor; in both cases, too, there is a central *pòrtego* large enough to be used as the focal room of the house rather than simply as an access corridor.

The third notable *casa padronale* in this part of the village is that at nos. 14–20, only a few metres from the first two houses. However, it is a different type, since it is built on three full storeys together with an attic. It has been converted into two houses but originally formed a particularly large, spacious farmers' villa. The form is conventional, tripartite and symmetrical and the detailing generally very restrained. The doorway is simple and the *pòrtego* is denoted by an equally simple paired light on both upper floors. The central

214 *Casa padronale* at no. 6 in Pellestrina; rather less elaborately detailed than no. 30, it is also more refined in its proportions.

gable has a similar window directly above the others, and is surmounted by a modest triangular tympanum. Of the few decorative features on the façade we may mention the prominent hood moulds to the *piano nobile* windows, and the large roof cornice. There are also stringcourses at the head and sill levels of all of the windows; these are a common feature of city houses of the seventeenth and eighteenth centuries where they are formed of simple bands of squared stone. They are rare here since they are a purely decorative feature, whereas almost all of the decorative forms at Pellestrina grew directly from functional necessity; here the stringcourses are usually formed of projecting courses of render, painted to contrast with the wall surface. The house has recently been restored, and also retains four fine and prominent Venetian chimneys of the pyramidal type. The form of the house on three storeys produces an overall volume that is almost an exact cube, and there are three or four other such *case padronali* on the *lido* of almost identical form, such as that at no. 231 at S. Vio and no. 176 at Porto Secco.

Most of the other *case padronali* in Pellestrina are more modest than these first three; a

215 *Casa padronale* at nos. 14–20 in Pellestrina; an example on three full storeys, now divided into two houses.

further three may be grouped together since they are very similar in appearance. These are at nos. 3, 27 and 219. All three are of two storeys and have little decoration other than the central aedicule. No. 3 is a very plainly detailed house with a rather unusual asymmetrical arrangement of six bays; it is in very poor condition and the only decorative detailing is that to the dormer, with a triangular pediment and flanking volutes. No. 27 is also a fairly small house and equally simply detailed apart from the aedicule, which again is flanked by simple baroque volutes and capped by a curved pediment; the only other decoration on its asymmetrical four-bay façade is the simple hood-moulding to the window heads.

The third house, no. 219, is a little more imposing. It has been altered at ground-floor level by the insertion of a shopfront, but is of five bays with a traditional plan and façade, which appears to be contiguous with an extension to the south. The chief feature of the house, however, is the complex aedicule in the roof containing a central round-headed light and flanked by two small rectangular lights. Separating the lights are four attached

216 Façade of house at no. 219 in Pellestrina, a modest structure but with a complex aedicule to the attic.

columns with high bases and cushion capitals; there are small volutes to the sides and above this miniature temple-front is a baroque pediment of some complexity and capped by three small obelisks. This very small but exuberant piece of decoration is unique on the island and contrasts curiously with the simple detailing to the rest of the house.

The last four *case padronali* form a disparate group scattered down the length of the village. No. 57 is a fairly large square house on three storeys, unusual in that it has no dormer in the roof; it is probably later in date than most of the others, and possibly of the early nineteenth century. The detailing is very simple apart from the stone cornice and the unusual facing of the façade with stone up to the level of the ground-floor window heads. No. 240 is an atypical house in that it is built over an arcade facing the waterfront. *Sottopòrteghi* are fairly rare here: there are seven in Pellestrina, all concentrated in the crowded *sestieri* of Busetti and Vianello and indicative of the scarcity of available building land here in the *settecento*. The house originally stood on the water's edge, like such houses at Murano: the land in front has been reclaimed. The house has been much altered by later extension but the original arcade is supported by large columns of Istrian stone, while there is a semicircular arch at each end. Detailing is very simple, although there is a large roof gable with its moulded pediment.

Finally there is the house at no. 427, near Ognissanti church, and now divided into two. It has much in common with houses such as that at nos. 14–20 as it is on three storeys with an attic. The form is symmetrical and the detailing again simple with the typical exception of the cornice and hood moulds to the first-floor windows. The door is flanked by oval

217   House at no. 240 in Pellestrina (left), with a colonnade onto the waterfront.

oculi characteristic of the seventeenth and early eighteenth centuries. In front of the house are two tiny one-roomed cottages that partially obscure the façade, but illustrate very clearly by this proximity the wide range of house types to be found on the *lido*.

4 *Case Padronali* at S. Vio

As at Pellestrina, the farmers' villas here take several forms; we may mention firstly the houses built on three storeys, all of which have a close resemblance to those noted above. The most imposing is that at no. 231 (Fig. 116), which is at present the post office; it has three particularly generous storeys although the detailing generally is spare, and even austere. Nevertheless, there are characteristic hood moulds to the ground- and first-floor windows, and a typical roof gable with volutes and tympanum. There is a spacious *pòrtego* to both upper floors, its location indicated by a simple paired light.

Very similar again is no. 111–113–114, which has now been divided into three separate houses. The original villa was of some size, indeed it was one of the largest on the *lido*, with a symmetrical façade nine bays long. This consists of a paired light to the central hall and four single lights on each side. Despite its size, the house is once again very simply detailed, the only notable feature being a prominent tympanum to the roof gable.

The last three-storey villa in this small group is at no. 174–5; this house and that adjacent to it are today in the same ownership so that their façade decoration is now also contiguous. No. 174, the larger house, is very similar to the two noted above, but has prominent stringcourses at window head and sill level, and a large central gable with volutes and pediment of more than usually complex profile. The smaller house (no. 175) cannot be

218 A very substantial *casa padronale* at nos. 111, 113 and 114 S. Vio, on three storeys and originally nine bays wide. It is now divided into three houses.

219 A pair of houses at nos. 174–5 S. Vio, of which the larger is a typical three-storey *casa padronale* of the later seventeenth or early eighteenth century.

220 House at no. 233 at S. Vio with traces of *trompe l'œil* decoration to the façade.

considered a *casa padronale* although it shares some of the same features as the larger and is again on three storeys. Both have been recently comprehensively restored.

The remaining *case padronali* at S. Vio are all of two storeys, and are typical of the genre. We may mention the house at no. 88 and its neighbour at nos. 90–3 (now two houses), both very similar indeed, fairly large houses of five bays, and both with very prominent roof gables. In both cases, too, the triangular tympana are capped by small obelisks, a further characteristic of several of these houses. The houses are very simple in their detailing and quite conventional in their form.

More interesting is the fairly small house at no. 233; in most respects it, too, is typical of the smaller farmers' villas of the lido. However, it is the only surviving house on the littoral to retain *trompe l'œil* decoration on the façade which appears to be original. The house is of two storeys and five bays with generally very simple detailing. The fresco work consists of painted triangular pediments and sills to the side windows and a painted surround to the central *pòrtego* window; there is also a painted cornice to the roof eaves and traces of a surround to the gable window. The work is now very faded but still identifiable. It was not uncommon to fresco façades in Venice, chiefly in the later *cinquecento* and the *seicento*, although the full extent of the practice may never be known since almost all examples from these periods have now been lost, apart from a few faded fragments. It must have been extremely rare in the lagoon, however, and no examples are known other than the much more notable Palazzo Trevisan at Murano, also of the *cinquecento*. There is certainly no known tradition of fresco painting at Pellestrina; indeed,

221 No. 281 at S. Antonio, one of a group of three such houses in this zone, all with prominent pedimented gables.

the *lido*'s very exposed position rendered such work even more subject to degradation by the elements than it was in the city centre.

Finally at S. Vio we may mention two further fairly compact houses that illustrate the difficulty of the precise definition of the *casa padronale*; no. 125 is a five-bay house on two storeys and fairly unremarkable in appearance, although it is clad with stone up to the top of the ground-floor windows and has a very modest balcony. In size it compares with the small group of *borghese* houses at Burano, and epitomises the lesser farmer's villa. The house at no. 160–1 is more substantial but virtually devoid of decoration, with the exception of the little triangular pediment to the roof gable. In plan it is symmetrical and traditional and may be seen as an example of the larger working farmhouse with some very modest architectural pretension, but which cannot really be considered a *casa padronale* as it is almost without decorative detail.

222 House at nos. 175–8 S. Antonio, now divided into two, but of the same type as no. 281.

5 *Case Padronali* at S. Antonio

Urban development at S. Antonio consists almost entirely of a single strip of housing along the lagoon shore. There are perhaps half a dozen noteworthy houses here, the first three of which may be grouped together as they are stylistically very similar and are also fairly close together; they are at nos. 221, 227 and 281. All three are symmetrical, five-bay houses on two storeys, and all have a prominent central roof gable crowned with a triangular pediment. In each case, too, a simple paired light indicates the *pòrtego*, and there is a similar light in the gable. One of the three has a large central balcony, while two of them (nos. 221 and 227) are decorated with three small obelisks on the corners of the pediment. The other house has the portal flanked by oval oculi; in all other respects the three are virtually identical. A very similar house can be seen at no. 175–8, which today is divided into two. We may also mention no. 145, another five-bay, two-storey house notable for the very curious parapet, consisting of three short pinnacles of profiled brickwork. As in a number of such houses, the ground floor is faced with slabs of stone up to window-head level.

Finally at S. Antonio, we have a very substantial house at no. 95, on the corner of Campo Paulotti. It is built on three floors but extremely simple in appearance, and almost devoid of decoration. Nevertheless it is the largest house in the zone, with a traditionally symmetrical plan and façade, although the interior has been much alterered and converted into smaller apartments (see fig. 30).

223   Porto Secco: house at no. 176, the finest farmer's villa in the little village.

6 *Case Padronali* at Porto Secco and S. Pietro in Volta

Porto Secco and its northern neighbour were historically the poorest of all the lagoon communities. Both villages were remote and isolated, on the furthest part of the *lido* from Chioggia but also some considerable and inconvenient distance from the capital. Most of the larger farmers and landowners of the littoral naturally chose to build their principal homes in or near Pellestrina itself, the village that has always been the socio-economic hub of the island. It is not surprising, therefore, to find that there are very few substantial *case padronali* in either village, although we will record these few here.

There is only one such house at Porto Secco, although it is a particularly fine example, at no. 176, a little north of the parish church. It is a large, square villa on three storeys with an attic, and recently restored. The detailing is very simple but the overall proportions quite refined; the roof gable is extremely simple, with no crowning pediment, and the only decorative feature on the façade is the characteristically bold hood-mould above the ground- and first-floor windows. The house also has three fine, large Venetian chimneys.

Further north at S. Pietro there is a handful of houses worthy of mention. Three are fairly typical smaller farmers' villas, with very simple façades and hardly any decorative features; these are at nos. 13, 16 and 85–6, the last now divided into two small cottages. No. 16 (also now subdivided) is the largest of the three, but despite its broad spacious elevation it, too, is almost devoid of decoration apart from the ubiquitous triangular pediment to the attic storey.

Two other houses are a little more unusual: that at no. 131, next to the parish church, has an elevation with a full-width gable and substantial accommodation in the roof. Not

224 A very simple *casa padronale* at no.13 S. Pietro in Volta.

225 The waterfront at S. Pietro, with the colonnaded house at no. 8 in the background.

226 The curiously embellished villa at no. 95 in S. Pietro, with 'Gothick' window heads.

far away at no. 160 is another atypical house with a broad façade of seven bays and again a double-pitch roof which is expressed on the façade by a very large gable. It is very simple in its detailing although it is certainly the largest house in the little village.

We may also mention the house at no. 8, which has a colonnade along the quay and two floors of accommodation above. The upper floors are supported by very large brick piers which thicken out to form buttresses for additional stability. Lastly, there is a most unusual house at no. 95, with its main façade at right angles to the quay. It was probably originally a fairly conventional two-storey, five-bay farmer's villa, but was later embellished with some highly eclectic decoration, probably during the last century. The two-light *pòrtego* window has been decorated with 'Gothick' Venetian trefoil heads, as have the four flanking windows and the two side wings are surmounted by an elaborate balustrade behind which is a roof terrace. The central bay rises to the second floor and is crowned by a broken pediment with a somewhat baroque profile.

7 The lesser farmworkers' houses

The *case padronali* form a fairly well-defined group, distinguished by their symmetrical plans and elevations, their classical detailing (however crude or minimal) and by the fact that most were designed as freestanding houses on their own sizeable plots. However, most villagers did not live in such houses but in a wide variety of lesser accommodation from tiny cottages to quite large but very simple farmhouses with no architectural aspirations at all. Pellestrina's houses have many sizes, shapes and plans and are far less easy to analyse than the cottages of Burano. We may briefly summarise the chief characteristics of the lesser houses in each of the built-up zones of the island.

Sestiere Busetti is densely built up. Because of the acute shortage of space, almost all houses here are on three storeys, with several on four floors. There are several fairly large houses, but a much larger number of tall, narrow houses much like those of Burano; many have asymmetrical plans and elevations. There are very few tiny cottages here as land was simply too scarce to be left so underdeveloped.

Sestiere Vianello is almost contiguous with Busetti and nearly as highly developed. There are a few *case padronali* here, mostly at the northern end, although again the most common house type is the narrow three-storey cottage. There is also at least one example of a speculative terrace, built along the waterfront. Sestiere Zennari is not highly urbanised and development is mostly confined to the waterfront strip. It does contain a good cross-section of house types, however, with two speculative terraces, several *case padronali* and examples of almost every house form between these two extremes.

Sestiere Scarpa is the largest of the four, with a very long shoreline; because of its distance from the centre of Pellestrina it has become virtually another self-contained village. There are several farmers' villas here, as well as number of large, simple farmhouses and smaller cottages. There are few four-storey houses but many smaller two- and three-storey cottages.

Porto Secco contains few larger houses, but again a good selection of lesser types; there are also a number of very small one- and two-roomed cottages. S. Pietro in Volta has a similar pattern of house types; even the few larger houses are very simple in appearance as S. Pietro was almost as poor and isolated as its neighbour.

If we proceed down the social scale from the *padroni* we come next to the builders of large but architecturally very simple farmhouses, and we may cite a few examples here. A house at no. 177 in Pellestrina well typifies the genre; it is a substantial structure, square and solidly built but with no architectural ornament whatsoever. In form it is roughly symmetrical although the two flank walls are very informally fenestrated, and there is a simple double-pitched roof. The most prominent features of the exterior are the large chimneys; all of the windows are small, simple rectangles. A similarly large and plainly detailed house is at no. 137 at S. Vio, in this case built on three storeys. Again there is no decorative detail to the façades, which are extremely plain, even austere, in appearance. There is some evidence that it was built as a semi-detached pair of houses, an unusual form here, and it was clearly a freestanding structure, capped by a simple four-way pitched roof. A third house of similar size to our first example (at no. 80 S. Antonio) has some claim to be classed as a small *casa padronale* with its symmetrical façade, carefully detailed hood-moulds to the windows and large prominent pediment for the full width of the façade.

We must now consider the larger cottages of the littoral. This group of houses is extensive and numerous and distinguishable from the *case padronali* and the other larger houses in two ways: firstly they are almost always asymmetrical in their plan and

227 A characteristic group of narrow-fronted cottages at nos. 107–26 S. Antonio; houses of four storeys are not uncommon where the frontage to the quay was so narrow.

elevational treatment, and secondly they are not designed as freestanding structures but almost always as elements in a terrace. They nearly all have narrow frontages and deep plans and all rise to three and sometimes four storeys. They are naturally concentrated in the most densely built-up zones and very closely resemble the three-storey cottages of Burano, both in plan and in appearance. That it was sometimes considered worth the expense of building to four storeys is clear evidence of the acute pressure on waterfront land for development, mostly in the first decades of the eighteenth century; such houses are prominent in Busetti but can be seen in several other locations further up the littoral.

Like their equivalents at Burano, these houses usually have two rooms on each floor, one behind the other, and the stair usually rises directly out of the rear room. Fireplaces are often built on the rear wall to serve the kitchen, but this position is by no means universal and sometimes they are on the flank or party wall and in a number of cases chimneys rise up the front façade.

Two or three examples, or groups of examples, will serve to illustrate the genre. The first is a group of houses at nos. 31, 35, 38, 40 and 46 in Pellestrina village, just south of S. Vio church. The five houses are separated from each other by parallel *calli* (here called *carrizzade* or lanes) which follow the old plot boundaries of the *lido*; all five are of three storeys, with fairly narrow façades but comparatively deep plans. They are all very similar in size but vary slightly in detail; four of them have double-pitched roofs with the gable on

228 A group of cottages on Campo Brasiola in S. Antonio, here all on three storeys.

229 Three-storey cottages at nos. 140–3 in S. Pietro in Volta.

the front façade; two have chimneys up this front elevation while the other three have their fireplaces on the flank or rear walls; two of the five have symmetrical façades with a central doorway, while the other three are asymmetrical.

There is a second group of rather smaller three-storey houses in S. Antonio on Campo Brasiola (nos. 31–48). They have extremely narrow façades (one of them is only about 2.5 metres wide) but deep plans; all are asymmetrical and very informal in appearance and one of the group is built over a *sottopòrtego*. Such houses are very similar to the archetypal Burano cottage and, like them, have no decorative detail in their appearance at all.

A third, final, example is a small group of four such houses at S. Pietro in Volta (nos. 140–3). Again all are on three storeys, with somewhat wider façades than the last example but in most other respects very similar in appearance.

8 The smallest cottages

The archetypal lagoon cottage can be found in its greatest numbers at Burano as a direct reflection of the remarkable social cohesion of the village. Pellestrina's cottages vary more widely in size and shape, and partly as a result of its poverty and isolation some parts of the *lido* retain a number of extremely small cottages. Although Pellestrina contained a number of *padroni* and a larger number of modest farmers, it also contained a significant group of disinherited, landless *mezzadri* and farm labourers, some of whom continued to live in great poverty until very recent times; their own tiny cottages can be seen in all parts of the littoral. There is some variation in their size and form depending on their location; in some zones they are on two storeys and sandwiched between larger houses, while in others they are detached single-storey cottages. Again we may cite a few examples to indicate the range of forms that may be seen.

An example of a very small cottage within a terrace is that at no. 176 in Pellestrina; it is on two storeys but has an extremely narrow frontage of barely 2.5 metres. There are two very small rooms on each storey, with the fireplace at the rear. No. 80, a little further north, is rather larger, again on two floors but with a symmetrical façade and a central roof gable surmounted by a triangular pediment, a very rare example of such a small house with architectural embellishments of this type.

There are several very small cottages adjacent to the church at S. Antonio, on Campiello dei Tre Gobbi to the south and on the quay just to the north. Most of them are on two floors with deep plans and narrow façades; we may note the group of three which abut the north flank of the church, and possibly built as a terrace. They have a wider elevation than many such houses but are extremely simple and with no external decoration whatsoever. Further very similar groups may be found at S. Vio, also near the church, and at Porto Secco.

There were still thirty-one cottages of timber on the *lido* at the beginning of the nineteenth century, although all have since disappeared; however, their survival for so long clearly illustrates the poverty of the island's underclass. For this group a simple one- or two-roomed hut was all that they could aspire to, and again, because of the isolation of the island, there remain several such cottages today – now of brick rather than timber – some time after these one-storey cottages have disappeared from Burano.

230 Pellestrina; the smallest cottages: a pair of tiny single-storey cottages at nos. 161–2 in S. Antonio.

In Pellestrina itself we may first mention the two tiny one-roomed houses at nos. 426 and 427 that were noted earlier. We cannot determine their age, although they are indicated on Monti's survey of 1840. Both of them consist of a single room measuring about three metres by five and with a simple double-pitched roof; the front façade consists of a central doorway flanked by two simple windows, and there is naturally no form of decoration at all.

There are two further examples of the genre at S. Antonio, at nos. 161 and 162, about 100 metres north of the church. They are built end-to-end and both again consist of a simple one-storey rectangle about six metres long and three in width. Again there is a double-pitched roof, but no perimeter gutter and no other form of architectural feature. One of the two cottages has been recently restored but the other has been uninhabited for some years and is now semi-derelict. On this part of the littoral there are seven other such basic cottages, usually with just a single room; we may cite as examples no. 1 S. Antonio, on the quay near Corte Amai, about 300 metres south of the church, and a similar group of three at the corner of Corte Gallina, some 200 metres north of the church. These last examples all have monopitch roofs but are otherwise very similar to the first cottages.

Nearly all of these smallest houses are built on or very near to the quay and with their long axis orthogonal to it. Most have a fireplace and chimney at one end, usually that away

231 Contrast at S. Antonio: a tiny one-cell cottage in the foreground and *casa padronale* behind it (nos. 80 and 81).

from the quay; the entrance is either at the other end, on the *fondamenta*, or on one of the long sides. The fenestration conforms to no particular pattern but followed the inclination of the builder, that is, probably the owner. Like the few such cottages in the capital they were almost incapable of internal subdivision, although cooking took place at one end while the other end was the all-purpose living room–bedroom.

9 Terrace developments

Our earlier observations on terrace development elsewhere, and particularly at Burano, all apply equally here. Large terraces are few and some that survive are of the nineteenth century. More common here are small blocks of houses containing perhaps four or five units, and sometimes only three. In contrast to the general pattern of urbanisation on the *lido*, most of the larger terraces lie parallel to the waterfront; however, these are fairly late in date and at least one is known to have been built on land reclaimed from the lagoon, and thus in front of the original quay of the village. Other longer terraces, such as the two parallel blocks next to S. Vio church, are quite modern and built with no regard for the traditional 'grain' of the urban structure.

The largest terrace in Pellestrina itself is at no. 214, between the *sestieri* of Busetti and Vianello. It is quite modern in date although it follows traditional forms fairly closely, with a row of prominent chimneys down the lagoon façade and typical detailing to doors and windows. A more authentically vernacular example is at S. Vio, about 100 metres north of

232 Terraces: a small terrace of broad-fronted cottages at S. Antonio, next to the church.

233 Terraces: a long terrace of nine cottages at S. Vio, several of which have been altered and enlarged.

the church, and consisting of a terrace of nine small cottages at the corner of Calle Capogianni. One or two of the cottages have been altered but most are largely un-modernised and consist of two rooms on each of two storeys. The houses have narrow frontages and are asymmetrically arranged; there is no form of decoration to their façades. The two modern terraces noted above are also nearby, at no. 268. Again the detailing is based on traditional forms but the scale of the terrace is out of character with the general urban context, and is simply too large and undifferentiated in appearance.

10 The use of colour on façades

We have mentioned the notable use of colour on façades at Burano; much of the extremely brightly coloured appearance of that island is of very recent origin, although there are many historical precedents for such decoration. Colour is also used to strong effect at Pellestrina, although usually in a slightly more muted way. Historically the render that protected houses was self-coloured by the use of brick dust or other additives as we saw in chapter 4. However, façades were also painted and this colouring is an important element in establishing the identity of a house and expressing the individuality of its owner. Many of the hundreds of small cottages at Burano and Pellestrina are very similar, indeed virtually identical, so that colour was one of the few ways in which the owner, at a modest cost, could 'personalise' his house. Traditionally, the façade colours were fairly muted, based on earth pigments, reds, browns and ochres. More recently, synthetic paints have led to the use of much brighter colours. We may note that at Pellestrina this decoration is often confined to the front façade onto the waterfront, and the rear elevation, towards the sea, is often left as render in its natural light grey colour. At Burano the colour is usually applied to all visible façades, although many cottages here are much smaller than those on the *lido*. The practice at Pellestrina is not confined to the smaller cottages but applies to all house types including the *case padronali*, many of which have been restored recently.

14

The rural and semi-rural environment, Mazzorbo, Torcello, Malamocco

Introduction

Mazzorbo, Torcello, Malamocco: these three islands today are small, still fairly isolated, and support modest communities traditionally based almost entirely on the land. In the medieval period both Torcello and Mazzorbo were thriving towns, each containing several thousand inhabitants, and with churches, monasteries, patrician villas, shops and warehouses. Both of them declined as Venice itself grew; our knowledge of the earlier history of both islands is so poorly documented that we can only begin to chart their history in detail from the sixteenth century. Already by this time they had both declined to become the sort of community that Sant'Erasmo has always been – small scattered villages of farmhouses and farmworkers' cottages. At Torcello we can still see a group of important buildings that give us an indication of the island's rich past, but today Torcello's lay population is smaller in number than that of any of the other settled islands of the lagoon, a mere hamlet.

As we saw at Pellestrina the dependence of a rural community on the land in the lagoon tended to produce a notably broader spectrum of wealth than we find in a community such as Burano, where almost all of the adult men were fishermen and all equally susceptible to fluctuations in their catch. All the rural communities have a similarly broad range of house types from substantial farmhouses to small cottages of the *mezzadri* (share-croppers). At both Torcello and Mazzorbo there were also a number of houses originally built by the nobility as hunting lodges or rural retreats, but the few of these that survived into the seventeenth century were by that time mostly leased to local farmers and thus also became simply working farmhouses.[1]

1 Mazzorbo

Mazzorbo is virtually contiguous with Burano, with which island it is connected by a long timber footbridge, a link that was established at least as early as the mid-seventeenth century. Medieval Mazzorbo, like Torcello, was famous for its monasteries, villas and

---

[1] Again the most important archival records for the demographic and urbanistic history of these three villages are summarised here:
   Mazzorbo: A.S.V. Dieci Savii B.459 and 472. See also the 1766 Anagrafe di Tutto lo Stato, and various *buste* in the series Podestà di Torcello, esp. B.433, 544.
   Torcello: the chief sources are as for Mazzorbo; see also B.549, 552, 554 in the Podestà di Torcello series; also Dieci Savii B.461; and Milizia da Mar B. 184; Catastico Napoleonico Lib.8.
   Malamocco: A.S.V. Dieci Savii B.458, 473.; Catastico Napoleonico Lib. 10; Milizia da Mar B.235 to 239; see also A.C. 766 for eighteenth-century surveys.

234 Mazzorbo: medieval house sometimes known as the Cà d'Oro, on the north side of the Mazzorbo Canal.

orchards; it had an equally important patrician element in its social history but also declined steadily during the fifteenth and sixteenth centuries as its canals silted and its nobility slowly abandoned the island for the capital.

By the later sixteenth century Mazzorbo's population was less than 500; most of the land was under vines or cultivated with vegetables. However, despite this decline, several medieval buildings still survived and three of them stand today. One is the gothic church of S. Caterina and the others are fine *case padronali* or *case coloniche* on the north side of the main channel, the Mazzorbo Canal. The houses are particularly important examples of such detached *casini* of the gothic era, very few of which have survived in these satellites of the capital. Unlike the roughly contemporary *palazzetti* of Murano which were all built in a fairly highly developed urban context, these two *casini* were built in a more remote suburban or semi-rural environment. They are both probably of the later fourteenth century, although the eastern house may be rather later than the other. It is not easy to reconstruct Mazzorbo's appearance in this period; it was probably still a community of some importance although its era of greatest prosperity and population had already passed. It is said that there were originally five parishes here, but these had already been reduced to only two by the end of the fifteenth century. The decline was very slow and protracted, however, and certainly at the time when these two houses were built it was still a significant settlement, with some important religious houses and undoubtedly a number of other substantial houses of the nobility.

The western of these *casini* is sometimes known as the Cà d'Oro and is a solidly built compact *casino* of the later medieval period. It may have been built by a branch of one of the noble clans of the capital, possibly as a base for hunting and fishing expeditions, and probably also as a working farmhouse with vines and orchards. The house is fairly modest in size, with the broad, comparatively shallow plan that we see in many other, later, *case padronali*. It was clearly designed as a detached house with no immediate neighbours on either side; the plan is a compact rectangle, on two storeys, with a four-way pitched tiled roof. The main façade to the Mazzorbo Canal is slightly asymmetrical, with the doorway off-centre; it has a simple square surround of Istrian stone. The three ground-floor windows have radiused heads, while all of those to the *piano nobile* have gothic heads; these consist of a two-light window to the *pòrtego* and three single lights. The plan is basically conventional and tripartite with the smaller rooms flanking the hall on both sides. There is little decoration to the exterior, apart from the stone window heads; the broad façade has a pronounced horizontality with proportions of about $1\frac{1}{2}$ to 1, and these dimensions and proportions compare very closely with many later *case padronali*, particularly at Pellestrina.

The second medieval house is situated about 150 metres along the same waterfront as the first. It appears to be of slightly later date and is of quite different proportions; like the first house, however, it was also apparently built as a detached, freestanding structure, and there are several outbuildings on one side. The façade to the canal has a double-pitched roof, with the gable facing the canal; there are two main storeys but also further accommodation in the attic. The elevation is symmetrical with the exception of the doorway, which is slightly off-centre; this portal, like that on the Cà d'Oro, is a simple frame of stone, although all the windows are gothic. They consist of two lights flanking the doorway, two others directly above them and a paired light to the *pòrtego*. Above this last, a single additional gothic window lights the attic. All of the windows have identical detailing except that to the attic which has a cusped intrados and extrados very similar to the windows of the Cà d'Oro. There is no further decoration other than a small stone panel set into the façade. The overall form and proportions of the *casino* are quite different from the first house; the plan is narrower but considerably deeper, and thus more closely resembles the plans of the contemporaneous city *palazzi*, which were built on sites of restricted width but adequate depth. Despite these urban qualities the house is another valuable survivor of such a *casino*.

The government land register of 1581 lists eighty houses at Mazzorbo of which fourteen were still owned by the patriciate, including five in the hands of the Zorzi. Most of these houses were quite large, and those rented out to local villagers realised rents three or four times as high as those for one of Burano's small cottages. It is clear, therefore, that many of Mazzorbo's houses at the end of the sixteenth century were the solid substantial farm-houses and *casini* several of which we can still see today, chiefly on the banks of the Mazzorbo Canal.

Earlier in the century the island had still been a popular place of resort for patricians seeking escape from the noisy, crowded city, but by the end of the *cinquecento* this interest

235 Mazzorbo: the second gothic *casa padronale*, also on the north bank of the main waterway.

had virtually ceased and only two of those noble *casini* were still used for that purpose. The community was indeed continuing its slow decline and by 1661 all of the houses still owned by the patriciate here were now let to local smallholders and farmers. A number of sizeable houses remained, however, and of the remaining 66, about 20 could be described as *casini* or *case padronali*; several of them can be identified with a high degree of confidence today. Most of the rest of the houses were much smaller farm workers' cottages with only two or three rooms, compared with the seven, eight or more rooms of the larger *casini*.

Mazzorbo's decline continued into the eighteenth century, however, and by mid-century only 43 houses remained; again they fell into two well-defined categories, the larger *case padronali* and the much smaller cottages. The village has changed very little since that date and most of the larger houses described below were probably built in the latter part of the *cinquecento* or the second half of the following century. Some were built by the nobility – mostly the older houses – and the remainder by local landowners for use as working farmhouses.

All of these larger houses, whether built by patricians or local farmers, have features inherited from the gothic *case padronali*, and in particular from the type exemplified by the Cà d'Oro. The chief of these characteristics are the overall dimensions and proportions of the houses; they have broad elevations with a strong horizontal emphasis and in many cases the width of the house is equal to or greater than its depth. This form is typical of

236 Mazzorbo: *casa colonica* of the seventeenth century near the two gothic houses, and recently restored.

houses built where land was not so scarce and pressures for high-density development not so acute; the *case padronali* of Pellestrina are nearly all of similar proportions as are some of Murano's villas. At Mazzorbo houses like the Cà d'Oro seem to have formed a local model for several later houses, as we see below; details of fenestration are naturally different in the *cinquecento* houses but the dimensions and volumes are very similar.

Mazzorbo is divided into two parts by the wide channel of the Mazzorbo Canal; nearly all of the modern hamlet lies on the east side, but there are four noteworthy houses on the other bank in addition to the two medieval *casini* noted above. Approaching from the south, that is from Venice, the first house is a substantial *casa colonica* probably of the later sixteenth or seventeenth century. In appearance it is fairly simple, with little decoration, although it is quite large with fine proportions, and a symmetrical façade two storeys high and five bays long. It is surmounted by a double-pitch roof into which is inserted a central gable with pediment and simple flanking volutes. All of the openings have square heads and simple stone surrounds; the only elements of sculpted detail are hood-moulds above the ground-floor windows and a stone cornice-gutter on corbels.

Like the other Renaissance houses along this waterfront it was built as a detached *casino*, and like most of the others it has annexes and outbuildings that indicate its function as a working farmhouse. In this and the other examples, we see features similar to those of the *case padronali* of Pellestrina – broad façades, usually of five bays, and often with a central gable, symmetrical tripartite plans, and arranged nearly always on two storeys. On plan the central *androne* and *pòrtego* usually take the form of a spacious corridor rather than a *salone* and there are usually four rooms to each floor; in essence, therefore, they closely

237 Mazzorbo: a fine example of the *casa colonica*, also probably of the early seventeenth century.

resemble the *borghese* houses of Burano and Murano, although usually on a slightly larger scale.

A little further along the canal is another detached house, unusual in this group in that it is built on only one storey, albeit with a large central roof gable. Again it is five bays wide, with a central doorway flanked by two oval oculi characteristic of the *seicento*. The next house to it, at no. 48, is perhaps the finest of these *casini*; it is similar in size to the first, and also dates from the later sixteenth or early seventeenth century. Again there is a symmetrical façade of five bays, but here more prominence is given to the first floor, which has windows with semicircular heads and a large central window to the *pòrtego* with a balcony. As is usual with these houses there is very little applied decoration, the only notable feature being a prominent cornice on corbels. However, the overall proportions of the house are particularly fine, and again may be compared with some of the *case padronali* of Pellestrina and the later villas of Murano. The plan is conventional and tripartite, with four large rooms in each corner, and a spacious central hall or corridor. As in most of these rural or semi-rural houses, the fireplaces and chimneys are placed on the gable walls; the range to the kitchen can sometimes be identified from outside as a much larger projection than the others, often containing an inglenook inside. Such arrangements are far less common in more densely built-up environments, where the kitchen range is thus more often positioned on the back wall.

238 Mazzorbo: a slightly smaller house of the same genre as the above, and only four bays wide, rather than the usual five.

239 Mazzorbo: house at no. 23, on the south bank of the Mazzorbo Canal: detail of the central bay of the façade, with highly eclectic stone detailing probably of the seventeenth century.

The last house in this small group is a smaller, more compact house, again of two storeys, but only four bays wide. The entrance is thus off-centre and the interior asymmetrical. The house has recently been restored (as have most of the others) but it is difficult to date its original construction. The openings are all square and very simple, the only decoration to the façade being a prominent cornice supported on an unusual row of miniature corbelled arches; in other respects the house broadly conforms to the *casa padronale* type, with a broad plan and comparatively shallow depth.

On the canal bank opposite this scattered string of individual houses there is an almost continuous row of structures of various sizes and types, most of which are of the seventeenth and eighteenth centuries. A few are large but very simple in appearance, representative of the working farmhouse as the hub of a large extended family rather than the *casa padronale* of a noble or other absentee owner. Of these larger houses, one (no. 23) is particularly noteworthy as the exception to this general observation. It is probably of the later seventeenth century and has unusual decoration on the façade. The house has a broad plan but is only one room deep; it is on two floors with a hipped gabled roof. The façade has probably been altered, since the ground floor has five bays and the first only three; two upper windows have probably been filled in. The central doorway is surrounded by rusticated stonework, and all four ground-floor windows have surrounds of coursed stone with elaborate volutes, scrolls and keystones in an odd, mannerist style. Above the doorway is a large window to the *pòrtego* and this is detailed in a correct but rather heavily classical manner with a triangular tympanum above and a robust stone balcony below. The two remaining outer windows to the first floor are undecorated. It is possible that these various embellishments were added to an earlier house in an attempt to 'modernise' it and there are no comparable examples of such detailing in any other house in these villages.

The Canale di S. Caterina, leading to the homonymous church, is the secondary axis of the little community, and on its banks are several substantial houses; two may be described as *case padronali* and the first stands adjacent to the timber footbridge. It is probably of the seventeenth century and built on two storeys, with a typical five-bay façade. The entrance is flanked by two oval oculi and above it a single large window lights the *pòrtego*. The plan is conventional, although the position of the two chimneys rising up the front façade is unusual; this is probably because the house is flanked on both sides by a pair of small cottages, probably for farmworkers on the owner's estate.

The other larger house is on the opposite bank, about 100 metres further towards S. Caterina. It has recently been restored and is a detached *casa padronale* of the conventional type, with five bays and built on two storeys; here there is also a prominent central gable with pediment and flanking volutes. In many ways the house epitomises the genre, although we cannot be sure whether it was built by the nobility, by a prominent local landowner or indeed by the Church, which owned a significant proportion of the land of Mazzorbo.

Of the smaller houses and cottages of the village, nearly all stand on the east bank of the main channel. They closely resemble the cottages of Burano in their appearance, most being simple two-storey structures, with two rooms to each floor. Few are worthy of individual mention since they conform closely to the narrow range of types discussed

240 Mazzorbo: houses along the main quay of the little village, a mixture of small cottages and fairly substantial, but very simple farmhouses.

earlier; however, we may mention one cottage adjacent to the ferry landing-stage which is a little unusual in its form – no. 50. It has a broad façade but is only one-room deep, and there is thus a central doorway with a single room on either side of the hall; there is only one full storey, although above the entrance is a large, oversized gable with a single room in the roof. The cottage also has a prominent carved stone cornice-gutter which, like the gable, appears to be far too elaborate for such a small dwelling.

2 Torcello

The general history and the long, slow decline of Torcello very closely follow the path of its close neighbour, Mazzorbo, and for similar reasons. Torcello reached its peak of importance in the early medieval period and from this apogee there began a decline that has continued almost uninterrupted until our own day, with only a brief respite in the eighteenth century. Of flourishing medieval Torcello, with its famous and powerful monasteries, its international trade and its noble villas we know very little indeed; and of the domestic buildings of that era, with only one exception, we similarly have no trace.

Torcello is a rare example of a community that has slowly withered away leaving hardly any of its shops, houses or workshops, but instead leaving to us only its public buildings, its cathedral and Palazzo Comunale. Torcello's civic square is still surrounded by its public buildings but the square itself is grassed as it was a millennium ago, and beyond it there is no city, not a town, hardly even a village, but only a handful of farmhouses and a few fields of vines and artichokes.

We cannot draw any detailed conclusions as to the appearance of medieval Torcello, and can only begin its documented history in the later sixteenth century, by which time there were only 30 houses and a bakery, which together with the civic buildings on the Piazza, constituted the entire community of 150 people. It is true that numbers slowly increased in the seventeenth and early eighteenth centuries but even by the census of 1766 the population had still not passed three hundred. In the seventeenth century most of the fifty-odd houses were owned by the several rich and influential monasteries that still flourished, and the rest were the property of Venetian nobles, relics of the earlier time in which Torcello had been an important community, 'capital' of the northern lagoon. By the mid-eighteenth century, half of the houses were still in Church hands, while ten noble clans retained their ancient estates and most Torcellani were thus tenants of absentee owners. They remained so until the Napoleonic dissolution of the monasteries in the early nineteenth century; by now the tide had already turned again, and Torcello began the decline that has continued to our own day. Today there are only a dozen houses standing; most are fairly large, substantial farmhouses, built probably in the period of slow expansion in the later seventeenth and early eighteenth centuries. Few have any notable architectural features and their importance simply lies in the fact that they have survived to represent the genre and to house the survivors of this once rich community.

The medieval legacy

Medieval Torcello was not only a populous and wealthy community, but the administrative centre for all of the northern lagoon. Its subject communities included nearby Burano and Mazzorbo, but also a number of settlements that have since entirely disappeared as a result of the lowering of land levels, of malaria and depopulation. These towns included Costanziaca, Ammiana, Ammianella and S. Cristina. Torcello's importance was thus partly based on its economic significance, partly because it was a major religious centre and partly as the geographical hub of this group of communities. It probably reached its maximum importance in the twelfth or thirteenth centuries, that is, the period after the construction of the two churches of S. Maria Assunta and S. Fosca. These structures are two of the most important early buildings in the lagoon, although a detailed analysis of them is out of place here. Nevertheless they epitomise Torcello's importance in the emerging Venetian state, an importance that had probably already begun to decline by the time of construction of the two little *palazzi* that stand on the square opposite these two churches. In Torcello's long history of decline, these two small civic buildings are nearly as significant as relics of the lay community as the churches are in assessing the island's ecclesiastical importance. They provide an almost unique insight into the physical environment in which the administration of the medieval town was executed. Both buildings stand on one side of the grassed Piazza that forms the hub of the present hamlet and formed its original civic focus. They are both very small; the Palazzo Comunale stands opposite S. Fosca, while the other, the Palazzo dell' Archivio is a little to the north and at right angles to the first. Between the two originally stood the residence of the *podestà*, the site of which is now indicated by a solitary brick wall, the only surviving

241 Torcello: main façade of the Palazzo Comunale onto the piazza of the hamlet.

fragment. Together, these three buildings formed a unified whole, a civic group that faced the ecclesiastical group across the square; this latter group consisted of the cathedral, the little chapel of S. Fosca, the baptistry that formerly stood in front of the cathedral, and finally the great bulk of the *campanile* rising behind them.

The Palazzo Comunale today houses the little Museo dell'Estuario and has recently been restored. It is a small rectangular building all of brick with stone detailing. The council chamber, which occupies the whole of the first floor, is approached by an open stair at one end, and above the doorway is a small *campanile* with a bell to summon the citizens to meetings. (A small additional stair has now been inserted inside the building.) The *palazzo* as we see it now is later in date than the adjacent Palazzo dell' Archivio; we know that it underwent extensive restoration in 1443 (see Appendix II) but we cannot be sure of the date of its original construction. The window detailing, however, is gothic, and the paired light to the first-floor hall has heads that suggest the later *trecento*. On the long façade towards the Piazza there is a very simple doorway flanked by two pairs of windows, all with flat segmental arched heads. The upper windows, though, are gothic and have the small pointed cusped extrados typical of the fourteenth century. Equally characteristic of the period is the detailing to the columns between the lights, with their rather flat relief and stylised Corinthian motifs.

The construction of the *palazzo* is simple and logical; the roof has a double-pitch with the ridge parallel with the long axis of the building. The floor of the council chamber is supported by the usual Venetian system of closely spaced timber beams, but they are strengthened by the insertion of a longitudinal spine-beam down the centre of the floor,

242 Torcello: façade of the Palazzo dell' Archivio.

which halves the span, and is itself carried by two stone columns. The council hall is quite small, and was intended to house no more than perhaps thirty or thirty-five men. It is consistent in scale with the adjacent *fòntego*, and the impression given by the two structures is that they formed the civic nucleus of a significant but by no means very large community, and certainly not a community of the size and wealth of Chioggia in the later thirteenth and early fourteenth centuries.

The Palazzo dell'Archivio was built to house the community's flour and grain supplies, and is considerably older than the Palazzo Comunale. Indeed, the form of the window heads on the first floor is Veneto-Byzantine in style, with stilted arches surmounted by a stone head with a small cusp at the apex, very similar in profile to those on city *palazzi* such as Cà Falier at SS. Apostoli and Palazzo Vitturi in Campo S. Maria Formosa, although simpler than those on the latter house. The small columns and capitals to the three-light window at first floor here are almost identical to those on Cà Falier, as are the mouldings generally. Arslan has suggested that Cà Falier is of the second half of the thirteenth century and so we may attribute a similar date to the *fòntego* here at Torcello. This conclusion means that this is perhaps the earliest structure in the lagoon outside Venice with the exception of the two adjacent churches and S. Donato at Murano.

In this early period Torcello was still a flourishing and important community; however, its provisions for its own citizens in time of war or famine seem to have been very modest,

243 Torcello: detail of the façade of the Palazzo dell' Archivio, showing the ground-floor colonnade. Like the Palazzo Comunale it has been altered on several occasions, and the square first-floor windows are later insertions.

as the size of the *fòntego* attests. Chioggia's *fòntego*, which was rebuilt in the 1320s, is considerably larger, and the granaries of the capital, as we might expect, were vast and extensive. It is unwise to speculate further on Torcello's size and wealth in this period, however, since there may perhaps have been another warehouse elsewhere or, alternatively, it may have been assumed that emergency supplies could have been obtained from the capital.

The *fòntego* is built on two storeys, the ground floor consisting of an open loggia with walls on three sides and the fourth open to the square. This façade is supported by a row of stone columns with larger brick piers to the corners; there are five bays, with a large timber beam supporting the first-floor warehouse, and which is strengthened by fine carved *barbacani* of complex profile. The first floor is approached by an open stair at one end, all of brick, and the room is lit by the three-light window noted above (in the centre of the façade) and two large rectangular lights, one on each side. The elevation thus suggests

244 Torcello: the most prominent of the few remaining houses is this *casa padronale* near the Palazzo Comunale.

that behind it there lies the traditional Venetian tripartite plan, although the *fòntego* almost certainly occupied the whole area of the first floor. The rectangular windows are not original, however, and only the central *trifora* allows us to date the building; it was undoubtedly restored on many occasions in the following centuries.

Both *palazzi* were built as freestanding structures (as was the house of the *podestà*), a further indication that even the most central zones of Torcello were never built up to the very high densities that prevailed elsewhere, in Chioggia, in parts of Murano and of course in Venice itself. The general offices for the administration of the northern lagoon were probably located in the ground floor of the Palazzo Comunale; a comparison between it and the Palazzo Comunale of Malamocco is instructive, as we see further below. The latter is considerably larger than that of Torcello, and contained not only the council hall but rooms for various other offices and possibly space for the storage of grain and other goods as well.

245 Torcello: a fairly typical substantial farmhouse, surrounded by vines and market-gardens.

The housing

The hamlet today contains barely a dozen houses, most of which stand on the banks of the Rio di Torcello, the main axis of the tiny community. The only surviving medieval house stands apart from this nucleus, towards the east. It is a substantial *casino* of gothic appearance, recently restored, which in size and general appearance resembles the two medieval houses on Mazzorbo. It is built on two storeys, and has similar accommodation to the Mazzorbo houses, although is perhaps of slightly later date. There is a fine example of an *altana* on the roof as well as some characteristic Venetian chimneys.

The remaining houses here are nearly all fairly large detached farmhouses, built at various times from the seventeenth to the nineteenth century. We may begin our brief survey in the Piazza; a few metres from the Palazzo Comunale is a large, fine *casa padronale*, the most imposing house in the village. It is probably of the seventeenth century, with a symmetrical five-bay façade and two principal storeys. There is also a prominent central gable with two small windows, capped by a tympanum and flanked by fairly simple volutes. The house was clearly designed as a detached villa, albeit a modest one, and the other three façades are detailed in a very similar manner to the front elevation.

Behind the *fòntego* is another substantial house, but considerably later in date, with a simple double-pitched roof, and a narrow, asymmetrical plan. Further south, we come to the Rio di Torcello and the Locanda Cipriani, which today consists of several quite small houses joined together to form this famous inn. The north wing is of very simple

246 Torcello: a very substantial three-storey farmhouse, with a particularly prominent fireplace containing a range and oven.

appearance, and probably originally consisted of three quite small cottages, with very little exterior decoration. The south wing was also a separate house, rather larger, but again with simple detailing. A few metres south again, and built right on the canal's edge is another typical Torcello farmhouse. It is on two storeys, with a comparatively long, narrow plan, with the axis parallel to the canal. The exterior is plain, the only ornamentation being a cornice of corbelled brickwork; all the windows are small, simple rectangles; the most notable feature of the exterior is the large prominent chimney with its characteristic *comignolo*.

Almost all of the other surviving houses line the west bank of the Rio di Torcello. Proceeding southwards, the first is set back some distance from the *rio*; it is a large, detached farmhouse difficult to date with accuracy but probably of the eighteenth century. The detailing is again simple, with no superfluous ornament, and the most notable features are again the prominent chimneys. The plan is rectangular, and the house is roofed with a double-pitch, but an asymmetrical one, an unusual form in such houses.

The next house down the quay is a comparatively low construction, on two storeys with a symmetrical five-bay main façade; it has been considerably modified in its recent transformation into a *trattoria*. A few yards further along the *fondamenta* is Torcello's largest farmhouse, a substantial structure on three floors. In some ways it has the appearance of a villa rather than a simple farmhouse, although there is once again little decoration. The form is entirely traditional, with a symmetrical façade and tripartite plan, and a balcony to the first-floor *pòrtego*. There are three prominent chimneys, two serving conventional fireplaces, while the third terminated in a large kitchen range and bakery oven, clearly expressed projecting from the north wall of the house. The house may have been built as a patrician *casino*, but was clearly intended to be a practical farmhouse as well. The house immediately adjacent to the well-known Ponte del Diavolo is somewhat unusual and probably one of the later houses to be built here. It is again of some size, with a symmetrical five-bay façade. Above the two fairly conventional lower floors is an attic storey which is lit on the front solely by two small oval oculi; above them the corbelled brick cornice forms the only decoration to this otherwise very simple façade.

3 Malamocco

Introduction: the Palazzo Comunale

Malamocco is a small compact hamlet near the southern end of the Lido of Venice. Although today an integral part of the littoral, its original natural site consisted of two tiny islets just off the lee, or western shore of the Lido, and it has become 'embedded' in the territory of the littoral as a result of reclamation both north and south of the village; its main street, formerly a canal, has also been reclaimed. The topography of the littoral closely resembles that of Pellestrina immediately to the south and its history in general also followed a similar course. The *lido* was sparsely settled until quite modern times, although the hamlet of Malamocco itself is of early medieval origin and thus historically formed the local nucleus for the scattered farmers on the littoral.

However, Malamocco has always been small and isolated; the two notable medieval buildings that survive there today reflect its modest importance as the administrative centre for the nearby *lido*, which was governed by a *podestà*, one of the four of the lagoon. Like the others, he was appointed by the Signoria and presided over meetings of the village council, which sat in the Palazzo Comunale that can be seen today near the lagoon waterfront. The little village also contained the spiritual focus of the *lido* in the form of the parish church, as well as the bakery and an inn or *osteria*.

Because of its proximity to Venice, the ownership of land on the *lido* was very mixed: the northern part was mostly in the hands of the Church and a number of noble clans, while the southern part was mostly owned by local farmers, although the parish church also owned many vineyards, particularly between Malamocco and Alberoni. Patrician interests here were broadly similar to those at Torcello and Mazzorbo: most estates were quite small, although several had substantial farmhouses built on them. A few were used as *casini* but most were let to local farmers as tenants or *mezzadri*. The little nucleus of Malamocco thus contained various facilities for the farmers and market-gardeners of the littoral.

The houses in the village today show a fairly wide range of types reflecting the comparatively broad social spectrum of the community and the *lido*. There were a few quite large estates as well as a number of very small holdings; of the larger holdings of the

247 Malamocco: the Palazzo Comunale from the lagoon shore, immediately after its recent restoration (1985–6).

nobility we may mention those of the Tiepolo who owned a *casino* at the east end of Malamocco's main canal, on the Piazza delle Erbe (see below). Most of the other larger houses also lined the main axis, which had a quay down each side, until its reclamation in the early nineteenth century. These larger houses that we see today are mostly of the later sixteenth and seventeenth centuries, built as a result of steadily increasing numbers, both in the village and on the *lido* in general.

Before this *cinquecento* expansion, medieval Malamocco was a compact little community, and in addition to the Palazzo Comunale and the house nearby, there are medieval fragments surviving in at least three other houses. Of these medieval survivors, the Palazzo Comunale is the most important and is another member of the small group of civic buildings from this period that survive in the lagoon today. In several aspects it resembles the contemporaneous private houses in the city, although it naturally had to accommodate quite different functions. The most important of these was the hall for council meetings, the council being drawn not only from the village but from the whole littoral as well, from as far as S. Nicolò near its northern end. There were also several local officials whose needs had to be accommodated in the Palazzo including the treasurers and the *cancelliere*. As at Torcello the hall is on the first floor, with ancillary accommodation below it. The Palazzo is a substantial building, larger than those of Torcello or Burano, possibly because it was also used for storing grain and other supplies; we do not know of

248 Malamocco: detail of the south-west corner of the façade, showing gothic stonework, probably of the mid-fifteenth century.

any separate *fòntego* here for this purpose, although the *fòntego* was usually a separate structure, again with the storage at first-floor level, to prevent damage by flooding or attack by rats.

The Palazzo Comunale is an important building and, like so many other noteworthy buildings in the lagoon, has recently been restored. It is on two storeys, with one main façade onto the village square, opposite the church, and the other facing the open lagoon. Both façades are nearly symmetrical; in the centre of each one is a fine three-light window indicating the position of the council hall. As in the case of the *fòntego* of Torcello, the position of this window in the centre of the façade recalls the typical fenestration pattern of the Venetian *palazzo*; here, too, the multi-light window is flanked by single lights, in this case two on one side and one on the other. The position of the council hall thus corresponds with that of the *pòrtego* in a private house and it is similarly flanked by lesser accommodation. All of the first-floor windows have gothic heads and are probably of the middle part of the fifteenth century. The flank walls have similar windows, with five single lights along the southern wall to light the ancillary accommodation. The ground-floor

The main door is that onto the Campo della Chiesa. The west elevation, to the lagoon, formerly stood almost at the water's edge, and the land in front is all reclaimed. The landward approach was the more important one here and indeed the secondary door is that to the *calle* at the side. Both of these main doorways have characteristic late gothic surrounds, with square heads, a broad flat architrave, and in the case of the entrance to the *campo* a typical dog-tooth moulding to the outer edge.

The façade to the square is embellished with various panels and inscriptions including a large stone lion of S. Marco in bas-relief which may once have been mounted over the portal. Most of the other details of the Palazzo are typical of the period and of buildings of such size, whether private or public. There are stone cornice-gutters along both main elevations; that to the lagoon has a carved lozenge pattern again characteristic of the period and is supported on carved stone brackets. Above the *campo* façade is a tiny stone frame supporting a bell to summon villagers to council meetings.

Since this is the last of the small group of civic buildings in this survey we may draw some general conclusions as to their design and appearance. Their planning naturally reflects the specific functions they were required to contain, but there was a conscious effort to accommodate those functions in such a way that the completed building closely resembled the contemporaneous *palazzetti* by which they were originally surrounded. This attempt to conform to these typologies is particularly clearly seen at Torcello and here at Malamocco where the disposition of fenestration precisely echoes that of private houses of similar size. The overall volume and scale of these public buildings also conforms to this pattern: a lower, simply detailed ground floor is surmounted by a higher, more important *piano nobile* (in these cases containing the council hall) and which again corresponds with the *piano nobile* of the private houses. The detailing reinforces this vertical zoning, with simple fenestration to the ground floor and taller, more elaborately carved windows to the first floor.

In all of these public *palazzi* the detailing generally, however, is fairly restrained. The buildings naturally reflected the status of the community that they served; none of these settlements was very large or prosperous and the quality of workmanship reflects the balance between the need to provide on one hand a suitable degree of dignity for the building that formed the civic focus of the whole community and on the other the extremely humble status of many of that community's citizens. The exception to the fairly modest appearance of these Palazzi Comunali was undoubtedly the lost Palazzo of Chioggia, demolished in the mid-nineteenth century. It was considerably larger than the others, as befitted the second city of the lagoon, and was a rambling structure originally built towards the end of the thirteenth century but restored and adapted on several occasions. Imposing in appearance, it nevertheless conformed to the general pattern with the hall of the Maggior Consiglio centrally positioned on the first floor, with a low ground floor of ancillary accommodation and a generally symmetrical façade.

These lesser Palazzi Comunali thus share several common features; all are fairly small and domestic in scale and character, and all are on two storeys, with the hall at first floor. Although their internal planning is not always precisely symmetrical, there is in every

249 Malamocco: house known as that of the *podestà*: general view of the façade showing the unusual central gable.

250 Malamocco: house of the *podestà*: detail of the central bay of the façade with gothic *bifora* and square portal.

251 Malamocco: a much altered gothic house on Rio Terrà, possibly the remains of the Tiepolo *casino*.

case an attempt to achieve symmetry on their main façades. The arrangement here at Malamocco closely follows the domestic tripartite form, with the hall in the position of the *pòrtego*, flanked by lesser accommodation on both sides. In the asymmetrical example at Burano we have a bipartite plan, with the main hall and only one side wing.

Medieval houses

Apart from the Palazzo Comunale there is only one intact medieval building in Malamocco, a house almost adjacent to the church in the same *campo* as the Palazzo. It is sometimes referred to as the house of the *podestà* and this may indeed have been the case; its location would certainly support such a conclusion. The house is conventional in some respects, but with the exception of the large gable above the first floor. The form is symmetrical, with a central portal with stone surrounds, simple and square in profile, and very similar indeed to that on the adjacent Palazzo Comunale. The ground-floor windows are simple rectangles, but on the *piano nobile* there is a paired light to the *pòrtego* flanked by two pairs of single lights; all of these have trilobate heads suggesting a date of construction of the late fourteenth or early fifteenth century, and hence possibly earlier than the Palazzo. Although the heads are different, the capitals, pilasters and sills are almost identical to those on the Palazzo Comunale, and strongly suggest that one building served as a convenient model for the other. The façade is conventional, therefore, apart from the wide gable which has a double pitch and a raised central section, surmounted by a brick cornice. The profile is unique in the lagoon.

252 Malamocco: a single gothic window is all that remains of another medieval house in Piazza delle Erbe.

The other traces of medieval Malamocco are very few, and consist chiefly of three gothic houses, all of which have been very much altered over the centuries. The first is at no. 46 Rio Terrà, together with the adjacent house; the medieval fragments consist of four gothic windows, irregularly disposed. In Gallo's survey of the lido in 1557 this end of the main axis of the little community was occupied by the large house owned by the Tiepolo, and the gardens of which occupied all of the south-east corner of the island. It is likely, therefore, that these gothic fragments are the much-altered remains of the Tiepolo *casino*, shown only as a pictograph by Gallo, but which was also only on two storeys.

Further along the south side of Rio Terrà, there is another medieval fragment at no. 14, adjacent to Sottopòrtego Povolato, where a single window head is all that can be seen of another, small, gothic house. The last medieval relic also consists of a solitary window, on the first floor of a house on the north side of Piazza delle Erbe, near the village gate. This window is of the trilobate type, with some quite fine detailed carving, suggesting that this was once a house of some distinction. The detailing is very similar to that on the house of the *podestà*, and is thus perhaps also of the early fifteenth century.

The later houses

Immediately adjacent to the church are two good examples of medium-sized *case padronali*: one is on the south side of Campo della Chiesa (Catastico Napoleonico no. 308) and the other on the east side of Piazza Maggiore (C.N. no. 773). Both are on two storeys, with broad and comparatively low principal elevations typical of the genre. Both have conventional tripartite plans, and simple façades, and probably date from the latter part of the

253 Malamocco: *casa padronale* on Campo della Chiesa next to the Palazzo Comunale.

sixteenth or early seventeenth century; one of them can be tentatively identified on Gallo's survey of 1557. As in the case of many of the smaller houses at Burano and Pellestrina, only the heads and sills of the windows generally are of stone; the jambs are of painted rendered brick. However, both houses are quite large and represent the small group of reasonably well-off local farmers, broadly the same socio-economic group as those who built the *case padronali* of Pellestrina.

There are several other larger houses in the village of the same type, but of rather later date. One of the largest stands next to the little bridge that joins Malamocco to the lido (C.N. no. 374); it is probably of the seventeenth century and has the broad spacious plan typical of these lesser villas and *case padronali*. The plan and façade are conventional and tripartite, with a large prominent central dormer containing three lights, flanked by large volutes and capped by a triangular pediment. Further down the Piazza, on the corner of the Merceria, is another substantial house (C.N. no. 326), very similar indeed to those at Pellestrina. Unlike most of Malamocco's houses it is on three storeys, with a compact, almost cubical form, probably as a direct result of the restricted nature of its site. The only similar house in the village is that diagonally opposite (C.N. no. 349) which is much later

254 Malamocco: a substantial seventeenth-century house next to the village gate and the bridge to the Lido.

255 Malamocco: a large three-storey house on the corner of the Merceria, very similar to a group of such farmers' villas at Pellestrina.

256 Malamocco: detail of the rear façade of the house in Fig. 255, showing typically simple robust detailing of the seventeenth and eighteenth centuries.

in date, probably of the latter part of the eighteenth century. It, too, has a compact, square plan, with three storeys and an attic.

A smaller house of the *casa padronale* type is that on the south side of Piazza delle Erbe (C.N. no. 219) almost adjacent to the Tiepolo house; this is probably of the seventeenth century and compares very closely with the smaller *case padronali* of Pellestrina and the slightly larger houses of Burano. These few larger houses at Malamocco were owned either by the handful of major local landowners or by absentees, who leased them to local farmers. A number of noble clans retained property here until the fall of the Republic; the Foscarini, Grimani, Correr and Erizzo were examples of these families and there were perhaps as many as a dozen others.

However, as well as the small group of major local farmers at Malamocco, there were naturally a large number of poorer *ortolani* (market gardeners) and the village also contains a number of their more modest houses and cottages, chiefly along the Merceria and in the short series of *calli* on the south side of Rio Terrà. Here, as at Murano, the larger, more imposing houses were naturally built on the best sites along the main axis, the former central canal, and the humbler cottages were relegated to the lesser sites in the narrow alleys giving off this axis. There are at least one or two examples here of most types of small lagunar house, from the tall, narrow three-storey type (common at Pellestrina and

257 Malamocco: a smaller, two-storey, five-bay house much like the small group at Burano.

parts of Burano) to the more widespread two-storey cottage (the most common type at Burano), either symmetrical or asymmetrical, and in some cases with only a single room on each floor.

A group of such two-storey cottages can be found along the north side of Merceria, while an example of a tall, narrow, three-storey house can be seen in the Campo dei Meloni, on the south side of Rio Terrà. Both cottages are extremely simple, and identical to those of Burano and Pellestrina. The use of stone here is also confined to the door and window heads, most of the cottages lacking even the almost universal stone cornice-gutter. In a number of cases, the fireplace is positioned on the front wall, either at ground- or first-floor level and the chimney thus runs up the façade approximately in the centre. Two good examples, recently restored, may be seen on the north side of Piazza delle Erbe. Both are of three storeys and have been converted into one house; the restoration has also provided them with chimney pots even more prominent than those that they originally possessed.

15

Conclusions

Venetian vernacular architecture is unique: a unique response to a very unusual and demanding environment. In its most characteristic form it is confined to a small, fairly well-defined area that comprises the Venetian lagoon itself and the coastal margins for some distance in both directions; it cannot be found in the many large mainland settlements – Padua, Vicenza, Treviso – that are physically very close but topographically quite different. All are cities of the Terraferma, of the 'normal' world of mainland Italy.

In the lagoon of Venice different conditions prevailed. Firstly the subsoil was different, and hence specialised forms of foundation had to be developed, some in the form of timber pads, others as piles driven into the lagunar clay. Certain structural maxims were almost essential for any substantial building to remain standing: floor loads had to be as evenly distributed as possible; buttresses were only rarely used, flying buttresses never, since they required complete rigidity of foundations to function effectively. Towers produced constant problems of differential settlement, and collapse was frequent. Framed structures with columns and vaults are almost entirely confined to churches and are hardly ever found in private houses or lesser public buildings. Even in churches timber or iron ties were necessary to redistribute excessive local loads and stresses. As a result of these vital structural considerations house design was developed with a basic form of parallel structural walls supporting closely spaced beams; until the later more extensive use of piled foundations after the fifteenth century houses were only very rarely more than three storeys high.

The second major constraint on the evolution of an indigenous lagunar architecture was the availability of materials. There are only two primary materials used in almost every house in Venice and its satellites, brick and timber, with a third element – stone – used extensively as a secondary element but hardly ever as a primary structural component. These three fundamental materials, together with decorative finishes such as render or stucco, comprise the basic framework of all lagunar housing.

Venetian vernacular architecture has a number of special features of design, all of them with a specific purpose; some of these purposes are unique to the lagoon, while others are a particular local response to a more general need. Chimneys, for example, fulfil a universal requirement in all housing, but their form here is a special response to the extremely high risk of fire in the crowded lagunar capital. Similarly, *altane* reflect the acute shortage of space in an urban environment circumscribed by nature and in which expansion was almost impossible. Again, the scrupulous attention to the detailing of rainwater gutters reflects the often urgent need to conserve drinking water in the underground cisterns.

The development of vernacular architecture in the lagoon is inseparable from the evolution of the *palazzo-fòntego*. This seminal building form almost certainly had its roots in an early tradition of fortified houses, but as it evolved here it became unique to Venice. Its key elements are symmetry of plan and of façade but also a lightness and openness of design as a direct result of the extraordinary security offered by the natural moat of the lagoon. The symbolic effect of its form was powerful and influential, and was imitated by many classes of society down to humble artisans and tradespeople. However, the visual symmetry of the *palazzo-fòntego* was entirely logical, a direct expression of the tripartite form behind the façade; this plan again grew out of structural and practical necessity, from the requirements of the merchant aristocrats for whom these great houses were built. Such a logical adaptable plan could be adopted by almost all social classes by simply modifying the scale, by reducing the number of storeys, even by reducing the great central hall, the *pòrtego*, so that it became merely an access corridor. In a similar way the *cortile* could be reduced to a light-well, or omitted altogether in the smaller *borghese* houses. This archetypal form thus engendered many thousands of descendants not only in the city but throughout its dependant communities, from the nobles' villas of Murano to the farmers' villas of Pellestrina and the modest *borghese* houses of Burano; all ultimately have their origins in the great Veneto-Byzantine palaces built on the Grand Canal in the twelfth and thirteenth centuries.

The importance of this lagunar vernacular architecture is considerable. While the whole political and social history of the Most Serene Republic is epitomised by the magnificent sequence of palaces that line the Grand Canal, the architecture of Murano, Burano and Pellestrina forms an essential counterpoint, representing the satellite communities that depended on the *Dominante*, but also on whose people the sea-city itself depended for many of life's necessities – fish from Burano, wine, fruit and vegetables from the *lidi*, salt from Chioggia, glass from Murano. Venice's contribution to our architectural heritage is priceless, and is quite justifiably the subject of the world's concern. But its satellites, too, have an invaluable contribution to make to our historic heritage; we are fortunate that these villages are also well preserved and that they will also be the beneficiaries of many of the great efforts being made to restore, repair and revitalise Venice.

Postscript

As I suggested in an early part of this book, there are several fields of research which I have only fairly briefly (and superficially) touched upon, and in which further investigation needs to be undertaken. Murano has been poorly served by social and economic historians, and not surprisingly it is the glass industry that has attracted most of the little attention given to this important satellite of Venice. Useful work could be undertaken into the detailed investments of the patriciate here, and also on the socio-economic history of the glassmaking families, their wealth and their relationship with the nobility and the government.

Further work also needs to be done on the basic organisation of the building industry, and in particular its fortunes in relation to general economic and political circumstances, notably in the fourteenth and fifteenth centuries, which saw extraordinary activity in palace-building by the patriciate. There is also room for much investigation of the lesser medieval houses of Venice; recent attention has still tended to focus on the great palaces, but we must not forget the many dozen important *palazzetti* from the medieval period that deserve better than a passing note in yet another eulogy on the palaces of the Grand Canal. Many of these houses are significant buildings, and in any city other than Venice would be the subject of considerable attention and concern.

However, the climate among architectural historians (indeed, among many architects as well) has fortunately changed radically in recent years, and our awareness of these lesser buildings has increased considerably. Venice, like other great historic cities, is no longer seen as a collection of individual jewels surrounded by the undifferentiated matrix of the city. It is now universally acknowledged that 'secondary' and 'tertiary' buildings fulfil a vital function in knitting the urban fabric together, and it is hoped that the smaller medieval houses of Venice will also receive the attention that they certainly deserve.

Appendix I

Some further notes on the lost villas of Murano

Palazzo Vendramin at S. Salvatore

According to Zorzi, the Vendramin house stood at the end of a *rio* that was reclaimed in *c*. 1820, about the time that the house itself was demolished. It was flanked on one side by the monastery of S. Andrea and on the other by S. Barnardo. If this location is correct then the house the remains of which still stand at no. 21 Fondamenta S. Lorenzo must be a second Vendramin villa, and it is this latter that was the property of Francesco, Patriarch of Venice in 1615.

Palazzo Balbi

This was a notable house of gothic appearance, which stood at the southern entrance of Rio dei Vetrai, very close to the surviving Contarini villa. It was built in the fourteenth century and stood until 1819 when it was largely destroyed in a storm. At the fall of the Republic it was owned by the Motta, a glassmaking family noted for the manufacture of mirrors.

Palazzo Benzon-Manin

The Benzon house stood on Fondamenta Giustinian, almost adjacent to the Tiepolo villa, between it and Palazzo Giustinian. According to Zanetti it was a 'bello e vastissimo palagio con deliziosissimo giardino' (*Guida di Murano*, p. 120). It stood until about 1866 when it was demolished. Little is known of its appearance; after its loss all that survived was a large hexagonal well-head with the arms of the Lippomano family.

Palazzi Corner

The Corner had extensive interests at Murano. As well as the *palazzetto* discussed in the text, there were the two great later villas in the north of the island, one of which was the house of Caterina, Queen of Cyprus. There was also a fourth Corner house, south of the Grand Canal, and which probably stood on the Fondamenta S. Giovanni Battista near the surviving Soranzo villas, and adjacent to those of the Grimani, Morosini and Giustinian. It was a large imposing structure, with a fine portal onto the quay. From the Corner it passed to Jacopo Vianoli, bishop of Torcello, and was finally demolished in 1814. Immediately prior to its loss it was the property of the Moratto, a local family.

Palazzo Giustinian at S. Giovanni dei Battuti

This villa stood on the quay of the Grand Canal and was one of the three important villas that stood between the two of the Soranzo; the others were the Grimani and Morosini. The Giustinian house belonged to the Zattere branch of this extensive and wealthy clan; it was lost soon after 1797 and we have no details of its appearance.

Palazzo Grimani

We are fortunate in having an illustration of this villa engraved by Coronelli in 1709. The house stood until about 1830, and was a two-storey structure rather like the Soranzo house on Fondamenta

Colleoni. There was a spacious *piano nobile* over a lower-ground floor; the façade was symmetrical with a central four-light window to the *pòrtego*, a stone balcony and semicircular window heads. A prominent cornice produced a strong horizontal emphasis to the façade, and the villa was probably of similar date to the nearby Soranzo house, that is, of the early *cinquecento*.

Palazzo Morosini

Adjacent to the last two, very little is known of this villa, although in Zanetti's day one room or hall survived and had been incorporated into the Toso glassworks. All three of these villas had large gardens behind them to the south and west.

Palazzo Giustinian at S. Matteo

Among the Giustinian family's extensive interests at Murano was a large, imposing *palazzo* which stood on Rio di S. Matteo near the present cemetery. Little is known of its history, and it was demolished in the early nineteenth century. Next to it was a second Giustinian house.

Appendix II

Builders' estimates

These documents are appended here for a number of reasons; the first example is particularly important as it is the earliest estimate that I have found for any significant building works in the lagoon villages. As such it represents typical builders' practice in the middle of the fifteenth century, and similar methods of scheduling and pricing work could be found throughout the city in this period. The estimate illustrates the type and nature of materials used, the sort of quantities necessary and the relative costs of materials. The method of pricing is a mixture of unit costs for materials and lump sums for labour costs; this method was refined over a long period of time, as our second document shows. Here much of the work is priced complete by the unit of length or of area.

The first document is the estimate for major works of restoration on the Palazzo Comunale at Torcello in 1443; it can be found in A.S.V. Podestà di Torcello B.554 Cassa della Comunità. The second is the quotation for the construction of a new house for the bishop on the same island in 1704, and this can be found in A.S.V. Milizia da Mar B. 186.

1 The Palazzo Comunale of Torcello 1443

1 For 1,700 small bricks for the wall of the *palazzo*	L.1.0
2 For interest [raxon] of L.7.10 per month	L.11.13
3 For two columns of marble for the above wall	L.2.10
4 For 14 piles for the orchard and the courtyard of the *palazzo*	L.4.4
5 For . . . 25 [gap in text]	L.1.5
6 For sand	L.1.16
7 For . . . [gap in text] carpenter, for work in the courtyard of the *palazzo* etc., for 3 days	L.4.4
8 For five planks [or slabs] for the *palazzo*	L.12.10
9 For seven planks of larch	L.2.16
10 For five beams of timber for the *palazzo*	L.8.0
11 For three ditto.	L.7.10
12 For steps [of stone]	L.4.16
13 For *moralij* of larch	L.8.0
14 For labour in working the above timber, and for expenses in food for the carpenter[s]	L.1.18
15 For nails of various types	L.5.9
16 Sixteen barrels of lime	L.4.16
17 Small bricks: 2,500 at the rate of L.7 per 1,000 and roof tiles 800 at the rate of L.13 per 1,000	L.27.18
18 Four barrels of [slaked] lime	L.2.0
19 Twenty barrels of lime from Padua	L.6.10
20 For the architrave [or lintel, beam]	L.8.11

346

21 To the craftsmen for executing the above work, for re-roofing all the *palazzo*, and
    . . . all of the ceiling of the *palazzo*, four craftsmen and three labourers   L.80.0
Item: for labourers to restore [re-point?] and *stargare* [?] the brickwork, and to clean
    out the courtyard of the *palazzo*   L.6.0
Item: for the oarsmen (for transport)   L.1.4

TOTAL   L.239.9 [*sic*]

2 The Bishop's House at Torcello 1704

1 To complete all of the walls and foundations in the total amount of 438 (square)
    passi at the rate of L.12 per *passo*   L.5256
2 The whole of the roof of new tiles, of 140 [square] *passi* at the rate of L.10 per
    passo   L.1400
3 A total of 98 [square] *passi* of terrazzo at L.12 per *passo*   L.1176
4 Windows of glass, total number 33   (–)
5 439 feet of timber at 44 *soldi* per foot   L.966
6 33 balconies of stone, 264 ft total length, at one *soldo* per foot [*sic*; should be *lira*]   L.264
7 Decking to the upper floor: 59 [square] *passi* at 5 *lire* per *passo*   L.295
8 For the demolition of the old house of the bishop (255 ducats)   L.1581
9 For two chimneys with ranges   L.403
10 The ditch around the perimeter of the house: 50 *passi* at 50 *soldi* per *passo*   L.125
11 For 80 *sorzoni* of larch for putting below the foundations   L.126
12 For shutters no. 16; 1248 *passi* at 12 *soldi* per *passo*   L.770 [*sic*]
13 For steps of stone   L.100
14 For the ceiling [soffit] of the staircase: 16 *passi* at 4 ducats per *passo*   L. 396
15 For doorways of stone 10 no.; 200 linear feet at 20 *soldi* per foot   L.200
16 For steps of stone 21 no.: 5¹/₂ feet each, which totals 116 feet at 28 *soldi* per foot   L.162
17 For the main entrance of stone with two steps   L.62

There follow several other very minor items. The bill also included works to the cathedral, including re-roofing the portico; this work totalled a further L.723. The grand total was L.18,187, a figure that the procurators considered too high; a fair price for the 'murer, terazer, tagliapiera e fenestrer' was agreed to be L.13,337.

Select bibliography

Abbreviations

A.R.   Architectural Review, London
A.V.   Archivio Veneto, Venice
C.I.S.A.   Centro Internazionale di Studi di Architettura Andrea Palladio, Vicenza

Introductory note

I have attempted to include a large number of works that are reasonably accessible to the more general reader. For a summary of much invaluable original archival material, see the bibliography to my earlier book, *Chioggia and the Villages of the Venetian Lagoon*, which also contains lists of works on the lagoon in general, on the history of Chioggia and the lesser villages. The present bibliography includes a few standard works, a number of authoritative monographs, as well as several more esoteric but useful essays and papers.

Archival sources: a summary of the main series in the Archivio di Stato, Venezia

Murano
  Podestà di Murano (generally)
  Milizia da Mar, esp. B.199 to B.234
  Dieci Savii   B.459 (estimo of 1581)
               B.461 (estimo of 1661)
               B.472 (catastico of 1740)

Burano
  Podestà di Torcello, esp. B.433–9, B.541, 544–6, 549, 551–4, 566
  Dieci Savii B.82, 232, 296, 331–2, 413, 459, 461, 472, 610
  Anagrafe di Tutto lo Stato 1766
  Catastico Napoleonico vol. 8
  Milizia da Mar B. 187–98
  Capi del Consiglio dei X: Lettere dei Rettori: Dogado B.78, 79

Pellestrina
  Dieci Savii   B.234, 299, 334, 413;
               B.458 (estimo of 1581)
               B.460 (estimo of 1661)
               B.473 (estimo of 1740)
  Capi del Consiglio dei X: Lettere dei Rettori di Chioggia: B.73–5
  Collegio V Secreta: Relazioni dei Podestà di Chioggia: B. 39
  Milizia da Mar B.684–6, 703, 704, 744, 761
  Provveditori alla Sanità B.606, 618, 619
  Anagrafe di Tutto lo Stato 1766

Catastico Napoleonico vol. 46
Savii ed Eesecutori alle Acque: Reg. 335; B.40, 41, 56–64

On Pellestrina there is also much material in the Archivio Comunale di Chioggia, particularly the following series:
AC 10–18 Ducali
AC 23–45 Riformagioni de' Podestà di Chioggia
AC 50–66 Officiali misc.
AC 67–71 Affitti circa Valli, Registro dei Livelli
AC 757, 766: misc. rent-rolls and censuses of the eighteenth century
Torcello
Podestà di Torcello, generally but esp. B.433–9 (Ducali), 541, 544, 549, 551–2, 554, 566
Dieci Savii B.459, 461, 472, 610
Anagrafe di Tutto lo Stato 1766
Catastico Napoleonico vol. 8
Milizia da Mar B.178–98
Capi del Consiglio dei X: Lettere dei Rettori; Dogado B.78, 79
Mazzorbo:
As for Torcello, but see also Milizia da Mar B.177
Malamocco
Archivi dei Reggimenti: Podestà di Malamocco
Milizia da Mar: B.235–6, 237, 239
Capi del Consiglio dei X: Lettere dei Rettori: Dogado B.77
Dieci Savii B.458, 473
Catastico Napoleonico vol. 10

Secondary sources

Ackerman, J. S., *Palladio* (Harmondsworth 1966)
    'Sources of the Renaissance villa' in *The Renaissance and Mannerism* (Princeton 1963)
Albertini, R., *I Porti Minori del Litorale Veneto* (Naples 1957)
Angelini, L., *Le Opere in Venezia di Mauro Codussi* (Milan 1945)
Aricò, A. C., ed., Marin Sanudo the Younger: *La Città di Venetia 1494–1530* (Milan 1980)
Armani, E., and Piana, M., 'Le Superfici Storiche Esterne dell'Architettura Veneziana': Conference –
    Restauro e Conservazione delle Facciate Dipinte (Genoa 1984)
Arslan, E., *Venezia Gotica* (Milan 1970)
Astengo, G., 'Il Risanamento Conservativo del Centro Storico e delle Isole': Conference – *Il Problema
    di Venezia* (Venice 1964)
Badile, G., 'Un architetto veneto del Settecento – Antonio Gaspari' in *Arte Veneta* (1952)
Barbacci, A., *Il Restauro dei Monumenti in Italia* (Rome 1956)
Barbieri, F., *Vincenzo Scamozzi* (Vicenza 1952)
Barovier Mentasti, R., *Il Vetro Veneziano* (Milan 1983)
Bassi, E., *Gianantonio Selva Architetto Veneziano* (Padua 1936)
    'Il Restauro dei palazzi' in *Critica d'Arte* (Jan.–Feb. 1951)
    'L'Edilizia veneziana nei secoli XVII e XVIII' in *Critica d'Arte* no. 19 (1957)
    'L'Architettura gotica a Venezia' in *Bollettino C.I.S.A.* VII (Vicenza 1965)
    'Venezia nella Storia Civile' in *Urbanistica* no. 52 (Turin 1968)
    Palazzi de Venezia (Venice 1976)
    Architettura del Sei e Settecento a Venezia (2nd edn Venice 1980)
Bassi, E. and Trincanato, E. R., *Il Palazzo Ducale nella Storia e nell'Arte di Venezia* (Milan 1960)
Battagia, M., *Cenni Storici e Statistici Sopra l'Isola Della Giudecca* (Venice 1832)
Baum, G., *Architettura e Plastica del Rinascimento Italiano nel Quattrocento* (Stuttgart n.d.)

Bellavitis, G., 'Rediscovering the Palazzo' in *A.R.* (London May 1971)

Bellavitis, G., *Palazzo Giustinian Pesaro* (Vicenza 1975)

Bellavitis, G. and Romanelli, G., *Le Città nella Storia d'Italia: Venezia* (Rome 1985)

Beltrami, L., *La Cà del Duca sul Canal Grande* (Milan 1900)

Berenson, B., *Italian Painters of the Renaissance* (New York 1952)

Berenson, B., *Italian Pictures of the Renaissance: Venetian Schools* 2 vols. (London 1957)

Berti, G., *L'Architettura a Venezia: Il Rinascimento* (Turin n.d.)

Bettini, S., 'L'architettura gotica veneziana' in *Bollettino C.I.S.A.* VII (Vicenza 1965)

de'Biasi, M., *Toponomastica a Murano* (Venice 1983)

Boldrin, G., *I Pozzi di Venezia* (Venice 1910)

Bonfanti, L., *L'Isola della Giudecca* (Venice 1930)

Boni, G., 'The Cà d'Oro and its polychromatic decorations' in *Transactions of the R.I.B.A.* III (1887)

Boschieri, G., 'Il Palazzo Grimani a S. Luca' in *Rivista della Città di Venezia* (Venice 1931)

Boschini, M., *La Carta del Navegar Pittoresco* (Venice 1660)

Burns, H., 'Le Opere minori del Palladio' in *Bollettino C.I.S.A.* XXI (1979)

Caiani, A., 'Un palazzo veronese a Murano' in *Arte Veneta* (1968)

Carboneri, N., 'Mauro Codussi' in *Bollettino C.I.S.A.* VI (Vicenza 1964)

Carlevarijs, L., *Le Fabbriche e Vedute di Venezia* (Venice 1703)

Cassini, G., *Piante e Vedute Prospettiche di Venezia* (Venice 1971)

Cattaneo, R., *L'Architettura in Italia dal Sec. VI al 1000 c.* (Venice 1870)

Cecchetti, B., 'Le Industrie a Venezia nel secolo XIII' in *A.V.* IV (1872)

    'Nomi di Pittori e Lapicidi antichi' in *A.V.* (1885)

    'La facciata della Cà d'Oro dello Scalpello di Giovanni e Bartolomeo Buono' in *A.V.* XXXI (1886)

Ceschi, C., *Teoria e Storia del Restauro* (Rome 1970)

Cessi, F., *Alessandro Vittoria, scultore 1525–1608*: 2 vols. (Trento 1961–2)

Cessi, R., *Storia della Repubblica di Venezia*: 2 vols. (2nd edn Milan and Messina 1968)

Chiminelli, C., 'Le scale scoperte nei palazzi veneziani' in *Ateneo Veneto* XXXV I (Venice 1912)

Cicognara, L., Diedo, A. and Selva G. A., *Le Fabbriche Più Cospicue di Venezia misurate, illustrate e intagliate* 2nd edn (Venice 1858)

Clasen, K. H., *Die Gotische Baukunst* (Potsdam 1930)

Cocke, R., *Veronese* (London 1980)

    The Drawings of Veronese (London 1984)

Connell, S., 'The Employment of sculptors and stonemasons in Venice in the 15th century'; unpublished Ph.D. thesis: Warburg Inst., University of London 1976.

Constable, W. G., *Canaletto, Giovanni Antonio Canal 1697–1768*: 2 vols. 2nd edn (Oxford 1976)

Cornaro, F., *Notizie Storiche delle Chiese e Monasteri di Venezia e Torcello . . .* (Padua 1758)

    Ecclesiae Torcellanae . . . (Venice 1749)

Coronelli, V. M., *Singolarità di Venezia*: 2 vols. (Venice 1709)

Correr, G., *Venezia e le sue Lagune*: 3 vols. (Venice 1847)

Costa, F., *Delizie del Fiume Brenta* (Venice 1750–56)

Cristinelli, G., *Baldassare Longhena, Architetto del 600 a Venezia* (Padua 1972)

Cuchetti, C. A., Padovan, A. and Seno, S., *La Storia Documentata del Litorale Nord* (Venice 1976)

Dalla Santa, C. and Paolillo, D. R., *Il Palazzo Dolfin Manin a Rialto* (Venice 1971)

Enlart, C., *Origines Françaises de l'Architecture Gothique en Italie* (Paris 1894)

Filiasi, J., *Memorie Storiche dei Veneti Primi e Secondi* (Padua 1811)

Fiocco, G., 'Palazzo Pesaro' in *Rivista della Città di Venezia* (Venice 1925)

    Paolo Veronese (Bologna 1928)

    Andrea Palladio Padovano (Padua 1933)

    Guardi (Florence 1937)

    'La casa veneziana antica' in *Rend. dell'Accademia Nazionale dei Lincei*: IV (Rome 1949)

Fontana, G. J. *I Cento Palazzi Fra i Più Celebri di Venezia. . .* (Venice 1865)

    Venezia Monumentale: I Palazzi (Venice 1845–63; new edn by L. Moretti, Venice 1967)

Forlati, F., 'Restauri di architettura minore nel Veneto' in *Architettura* IV (1926–7)

Foscari, L., *Affreschi Esterni a Venezia* (Milan 1936)

Franceschini, G., *Case Gotiche e Edifici Palladiani* (Vicenza 1925)

Franzoi, U. and di Stefano, D., *Le Chiese di Venezia* (Venice 1976)

Gaitanakis, G., 'Housing study' in *A.R.* (London, May 1971)

Galliciolli, G. B., *Delle Memorie Venete . . .* (Venice 1795)

Gallimberti, N., 'Architettura civile minore del Medioevo a Padova' in *Bollettino del Museo Civico di Padova* (Padua 1934–9)

Gallo, R., 'Corte Colonne a Castello e le Case della Marinarezza' in *Ateneo Veneto* no. 23 (1938)
  'Per la datazione delle opere del Veronese' in *Emporium* LXXXIX (1939)
  'Andrea Palladio a Venezia' in *Rivista di Venezia* (1955)
  Michele Sanmicheli a Venezia (Verona 1960)

Gasparetto, A., *Il Vetro di Murano dalle Origini ad Oggi* (Venice 1958)

Gazzola, P., *Michele Sanmicheli* (Venice 1960)

Gianighian, G. and Pavanini, P., *Dietro i Palazzi: Tre Secoli di Architettura Minore a Venezia 1492–1803* (Venice 1984)

Goldthwaite, R., *The Building of Renaissance Florence* (Baltimore 1980)

Goy, R. J., *Chioggia and the Villages of the Venetian Lagoon: Studies in Urban History* (Cambridge 1985)

Grevembroch, G., 'Pozzi e Cisterne' (Codice Gradenigo-Dolfin no. 607, Museo Correr, Venice)

Guiton, S., *A World By Itself* (London 1977)

Harvey, J. M., *The Gothic World* (London 1950)
  The Medieval Architect (London 1972)

Howard, D., *Jacopo Sansovino: Architecture and Patronage in Renaissance Venice* (New Haven and London 1975; new edn 1987)
  The Architectural History of Venice (London 1980; new edn 1987)

Lane, F. C., *Venice: A Maritime Republic* (Baltimore 1973)

Lane, F. C. and Müller, R. C., *Money and Banking in Medieval and Renaissance Venice* I (Baltimore and London 1985)

Langeskiöld, E., *Michele Sanmicheli, The Architect of Verona* (Uppsala 1938)

Lauritzen, P. and Zielcke, A., *The Palaces of Venice* (London 1978)

Levi, C. A., *I Campanili di Venezia* (Venice 1890)

Lieberman, R., *Renaissance Architecture in Venice 1450–1540* (London 1982)

Links, J. G., ed., *Views of Venice by Canaletto Engraved by Antonio Visentini* (New York 1971)

Lorenzetti, G., *Itinerario Sansoviniano a Venezia* (Venice 1929)
  'Gli affreschi della facciata di Palazzo Trevisan a Murano' in *Scritti Storici in Onore di Camillo Manfrin* (Padua 1925)
  Cà Rezzonico (Venice 1940)
  Venezia e il suo Estuario (Venice 1958) translated as: *Venice and its Lagoon* tr. J. Guthrie (Trieste 1975)
  Vita di Jacopo Tatti Detto il Sansovino di Giorgio Vasari (Florence 1913)

Lotz., W., *Studies in Italian Renaissance Architecture* (1981)

Loukomski, G. K., *Andrea Palladio* (Paris 1927)

Luxoro, M., *Il Palazzo Vendramin Calergi* (Venice 1937)

Mackenney, R., 'Arti e Stato a Venezia tra Medio Evo e 600' in *Studi Veneziani* V (Venice 1981)
  'Guilds and guildsmen in 16th century Venice' in *Bulletin of the Soc. for Renaissance Studies* (Autumn 1984)
  Tradesmen and Traders: the World of the Guilds in Venice and Europe c. 1250–1650 (Beckenham 1987)

Magagnato, L., 'I collaboratori veronesi di Andrea Palladio' in *Bollettino C.I.S.A.* (Vicenza 1968)

Magrini, A., *Memorie intorno la vita e le opere di Andrea Palladio* (Padua 1845)

Maretto, P., *L'Edilizia Gotica Veneziana* 2nd edn (Venice 1978)
  'L'Urbanistica veneziana del trecento' in *Bollettino C.I.S.A.* (Vicenza 1965)
  La Casa Veneziana nella storia della Città dalle Origini all'Ottocento (Venice 1986)

Mariacher, G., *Il Palazzo Ducale di Venezia* (Florence 1950)

352 *Bibliography*

'Il continuatore del Longhena a palazzo Pesaro' in *Ateneo Veneto* (1951)
Il Sansovino (Milan 1962)
Cà Vendramin Calergi (Venice 1965)
Guida Artistica di Palazzo Rezzonico (Florence 1966)
Vetri di Murano (Milan 1967)
Martineau, J. and Hope C., eds., *The Genius of Venice 1500–1600* (London 1983)
Marzemin, G., *Le più Antiche Arti a Venezia* (Bologna 1938)
Massari, A., *Giorgio Massari* (Vicenza 1971)
Mauroner, F., *Luca Carlevarijs* (Padua 1945)
Mazzariol, G. and Pignatti, T., *La Pianta Prospettica di Venezia del 1500 Disegnata da J. de'Barbari* (Vicenza 1963)
Mazzotti, G., *Le Ville Venete* (Treviso 1954)
Melzi d'Eril, G., 'Tipologia di palazzi veneziani prepalladiani' in *Bollettino C.I.S.A.* (Vicenza 1972)
Miozzi, E., *Venezia nei Secoli* 2 vols. (Venice 1957)
Molmenti, P., *La Storia di Venezia nella Vita Privata* 3 vols. (Bergamo 1906–8 and Trieste 1973)
Le Vere da Pozzo di Venezia (Venice 1911)
Molmenti, P. and Mantovani, D., *Le Isole della Laguna Veneta* (Bergamo 1925)
Calli e Canali in Venezia (Venice 1893)
Monticolo, G., *I Capitolari delle Arti Veneziane* 3 vols. (Rome 1896–1914)
Moretti, L., ed., *Francesco Sansovino: Venetia Città Nobilissima et Singolare* 2 vols.; facsimile of the 1663 edn (Venice 1968)
Moschini, G. A., *Guida per la Città di Venezia* 2 vols. (Venice 1815)
Guida per l'Isola di Murano (Venice 1807)
Moschini, V., 'Giorgio Massari, architetto' in *Dedalo* (March 1932)
Muir, E., *Civic Ritual in Renaissance Venice* (Princeton 1981)
Muntz, E., *Arte Italiana del Quattrocento* (Milan 1894)
Muratori, S., *Studi per una Operante Storia Urbana di Venezia* (Rome 1959)
Muraro, M., *Les Villas de la Venetie* (Venice 1954)
Nani Mocenigo, M., *L'Arsenale di Venezia* (Rome 1927)
Nepi Scirè, G. et al., *Arti e Mestieri nella Repubblica di Venezia* (Venice 1980)
Neri, A., *L'Arte Vetraria* 1st edn 1612; new edn by R. Barovier Mentasti (Milan 1980)
Norwich, J. J., *Venice: the Rise to Empire* (London 1977)
Venice: the Greatness and the Fall (London 1981)
Olivato, L. and Puppi, L., *Mauro Codussi* (Milan 1977)
Olivato, L., 'Antonio Visentini su Palazzo Trevisan a Murano' in *Bollettino C.I.S.A.* (Vicenza 1972)
'Storia di un'avventura edilizia a Venezia tra il Seicento e il Settecento' in *Antichita Viva* (1973)
Ongania, F., *Raccolta delle Vere da Pozzo in Venezia* (Venice 1891)
Ongaro, M., *Il Palazzo Ducale di Venezia* (Venice 1927)
Paganuzzi, G. B., *Iconografia delle Trenta Parrocchie di Venezia* (Venice 1831)
Palladio, A., *I Quattro Libri dell'Architettura* (Venice 1570; facsimile edn Milan 1945 and 1969)
Palluchini, R., 'Profilo di Vincenzo Scamozzi' in *Bollettino C.I.S.A.* (Vicenza 1961)
'Vincenzo Scamozzi e l'architettura veneta' in *L'Arte* I (1936)
Pane, R., *Andrea Palladio* (Turin 1948)
Paoletti, P., *L'Architettura e la Scultura del Rinascimento in Venezia* 3 vols. (Venice 1893)
Pavanini, M., 'Traditional house construction' in *A.R.* (London, May 1971)
Perocco, G. and Salvadori, A., *Civiltà di Venezia* 3 vols. (Venice 1973–6)
Perrot, P., *Three Great Centuries of Venetian Glass* (Corning, N.Y. 1958)
Perry, M., 'Cardinal Domenico Grimani's legacy of ancient art to Venice' in *Journal of the Warburg and Courtauld Insts.* XLI (London 1978)
Piamonte, G., *Venezia vista dall'Acqua* (Venice 1966)
Pignatti, T., *Piazza S. Marco* (Venice 1956)
Palazzo Ducale Venezia (Novara 1964)

Pittori, L., *Jacopo Sansovino Scultore* (Venice 1909)

Pullan, B., *Rich and Poor in Renaissance Venice* (Oxford 1971)

Puppi, L., *Michele San Micheli, Architetto di Verona* (Padua 1971)

Puppi, L., *Andrea Palladio: l'Opera Completa* (Milan 1977; new edn Milan 1986)
   Palladio e Venezia (Florence 1982)

Puppi, L. and Puppi, L. O., *Mauro Codussi e l'Architettura Veneziana del Primo Rinascimento* (Milan 1977)

Quadri, A., *Il Canal Grande di Venezia* (Venice 1838)
   Descrizione Topografica di Venezia (Venice 1844)

Raschdorff, I., *Palast Architektur Italiens* (Berlin n.d. [c. 1900])

Raschdorff, O., *Palastarchitektur in Oberitalien und Toscana vom XIII bis zum XVIII Jahrhundert* (Berlin 1903)

Romanelli, G. D., *Venezia Ottocento* (Rome 1977)

Romanin, S., *Storia Documentata di Venezia* 10 vols. (Venice 1855)

Romanini, A. M., *L'Architettura Gotica in Lombardia* 2 vols. (Milan 1964)

Ronzani, F. and Luciolli, G., *Le Fabbriche di Michele Sanmicheli* (Turin 1862)

Rusconi, G. A., *I Dieci Libri di Architettura . . . secondo i precetti di Vitruvio* (Venice 1660)

Ruskin, J., *The Stones of Venice* (London 1851–8 and later edns)

Sabellico, M. A., 'de Venetae Urbis Situ' in *Opera Omnia* (Basle 1560)

Sagredo, A., *Di Jacopo Sansovino* (Venice 1830)
   Il Fòndaco dei Turchi in Venezia (Milan 1860)
   Sulle Consorterie delle Arti Edificatorie in Venezia (Venice 1856)

Samonà, G. et al., *Piazza S. Marco: l'Architettura, la Storia, la Funzione* (Venice 1970; new edn 1977)

Sansovino, F., *Cose Notabili di Venezia* (Venice 1562) (see also under Moretti)

Sanudo, M., *Itinerario per la Terraferma Veneziana Nell'Anno 1483* (Padua 1847)
   'De Origine urbis Venetae' in *Rerum Italicarum Scriptores* ed. L.A. Muratori (Bologna 1938–42) (see also under Aricò)
   I Diarii ed. R. Fulin *et al.* 58 vols. (Venice 1879–1903)
   Cronachetta (Venice 1880) (see also Aricò)

Scamozzi, V., *Idea dell'Architettura Universale* (Venice 1615)

Scarpari, G., *Le Ville Venete* (2nd edn Rome 1984)

Scattolin, A., *I 'Casoni' Veneti* (Venice 1936)
   'L'architettura rustica lagunare' in *Atti del Congresso Nazionale delle Arti Popolari* (1940)

Scattolin, G., *Le Case Fòndaco sul Canal Grande* (Venice 1961)

Schultz, J., *Venetian Painted Ceilings of the Renaissance* (Berkeley and Los Angeles 1968)

Scolari, F., *Commentario della Vita e le Opere di Vincenzo Scamozzi* (Treviso 1837)

Sella, D., *Commerci e industrie a Venezia nel sec. XVII* (Venice and Rome 1961)

Selvatico, P., *Sull'Architettura e sulla Scultura in Venezia dal Medioevo ai Giorni Nostri* (Venice 1847)

Selvatico, P. and Lazzari, V., *Guida di Venezia e delle Isole Circonvicine* (Venice 1852)

Semenzato, G., *L'Architettura di Baldassare Longhena* (Padua 1954)

Serlio, S., *Tutta l'Opera d'Architettura et Prospettiva di Sebastiano Serlio Bolognese* (Venice 1619)
   The Five Books of Architecture (London 1611; facsimile edn New York 1982)

Serra, L., *Alessandro Vittoria* (Milan 1921)

Simonsfeld, H., *Der Fòndaco dei Tedeschi in Venedig* (Stuttgart 1887)

Sohm, P., *La Scuola Grande di S. Marco . . .* (Ann Arbor, Michigan 1981)

Tafuri, M., *Jacopo Sansovino e l'Architettura del 500 a Venezia* (Padua 1969; new edn 1972)

Tait, H., *The Golden Age of Venetian Glass* (London 1979)

Tassini, G., *Alcuni Palazzi ed Antichi Edifici di Venezia* (Venice 1879)
   Curiosità Veneziane (Venice 1933)
   Edifici di Venezia distrutti o Volti ad uso Diverso (new edn Venice 1969)

Temanza, T., *Antica Pianta dell'Inclita Città di Venezia* (1st edn 1781; new facsimile edn Venice 1977)
   Vite dei più Celebri Architetti e Scultori Veneziani del sec. XVI (Venice 1778)

Tiepolo, M. F. *et al.*, *Mostra Storica della Laguna Veneta* (Venice 1970)

Tiozzo C. B. and Semenzato, C., *La Riviera del Brenta* (Treviso 1972)

Tiozzo, I., *Chioggia nella Storia, nell'Arte e nei Commerci* (Chioggia 1920)

Torres, D., *La Casa Veneta* (Venice n.d. *c.* 1937)

Trincanato, E. R., *Venezia Minore* (Milan 1948)

   'The humble Venetian house' in *A.R.* (London, May 1971)

   'Salvaguardia e risanamento di Venezia' in *Urbanistica* no. 32 (Turin 1960)

   'Residenze colletive a Venezia' in *Urbanistica* no. 42 (Turin 1965)

   'Sintesi strutturale di Venezia storica' in *Urbanistica* no. 52 (Turin 1968)

   'Le Comunità della laguna veneta' in *Urbanistica* no. 14 (Turin 1954)

Trincanato, E. R. and Mariacher, G., *Il Palazzo Ducale di Venezia* (Florence 1967)

Trincanato, E. R. and Franzoi, U., *Venise au Fils du Temps* (Boulogne Billancourt 1971)

UNESCO, *Il Patrimonio Edilizio di Venezia Insulare* (Venice 1970)

Urbani de' Gheltof, G. M., *Venezia dall'alto: I Camini* (Venice 1892)

   Il Palazzo di Camillo Trevisan a Murano (Venice 1890)

Vasari, G., *Le Vite de' più Eccellenti Architetti, Pittori e Scultori* 1st edn Florence 1550; new edn in 9 vols.
     G. Milanesi ed. (Florence 1875–85; edited English version by G. Bull ed., Harmondsworth 1965)

Venturi, A., *L'Architettura del Quattrocento* (Milan 1923)

Visentini, A., *Urbis Venetiarum prospectus celebriores . . .* (Venice 1742) (see also Links ed.)

Vitruvius, *The Ten Books on Architecture* tr. T. M. H. Morgan 1st edn 1914 (repub. New York 1960)

Vuchetich, A., *I palazzi, le Case Storiche e gli Avanzi Storici di Venezia, Sestiere di Dorsoduro, Parrocchia
     dell'Angelo Raffaele* (Mestre 1896)

White, J., *Art and Architecture in Italy 1250–1400* (London 1966)

Wiener, S. G., *Venetian Houses and Details* (New York 1929)

Wirobisz, A., *L'Attività Edilizia a Venezia nel XIV e XV Secolo* (Florence 1965)

Wittkower, R., *Architectural Principles in the Age of Humanism* (3rd edn New York 1971)

   Art and Architecture in Italy 1600–1750 (Harmondsworth 1973)

Zanetti, V., *Guida di Murano e delle Celebri sue Fornaci Vetrarie* (1st edn 1866; new facsimile edn Venice
     1984, U. Stefanutti ed.)

Zanotto, F., *Venezia e le Sue Lagune* (Venice 1847)

   Nuovissima Guida di Venezia . . . (Venice 1856)

   Il Palazzo Ducale di Venezia 4 vols. (Venice 1853–61)

dalla Zorza, A., *Andrea Palladio* (Vicenza 1943)

Zorzi, A., *Venezia Scomparsa* 2 vols. (Milan 1971, Vicenza 1972)

Zorzi, G., *Le Opere Pubbliche e i Palazzi Privati di Andrea Palladio* (Venice 1965)

   Le Chiese e i Ponti di Andrea Palladio (Venice 1967)

Zuccolo, G., *Il Restauro Statico dell'Architettura di Venezia* (Venice 1975)

Anon. *Raccolta di Terminazioni et Ordini de Mag. Eccellentissimo de' Provveditori di Comun* (Venice 1746)

Anon. *Teatro delle Fabbriche più cospicue . . . della Città di Venezia* (Venice 1754)

Index